Money in Crisis

From its origins in ancient Mesopotamia through the advent of coinage in ancient Greece and Rome and the invention of paper currency in medieval China, the progress of finance and money has been driven by technological developments. The great technological change of our age in relation to money centers on the creation of digital money and digital payment systems. *Money in Crisis* explains what the digital revolution in money is, why it matters, and how its potential benefits can be realized or undermined. It explores the history, theory, and evolving technologies underlying money and warns us that money is in crisis: under threat from inflation, financial instability, and digital wizardry. It discusses how modern forms of digital money (crypto, central bank digital currencies, etc.) fit into monetary history and explains the benefits and risks of recent innovations from an economic, political, social, and cultural viewpoint.

IGNAZIO ANGELONI is a policy fellow at the Leibniz Institute for Financial Research SAFE (Goethe University Frankfurt) and the Institute for European Policymaking (Bocconi University). He has held high-ranked positions in the European Central Bank, Italy's Ministry of Finance, and the Bank of Italy. He is the author of several books and articles published in leading international economic journals.

DANIEL GROS is a professor of practice at Bocconi University, Milan. He contributed to the Delors Committee, which drew up the plans for the euro, and has advised numerous central banks and governments on financial affairs. Previously a long-time director of a major EU think tank in Brussels, he coauthored the leading textbook on European monetary integration. He has published widely in leading international journals.

Money in Crisis

The Return of Instability
and the Myth of Digital Cash

SAFE Institute for Financial Research

DANIEL GROS

Bocconi University

CAMBRIDGE
UNIVERSITY PRESS

CAMBRIDGE
UNIVERSITY PRESS

Shaftesbury Road, Cambridge CB2 8EA, United Kingdom

One Liberty Plaza, 20th Floor, New York, NY 10006, USA

477 Williamstown Road, Port Melbourne, VIC 3207, Australia

314–321, 3rd Floor, Plot 3, Splendor Forum, Jasola District Centre, New Delhi – 110025, India

103 Penang Road, #05–06/07, Visioncrest Commercial, Singapore 238467

Cambridge University Press is part of Cambridge University Press & Assessment, a department of the University of Cambridge.

We share the University's mission to contribute to society through the pursuit of education, learning and research at the highest international levels of excellence.

www.cambridge.org
Information on this title: www.cambridge.org/9781009390149

DOI: 10.1017/9781009390101

© Ignazio Angeloni and Daniel Gros 2025

When citing this work, please include a reference to the DOI 10.1017/9781009390101

First published 2025

A catalogue record for this publication is available from the British Library

A Cataloging-in-Publication data record for this book is available from the Library of Congress

ISBN 978-1-009-39014-9 Hardback
ISBN 978-1-009-39013-2 Paperback

History is an organic process, a continuity of related events, inexorable yet not inevitable.

Stanley Karnow

Contents

Preface   *page* ix

1   Hopes and Reality of Digital Money   1

2   Money and Technology in Ancient Times   14

3   Money and Technology in the Modern Age   46

4   What Money Is and Does for Us   77

5   The Paradox of Cash   105

6   Banks as Creators and Stores of Money   133

7   Cards and Apps from Above and Below   158

8   Promises and Failures of Crypto   178

9   Stablecoins or Troublecoins?   229

10   Central Bank Digital Currencies   257

11   Money and Freedom   289

12   Money in the Global Power Game   304

13   The Return of Instability   335

14   Money in Crisis and the Possible Future   353

Index   362

Preface

The past is an inheritance, a gift and a burden.

Jill Lepore

Those who followed economic and political affairs in the 1990s can hardly escape the feeling that the new century marked a break from earlier trends and beliefs. As soon as the December 31, 1999, page was stripped from the calendar, the worldview built on free markets, globalization, and liberal democracy stumbled into multiple crises: all unexpected, all different yet somehow connected, all near-existential. The old times may one day be regarded as a Golden Age. What is clear already is that they were a step in history, not the end of it.

The sequence of those crises is worth reminding. The terrorist attacks of 2001. The financial meltdown of 2008 and the economic recession that followed. The COVID pandemic in 2020–21. Environmental disasters, epitomized by wildfires in North America and elsewhere. The return of commodity shortages and global inflation. Lastly – as we write, at least – Russia's attack on Ukraine, the Middle Eastern crisis and the freeze of East–West relations, reminiscent of the Cold War. In Western societies, the seemingly unstoppable divergence in living standards between the rich and the poor. Superficially, these things have little in common. At their core, all of these elements have brought with them cracks or utter failures in the assumptions underlying democratic liberalism, based on a shared trust in legitimate leadership, institutions and political representation.

As the political pendulum swings back toward centralism and control, the responsibility of politicians is to promote balance, mitigating the tendency toward the extremes of public opinions increasingly divided into opposite camps. Our times may well require a stronger presence of the government in the economy, more attention to national and even certain vested interests, a narrower scope of private markets, and more governance of globalization processes. But this tendency must be controlled. The perimeter of private, open, and competitive markets should not be restricted to the point at which they lose their creative force. Their contribution to collective welfare has been demonstrated and should not be lost.

From ancient Greece to modern times, philosophers and historians have seen history as evolving in cycles, from birth to development to maturity and decline, possibly followed by rebirth and a new cycle. That vision has been reproposed in the so-called theory of turnings, according to which ages go from high to awakening, then to unravelling and to crisis. Supposedly, each phase lasts about a quarter century and we are now in the last, the crisis one. This theory may not have much scientific value in the commonly intended sense, but its descriptions resonate with much of what we see happening as we move deeper into the twenty-first century.

In this book we reflect on these developments through the prism of one of the most ancient and fundamental societal institutions: money. Both of us have put, in different ways, money at the center of our lifetime professional interests. But there are other reasons as well. Money is a mirror of society – the litmus paper that reveals the deepest drivers, contradictions, strengths, weaknesses, and failures of the societal order at large. Money not only reflects society's development and destiny but also shapes them. That is why monetary institutions are so important and worth upholding and protecting.

To our mind, the expression "money in crisis" combines different ideas. The etymology suggests a state of disease and also a situation in which transformation takes place and decisions need to be made. But we are also interested in understanding what happens to money when societal tenets and values enter into a crisis and politics and policies take new directions.

Like history more broadly, monetary history has gone through phases recently. The foundations of contemporary monetary institutions reside in the postwar arrangement agreed in 1944 at Bretton Woods. The initial phase lasted a quarter century, until the early 1970s when that system broke down. The following stage, one of development and progress, lasted through the 1990s. It was dominated by the opening of global finance, the buoyant expansion of international capital flows, and the triumph of free markets. Then cracks began to appear. We are now into the next phase, in which traditional money is undercut by monetary and financial instability and challenged by new forms of money engineered by the private sector, some more cryptic than others, all threatening the status quo. One manifestation is a lack of trust in the ability of central banks to foresee and govern economic outcomes. Again, this mirrors society: If society is divided, it is more difficult for money and its institutions to be strong and stable.

In our advanced democracies, monetary and financial governance is largely entrusted to independent institutions with mandates spanning longer than the political cycle: central banks, capital market regulators, competition authorities, banking supervisors, and the like. Those institutions, unelected but essential to the democratic architecture, share with politicians the responsibility to exercise a restraining influence in our increasingly divided societies. In particular, they should resist the opposite temptations of unduly relaxing prudential standards or overregulating the economy by replacing private markets. We suggest that this applies to two areas: financial regulation, where it is increasingly apparent that the lessons of past crises have been insufficiently heeded or prematurely forgotten, and the payment industry, where the tumultuous innovations of the last decades are tempting central banks to start offering their own payment means.

What lies ahead? Like history in general, the history of money is open; inexorable yet not inevitable, it cannot be stopped but can be changed. In our attempt to provide some answers, we build on two convictions.

The first is the heuristic value of history. A careful review of history goes a long way toward telling us what money is, what purpose should it serve, and how should it accordingly be designed and governed.

The second conviction is that the fundamental purpose and requirements of money do not change through time or space. What changes are the manifestations of money, its forms. Technology helps money serve those purposes and requirements better. It was true in the past and continues to be true today that most technology is digital. Like digital gadgets often make children lose concentration and disrupt their thoughts, digital money risks distracting us from what money is and should always remain: a stable, simple, friendly, and recognizable tool to measure the value of things we need, use, produce, possess, and exchange.

We hope that the story we tell and the reflections we make are of interest to some. We will have achieved our purpose if they stimulate and help the reflections of others.

I Hopes and Reality of Digital Money

Never mistake activity for achievement.

John Wooden

Digital monies are part of our daily life. Payment cards, smartphone apps, and online platforms have become routine ways to make payments, familiar to most of us. A minority of people – but a growing one – moved ahead, entering the mysterious, ethereal world of cryptocurrencies. Money, once seen and touched, pocketed and handed, now increasingly takes the form of electrons or waves travelling on air and wire at the speed of light, dispatched by a fingertip. The technological upheaval is apparent, but users are typically unaware of what happens below the surface. What has changed? Is it just the fact that payments are easier, quicker, and cleaner? Or are we losing something, together with the materiality of money? Are there pitfalls that ordinary people, even experts, fail to see? What do we need to know and understand, to stay safe in one of the things we care about the most – our money?

If readers feels disoriented, they are not alone. We all are. Disputes about the real nature of the alleged "monetary revolution" are raging. Virtually no week passes without media reporting on news, opinions, debates, initiatives, or controversies around digital money. And this is just the tip of the iceberg: Less visible but equally intense debates take place within closed halls in financial institutions, high-tech companies, official agencies, universities, and circles of experts. Initially concentrated in technologically and financially advanced countries, the phenomenon now garners global attention: Emerging countries often take the lead in the most technologically advanced monetary solutions. Like all activities at the frontier of thinking and innovation, the digitalization of money features its high share of enthusiasm, creativity, experimentation, confusion, and failures.

In the literature and the press one often encounters expressions like: the payments revolution; the reinvention of money; a new digital; the rise of a new monetary order; governments and central banks better catch up or will be left behind. The atmosphere is one of excitement, especially among newcomers. Legions of high-tech wizards, largely millennials, entered the field thrilled by the prospect of applying their specialist knowledge to a subject that has never failed to inspire fascination and attraction: money. Even more attractive is the prospect of actually *making* money – a lot of money. In the heyday of crypto markets (2020–21) Bitcoin investors made millions out of nothing: a fortune for most involved, largely youngsters with little more than a laptop, a desk, and a chair to sit on. Most of that money was then lost, but this mattered little: The hope of getting rich by pressing a keyboard survived, and the fascination too. Money, fun, and youth, all riding on a revolution. Can you think of anything better?

For those who spent part of their life studying money in academia or practicing it in financial markets or as civil servants, this alleged revolution raises several questions. Can money, one of the most ancient institutions of human civilization, change in such a radical way? If it can, is this a good thing? Can digital money make life better for the ordinary citizen? How can we ensure such an improvement? How should the boundaries between private enterprise and government be designed? Last but not least, what are the risks involved?

Addressing some of these questions inspired us to write this book. As authors, we share two characteristics, of dubious desirability in themselves but helpful in this endeavor. First, we are old enough to have lived through some of the changes in the arrangements and uses of money during and after the second half of the twentieth century. Economic phenomena tend to repeat themselves: Historical perspective helps assess novelties and their possible consequences. Second, as part of our professions, we have spent a lot of time thinking about such changes, researching their nature, and working both within and with institutions mandated to promote and defend the collective interest in the realm of money. If, as we believe, money is not primarily a private matter but a social construction essential for the lives of all, then such thinking, research, and work can (indeed should) be put to use to understand the nature and consequences of this new "digital revolution."

Here, however, comes an obstacle. Technology is complex, the digital one no less than others. Money, with its theory and practice, is also more complex than it appears at first sight. Yet since the topic is important to all, we wanted our argument to be accessible to anybody, with no more than minimal knowledge in either field. We have therefore tried to reduce technicalities to a minimum and offer our arguments in plain words as if our readers were complete beginners. At least some of them will be, we hope. We also thought we should not write a heavy tome: This is not a treatise – it is an introduction to the topic shaped by our own views. We have added a number of footnotes with bibliographical references to help readers go deeper if they want. Hopefully, our approach has not gone too much at the expense of correctness and completeness.

Digital money is a catchword for many things. Even traditional forms of money are mostly digital today, and they have been for quite a while. Yet only the newest payment technologies are labelled digital money in the common discourse. Some of them are "cryptocurrencies" because they rely on cryptographical algorithms to produce and exchange value: Bitcoin on top, and countless less well-known ones. Then there are forms of money that are not crypto but still are new and digital. Most of them stem from private initiatives: instruments located at the boundary between money in a proper sense (we will define this more precisely) and payment means, such as Apple Pay, PayPal, Google Pay, and Alipay. We regard those as interesting applications from the viewpoint of facilitating the use of money and enhancing its benefits for ordinary citizens. Then there are officially managed digital monies, still in an experimental or planning phase: the so-called central bank digital currencies, or CBDCs. All these instruments, all different but related, are dealt with in this book.

Given our premises, it should not be a surprise that our journey starts with the history of money. We are not historians, so we enter this terrain at our own risk. But history helps a great deal in understanding what money is and what purpose it serves. It also uncovers its intimate relationship with technology. The link between money and technology, the alternation of long pauses and sudden leaps that characterized the progress of monetary technology, has accompanied the history of civilization. Digitalization is only the most recent step in a sequence of repeated occurrences.

We deal with the relation between technology and money through ancient and modern history in Chapters 2 and 3. In monetary terms, ancient history lasted about five millennia. Modern times started more or less when telecommunications entered the world of money, in the early twentieth century. Ancient monetary history is fascinating, but the modern one is also enlightening because it illustrates the oft-overlooked fact that the transition to immaterial forms of money (electronic and digital) is much older than commonly assumed. In essence, it was already complete before any of today's "new forms" of digital money (crypto, apps, and the like) even appeared.

Economic theorists have noted that money conveys information – standardized and verifiable information on *where* value is and *how much* there is of it. Always and everywhere, information travels on the best available technology. In ancient Mesopotamia, information circulated on clay tablets. The Greeks and the Romans stored that information in coins – that lasted for centuries. After the second century AD, when the information content of coins started to degrade, the Roman world also declined. The combination of paper and printing technology in the Middle Ages, migrating from China to Renaissance Europe, improved upon earlier forms, leading to the birth of the modern monetary system combining private banks handling commercial transactions and state institutions guaranteeing monetary stability. That wasn't an endpoint, because technology constantly evolves. With the rise of electronic and digital communications, it was only natural that money would assume that form, sooner or later.

We articulate these ideas in Chapter 4, where we discuss the economic functions of money. Money is distinct from wealth or productive assets; it is that part which is directly exchangeable for goods and services. Economists argue that money performs three functions: medium of exchange, to procure goods or services that fulfil the people's ultimate needs; unit of account, to measure more easily the terms at which those goods and services are exchanged; and store of value, to maintain over time the possibility to enact those transactions in the future. Some economists have gone further, extending those properties to the encompassing notion of "liquidity value." Money's liquidity value allows the bearer to execute purchases at any time, including unexpected ones, promptly and without value loss or added transaction costs. Seen in this light, money is not only information but also insurance against uncertainty.

Here one departs from economics and enters the realm of psychology – assuming the two are really distinct. By being immediately usable to procure goods and services, money fulfils deeper and immutable human desires: sense of certainty, control of oneself, openness to opportunities, and freedom of choice. Those aspirations are constant throughout history: They will stay with us as long as humans continue to live, own, and exchange. It follows that some of the most basic conditions money is supposed to satisfy are also immutable. It must be easily procurable and usable, immediately recognizable, mutually accepted, simple to understand, and stable in value. These are the characteristics that institutions and authorities, central banks primarily, are to promote and defend. They are the yardsticks we should use to assess the quality of digital money as well.

Chapter 5 deals with the most concrete and material form of money: cash. Cash is the signature product of central banks, an expression of the unique power, exercised on behalf of all citizens, to extinguish obligations by force of law. In earlier times, banknotes embodied a promise of conversion into precious metal; now they only promise to purchase goods and services, and even that at an uncertain price. Today some suggest that the disappearance of cash will follow the rise of digital money; some even argue that cash *should* disappear. We respectfully disagree with those views. As a matter of fact, cash is not disappearing, except in limited parts of the world. The demand for it is resilient, suggesting that its benefits are also resilient. Digital means are convenient for some, even most, people: not necessarily for all. Diversity of opportunities and freedom of choice should be preserved. Cash also guarantees privacy like no other payment means can; privacy is harmful when it supports crime, but not all demand for privacy is criminal. Last but not least, cash is unique in that it requires no infrastructure to function (except the technology to produce the banknotes themselves). For this reason, cash is a valuable component of a diversified and sustainable payments ecosystem.

A banknote with legal tender status is a non-interest-bearing debt of the issuer: a state in most cases or a combination of states in more unusual circumstances, like today's eurozone. The state (the "seigneur" in the old times) can oblige its subjects to accept it even when debased (i.e., when its value deteriorates). In medieval China, where paper money first appeared, death was the penalty for those refusing to accept it. Seigniorage extracts value, tempting the state to print more script or debase coinage to pay for wars or court expenses. In modern advanced countries this temptation has been hemmed in by making central banks independent. Occasionally today some governments resort to the printing press, like that of Venezuela, which issued in early 2021 1-million-bolivar notes (then worth about 50 cents). Later that year a new currency was introduced, ironically called the "digital bolivar," with banknotes showing six zeros less than the old ones.

Today, cash is but a small part of all money in existence: roughly, no more than 10 percent in the United States and in the eurozone. Most of the burden and the privilege of offering monetary means and services is entrusted to commercial banks, whose role is discussed in Chapter 6.

Banks, an Italian invention, spread over the whole of Europe during the Renaissance and are still the most important financial institutions in existence. Their activities span a broad range: payments, depository of savings, asset management, diversification, lending of first resort to individuals and firms, corporate-related activity and consulting, and others. Today their primacy as money issuers is increasingly challenged by new forms of digital money. To appreciate the role of banks as creators, managers, and stores of money, one needs to focus on three aspects of them.

First, they are private institutions. As such, they are subject to competition and incentives to innovate to enhance their efficiency. Second, their broad span of activity generates synergies: Payments are directly linked to deposits, deposits in turn often originate from lending activity, client networks demand multiple services, like portfolio management and consulting, and so on. The client base is the network where those synergies are exercised. Third, they have long-dated and multiple relations with central banks, on which they depend for reserve holdings, lending of last resort, open market transactions, prudential supervision, and so on. This linkage is critical to ensure the good functioning of money, a public good immersed in the private domain. We argue that the benefits stemming from this public–private mixed arrangement are important and difficult to replicate in any alternative setting. The enhancement of digital monies should therefore occur in a way that avoids any abrupt and uncontrolled disintermediation of banks.

Fortunately, this need not be the case. The most successful new digital forms of money are compatible with banks – in fact, complementary to them. The "mixed system" comprising banks (the "private" side) and central banks (the "public" side) works well, in the sense that it has not impeded, actually it facilitates, technical progress in the field of means of payments. In Chapter 7 we review the main payment technologies in use today. We explain that this has coincided with the demise of the use of personal checks and, to a lesser extent, a decline in the use of cash for many types of transactions. We start with the oldest forms, credit and debit cards, and move on to more recent applications like PayPal, Apple Pay, Alipay, and Google Pay. It is important to look at them "from above," that is, from the perspective of the user, and "from below," what actually happens after the payment is made and until it is finally settled. All transactions using these applications have a counterpart in the movements of bank and central bank accounts; this guarantees their certainty and finality. While the "above" part is apparent, it is the "below" side which makes the system solid. Far from challenging the mixed private–public combination of banks and central banks, cards, apps, and online platforms are integral parts of that arrangement.

A similar arrangement can support cross-border payments as well. The euro area today is a unique example of a smooth, seamless cross-border payment area. We show that the payment system of the eurozone (including both its interbank and client-based components, Target and the Single Euro Payments Area) is characterized by an elevated level of efficiency, low cost, and high security for users, both domestically and across national borders. By contrast, the US payment system still features a large use of personal checks and a high fragmentation and elevated fees applied to retail clients. We are inclined to consider the system of today's eurozone, as it emerged from over twenty years of construction and reform as state-of-the-art globally in terms of its retail efficiency and quality of service.

In Chapters 8–10 we discuss the newest forms of digital money: cryptocurrencies, stablecoins, and CBDCs. The first two are private (and, as of today, unregulated). The third one is public, and as such fully regulated, and in most countries it is still at the planning or testing stage. These instruments differ from the earlier ones in that they are potentially an alternative to the existing arrangements: The complementarity element is less clear here, whereas the "competition" element is stronger. Crypto instruments and CBDCs are related to one another in the fact that CBDCs originate largely as a reaction to the perceived threats posed by crypto instruments.

Cryptocurrencies are the easiest to deal with in our context since they are not money in the sense we have tried to define. We review the developments of Bitcoin and other similar instruments, describing how they work and assessing them from the viewpoint of fulfilling the function of money. We conclude that they stand no chance of replacing money for any of its crucial functions. Over time, however, under certain conditions, they may establish themselves as a "niche" speculative asset class, potentially useful to complete the financial market. This outcome is possible but still uncertain, and out in the future.

Stablecoins are more difficult to assess, largely because they are still in their infancy. The most prominent among them, Libra (subsequently Diem), launched in 2017 by Facebook (now Meta), was eventually abandoned – a sign that maybe this is not the future of money. Others survive and others are yet to be born. In essence, stablecoins are banks, just more specialized. Like banks, they offer a special service – liquidity transformation – which is both essential to the economy and risky. Their ambition is to offer instruments that are as safe as bank deposits, with associated payment facilities, backed by a pool of assets or by trading algorithms. The main concern about them is their fragility, inherent in the maturity and risk transformation that occur in their balance sheets. The risk is compounded by them being still unregulated and unsupervised – unlike banks, with which they compete. However, were they regulated, they may find it difficult to compete with traditional intermediaries. We conclude that while the trade-off between security and cost does favor them in comparison to other crypto assets, the jury is still out, because the sector is still evolving and a proper prudential framework is still in the future.

Central bank digital currency is a catchword for proposals discussed in central banking circles at present to indicate digital cash issued by central banks. Leaving details aside, the basic idea is that CBDCs should be like bank deposits, except that they would be recorded in the books of the central banks rather than those of the banks. This would evidently short-circuit the complementarity between banks and the central bank: The two would end up offering similar services, thus becoming substitutes more than complements. No major central bank has yet issued a CBDC, with the partial exception of the People's Bank of China. The main Western central banks – the Federal Reserve, the European Central Bank, and the Bank of England – are conducting studies and will make decisions within the next few years.

In Chapter 10 we go deeper into the pros and cons of this idea. From the perspective of individual users, successful retail CBDCs would be indistinguishable from bank deposits. They could be supported by any of today's digital means (cards or apps). The person approaching the cashier in a store would have in their pocket another card or a smartphone app, which directly or indirectly (the precise way is unclear at the moment) would be linked to a customer deposit in the central bank. Payments could be instantly registered with a central bank and be interfaced through a bank acting as an operational platform. All the difference would be "below the surface," not visible to or understandable by the unsophisticated user. Assuming the central bank were able to remain technologically at the frontier – something which is far from granted – the CBDC would compete with other instruments, already established and which work well, without clear user advantages.

We also discuss potential complications arising from CBDCs for monetary policy, financial stability, and other reasons. Given the limited advancement of CBDC projects, it is impossible to see what their future may be – if, in particular, they eventually see the light and find their niche in a complete and diversified payments ecosystem, or risks will arise which will outweigh their benefits.

In Chapter 11 we consider whether digital monies can redesign the boundaries between market forces and government, ultimately between individual freedom and public control in the monetary sphere. Supporters of this view often refer to the Austrian school, which in earlier centuries advocated free markets in both money management and banking. The digital revolution potentially makes steps toward "free banking" and privatized forms of monetary management easier. By contrast, CBDCs are a reaction to it, aiming at reestablishing central bank monopoly in a stronger form. Competition, advocates believe, can improve the quality of money. Privacy is a dimension of freedom: If a payment cannot be traced, it cannot be controlled either. But it can be socially harmful, if criminally motivated.

We conclude that the scope of digital and crypto instruments to enhance freedom, competition, and privacy is limited at best. These instruments are all traceable; even if legal safeguards are put in place, they may not resist pressure toward disclosure. Competition always requires rules to function, and digitalization makes this need more compelling because it increases the risk of exploitation for opaque or fraudulent purposes.

In Chapter 12 we look at money as a weapon in global power strategies. The role played by monetary dominance in world politics is far from new: suffice to remind the importance of sterling as a pillar of the British empire in the nineteenth century and that of its successor, the US dollar, in the post–World War II world order. The weaponization of money has become more extensive in the twenty-first century: Banking systems and payment infrastructures, such as SWIFT (Society for Worldwide Interbank Financial Telecommunications), have been used, for example, as part of the war on terror and to uphold the sanctions against Russia during the Ukrainian war. CBDCs, it is sometimes argued, can foster the global role of the respective currencies. This idea adds fuel to the long-standing debate on whether the US dollar is declining as a leading global currency, possibly to be replaced by the Chinese renminbi or the euro. Currency dominance, we argue, has deeper-rooted determinants: the size of the economy, the breadth of financial markets, the efficiency and stability of banking and payment structures, the quality of regulation, and, more broadly, the standing of the respective jurisdiction and the authority it commands on the global scene. No financial market today can compete with that of the United States once the full constellation of relevant characteristics is accounted for. It is unlikely that the mere digitalization of money, by an emerging power like China or even by Europe, could by itself be decisive. Over time, tectonic movements may occur, though. An efficient monetary digitalization can contribute, with other factors, to shifts in geopolitical power.

In Chapter 13 we delve into the possible reasons for the acceleration in the digitalization of money observed in the last fifteen to twenty years. We identify those roots in the return of instability in the global economy and financial sector after decades of relative calm, sometimes called in academic debates "moderation." The launch dates of many digital start-ups are revealing: 2014 for Apple Pay and 2011 for Google Pay. The foundational document of Bitcoin by the pseudo-named Satoshi Nakamoto dates 2008. PayPal is older (1998), but its development phase really started after the spinoff from eBay (2014) and the launch of a new strategy as an independent platform. The financial environment after the financial crisis of 2007–08 provided a fertile ground for the rise of digital monies, in various forms. The crisis shattered public confidence in banks and other established financial institutions, encouraging solutions outside the traditional sector. The wave of bank regulation that followed the crisis facilitated the shift of resources and business toward the less-regulated financial sector, which became the cradle and incubator of fintech. Massive liquidity injections by the central banks compounded the process by fueling risky investment, part of which was channeled toward crypto markets. It also provided finance to corporate buyouts, part of which took place in the tech sector.

That phase has now ended; interest rates have returned positive and central banks are mopping up the mass of liquidity created by their "quantitative easing." Will the reversal extend to the digital money world? Shall we see a retrenchment in the use of digital monies, less innovation, and a return to traditional payment practices? Experience suggests that interest rate fluctuations often trigger new phases of financial innovation. A similar experience may repeat now. Online payment facilities will increasingly dominate the retail sector, with fierce competition among networks being fatal to many competitors, especially the smaller ones, leading to more concentration and market power. Cryptocurrencies and stablecoins may not have an easy life in the "new world" of higher inflation and interest rates. They may offer some value in diversified portfolios, especially if supported by regulation enhancing their transparency, protecting investors, and combating crime. In one sentence: Crypto instruments will not always be the same but will always be with us.

We conclude, in Chapter 14, highlighting possible future directions. We argue that central banks – partially independent and accountable agencies with a mandate and technical expertise – are not replaceable, in the foreseeable future, as guardians and administrators of monetary systems as they move deeper into the digital era. They should remain the base of a monetary pyramid that includes private banking institutions and a constellation of related and connected private payment solutions, constantly evolving and improving. The critical element to be maintained is the complementarity between the private and the public side of this construction. The first is the engine of innovation, the second ensures the competitive playing field and financial stability. A well-functioning monetary and payment ecosystem requires regulation and supervision. For the world of crypto, rules have to be set up from scratch – using experience from other areas. Innovation should be encouraged and, even before that, *permitted*. This is why, in our opinion, CBDCs are not helpful and may even become a threat. Competing with private providers from a privileged position (central banks are financed by taxpayers and cannot go bankrupt) they risk altering the playing field, upsetting the equilibrium between the private and public components and stifling technical progress. If CBDCs see the light eventually, they should be carefully designed in a way to preserve that equilibrium.

2 Money and Technology in Ancient Times

Et maiores et posteros vestros cogitate.

Cornelius Tacitus

Ask two economists a question, and you will get three different answers – so a popular joke goes. This is an exaggeration, but with a grain of truth: Economists often disagree with one another, perhaps because their theories are so difficult to prove or disprove. When they agree, it may happen that their proposition is disproved by other scientists. This happened to a theory that interests us here: that of the origin of money.

Adam Smith, the father of classical economics, in his 1776 magnum opus *An Inquiry on the Nature and the Causes of the Wealth of Nations*, argued that money arises spontaneously from labor specialization.[1] In primitive societies – so his story goes – each person procured the necessary for the self and the family and no exchange took place. Procurement and consumption remained confined within the same person or small community. As soon as hunter-gatherers settled down and became farmers and ranchers, which happened some 10,000 years ago, they realized that labor was more productive if each person specialized. With specialization, more can be produced, but exchange must take place; a producer of a certain good has too much of it, hence they must trade with those who have less of it than desired. Here is where money enters the picture. It is very difficult for a baker (this is the example Smith makes), who has a lot of bread – a perishable good – and no meat – another perishable good – to find at that exact moment a butcher who desires that amount of bread and has that amount of extra meat to give away. According to Smith, Barter exchange is "clogged and embarrassed"[2]: A well-balanced diet becomes unlikely. The problem is overcome with an intermediate means of exchange – call it money – recognized and accepted by both. The baker can sell bread to anybody and use the monetary proceeds to buy meat, at the same or at a later time. The requirement of simultaneous desire – the double coincidence of wants, as economists call it – is eliminated; the acts of selling and buying are delinked. A more efficient "monetary" economy is born.

This reasoning suggests a time sequence: Separation of labor gave rise to barter first; this gave rise to the invention of money and to an economy based on monetary exchange.

This story is logical and prima facie convincing. It also fits nicely into Smith's philosophical mind frame, in which human actions are driven by individual incentives. People specialize because by doing so they produce more; then they "invent" money to better exploit the value of that added production. The whole process is market-driven; money arises spontaneously from private tastes, decisions, and actions. No social coercion, no consensus gathering, and no government action or ruling are needed.

The problem with this theory is that no evidence was found to support it.[3] Anthropologists gauge ancient peoples' customs from archaeological sites, and by studying modern primitive communities, under the admittedly dubious assumption that they behave like the ancient ones. From neither of these sources has anthropological research found any trace of barter leading to monetary exchange. Evidence of the contrary was actually found: Barter typically arises among people already accustomed to money, for example, if for whatever reason money becomes scarce or unusable. We will see an example later in this chapter. In primitive societies, barter and money may complement each other, for example, when trades of goods of unequal value need balancing. Some small communities rely on kinship to transfer goods without immediate compensation; "gifts" are offset at a later date, supported by bonds of trust in a sort of informal credit system. All these practices are interesting and tell something about how money can usefully serve basic human needs. And there is evidence of each of them. But none of them remotely resembles barter as intended by Smith.

By contrast, history offers repeated examples of a close link between the "forms of money" – the physical support that embodies the monetary concept – and the technology prevailing at any given time. Across the ages, money adopted the most advanced techniques available at each given time with the purpose of ensuring the fulfilment of certain desirable characteristics. Technology evolves over time, usually improving; so does money.

We will return to those characteristics in Chapter 4. Suffice here to say that a well-functioning monetary instrument must satisfy four broad requirements: be commonly familiar and accepted by all – which implies it should be hard to falsify; be transferable across space – meaning, easy and safe to handle and to carry; be efficiently transferable over time – meaning, not perishable in quality and value; and be easily divided into subunits – so as to serve as a convenient unit to exchange goods of different value. In catchwords, and not necessarily in order of importance, money should be: *generally recognizable, movable across space, movable over time,* and *divisible.*

In its essence, the history of money – a branch of history for which a large literature exists – tells the ways in which these requirements were gradually fulfilled across the epochs, by means of technology and institutions. A long process, unfinished to this day, featuring advancements and setbacks, breakthroughs and mistakes, discoveries and occasional mischiefs. Most of the time, users of money faced trade-offs among the different requirements: Instruments convenient for measuring, such as the barley or cocoa beads used by ancient civilizations, were too perishable and were abandoned; more resilient ones, like gold ingots or silver coins, could not be easily transported in large quantities and also featured security problems, hence were also superseded. In the end, technology mitigated the trade-offs and allowed progress in all dimensions. A regular intruder in this process was the state, with its temptation to exploit its monopoly over the currency as a firm of taxation: the so-called seigniorage.

We will now tell the story of the three main technological milestones of monetary history prior to the modern age. This will bring us from the dawn of human civilization until the end of the nineteenth century – a period during which money took mainly three forms: clay, coined metal, and paper. The remaining and more modern part of the story, from the twentieth century onward, is the subject of the rest of this book.

Our journey starts five millennia years ago, in the so-called land between two rivers: Mesopotamia.

CLAY

Ashurbanipal, King of the Universe (how he liked to be called), king of Assyria, conqueror of Egypt, reigned between 668 BC and 631 BC. A skillful ruler and military commander, he was also, or perhaps mainly in his heart, a collector of books. More precisely: the greatest collector of books in ancient history. We owe him much of what we know about ancient Mesopotamia today. And, in particular, that we understand the remarkable role that the "land between two rivers" played in the history of money.[4]

By "books" we do not mean stacks of paper bound on one side and opened on the other that we intend today. We mean tablets made of dried clay. Mesopotamia was, and still is now that it is called Iraq, the ideal place on earth to manufacture those kinds of tablets: rich in good clay from the banks of the rivers, fresh flowing water to mold the tablets, and a powerful sun to dry them up. Using those resources and developing unprecedented skills in the necessary technique, the Mesopotamians became the greatest masters in the craft of manufacturing clay tablets history remembers. Many important things followed. For one, the invention of modern writing: cuneiform, the intermediate step between ancient ideograms and modern alphabets. Being skillful writers, with lots of good tablets on hand, the Mesopotamians developed the habit of recording virtually everything that mattered in everyday life: from literature to inventory catalogues, from customs to price lists, letters and memo pads, legal contracts, and financial statements.

An intellectual before being a king, Ashurbanipal wanted to establish the greatest library of his time. For this purpose, he collected all tablets he could find in his own kingdom or loot in the territories he conquered. Remains of that library survive in the ancient city of Nineveh, today Mosul, after resisting the corrosion of time and more recently the barbarism of the Islamic State. Those remains witness the intention of the farsighted ruler to pass on knowledge to future generations, besides preserving his own name. His intention would not have been borne out, however, if not for an unforeseen event he would have considered a misfortune had he been able to predict it.

Shortly after his death, the city of Nineveh was conquered, and the library destroyed by fire. We don't know how many documents made of combustible materials perished; what we do know is that the clay tablets were "cooked" by fire, hence vitrified and made fit for eternity. Discovered by British archaeologists in the mid nineteenth century, Ashurbanipal's library is now kept largely in the British Museum, the object of active research between British and Iraqi scholars.

With countless others found elsewhere in the region, those tablets offer a detailed picture of the financial arrangements in use in the Sumerian–Babylonian–Assyrian civilization starting from around 3000 BC – a picture that is as fascinating as it is startling because of the many similarities it shares with modern financial and banking practices.

The fundamental monetary value for the Mesopotamians rested on two goods: barley and silver. They had, therefore, like others in later history, a two-commodity monetary standard. In contrast with later experiences with multiple standards, however, it is hard to imagine two more radically different monetary means coexisting. Barley can be finely divided and amassed, therefore providing an excellent metric. But it is highly perishable, hence difficult to maintain through time. Silver ingots, by contrast, are not affected by time but are cumbersome to carry and difficult to divide into subunits.

Perhaps complementarity was precisely the reason why the ancient Iraqis used barley and silver together.

The two forms of money were stored in temples and supervised by priests. Priests scrupulously recorded deposits and withdrawals, took care of good and orderly storage, administered the records of depositors and borrowers (the two types of money were also lent out), controlled the authenticity of the material, and certified it by means of specific seals. They were, in all effects, "bankers" responsible for the good administration of the monetary values entrusted to them. Gradually, the profession moved outside the temples, and families of bankers started to perform a similar role.

All contracts, transactions, arrangements, certificates of authenticity, deposit or loan operations, and so on related to barley and silver were recorded on clay tablets. Some of them displayed seals certifying the quality of the underlying values under the authority of the issuer – priests or others.

Some historians believe that tablets could also function as "bearer securities," representing the underlying asset, and could change hand – much like today's transferable bank checks. The exact extent to which monetary circulation took place through movements of the underlying values, as opposed to simpler transfers of tablets, is unknown. One can conjecture that the ease with which Mesopotamians manufactured and handled tablets and the complexity and risk of moving barley and silver outside the safety of the temple provided a powerful incentive to execute a good part of monetary transactions by a simple transfer of tablets.

We are witnessing here a skeleton banking system, with bankers (priests or specialized families) receiving deposits and lending out, guarding the real value (commodity in the form of barley and silver, sort of bank reserves), and ensuring that all transactions were always legitimate and based on the underlying value. Depositors (usually merchants) would use clay tablets to record contracts and exchange, according to the needs of their business. A major difference with today's banking operations, of course, was the absence of credit multiplication: Priests operated effectively on a 100 percent reserve constraint. Other differences seem largely cosmetic.

This system was good enough to survive for millennia. In the end, however, the Mesopotamians' highly sophisticated practices based on clay were not bound to last: technological advances led to their demise. The ashes of Ashurbanipal's library were barely cold when another monetary revolution was in the making, about a thousand miles west of Nineveh near the coast of the Aegean Sea.

GOLD (AND OTHER PRECIOUS METALS)

Croesus, king of Lydia (a region corresponding to the western part of today's Turkey) around the middle of the sixth century BC, was no modest man: Credited with the biggest wealth of his era, his name is still the archetype of extreme richness. Part of his wealth derived from the usual channel of sovereigns: taxes; the rest, from a gold-soaked river where, according to the legend, his mythical predecessor King Midas (the one with the "golden touch") used to swim.

The kingdom of Lydia was very advanced economically, commercially, and technologically. Its metal processing specialists were the first to discover a technique to separate base metal from precious metal, thereby obtaining pure gold. Gold nuggets contained a percentage of silver, giving rise to a league called electrum. Ingots or coins made of electrum could not be trusted because the gold content was uncertain. After the discovery of that technique, those minted in Sardis (Lydia's capital) became the first authentic and guaranteed gold coins in history.[5] Oval ingots of pure gold started being minted, with a stamped profile of a lion, which was a trusted guarantee of quality. This stamp is, incidentally, the reason why coins still have a flat shape today.[6]

Like Ashurbanipal, Croesus was the last king of his dynasty: Defeated by the Persians, he lost his kingdom and his life. His conqueror, King Cyrus of Persia, wasted no time in adopting the Lydian minting technique. The era of coinage was in full swing. It hasn't ended yet.

The advent of coinage on the eastern shores of the Mediterranean in the sixth century BC is arguably *the most important* event in monetary history to date. Mankind would have to wait for well over 1,000 years before seeing another comparable technological advancement: paper money. Coins still circulate today and show no sign of being abandoned. They, therefore, represent the oldest still used monetary instrument.

Coins represented a major leap forward for several reasons. First, minting allowed standardization. Standardization made coins superior to beads and other natural commodity monies, each piece of which is different. Moreover, minting technology was not widely available, hence limiting forgery. Coins also outperformed barley and any other form of commodity money in terms of resilience and duration, thus making them better stores of value. They could be transported easily, at least in small quantities.

Coins also arose at the other end of the Eurasian landmass. But the Chinese followed a different path. At first, they replicated the form of cowry shells in copper. Sometimes they also gave copper ingots the form of knives, but these irregular forms were not practical and were soon abandoned. Starting from the second century BC the first unified dynasty standardized the currency, issuing copper coins with one practical innovation: a hole in the middle to make them easy to transport and count, if held on a string. This illustrates the importance of standardization and divisibility, a property that other forms (like metal cowry shells) did not have. Round copper coins with a square hole in the middle remained the basis of Chinese money for the next 2,000 years. This resistance of the Chinese monetary system to change over two millennia is a mystery.

A first distinctive aspect of Chinese coinage was the technology used: Western coins were minted (i.e., the piece of metal was hammered on a die), whereas Chinese coins were cast (the liquid metal was poured into a mold). Casting has the advantage that it is possible to make a hole in the middle. This would be very difficult to achieve in minting (no European coins had a hole until modern times). The disadvantage of casting is that finer details are often lost. This facilitates the work of forgers who can just produce a mold from a legitimate coin. Nevertheless, the Chinese continued to use almost exclusively casting instead of minting, which was known and used in surrounding countries.

The second distinctive aspect of the Chinese monetary system was the continued reliance on copper or bronze coins only. Although it was clearly inconvenient to use kilos of copper coins to make major purchases, the Chinese did not adopt silver coins until modern times. Silver was known in China and considerable quantities were imported but was used only in the form of ingots for major transactions, never coined or minted on a large scale.

Despite these disadvantages, the Chinese never changed their system while Europe continued to experiment with gold and silver coins, leaving copper ones to small denominations.

The little round pieces of gold of the Lydian king were recognizable after being stamped with the lion's head. Their value was inherent, embodied in the coin itself, controllable "by sight" and therefore widely trusted. The king accepted them for taxes and other payments. The stamp of the king provided an authoritative certification of their value.

But precisely here lay a snag.

The technology to determine the exact content of a metal alloy was in the sovereign's hands. Sovereigns could mint honest coins, of value equal to the declared one, but didn't have to. They soon learned that by not doing so, they could extract value from their citizen using coin production – a covert channel of wealth appropriation that the Sumerian system, where real value remained safely stored, did not allow. Sovereigns are among the most cash-hungry individuals in history, especially in times of war. Coinage, therefore, delivered to the sovereign a very effective new means of taxation: debasing the currency. The era of "seigniorage" had started.

The Greeks wasted no time in learning the trick. Politically fragmented in city-states constantly at war with one another and outside enemies, Greek rulers were often in acute need of money. When overt taxation did not suffice, coinage was available. The best-known case, unveiled in 405 BC by the playwright Aristophanes in the premiere representation of one of his comedies,[7] happened in Athens. Short of species during the Peloponnesian War, the Athenian leaders introduced bronze tokens to temporarily remedy the scarcity of more valuable coins. Whether the move was transparently communicated to the people or not is still debated by historians, but the reputational damage for Athens, the political and cultural leader of that time, was unquestionable. The scandal was compounded by the fact of being exposed, with irony, by the city's most popular comic author. As a result, the bronze tokens were quickly withdrawn and replaced by coins with proper silver content.

The debasement of coins in ancient Greece remains on record mainly because of that colorful episode, which also showed the limited scope Greek city-states had in manipulating the quality of their coins. They were likely to be discovered, and citizens could easily adopt coins of neighboring and maybe rival cities. Currency competition helped maintain the quality of coins stable. Especially after its failed attempt with copper coins, Athens made sure its coins would set the standard for others. Anybody could bring its silver to the mint in the city and, for a small fee, have it minted into Drachmas. This meant that the Athenian rulers could not debase their silver coins, which became the standard throughout the entire Greek world.[8]

But while the Greeks were enjoying Aristophanes' plays, another power arose gradually further west, on the shores of the Italian peninsula. Rome over time conquered most of the known ancient world. Its history provides an example of both unparalleled monetary stability and equally unparalleled monetary debasement six centuries later. Historians disagree on whether monetary debasement was the consequence of, the cause of, or just a sideshow in the decline and eventual demise of the Roman empire.[9] What is certain is that the phenomenon was unprecedented. Even today, economic historians refer to the Roman monetary debasement of the third century

AD when they want to prove or disprove theories regarding the consequences of bad monetary management for inflation, economic prosperity, and the broader political fortunes or ills of civilizations.

Rome rose as an agricultural republic in which independent farmers had little need of money, using mainly coins from the Greek city-states in southern Italy. However, this changed as the republic grew in power and extension. The first major Roman coin, the *denarius*, was created in republican times, in 211 BC – just when Rome was winning the war against its major Mediterranean rival: Carthage. This coin would last five centuries and pass on its name to many descendants until our times. The *denarius* was divided into ten parts (hence the word *denarius*) and was initially almost pure in its silver content. The Romans mastered the minting techniques and could perfectly measure the purity of metal, having learned that from the Greeks.

As in other areas, the Romans did not innovate the technology. They only exploited it like no others.

The main contribution of the Romans to monetary history was organizational. A gold coin is of little use in everyday life. It can be used to pay taxes (or bribes, the difference was not always clear in ancient times), but not to buy a loaf of bread on the market. The Chinese copper coins worked much better for this purpose. An entire system of coins with a wide range of different values is thus needed to fully exploit the advantages of coinage.

Modern cash spans a range of 10,000 to 1, going from a 100-dollar or 200-euro banknote to a single cent (euro or dollar). Such a range is difficult to achieve with coins made of one metal. The largest coin would have to weigh 10,000 times more than the smallest. The combination of banknotes makes this vast range possible. The Romans achieved something similar more than 2,000 years ago by using a single scale based on three different metals: gold, silver, and copper.[10] Such a system is now usually called bi-metallic because the role of copper as "small change" is disregarded in the classification of monetary systems.

The first emperor, Augustus, overhauled the silver-based system inherited from the republic. The imperial monetary system was based on four coins: The gold *aureus* was equal to 25 silver *denarii* or 100 silver *sestertii* or 400 copper *as*. The range was 400:1. The weights (*aureus* 8.09 grams of gold, *denarius* 3.9 grams of silver, and *as* about 10 grams of copper) were roughly similar to modern coins. Roman literature reveals that the *sestertius* was by far the most common unit, followed by the *denarius* and then the *aureus*.[11] Their real values can be grasped if one considers that one month's pay of a low-ranked legionary in the early empire was equivalent to one *aureus*, or 25 silver *denarii*, weighing about 100 grams – still manageable. One would need two to three kilograms of the brass *sestertius*. Paying in *as* would require four kilograms of coins – clearly inconvenient. Ordinary Romans, including most legionaries, would rarely see an *aureus* in their life, but that unit was useful for measuring tributes from Rome's provinces or paying for a shipload of Greek wine.

The advantage of this system was that it provided coherent metric to accommodate a large range of small and large transactions – much better than the multitude of small Greek silver coins or the copper-only Chinese system. Using three different metals was crucial to having a wide range of values. In ancient times gold was worth about twelve times its weight in silver and silver was worth about forty times its weight in copper. About 480 units of copper would be needed for the same quantity of gold.

For a simple salary earner, the *denarius* was as valuable as the US dollar around 1900. At that time the average wage for an unskilled worker in the United States was about 1 dollar a day, compared to a daily salary of around one *denarius* in imperial Rome.[12] The quarter dollar is now the largest denomination US coin and plays a minor role in daily life. But back in the 1900s, the quarter constituted a significant value, about as important as a *sestertius* for an average Roman.[13]

A second distinguishing feature of the Roman monetary system was its stability for centuries, followed by accelerating decline. The eventual decline naturally attracts more attention than the long period of stability that preceded it. But while many monies in history have come and gone, few have survived and stayed as stable and long as the *denarius*. Its silver content was still essentially unchanged 200 years after its first introduction, when the republic morphed into an empire in 23 BC. The mint, located in the noblest site of the Eternal City, the top of the Capitol, was dedicated to the goddess Juno Moneta – whence comes the name "money." The heydays of the *denarius* would last another two centuries. Early signs of danger came already in Augustus' family, when his great-grandson Nero, who reigned between AD 54 and AD 68, chopped off 5 percent of its value. That was a one-off event, nothing compared to what would follow later.

We do not have statistics on prices from ancient Rome. The one reliable indicator of inflation is the pay increase of legionaries, which was carefully recorded and whose evolution indicates the progression of the currency's debasement. The records indicate that around AD 200, under emperor Septimus Severus, the pay of soldiers had about doubled compared to the reign of Augustus. A doubling of the price level may seem like a lot, but in fact this corresponds to an annual inflation of about 0.5 percent. Today we regard a 2 percent inflation as "price stability." But price increases at 2 percent per annum, which would cumulate in 200 years to an increase of the price level of about fifty times. The *denarius* was thus extraordinarily stable by today's standards.

The currency debasement that started in the third century originated in the economic structure of the empire. Rome (the city) produced virtually nothing: It received everything from the territories it conquered. Formidable as engineers, administrators, and warriors, but not equally good as producers, the Romans increasingly faced a conundrum as their dominance expanded beyond the Italian peninsula. Their conquests procured the resources necessary to support their large territory and to satisfy the sophisticated desires of wealthy Romans for imported luxury goods. But those conquests required an ever-increasing army, initially to expand and later to defend the ever-growing borders of the empire. At some stage, military costs became overwhelming; looting and taxing were no longer enough. Recourse to seigniorage, greatly facilitated by the enormous diffusion of the *denarius* within the empire and beyond, became necessary.

The process accelerated at the beginning of the third century AD under the Severians, a dynasty of emperors of military origin. One of them, Caracalla, familiar today mainly because of the monumental thermal baths whose ruins still impress tourists in the center of Rome, is reported to have said: "Nobody in the world should possess money but me, so that I can give it to my soldiers." No clearest statement was ever made by any ruler of his intention to exploit his own citizens by means of money. For that purpose, he introduced a different technique, or rather a smarter trick: rather than melting coins and reminting them with lower content, simply restamping them with a higher number. Easier and quicker.

The debasement of the *denarius* continued relentlessly throughout the third century; in a period of intense crisis, during which the average tenure of emperors was less than three years, the empire morphed into a military dictatorship and the borders of the empire became increasingly permeable and insecure. Under Diocletian (AD 284–305), the *denarius* had virtually lost all its value; it was replaced and continued to be minted only for ceremonial purposes. Gradually, the economy based on money exchanges ceased to function, alongside the loss of trust in the authenticity of the means. At the end of the Western Roman Empire (AD 476), the process was complete. The mint on the Capitol Hill ceased to function and was transferred to Constantinople, the new capital of the East founded on the Bosphorus.

From that time, and thereafter for centuries, the economy of Western Europe shrank, clustering around castles inhabited by the nobility surrounded by cultivated land. Most of the population engaged in subsistence agriculture, which did not necessitate much market exchange. Not many records of trade during that epoch survive. Money was known as a concept but was used little. No undisputed central authority was available to guarantee its value. For example, the duties of the serfs were determined by days of labor or wheat to be delivered, and the mill received a percentage of the grain to be transformed into flour. With the splintering of the Roman administration into small kinglets or fiefdoms of various and shifting shapes, there was no common institution to issue trustable monetary means.

For the few trades that took place in an impoverished economy, people made increasing recourse to exchanges in kind: The monetary economy morphed, to a large extent, into a barter economy. This practice is believed to have survived for long, during the era we now call the Middle Ages.[14]

PAPER

Civilization was just emerging from that dark period, socially, economically, and politically, when the Venetian Marco Polo undertook his travels in the Far East. Rich merchant in a rich city, explorer and writer, Marco Polo reached China through the Silk Road and visited it extensively between 1271 and 1295. After returning, he joined the war Venice was waging against Genoa, was captured, and spent years in a Genoese prison. There he dictated his memoirs, known as *Travels of Marco Polo*, or *Il Milione*.

A passage of that book is worth reproducing here:

> In this city of Kanbalu is the mint of the Grand Khan, who may truly be said to possess the secret of the alchemists, as he has the art of producing money by the following process. He causes the bark to be stripped from those mulberry-trees the leaves of which are used for feeding silk-worms, and takes from it that thin inner rind which lies between the coarser bark and the wood of the tree. This being steeped, and afterwards pounded in a mortar, until reduced to a pulp, is made into paper, resembling (in substance) that which is manufactured from cotton, but quite black.
>
> When ready for use, he has it cut into pieces of money of different sizes, nearly square, but somewhat longer than they are wide. Of these, the smallest pass for a denier tournois; the

next size for a Venetian silver groat; others for two, five, and ten groats; others for one, two, three, and as far as ten besants of gold. The coinage of this paper money is authenticated with as much form and ceremony as if it were actually of pure gold or silver; for to each note a number of officers, specially appointed, not only subscribe their names, but affix their signets also; and when this has been regularly done by the whole of them, the principal officer, deputed by his majesty, having dipped into vermilion the royal seal committed to his custody, stamps with it the piece of paper, so that the form of the seal tinged with the vermilion remains impressed upon it, by which it receives full authenticity as current money, and the act of counterfeiting it is punished as a capital offence.

When thus coined in large quantities, this paper currency is circulated in every part of the Grand Khan's dominions; nor dares any person, at the peril of his life, refuse to accept it in payment. All his subjects receive it without hesitation, because, wherever their business may call them, they can dispose of it again in the purchase of merchandise they may have occasion for; such as pearls, jewels, gold, or silver. With it, in short, every article may be procured.[15]

All key aspects of modern banknote production and circulation, down to most minute details, are present in this passage. The production of paper, starting from wood transformed into wood pulp and eventually to the production of paper sheets. The cut into different sizes and shapes, according to the denominations of the banknotes. The print by means of colorful ink. The precautions adopted to authenticate the banknotes and limit counterfeiting, which was punished with a capital penalty. Finally, the enforcement of the value of money by law, resulting in its acceptance by everybody for all purposes.

The paper money of the Yuan (Mongol) dynasty constitutes the first fiat money in history. Some forms of paper money existed under earlier dynasties, but in a limited form and mostly as private depositary receipts, called flying money. The Yuan emperors decreed its value and ensured acceptance by means of the capital threat – not, as later in Europe, by promising redemption in precious metal.

Paper money did not survive very long in China, however. It was only as strong as the state that issued it. A useful invention, its weakness was in its top-down nature, based on command. When the top weakened, the entire system stopped working. Even a death threat may not be enough for people to surrender real for face value if they believe the paper is worthless. Paper money disappeared in China around the fifteenth century, just when it appeared in Europe in a different form.

Scholars debate why China's monetary sector developed in this way, under the aegis of the state rather than giving rise to a banking system, as happened in Europe. The experience of Europe, to which we now turn, provides a hint: It might be that in China private financial institutions could not find enough space to rise and develop as independent centers of operation and power, due to the overwhelming influence of the state.

At the end of the Middle Ages, conventionally dated by historians around the fall of Constantinople to the Ottomans in 1453 and the discovery of America in 1497, Europeans had not yet realized the potential synergies that existed between paper, which was well known, and the production and usage of money. Paper had been produced in Europe for centuries, but instead of using the bark of a tree, Europe had imported from the Arabs the technique of using rags as the raw material. With Marco Polo the idea that sheets of paper could acquire monetary value became known but was not exploited immediately as such. More fragmented politically than China, hence free from the dominance of a unified state, the European continent featured powerful private financial clusters around banking families, in Germany, Italy, and elsewhere. The monetization of paper thus started in a very different way.

Over the course of the late Middle Ages commerce started to revive. But longer-range trade was hindered by a fragmented monetary system with hundreds of coins and a shortage of good quality high value coins. This led, bottom-up, to the emergence of promissory notes and bills of exchange issued by merchants and negotiated by resourceful bankers. Promissory notes entitle the bearer to receive valuables at given locations from given persons or institutions – a bit like the Sumerian tablets – and they could comfortably change hands. The value of bills of exchange depended of course on the notoriety of the issuer as somebody who would reliably honor promissory notes. But not every merchant could know the solvency of every potential trading partner in a distant city. There was thus a need for a small number of well-known institutions (in fact mostly families) that could provide intermediate services. The usage of paper in the form of promissory notes proved to be complementary to the rise of banking in Europe.

Originating in Italy in the late Middle Ages, banks were expanding their activity in Italy (Venice, Genoa, Florence), and northern Europe (Holland, Germany, Spain) while Marco Polo was writing his memoirs. The ancestors of modern credit institutions centered around rich families, like the Bardi and the Medici in Florence, or later the Fugger and Beremberg in Germany, leveraging on their established wealth to finance a variety of private and sovereign enterprises. Banking in the Renaissance was remarkably cross-border: The Florentine families, for example, played key roles in financing such important endeavors as the British crown's participation in the Hundred Years War, the ships which brought Columbus to America (which sailed from Spain), and in Italy the works of artists such as Leonardo da Vinci, Michelangelo, and Raffaello.

Banks did not issue sight deposits redeemable at par as they do today. They rather operated with a number of contracts written on paper. In some cases, those instruments closely resembled modern instruments currently classified as "money," or close substitutes of them. A key difference was that every "deposit" was, unlike today, an individual contract. This made it impossible to transform these deposits into widely circulating money.

There is evidence that banks in some jurisdictions accepted written pay orders on their accounts.[16] These differed from modern checks, however, in that they were issued not by banks but by individuals, hence less easily recognizable and more prone to fraud. This practice was not universal, due to the inherent risks, but gradually spread. The use of promissory notes was common during trade fairs, as were bills of exchange guaranteed by a bank, which the bearer could discount. Settlement, with possible netting, would take place usually at the end of the fair. Over time, these paper instruments became exchangeable, subject to specific provisions, and circulated in representation of the underlying debt obligation.[17] There was a major difference relative to the tablets of ancient Mesopotamia: Renaissance banks would keep only part of the deposited species in their vaults and lend out the rest. This gave rise to fractional banking, the multiplication of credit, and the expansion of "bank money" (deposits recorded in the banks' ledgers) alongside "base money" (species in the vaults of the banks).

It should be emphasized that these activities were all private; the state was not involved as a direct actor. The state was never too far away, though. For starters, some of the banking families either coincided with the government (as was the case for the Medici in the city of Florence) or had close ties with the government. Moreover, the state would normally intervene with laws to ensure the correct conduct of business. For example, contracts regarded as too risky could be banned in more conservative jurisdictions, while being allowed elsewhere. That was, for example, the case of checks, which were outlawed in Venice until after the sixteenth century.

It was only with the rise of central banks that the relationship between paper and money, until then one of cohabitation, albeit a very stable one, became an official marriage. A new industry was born: that of banknote production, soon to become the core business of central banks. The relevant technology that allowed or at least greatly facilitated this transition was the printing press using standardized moveable type. Invented – once again – in China, this revolutionary technology was first applied in Europe around the middle of the fifteenth century by a resourceful goldsmith in the German city of Mainz: Johannes Gutenberg. His first output was, predictably, the Bible. But once introduced, the new technique could easily be extended to a more material realm: money, in the forms of banknotes and checks.

Together with banknotes, checks, or the more French-sounding cheques, are one of the oldest forms of payment still in existence. The word is thought to derive from the Arabic *sakk*, meaning certificate or payment order. This type of financial instrument – an order issued by an individual, the drawer, to its bank to pay a sum to another party, the payee – was in use at the end of the first millennium AD among Muslim communities in the Eastern Mediterranean. Like other banking practices, it came to Europe from the East, probably during the Crusades between the eleventh and thirteenth centuries AD. In the Renaissance, banks contributed certainty (hence popularity) to checks and bills of exchange (promises to pay between two parties) by requiring the physical presence of both parties at settlement. In their absence, checks were considered risky because of the possibility of forgery, so much so that at times they were forbidden – for example, as we have seen, they were for long outlawed in Venice.

Checks started to be negotiated – that is, to circulate after being issued – late in the sixteenth century in the Netherlands, partly to obviate strict regulations imposed on banks. Negotiability initially concerned bills and promissory notes, then it extended to checks. The receiver of a check would simply write on its back "payable to ...." This would oblige the bank on which the check was drawn to pay this other person or company. Eventually, the practice of "endorsement" (derived from the French "*dos*," or back, implying that they may be signed on the back) made the checks negotiable. Interestingly, the term "endorsing" has escaped the monetary sphere, being now used to mean confirming in every sense.

A specialized institution to clear and settle checks, the ancestor of the modern check-clearing function of central banks, was first founded in Amsterdam in the early seventeenth century. In England

and its colonies, first and foremost the United States, the importance of checks increased with the rise of the deposit bank, institutions whose primary business was to collect deposits and grant credit. A boost to checks came from the restrictions imposed on banks on the issuance of banknotes. After the Civil War (1861–65), bank deposits in the United States rose sharply, and their popularity increased after the newly founded Federal Reserve put in place an efficient clearing system. This early lead in check processing might be in the United Stone reason why checks still play an important role in the United States, as we note in Chapter 7.

A SHORT HISTORY OF CENTRAL BANKS

Economists disagree on what sparked the rise of central banks. Some argue that they arose spontaneously from the need of private banks to organize themselves, ensuring stability to their business: like players who decide to join a "club" because they need common rules for their "game" to function. According to this view banks "need" a central bank, because the nature of their business inherently entails a risk of abuse and the possibility of destabilizing contagion. Most historians reject this explanation though, pointing to the key role governments always played in the establishment of central banks.[18] They argue that central bank monopoly over banknote production is not a natural outcome but a political construct, whose carefully concealed motive is for the government to have an easy channel of finance: seigniorage in disguise.

History sheds some light on this issue. It shows that, in fact, both elements were present at the outset, in a complex mix that depended on the national circumstances of the time. The state, no less than banks, has an interest in financial stability, which central banks are tasked to maintain. Some central banks evolved from pre-existing private banks; others, like the US Federal Reserve, were created anew to protect the banking sector from financial crises. In most cases, however, the rise of central banking was not entirely spontaneous but always undertaken or facilitated by state intervention.

The availability of the printing press constituted in all cases a crucial backdrop; revealingly, all central banks immediately set up printing shops. It is difficult to imagine the rise of central banks without this technology.

The Swedish Riksbank, the oldest central bank in existence, was founded in 1668 by the transformation of a private bank, Stockholm Banco. The latter had enjoyed the privilege of issuing banknotes by appointment of the sovereign, which, in exchange, exercised broad powers in the bank's management. In spite of this, Stockholm Banco eventually abused the trust of the sovereign by issuing banknotes in excess of its reserves and went bankrupt. Hence, the decision to "nationalize" the function, by creating a national bank under the auspices of the parliament. This feature is still reflected today in the role the Swedish parliament plays in the management of today's Swedish central bank, the Sveriges Riksbank, a role that has no equal in other jurisdictions.

For the second central bank, the Bank of England, created a quarter century later, the role of the sovereign was even clearer. Here the basic motivation behind King William III's decision to establish a new financial institution under the government's direct control was to raise funds to finance his naval war against France. The subscribers of the government's loan were incorporated into a joint stock company, which was given the monopoly of issuing banknotes. Only subsequently, due to the trust enjoyed by the tender issued by the Governor and Company of the Bank of England – its name at the time – did the newly established financial institution develop into the role of "bank of the banks," or the "leader of the club."

The next great European power to establish a central bank was France in 1800. The situation of France at that time was somewhat similar to that of England a century earlier: The Napoleonic empire, at war with England and almost everyone else, was in need of finance. But the relation between the Banque de France and the British Isles runs much deeper and earlier than this. This story is relevant for the history we tell, and quite interesting in itself.

An attempt to establish something similar to a central bank had already been made by France under the reign of King Louis XV (1715–74). Five-year-old when he rose to the throne, the king was assisted by a regent, the Duke of Orleans, when a Scottish adventurer named John Law emigrated to France. Adventurous and hot-blooded, Law had killed a man in a duel; condemned to death in England he fled across the Channel into France, where he decided to establish a bank based on his economic principles. An economist and financier, Law is often credited for inventing paper money, though this is an overstatement – as we have seen, the Chinese had made this invention centuries earlier. As an economist, he introduced important ideas like the law of supply and demand, later developed by his compatriot Adam Smith.

The real novelty of Law's Banque Générale Privée was that it was funded by issuing banknotes. In Law's opinion, if banknotes were backed by sound credit extended by the bank to finance the production of goods, they would not cause either financial crises or inflation. This was another of Law's economic ideas, called the "real bills doctrine": a theory which would later be discredited, but not before causing considerable damage in France and in other countries. The French kingdom was close to bankruptcy due to the wars waged by the young king's predecessor: Louis XIV, the *"Roi Soleil"* or *"Louis Le Grand."* In need of money and not particularly versed in economics, the child and his regent endorsed Law's ideas and granted his bank the monopoly over the issuance of banknotes in France.

An embryo of Banque de France in all but the name was thus born in 1716, named Banque Royale. For the first time in history, paper banknotes were accepted for payments as well as for taxes.[19] This early experiment of central banking did not end well. While Law was distracted by other businesses, Banque Royale started overissuing banknotes; extended beyond its reserves, it collapsed in 1720. A disaster for private investors but a bonanza for the sovereign, who managed to reduce France's national debt. The oversupply of money caused inflation to rise – an early refutation of the "real bills doctrine." As a result, banking became so unpopular in France that another attempt to establish a central bank could happen only after the revolution and by the initiative of an absolute ruler: Napoleon Bonaparte. At the top of its power, Napoleon founded the Banque de France as part of his effort to rebuild the nation's institutions, but mindful of the earlier disaster he wanted the new creature to remain largely under state control[20] – a state of dependence from which the Banque de France was freed only late in the twentieth century.

Our chronicle of the central bank build-up in the seventeenth to nineteenth centuries continues with two prominent examples, in Germany and Italy. These two examples bear some similarities, both illustrating the intricate link between money and the state.

The German Reichsbank, founded in 1876 shortly after the unification of Germany under the aegis of Prussia, was the brain-child of Otto von Bismarck, the mastermind of German unification and the chancellor of the country until 1890. Clear in his mind were the precedents of central banking in Britain and France, including their failures. Before unification, several banks of issue had existed in the territory of what would become Germany, and this had generated confusion in the circulation and the use of money in the constitu-ent states. The newly established Reichsbank was supposed to end this confusion and provide a sound monetary basis for the nation's finances, within the framework of the Gold Standard (to be defined and described in Chapter 3).

The legal act establishing the Reichsbank is of particular interest.[21] The new state bank of the German empire adopted from the outset a markedly "legalistic" imprint, which German central banking would retain until modern days. Today's readers cannot but be struck by the similarity of the Reichsbank with the post–World War II central bank, the Deutsche Bundesbank. The latter would in turn exert considerable influence over the treaty establishing the European Central Bank, founded in 1998.

The Reichsbank Act established the bank's monopoly over the creation and circulation of German banknotes. It listed in detail the types of credit operations that the bank could conduct, hence determining the broad structure of the central bank's balance sheets. Special provisions stipulated the backing of the banknotes with gold, legally establishing Germany's adherence to the Gold Standard. In particular, the Reichsbank should stand ready to exchange banknotes with gold at a given parity and hold a given ratio of gold reserves in its vaults. Of interest from a modern perspective are the articles regarding transparency: The bank should publish information on its balance sheet and the conditions applied to credit operations. Among the latter, was the so-called Lombard Rate, which the German central bank would continue to use for lender-of-last-resort operations until the adoption of the euro in 1999. The Act stipulated that the bank would be tax-exempt but as a counterpart of that should provide cashiers and other monetary services to the German empire. The profits of the bank should be split between its shareholders and the empire. The bank thus maintained a trace of private ownership inherited by its ancestor, the Prussian Bank; full nationalization would come decades later by a decision of another and more infamous chancellor: Adolf Hitler.

Like the German one, the Italian state originated from a merger, in 1861, of several previously autonomous regions, each of which had its own currency, institutions, and conventions. A new national currency, the lira, was created, but there remained initially five banks entitled to issue liras – or rather six, including the Banca Romana, which joined after Rome, previously held by the pope, became the capital of the unified country in 1871. For about two decades, there were multiple banks issuing lira banknotes, all convertible in gold. These multiple currencies competed with one another subject to restrictions and state supervision concerning the extent and modalities of their issuance.

Several circumstances contributed to the collapse of this system. At the heart, here again, was the perennial risk of currency management by private banks: overissuance of banknotes. Banca Romana was involved in multiple scandals regarding the financing of politicians, which gave rise to a conflict of interest in the exercise of surveillance. Moreover, in the decades after unification Italy underwent a real estate boom, especially in Rome, fueled by inflows of inhabitants after becoming the capital of Italy. Banca Romana and other banks financed real estate developments largely by issuing banknotes redeemable on demand. Last but not least, serious banking irregularities were discovered in the Banca Romana. When the construction bubble burst, at the turn of the 1890s, a scandal erupted as the attempt by the government to cover up irregularities was revealed. In 1893 Banca Romana was liquidated and the other banks of issues in the Center–North merged into a new entity, Banca d'Italia, while two other banks in the South continued to operate as issuers to a smaller scale until Mussolini centralized banknote issuance into the Banca d'Italia in 1926.

WHAT LESSONS FROM THESE EARLY EXPERIENCES?

As our narrative moves forward to the twentieth century and beyond, a "new era" dominated by electronic and digital money, it is worth reflecting on what these more ancient monetary experiences can tell us, in spite of their diversity. We are interested in whether such experiences may bring lessons which, though coming from far back in time, remain valid today.

The first message to be drawn is that a successful "monetary function" – creating money, guaranteeing its quality, and administering its orderly circulation – requires a mix of two elements: a "public administration" element, consisting of institutions and individuals pursuing the collective benefit, and a "private interest" one, with subjects acting freely to pursue their own benefit. The ancient Sumerians founded their system on the cooperation between merchants, deciding what money would be used, and priests, the guardians of reliability and trust. The Romans upset the partnership when an overwhelming and oppressive imperial power debased and finally debauched the currency. Similarly, paper money did not survive in China because there were no well-established private forces to limit the power of the state to misuse money. In Renaissance Europe, the pendulum swung to the opposite side, to a system relying excessively on the power of private bankers.

The existence of multiple issuing banks would eventually become a factor of fragility in the absence of enforceable rules and effective supervision. However, partly due to Europe's political fragmentation, a bank-based monetary issuance system lingered on for long after the Renaissance. When banks exploited their issuing power, financial crises and inflation set in. Banknote-issuing banks were eventually bound to disappear, replaced in each country by a monopoly of issuance exercised by a single institution: the central bank.

The central bank exercises in essence a public function regardless of its legal form – even when it is a privately owned joint stock company subject to the civil code as well as constitutional provisions. The rise of central banks in Europe, and subsequently elsewhere, restored the balance between private finance and the power of the state. Yet even in modern times, this balance remains delicate and always at risk of being upset.

To use a popular expression, money is a *public–private partnership*. And for good reasons, because it is both the means through which private economic interest is pursued and preserved and a basic collective infrastructure allowing the economy to function for the benefit of everybody. To be clear, we refer here to market economies; centrally planned systems tend to make money disappear, as we will see in Chapter 3. In a recent book, economists Daron Acemoglu and James Robinson, both Nobel Prize recipients in 2024, have made a more general argument, theorizing that well-functioning liberal-democratic societies are based on a mix of public institutions and private initiative: They represented this graphically as a "Narrow Corridor" at the center of a diagram where the axes represent the power of the state and the power of society.[22] Inside that corridor, the state is strong enough to guarantee basic public goods like safety and the enforcement of contracts but not strong to the point of unduly repressing individual liberties, rights, and interests. Money, a key institution of a free society, must stay within that narrow corridor as well.

A second point that needs to be stressed is the complementarity between money and technology – the technology of clay first, then that of minting good and well-accepted coins, and eventually the technology of instilling value into printed paper. By the end of the nineteenth century, the whole monetary construction was largely run on paper, based on technologies Europe had imported and adapted from the Chinese. Six centuries after Marco Polo visited the reign of the Grand Kahn, most of Europe (and later in the United States as well, as we shall see) was using roughly the same "pulp ... pounded by a mortar... made into paper," which had amazed the Venetian traveler. Paper to compile and maintain ledgers. Paper to record all documentation relating to deposits, among banks and between banks and their clients. Paper to exchange money deposited at banks among individuals and businesses in the form of checks. Paper to draft contracts regulating all banking activities. Finally, paper as physical money itself, in the form of banknotes.

A European innovation, or rather an improvement on a Chinese one, the moveable type, proved decisive. The European alphabet, with its limited number of letters, is much more suitable to moveable type than Chinese writing with its very large number of characters. Printing with moveable type provided economies of scale and at the same time a good protection against forgery because setting up a printing press involved a lot of know-how and a heavy investment. As mentioned already, money must be an effective channel to convey information: high-quality, standardized, and verifiable information on the underlying value. In Mesopotamia, clay tablets were able to transmit such information. Precious coins improved on that technology, until they were debased. Coins were eventually largely replaced by paper. The combination of moveable type and paper vastly improved the ease at which information could be transmitted, in a standard format and relatively straightforward to verify.

At the end of the nineteenth century, the age of paper money was at its peak but also about to end. Money was ready to move on to new technology.

BEYOND MATERIAL MONEY

Transmitting signals at long distances, by rapid and immaterial means, has been a human aspiration since the earliest times – like flying, with which it has some similarities. The Greeks had keywords we still use to express the concept: *tele*, or far away, and *grafé*, or writing, hence telegraphy. Early forms of telecommunication used optical means. The Greeks used them for military purposes; historians report that optical signals helped ensure their victory against the Persians at Marathon. After them, optical telegraphy was used for centuries: from Roman soldiers to Medieval knights, from sailors engaged in discoveries and trades to Native Americans. There is no evidence that visual signals were ever used for financial messaging, though it is not inconceivable that this may have happened.

In modern times, the French mastered the practice of visual telegraphy. A young French engineer, Claude Chappe, introduced in the eighteenth century the largest network of optical telegraphs ever. In its height, the "Chappe system" extended 5,000 kilometers over the whole of France, with hundreds of nodes. Particular shapes and colors conveyed signals at long distances, using a code developed by a resourceful engineer. The revolutionary government recognized the strategic value of this invention: Robespierre, the mastermind of the Reign of Terror (the final phase of the French Revolution), authorized Chappe to remove all obstacles (trees, buildings, or anything else) that obstructed his signals. In 1794, the Chappe system brought to Paris the news of the victory of the revolutionary army against Austria and Prussia. Unfortunately for him, Robespierre could not rejoice: His head had already fallen under a guillotine.

While that system was still operating, experimentation with electrical telegraphs had already started in several places. Initially, they were rudimentary devices, sending basic signals at a short distance. A breakthrough came with the Morse alphabet, developed in the United States by painter Samuel Morse. The strength of Morse's system was in combining the telegraph with a dedicated cypher, the well-known sequence of points and dashes. The system rapidly developed in the United States for military means: Cables laid in the early 1860s helped the Unionist forces win the Civil War. More sophisticated transmitters and receivers were quickly introduced, eventually with telegraphic printers which greatly facilitated the receiving end of the messages. Cables laid under the sea connected islands and eventually continents. By the end of the nineteenth century, an extensive network of telegraphic cables had been established, permitting electrical telecommunication on a global scale.

At this point, everything was ready for money to start traveling on electrical signals, eventually in digital form.

NOTES

1. Adam Smith, *An Inquiry on the Nature and the Causes of the Wealth of Nations* (1776), book 1, chapter 4.
2. Smith, *Wealth of Nations*, book 1, chapter 4.
3. Ilana E. Strauss, "The Myth of the Barter Economy," *The Atlantic*, February 26, 2016.
4. On finance in ancient Mesopotamia and the role played by clay tablets therein, see Odoardo Bulgarelli, *Il denaro alle origini delle origini* (Spirali, 2001) and Odoardo Bulgarelli, "Le banche nell'antichità (II e III millennio a.C)," *Mondo Bancario*, 1999; for a general reference on money in ancient times, see Glyn Davies, *History of Money: From Ancient Times to the Present Day* (University of Wales Press, 2016).
5. Jacques Melitz, "Reasons for the Lydian Electrum Coins and the Succeeding Greek Silver Coins in Antiquity," Vox EU Column, December 15, 2019. See also Jacques Mélitz, "*A Model of the Beginnings of Coinage in Antiquity*," European Review of Economic History, 21, no. 1 (2017): 83–103.
6. For the early history of coinage see, among others, John Weatherford, *The History of Money* (Three Rivers Press, 1997).
7. Aristophanes, *The Frogs*, act 1, scene 3.
8. George C. Bitros, Emmanouil M. L. Economou, and Nicholas C. Kyriazis, *Democracy and Money: Lessons for Today from Athens in Classical Times* (Routledge, 2022).

9. Charles A. Kupchan and Paul Kennedy, "Empire, Military Power, and Economic Decline," *International Security* 13, no. 4 (January 1, 1989): 36, or Willem Jongman, "Gibbon Was Right: The Decline and Fall of the Roman Economy," in *Crises and the Roman Empire* (Brill, 2007), 183–99. For a wider discussion, The Editors of Encyclopedia Britannica, "The Decline and Fall of the Roman Empire | Rise & Fall, Causes, Consequences," Encyclopedia Britannica, December 1, 2023,

10. In reality the Romans used four different metals, gold, silver, copper, and bronze. Bronze (orichalcum for the Romans) was considered, by weight, to be about double the value of copper. This is why the *half-sestertius*, the *dupondius*, was around the same size and weight as bronze was but was worth two *as*.

11. Alfred Wassink, "Inflation and Financial Policy under the Roman Empire to the Price Edict of 301 A.D.," *Historia: Zeitschrift für Alte Geschichte* 40, no. 4 (1991): 465–93.

12. See Gilson Willets, *Workers of the Nation: An Encyclopedia of the Occupations of the American People and a Record of Business, Professional and Industrial Achievement at the Beginning of the Twentieth Century*, vol. 2 (P.F. Collier and Sons, 1903).

13. For what one could buy in the United States of 1900, see Shannon Quinn, "30 Things You Could Buy for $1 in 1900," *History Collection*, August 30, 2021, https://historycollection.com/30-things-you-could-buy-for-1-in-1900/.

14. Recent research has found evidence that coins were more common in post-Roman times than previously thought; still their use was confined to specific circumstances and classes of people. See Rory Naismith, *Money and Power in Anglo-Saxon England: The Southern English Kingdoms, 757–865* (Cambridge University Press, 2014).

15. Marco Polo, *Travels* (J.M. Dent and Sons, 1914), book 2, chapter 18.

16. Abbott Payson Usher, "The Origins of Banking: The Primitive Bank of Deposit, 1200–1600," *The Economic History Review* 4, no. 4 (1934): 399–428.

17. Stephen F. Quinn and William Roberds, "The Evolution of the Check as a Means of Payment: A Historical Survey," *Economic Review Federal Reserve Bank of Atlanta* 93, no. 4 (January 1, 2008): 1–28.

18. Charles Goodhart, *The Evolution of Central Banks* (MIT Press, 1988); Michael Bordo, "A Brief History of Central Banks," Federal Reserve Bank of Cleveland Economic Commentary, December 1, 2007.

19. Lawrence Lande and Tim Congdon, "John Law and the Invention of Paper Money," *RSA Journal* 139, no. 5414 (1991): 916–28.

20. This following sentence attributed to Napoleon – "Je veux que la banque soit dans la main du gouvernment, mais qu'elle n'y soit pas trop!" ("I want the bank to be in the hands of government, but not too much!") – suggests that he was aware of the opposite risks of both excessive dependence on and excessive independence from the state. See also Jean-Marie Thiveaud, "1814: La Banque de France au Défi de Son Indépendance – La Question Cruciale de La Confiance," Revue D'économie Financière, January 1, 1992.

21. National Monetary Commission, "German Imperial Banking Laws" (Government Printing Office, 1910).

22. Daron Acemoglu and James A. Robinson, *The Narrow Corridor: States, Societies, and the Fate of Liberty* (Penguin, 2020).

3 Money and Technology in the Modern Age

History is the flow of thought-stuff.
Thought-stuff goes through phases like water.

Henry Adams

In the late 1800s, world monetary arrangements seemed to have reached a stable and lasting form. Banking practices in the advanced world, which at the time meant essentially Europe, mirrored those of Great Britain, the world leader of the time. Encompassing one-quarter of the world's land and a higher share of its population, the British Empire dominated the globe economically, politically, and militarily. Its colonial system, the Commonwealth, accounted for most of the world's trade and capital flows and encompassed all elements of a well-functioning economic system: ample availability of raw materials; a powerful industrial base; vast markets for consumer and investment goods; and, last but not least, a well-run political system, with liberal institutions supported by dominant military power.

Other European countries' monetary and financial structures tended to align with Britain's. At the core of most national financial systems was a central bank with exclusive or predominant power of issuing banknotes which everybody was legally or de facto obliged to accept for payments and the extinction of debts. Central banks oversaw the financial sector and conducted a variety of transactions with banks. These practices would evolve into what we call "monetary policy operations" today, mainly the rediscounting of notes and purchases or sales of securities. The banking business involved collecting deposits and extending credit, today's bread and butter of retail banking. European banks at the time entertained a vast web of cross-border transactions; never before, and rarely later, have the world's frontiers been so open to international trade and capital movements.

In the United States, safeguards were introduced after the Civil War to prevent the overissuance of banknotes by state-chartered banks (under the earlier "free banking" period), including the creation of a new authority, the Office of the Controller of the Currency. Yet amid brisk economic expansion, until the establishment of the Federal Reserve (1913) the US financial system continued to be punctuated by recurrent crises.

The years around the turn of the nineteenth century have been called *la belle époque* – the beautiful era. This French expression conveys, together with the gallic flavor of much of the culture and style of the time, the sense of a "golden age" carrying the promise of endless welfare and progress. It was indeed a remarkable era, with peace, stability, advances in scientific knowledge and living standards coexisting and reinforcing one another. The aristocracy, back in power after the French Revolution, the Napoleonic Wars, and the Restoration, had initially attempted to resist the rise of the middle class,[1] but eventually shared power with it giving rise to mixed political arrangements – the "constitutional monarchies." The wars and revolutions which had ravaged the continent until recently seemed gone for good. It looked like the end of history: Nothing suggested that the beautiful era would soon end, followed by the Great War and the horrors of the twentieth century. Or that humans would soon radically change their ways of living. Including – a sideshow perhaps – their ways of dealing with money.

Before we enter the "new world," we need to look a bit more at the old one. Its monetary architecture was the Gold Standard, an arrangement introduced by Britain in the first half of the nineteenth century as the "monetary heart" of the Commonwealth and subsequently adopted by other nations. Because of the enduring and almost mythical fascination it still enjoys, and its importance for the history we tell, it is worth pausing a moment to understand what the Gold Standard really was, what it was not, and how it worked.

A MOUNTAIN OF PAPER ON A PLINTH OF GOLD

In essence, the Gold Standard is simple and intuitive – not surprisingly, since it originated from the rationalist philosophy called the Enlightenment. Few other topics have attracted so much fascination and attention from economic researchers. Among them, nobody has analyzed its properties, advantages, and limitations as persuasively as the Belgian-born Yale economist Robert Triffin, who wrote extensively about it between the 1960s and the 1980s.[2]

In the Gold Standard the values of currencies were fixed in terms of gold, hence against one another. However, the actual money ordinary people had daily contact with usually did not involve gold. Small transactions used silver or even copper coins; viler metals were used because in gold they would be too small to be practical. Rich households might use gold coins for pricey purchases; the poor might never own a single gold coin.[3] Large financial market transactions would have been cumbersome and risky if executed in gold. Banks' deposits, credit, and other operations were thus conducted mainly on paper, including bank notes and gold certificates. Banks in each country were financed by the central bank through rediscount operations and purchases and sales of bills.

In spite of the name, in the Gold Standard gold was actually seen only in rare circumstances. Most of it remained in the vaults of central banks, much like seeds and silver in the temples of ancient Mesopotamia. Monetary circulation took the form of paper-based banking transactions: paper in the form of banknotes issued by banks or the state; paper to transfer bank deposits in the form of money orders; paper to record transactions in bank ledgers; paper to describe and certify contractual arrangements.

There was one situation, though, when gold did come back to life and played a fundamental role, namely as a mechanism to ensure adjustment to international trade imbalances. When a country imported more than it exported, the payments for the net import would result in a scarcity of money in the deficit country, leading to an increase in interest rates (the price paid to obtain money from banks or other lenders) in that country. The increase in interest rates would then stimulate monetary flows from the surplus country, attracted by the higher interest. That was one way in which adjustment could take place, but not the only one. The scarcity of money would also induce prices to fall in the deficit country, because less money normally leads to lower demand for goods and services and a decline in their price. The deficit country would become more competitive (lower domestic prices relative to foreign prices), which would stimulate exports and hence reduce the original imbalance.

Only when the mechanisms just described did not work well, or not fast enough, did gold see the light and actually move. The increasing demand for foreign currency to pay for its net imports tended to drive its price relative to the domestic currency (the exchange rate) up. Beyond a certain point, it became convenient to pay imports in gold, rather than in currencies; gold hence moved out from the deficit country, reducing its gold reserves and increasing the reserves of the surplus country. To the extent that this stimulated credit extension and deposit taking by banks in the surplus country, and the opposite in the deficit one, this mechanism tended to reinforce the price mechanism that we have referred to – an apparently infallible mechanism to restore and maintain balance, the monetary equivalent of the "communicating vessels" in physics.

This is how the theory went. In fact, as Triffin explained, the Gold Standard rarely functioned as its rulebook predicted.

The "rules" required that the counterbalancing movements in prices and interest rates were allowed to happen. Central banks, however, were powerful enough to prevent that from happening, at least in full. And they did. By extending credit to commercial banks, via rediscounting of paper or outright purchases of it, central banks in deficit countries compensated to a large extent the outflows of money deriving from external trade imbalances. The reason for doing so stemmed from domestic considerations: Declines in prices and wages faced stiff opposition at a time in which organized labor was

rising as a political power. Central banks were thus tempted to neu-
tralize (professional economists would say "sterilize") the monetary
outflows via the external sector by means of domestic monetary creation. The limit to neutralization was given by the availability of gold
in the central bank vaults. As soon as the parity approached the "gold
points," making it profitable to pay directly in species, gold tended
to flow out. Central banks experiencing gold scarcity were compelled
to follow the "rulebook," letting money shrink. This was often the
case with Britain, for example, whereas France, more gold-rich, could
afford to be less disciplined.

Economic historians debate whether the Gold Standard contributed to economic stability and financial order or rather hindered
them. For us, what is of interest is what that system implied for the
use of money. We can metaphorically describe the Gold Standard as
a mountain of paper standing on a foundation of gold. The foundation
was small relative to the mountain. Around 1900, that paper mountain not only was far bigger than its golden pedestal but was growing faster. On Triffin's calculations, between 1885 and 1913 the total
amount of money circulating in the eleven major economies (United
States, United Kingdom, France, Germany, Italy, Netherlands,
Belgium, Sweden, Switzerland, Canada, and Japan) grew threefold,
from 8.4 billion to 26.3 billion dollars. In that same period, the price
level remained broadly unchanged, oscillating up and down over
shorter periods. This indicates that the growth of money in circulation was very large not only in itself but also in relation to the
goods or services it could purchase. The increase was almost fully
accounted for by the increase in what Triffin calls "credit money,"
namely banknotes and bank deposits, whose volume increased from
5.6 billion to 22.4 billion dollars. The "base" of the mountain, represented by gold, and for a minor part silver, increased only from 2.8
billion to 3.9 billion dollars.

These numbers demonstrate that while gold with its intrinsic value provided the essential element of trust, most of the actual
"work" of the monetary system relied on paper. Except that, on the

eve of the twentieth century, the paper was already obsolete as an information-transmitting technology. New discoveries had started to replace graphical messages with telegraphic ones in an increasing number of applications. As with many revolutions, this one too started slowly, but then hastened and became irresistible. After the turn of the century, the face of money was about to change again, forever.

THE "GREAT ACCELERATION" OF THE EARLY TWENTIETH CENTURY

There are times when history accelerates and events happen more frequently in sequence, each leading to another. The European Renaissance was one: Advances in arts, scientific progress, and geographical discoveries all happened at the same time after centuries of near-immobility. Another one of sorts took place in the seventeenth and eighteenth centuries, with the Industrial Revolution, followed by political upheavals shifting the fulcrum of power from the aristocracy to the middle class.

As the nineteenth century was ending, a new acceleration was firing up in science and technology. The wave of discoveries in that period can hardly be overestimated. Wikipedia's list of major inventions counts one every ten years in the seventeenth century,[4] one every three years in the eighteenth century (concentrated toward the end), and more than one per year in the nineteenth century and early twentieth century. These dry numbers still do not convey the importance of each of those innovations. Most of them are still with us: electric and combustion engines for autos, ships, and airplanes, wired and contactless communication devices, medical substances and techniques, plastic materials, cement, batteries, light bulbs, and so on. The list extends to such mundane but essential things as paper packaging, cameras, vacuum cleaners, ballpoint pens, and even the zippers which hold our pants up.

The American historian Henry Adams, a Harvard-educated scion of a prominent Bostonian family counting two US presidents, tried to explain this scientifically. In 1909 he conjectured the existence of inner laws explaining historical accelerations. He imagined the existence of similarities between physical and historical laws. Like matter, history would occasionally "heat up," changing state from solid to liquid and from liquid to gas, accelerating its motion in the process.[5] His era, he thought, was one of those periods. Adam's fanciful theory got nowhere: Lacking proper arguments or evidence, it was dismissed by contemporaries and disregarded by later scholars. Yet it captured the zeitgeist, the enthusiasm and creativity of those tumultuous years. Only his imagination ran a bit too fast even for them.

The technological progress in those years was firmly rooted in major scientific advances; that is when scholars of nature ceased to be philosophers and became "scientists." In the span of a few years, our knowledge of nature changed forever. In physics, the explanation of the common nature of electrical and magnetic forces eventually led to Einstein's theory of relativity. Chemists compiled the catalogue of basic elements and identified their atomic structure. Medical research gave us vaccines, antibiotics, anesthetics, and radiology, just to name a few.

The wave of discoveries in that era resulted also in the replacement of paper as the predominant support of money, after centuries of domination. The new conduit, telegraphic and radio signals, allowed a much smoother and swifter performance. We already mentioned Chappe's "semaphores," sending light signals through revolutionary France. While those devices were still in use, in the mid nineteenth century, inventors were experimenting with forms of wire communication.

In 1816, the Londoner Francis Ronalds constructed the first machine to transmit writing over wires. His telegraph transmitted signals over a distance of eight miles. Grasping its military potential, he wrote to the British Admiralty presenting his invention as "a mode of conveying telegraphic intelligence with great rapidity, accuracy, and certainty, in all states of the atmosphere, either at night or in the day, and at small expense." The military dismissed the invention, arguing that, with Napoleon already defeated, visual semaphores were more than enough. Military myopia did not stop progress, though. In 1841, Alexander Bain, a Scot who had already patented the electrical clock, constructed a printer-connected telegraph, put to use to regulate railway traffic between Edinburgh and Glasgow. He later went further, patenting a prototype scan-fax machine equipped with a pendulum to detect printed letters and then transmit them telegraphically. Fully aware of the potential of his invention, Bain farsightedly predicted that one day any printed surface would be wire-transmittable.

As usual, the new technique was widely adopted when it could be put to practical use. In 1840, the Samuel Morse patented the line-and-point language that bears his name. This was the "killer app" because it allowed to convert the crude on/off signal arriving over the wire into text. After that, telegraphic messaging developed quickly across the Atlantic. Suited to long distances, at a time when the colonization of the West and the construction of the railways made communication critical, wire services became a flourishing business in America. At the mid nineteenth century, the Associated Press opened up in New York to provide telegraphic services and wire-transmitted news. A similar business was established in France by a gentleman whose name, Paul Julius Reuters, still rings loud in today's wire services industry. In the late nineteenth century, telegraphic transmission was in full swing. In America, it proved critical in the Civil War and the colonization of the Western territories. Railways and telegraphs moved West together, exploiting logistical complementarities; telegraph offices bloomed, usually combined with post offices. In 1881, when the sheriff Wyatt Earp, known for his gunfight at OK Corral, needed to recruit gunmen, the telegraph office of Tombstone (Arizona) was the place he visited first. Telecommunication was less advanced in Russia; still, Leon Trotsky made sure the St. Petersburg telegraph was controlled by Red Guards before storming the Winter Palace on November 8, 1917.

The telephone, which transmits voice, developed later and separately from the telegraph. Initially, it was complementary to telegraphy, for example, when wire transfers needed to be confirmed by voice for additional security. However, the two technologies differ, and early inventors initially struggled with the problem of recognizably transmitting voices. The story of how the telephone was invented is one of the most hotly contested chapters in the history of technology.

In the 1850s, the Italian-born Antonio Meucci developed an embryo voice transmitter to connect different parts of his New York home, which he needed to assist his ailing wife. The device, a development of an earlier model he had constructed while still in Italy, was composed of a vibrating diaphragm connected by an electrified wire to another diaphragm. He left but scanty written descriptions of his "telettrophone" (as he called it) and did not patent it. Years later Meucci's regular candle-producing business went bust; when he finally decided to patent his invention, he lacked the money needed for that. In 1876, Alexander Graham Bell submitted a patent application for a well-functioning telephone, complete with a proper technical description. Since then, the Canadian-naturalized Scotsman is generally recognized as the inventor of the telephone, in spite of numerous court cases brought by Meucci and his supporters. In 1877 the Bell Telephone Company was founded, which would eventually evolve into what is today's giant AT&T Corporation.

By the end of the century, well-functioning devices to transmit telegraphic and voice signals at long distances were available, including connections between Europe and the United States. Transoceanic cables had been laid on the Atlantic seabed since the 1860s. On the eve of the twentieth century, another Italian, Guglielmo Marconi, was successfully experimenting with radio transmission. All was in place for money to abandon its long-standing and comfortable support, paper, and start travelling securely and fast on wire and later on air.

MONEY GOES ON WIRE

Paper was still used for payment messaging and bookkeeping when the US Federal Reserve was founded in 1913. What happened next is so important for the history of money that it merits recounting in some detail. The reader will pardon a few technicalities and a brief step back in time.

After the demise of the Second Bank of the United States (1834), until the Civil War the United States practiced what we called "free banking." A single monetary denomination, the US dollar, had existed since the Founding Fathers. Its name was inherited from the Spanish American colonies, and with a root ("Tal," or valley) deriving from the German location where silver mints were originally located. US dollars were available in two forms, coins minted in species and paper notes issued by banks. US dollar coins were minted only by one federal institution and were thus the same everywhere. However, banknotes were issued by many different private banks and were not always exchangeable at their nominal value.

Banknote issuance by private banks always embodies an inherent conflict between the necessity to keep their value stable in terms of gold and the temptation to issue more banknotes as a cheap form of finance. Banks were chartered by states, hence their trustworthiness depended on their own intrinsic soundness and the financial condition of the respective state. By and large, banks located in northern states (like Massachusetts or New York) were sounder than those in southern and western states (e.g., Alabama, Louisiana, but also Wisconsin). An astonishing one-half of all the banks in that region went out of business during the free banking period, and in one-third of the cases depositors suffered losses.[6] During the same time there were very few bank failures in New York and other northern states. It is thus not surprising that the banknotes issued by banks in these states traded closer to par.

The southern states had resisted tighter regulation fearing that their banks could not compete. But after the Civil War their influence declined, and the more financially conservative northern states prevailed. With the National Banking Act of 1863, this arrangement changed in two ways. First, the Union started issuing Treasury notes with legal tender status. Once the war was over, those banknotes were naturally more trustable than the ones issued by banks. Second, to strengthen the banking system, banknote issuance was restricted to a limited number of authorized "nationally chartered banks," subject to control by a newly created federal supervisor, the already mentioned Office of the Comptroller of the Currency. This institution printed all banknotes, thus guaranteeing their physical quality; it also supervised the national banks, ensuring they had sufficient capital and a sizeable portfolio of Treasury securities. This legislation, extended to the whole nation after the end of the war, de facto ended the "free banking" era, by establishing a much tighter federal control over banknote issuance. But, as we shall explain, it did not yet give rise to a fully integrated dollar system in the whole US territory.[7]

In spite of the single monetary sign, the actual value of dollar banknotes differed from one place to another: by a lot under "free banking" but still to some extent after the Civil War. The reason was technological and institutional. Monetary transfers could not be faster than the time needed to move paper notes across main trading cities – New York, Chicago, and New Orleans principally, but also Kansas City, Savannah, Detroit, and Omaha. Travel by horseback took several days, preventing arbitrage from equalizing monetary values across different locations. It was also risky: Stagecoaches were occasionally attacked by bandits, as we learn from Western movies.

Absent a central bank, transfers took place not on the books of a central clearinghouse but on those of the banks themselves, through "correspondent" account banks maintained vis-à-vis one another. The US monetary system, far from being the unified whole it is today, was in fact a sort of "domestic Gold Standard" where dollar parities depended on paper or even gold transfers across cities. Parities fluctuated within bands defined by "paper transportation points," or "gold transportation points," which depended on the times, costs, and risks of moving paper or gold from one place to another. The US inner system worked like a miniature of the international monetary system.

Gaps in dollar values were to be completely removed between 1913 and 1918 by the combination of two innovations: one institutional, the creation of the Federal Reserve System (Fed, in short), and one technological, the wired fund transfer network among Fed regional branches.[8] Called the Leased Wire System then, the system is today normally referred to as Fedwire.

Before 1913, exchange between traders at different locations required movements of valuables, either gold or trusted paper certificates, like Treasury notes or banknotes. Bank correspondent relations intervened to simplify these trades and reduce their costs. The traders in the two cities would adjust their deposits at the local bank, and the banks would settle the amount on their correspondent accounts.[9] Correspondent banking, largely superseded within-country today, still dominates international transactions, as we will see in Chapter 12.

Transportation costs could thereby be eliminated, but in practice their elimination required two conditions never completely fulfilled: seamless communication and full reciprocal trust between the two banks. Correspondent banking did reduce geographical differences in dollar parities but did not eliminate them entirely, the remainder depending on the efficiency of the transmission technology in place. Parity fluctuations also depended on whether paper or gold was actually transferred since transportation involved significant costs and risks.

The situation changed after the creation of the Fed and its Fedwire system. After that, both banks had accounts with the central Fed's regional offices at the two locations. The transaction no longer required movements in correspondent account; bank settlement happened more swiftly and securely through changes in the bank's accounts with the Fed regional offices, settled eventually on their central accounts. A Gold Settlement Fund was also created, eliminating gold transfer costs. Effectively, the Federal Reserve System became the correspondent bank of everybody.

This new arrangement was vastly accelerated by the best technology of the day – telegraphic communication. The immediate result was that dollar values stabilized and parity differences across regions permanently ceased. The United States had, for the first time, a unified monetary system.

These two reforms transformed the domestic US monetary system and the form of money itself. But they did not make paper and gold disappear. The link of the US dollar with gold remained, save for the wartime period, to anchor the value of the currency to a tangible commodity possessing intrinsic value. The Gold Standard would be abandoned by the United States and all other nations only later, during the Great Depression of the 1930s. Paper money expanded its circulation among ordinary household investors, in the form of personal checks as well as banknotes. Wire-transmitted technology was not yet accessible to individuals, limited for the time being to central bank and interbank transactions.

PAYMENT FINALITY AND THE ROLE OF CENTRAL BANKS

The transition just described brought another and deeper change, regarding the "finality" of payments.

Payment finality is a crucial feature of any well-functioning monetary system. A payment is "final" when the receiving side is confident that the sum involved is unambiguously and irrevocably in its possession. In other words, when the receiver of the money (the payee) considers that the sum is definitively owned, free of the risk that the payment be reneged or reversed by the giver (the payer). Evidently, reaching finality fast is vital, especially from the payee's side.[10]

In the system that prevailed in the United States between 1834 and 1863, a payment was final only when the payee had in their hands the corresponding amount of gold – not banknotes, because banknotes were subject to banking risk. After 1863, federal banknotes redeemable in gold or equivalent certificates were suitable surrogates for gold, but still some cost and risk premia persisted across different locations. After 1918, the mechanism ensuring the finality of US dollar payments changed. Once the regional Fed at the payee's location received the sum in its Federal Reserve account, it meant that the regional Fed of the payer's location had released that amount and therefore the commercial bank involved was assured that the importing trader had delivered, or was certain to deliver, the corresponding amount of gold or trusted notes. At that moment the payment was final. The authority of the Federal Reserve and the way the system worked acted as a substitute for the physical possession of species or Treasury notes.[11]

In essence, telegraphic messages substituted gold or paper as a means capable of enacting final monetary transfers. If by "money" we intend the instrument through which final payments can be made, then in the new system electrons travelling on wire had effectively replaced tangible objects like paper and gold as legitimate monetary representations.

Note that "finality" implies nothing about the "real" value of the sum involved, in other words, about how many goods and services that sum can buy. Finality is a "nominal" concept, simply meaning that a certain number of monetary units have changed hands. The "real" value depends on the price of goods and services evolved. It is entirely possible that a final payment may deliver a sum that can later buy fewer goods than originally thought if the price of goods and services in the meantime has changed. The link to gold provided by the Gold Standard in that period was precisely intended to ensure that the "real" value of money would be preserved through time. In a rather imperfect manner, we should say, since the price of gold itself is very unstable relative to the prices of most goods and services that people normally buy.

By all accounts, Fedwire is one of the most enduring and successful monetary infrastructures in history.[12] It still operates today as the backbone of the US dollar, supporting not only the domestic economy but also the international role of that currency, which has grown constantly and massively after World War II. Fedwire was a precursor, but it did not remain alone. Comparable systems were set up in other countries in the course of the following decades. Moreover, other systems have flanked it at a later time, also in the

United States, with a complementary role. The most important is the Clearing House Interbank Payments System (CHIPS), a privately run system that processes large-value transactions among a limited number of large financial institutions. This system had become so important after the 2008 financial crisis that CHIPS was designated a systemically relevant financial market infrastructure supervised by the Federal Reserve. In all such systems, central banks perform a supervisory role and, in most cases, directly run the system.[13]

The introduction of telegraphic payments in the United States and elsewhere was the first step in a process leading, over more than a century, to the later forms of digital currencies. Initially, wire-transmitted information arrived in Morse code transcribed manually by human operators. The transcription from Morse code had then to be put into the (literal) books of the banks. The operators reading and transcribing the telegraphic messages were carefully selected skilled professionals, but occasional mistakes were unavoidable. Great care had to be taken to ensure the accuracy of the recording. The transactions were recorded on the books of the twelve District Federal Reserve banks, which in turn had to communicate their balances to the Federal Reserve Board in Washington daily at 10 am. This represented a big improvement from the weekly settlement that had been possible earlier.[14] The leased wire system could thus be characterized as electric but not digital. Digitalization came in only when the first computers arrived in the 1950s – a step we describe in a moment. Transaction information had to be digitalized to be processed; ever-faster computers gradually took over the processing work. The term "book entry" survives, but today it usually means an entry in an electronic registry.

Modern Real Time Gross Settlement payment systems generally imply that payments are enacted immediately, without the need for end-of-day netting and settlement. This speeds up the finality and enhances the certainty of payments. Again, this progress was made possible by the technical improvement in information technology, which now permits handling large numbers of payments in electronic form in fractions of seconds – another example of technology at the service of reliable and functional money.

DIGITALIZATION

Bank of America occupies a special place in the history of money. Today the second bank in the United States by assets and the fourth globally, if one excludes Chinese banks, with its presence in some thirty-five countries through nearly 5,000 business points, BofA – in short – offers its clients the full range of bank insurance services, from retail lending to deposit taking, from payments to investment banking, from merger and acquisition to insurance products, portfolio allocation, and more. That said, what makes BofA really special is its history. Unknown to many, the bank played a major role in the development of electronic and digital money.

An embryo of BofA was founded in 1904 by Amedeo Giannini, the son of Italian immigrants in California. He initially called it Bank of Italy, echoing the homonymous Italian central bank founded in Rome a few years earlier. Two years later the city where the bank was headquartered, San Francisco, was destroyed by an earthquake. Not discouraged, Giannini lent all the cash he had been able to save to small clients who wanted to rebuild homes and restart businesses. He believed in lending to ordinary people, not to the big guys. From scratch, starting from what was left after a major disaster, he turned his creature into the prototype retail consumer bank and one of the most prominent in history. At some point, he reckoned not unreasonably that in his whereabouts a name like "Bank of America" would probably sound more attractive. The merger with another start-up with that name gave rise in no time to the largest bank in the rapidly developing state of California.

After World War II, BofA faced a conundrum. The postwar recovery multiplied the opportunities for profitable banking and the number of payments. The rising flow of personal checks – some 30 million were written during those years in a single day – could not be processed with the techniques of the time. Each one needed to be processed manually by the receiving bank. This involved identifying the issuing bank and branch, verifying the signature, inserting the amount into a mechanical calculator, separating the checks drawn on the own bank from the others, and sending the latter to the Federal Reserve. The Fed would then distribute all checks to the respective issuing banks, where all controls had to be redone before debiting the account of each client in the bank's ledgers. All this by hand.

When Giannini died in 1949, BofA, already the largest bank in America, faced a crossroads: The burden of check handling was putting the future of the bank at risk. The solution came almost by coincidence. Giannini had enrolled as manager one Clark Beise, a man with a keen taste for technological solutions. A few miles away from headquarters, in Menlo Park, stood one of the main concentrations of applied scientists in the world: the Stanford Research Institute (SRI), a nonprofit unit with the mission of developing technological solutions for public institutions and businesses. The partnership between BofA and SRI would produce the next revolution in monetary history, and one of the biggest ever.

The Stanford researchers set themselves to design a machine capable of performing, within each business day, all main functions in the check-handling cycle: authenticity controls; identification of the parties involved (payee, drawer); recording of transactions; crediting and debiting all client accounts, rejecting blank or faulted checks; and updating all client ledgers. The task was complex, partly because the bank refused to modify the checks' format. Yet after five years Beise was able to announce the introduction of ERMA or Electronic Recording Machine Accounting – a giant mainframe computer weighing twenty-five tons, with 300 kilometers of wire and thousands of diodes and "vacuum tubes" – ancestors of modern semiconductors. The processing system included two critical advances: magnetic ink character recognition, or MICR, the code recording check number, account number, and amount, which still features in personal checks today; and the electronic ledger. Similar or better machines, produced by General Electric and other companies, were soon adopted by all major banks. The path to digital banking, eventually to digital money, was wide open.

Somewhat paradoxically, the advent of electronics did not make paper disappear from the monetary system; on the contrary, automation made processes easier and smoother. The role of checks was far from over at that time. We will tell the rest of their story later. But before that, we need to tell the story of another exploit of BofA, this time having to do with plastic. While ERMA was cranking its first numbers, the era of money-on-cards was about to begin. That innovation was, once again, Giannini's brainchild.

FROM PAPER TO PLASTIC

According to a popular story, the credit card was invented in 1949 in New York by a finance executive named Frank McNamara. He went to lunch at a restaurant one day, and when the bill arrived, he realized he had forgotten his wallet and had to borrow the money. Back home he thought of a system where restaurant meals could be paid without cash: The Diners Club and the card that bears the same name were the results. This story is nice but rather implausible: When one forgets the wallet, the cards in it are forgotten too. A cellphone, a separate object less likely to be left behind, is probably more useful if equipped with an app or an e-wallet. But that marvel was still in the distant future.

Legends aside, one thing is certain. Around the 1950s the US financial system was ready for the next big leap: payments without cash or checks. As we have seen, retail banking was exploding, and personal clients were growing by the thousands every day. The economy was booming, driven by consumer spending. Banks were in pain to manage the torrent of checks coming in every day. The most ingenious of them, Bank of America, was on the verge of finding the right solution, moving check handling and transaction recording to a mainframe computer, and others would quickly follow suit. The road to technological banking was open and with it a world of lighter, more efficient, and secure means of payment.

The payment card, initially a toy for rich club members in a rich city, would one day become the most astonishing success in the whole history of finance. Visa and Mastercard, today's kings of the card networks, are worth more than most US banks by market cap. In terms of compatibility standards, the card is a miracle. The round-cornered rectangle measuring 85.6 by 53.98 millimeters (corner radius is 3.18 millimeters) is familiar to everybody, having been adopted in exactly the same shape world over. Even China, when it established its own card network, UnionPay or UPI, used that format. Unified global standards are elusive in many areas such as electrical plugs, cellphone recharge cables, and information technology operating systems. Not for "major" credit cards, which are accepted virtually everywhere.[15]

The initial Diners Card, while remarkable, was still quite archaic. For once, it was made of cardboard. Moreover, it was single purpose as it could only be used for meals at associated restaurants. Other cards issued in that period by stores shared that same limit. All payments had to be settled within standard cycles, typically a month. BofA made the big leap, once again. Its BankAmericard, introduced in 1958, was multipurpose: It could be used at every retail outlet, if, of course, the seller accepted it – which was very likely to happen, as we shall explain. As a second innovation, leveraging on its unique experience in the retail credit market, BofA added a revolving credit facility to the card. Cardholders were allowed to pay only part of the amount due at the end of the month, borrowing the rest from the bank at interest. Effectively, the BankAmericard provided two services, credit and a means of payment.

As the saying goes, imitation is the sincerest form of flattery. Other banks soon started to issue their own cards. However, smaller banks could not sustain the cost of setting up a card network. They thus formed the Interbank Card Association, which later became Mastercard.[16] Bank of America then had the choice of trying to continue on its own or to entice other banks to participate in its system. Bank of America was big, but it had only a fraction of the entire US banking market. Wisely it chose to open its system to other banks, which were nominally its competitors, and later gave up even control over the card it had invented to a cooperative involving many banks, which later became Visa.[17] Bank of America thus avoided the fate of another large US bank that tried to impose its own standard for international transactions on others. We describe in Chapter 12 how this attempt led to the formation of a rival consortium of banks, known as the Society for Worldwide Financial Telecommunications or SWIFT.

The cooperation among banks made possible the dizzying expansion of credit cards via what economists call the "network effect": The more people use cards, the more retailers find it advantageous, and eventually necessary, to accept them, investing in the required technology, lest being driven out of business. The more this happens, the more other individuals feel compelled to have cards because they can be used everywhere. Imitation and competition lead to further expansion among retailers and consumers, in a self-feeding circle.

But there is more than this. Behavioral scientists have demonstrated that people using cards are more inclined to spend; they make more purchases and also spend more on each of them. Why?

One reason is related to what economists call "liquidity constraints": Simply stated, people like McNamara who have no cash on hand (or even in the bank) can still spend using a card, which in essence means buying now and paying later. Evidence shows that the effect is stronger if the card allows for revolving credit: The more the settlement is procrastinated, the softer the liquidity constraint. But this motive does not explain all: Even debit cards that clear instantly on bank accounts seem to produce a positive effect on spending.

Two cognitive mechanisms are at play. The first is called "pain reduction." Procuring banknotes, extracting them from the pocket, counting them, and handing them over to the seller or, alternatively, extracting the checkbook, writing and signing the check takes time and effort, increasing the buyer's awareness and the perceived pain from parting with the money. This makes the buyer more cautious and reluctant to spend. By contrast, handing over the card is faster and allows the buyer to psychologically separate the purchase from the payment, generating a momentary illusion that the purchase is not actually paid.

The other more subtle effect is called "step in the gas." Neuroresearchers have found that card spending stimulates regions of the brain called "dopaminergic reward centers," normally associated with other forms of excitement and pleasure. The reaction is akin to that associated with forms of addictive behavior, for example, the assumption of drugs or other forms of excitement. According to recent research, these mechanisms "expose important consumer vulnerabilities that will require attention as payment methods rapidly evolve."[18]

The psychological reduction in the barriers to spending helps to explain the astounding success of credit cards. Another factor is that card payment costs are entirely borne by the retailer. The buyer normally is blind to the costs inherent in the credit card payment process. The price paid is the same regardless of the payment method used. The typical cost structure of credit card payments consists of a fee ranging between 1 and 3 percent charged on the seller, which goes in different parts to the two banks involved, that of the seller and the one issuing the buyer's card. A smaller fee – but multiplied by a much higher number of transactions – goes to the card network, Visa, Mastercard, or others. Sellers usually have little choice but to accept the cost, lest they lose clients to their competitors. The buyer enjoys the pleasure of the purchase, including the psychological one, apparently at no cost. The word "apparently" is necessary, of course, because eventually, costs are likely to affect the purchase price one way or another.[19]

Credit cards are an extraordinary brand marketing success. Most affluent consumers in the Western world have more than one. The cards we carry around are in reality issued by our local bank, not by Visa or Mastercard or whatever the logo that appears on them. It is logical that in reality banks issue the cards, because only they know how much credit we deserve. The credit card companies provide only the standard and the contact with retailers. This implies that the bank also bears all the risk. Spending more, especially if in a state of excitement, can lead to reckless spending beyond one's means. This in fact happened when credit cards spread in the United States. As credit card debt rose in relation to people's incomes in the 1980s and 1990s (from 0 to 10 percent in a few years), delinquency rose too, up to rates of 5 to 6 percent before the turn of the millennium and almost 7 percent during the Great Financial Crisis of 2008–09. Today's delinquency rates are back to around 1 percent, due to improvements in creditworthiness assessment methods introduced, again, as a result of new technology applied to money. We will return to this in a moment.

Brilliant inventions as they were, credit cards at first had very little technological content. The underlying processes were still "paper-based." Readers in their senior age probably remember the "click-clack" machine, a metal device with a rectangular base and a sliding bar on top. The retailer would impress the information embossed on the card on a triple carbon copied paper. One copy would stay with the merchant, one would go to their bank (for further transmission to the issuing bank), while the third was returned to the purchaser for their own records. Bank settlements still required considerable processing done by hand.

A turning point came in the 1970s, following a new technological breakthrough: the magnetic stripe, an imprinted string of electronically readable information. With that, the days of the triple-copier were counted: Paperless transactions took hold at a rapidly growing number of locations worldwide and cards became ubiquitous. "Don't leave home without it" – so went a well-known American Express slogan launched in 1975. The stripe was later to be superseded by the chip-and-PIN (Personal Identification Number), still in place in the 25 billion cards existing today in the world: an engraved microcircuit containing all the card's information and activated by a four-digit PIN.[20]

Banks responded to the challenge by embracing cards but also by developing alternatives. Credit cards presented a challenge to conventional business models grounded on deposit collection and the associated payment services, like checks and money orders. Banknote hoarding competed with bank deposits, while Federal Reserve regulation still prohibited interest on deposits – the prohibition was lifted only in the 1980s. Withdrawing cash at the bank presented a hurdle: One had to physically go to the branch and probably wait in line. More sophisticated competitors were money market funds (MMFs), offering interest-bearing instruments with automatic transfers to demand deposits. To maintain an edge, banks needed to modernize deposits by developing their "spendability." The response was twofold. The first was the automated teller machine (ATM). Inserting the electronically enhanced card in the machine, depositors obtained cash without trips to the bank and lengthy queues.[21] The second was the debit card, in all appearance similar to a credit card but with direct clearance on the bank deposit. With a single chip-and-PIN card, the bank customer could, depending on need, obtain cash at the ATM or directly spend at retailers equipped with the electronic POS (Point of Sale), drawing on her bank deposit. Credit and debit cards were also available to enact purchases over the phone, a rapidly growing form of commerce impossible a few years earlier.

The commercial success of the debit card continues today. They are easier to obtain and use than credit cards because they spare the bank most of the complexities and risks involved in rating the client's creditworthiness. Their simplicity makes them suitable for unsophisticated users, hence increasing financial inclusion. Their expansion surpassed that of credit cards, especially in Europe, where banks play a central role in the financial structure.

Though each of the elements just described – the digital card, electronic computing, and wire communication – is relevant on its own, it is their combination that opened the door to real advancement in monetary arrangements, domestically and globally. What was still missing at the time we are describing here was a technology enabling computers to communicate with one another. The internet would fill this gap in the 1990s. In the meantime, while the system was growing technologically from a number of private initiatives, central banks were enhancing their oversight role, surveying the payment system, ensuring the "finality" of payments, and, after the end of the gold-based monetary standard in 1971, maintaining money's purchasing power.[22] The private and the public side needed each other, and the efficiency and solidity of the whole system depended on the balance between the two.

Interestingly, while money was turning digital, two notable exceptions stubbornly persisted. Much like frogs and salamanders withstood the glaciations and floods that killed the dinosaurs and still populate our countryside, two monetary survivors outlived the digital age and persist today pretty much in their original form.

The first is cash: physical banknotes issued by central banks. Their extinction has been announced many times, but, similar to the death of Mark Twain, the announcement was always exaggerated. As we will show in Chapter 5, cash holdings are actually increasing almost everywhere in the world.

The second exception is personal checks. It may seem surprising that at a time when transferring money anywhere, quickly and safely, takes just a few touches on a cellphone, people still take the time and pain of writing and handling personal checks. But this is indeed what happens in one not-insignificant country: the United States. We discuss the endurance of checks in the United States in Chapter 7.

Before moving on from here, we should debunk a popular myth, or at least clarify a semantic misunderstanding. The word "digital" applied to money can mean two different things. Literally, "digital money" refers to digital instruments to enact payments and to maintain money balances as digital units (bits and bytes) in the electronic ledgers of central banks and private credit institutions. According to this definition, when the second millennium was nearing its end, the digitalization of money was already virtually complete. In the 1999 United States, the share of broad monetary aggregates – the definitions of money published by the Federal Reserve – held in the form of digitally recorded deposits or other forms of liquid instruments offered by banks had already surpassed 90 percent.

More recently, however, the popular press refers to "digital money" as monetary technologies developed outside the banking sector – mainly crypto and other related instruments. Here the discriminant is not digital technology but the decentralized nature of the platforms where these instruments are created and exchanged – the so-called Decentralized Finance, or DeFi. The same term is used to refer to the myriad of payment apps and platforms available today, mainly offered by tech firms. It is used, finally, for the central banking version of these apps, the central bank digital currencies or CBDCs, still in the planning phase. "Digital money" in this sense is a much more recent phenomenon, which continues to evolve and grow. We will describe these new forms of digital money in later chapters of this book.

INTERNET CLOSES THE CIRCLE

In the 1980s, banks had already started offering home banking applications via phone or video. These facilities were never successful though, in part because of the imperfect functioning of the underlying communication infrastructures. Meanwhile, early versions of the internet were starting to be used in the United States in certain circles, mainly to connect research communities and government agencies. In the 1990s and early 2000s, the Web became ubiquitous in business, finance, and the public at large. The global number of users exploded from 2 million to 400 million in the 1990s and up to 2 billion in the next decade. After the internet entered the communication ecosystem, banks started offering web-based facilities to perform basic banking operations without leaving home. Nonbank payment service providers also began to appear. Once more, self-propelled technological and financial acceleration marched together.

Providing a full account, or even a meaningful summary, of the universe of digital payment applications and platforms existing today in the world is nearly impossible. It is a virtually boundless and ever-changing universe. Some common traits exist, nonetheless. First, all the new payment tools are accessed from existing personal devices such as computers and, increasingly, smartphones. Second, communication transits through the existing mobile and fixed-line infrastructure. Third, this is possible only because of shared standards.

This convergence of operational standards is a notable feature of the present environment in contrast with historical precedents and confers an inherent momentum to the process. Consumers and merchants in earlier epochs used multiple processes to enact payments, depending on needs and transaction parties. No longer: Payment acts increasingly resemble one another and are similar to other acts of communication that pervade our daily lives.

The digital payments community is very large and constantly growing, in economically advanced areas and increasingly elsewhere as well. If one adds up the user numbers of PayPal, Apple Pay, and Google Pay, admittedly not a legitimate sum because many people use more than one platform, the total number is higher than the combined populations of the United States and Europe, the areas where those platforms are predominantly used. But less-developed areas are catching up: The single most important digital payment platform in Africa, M-Pesa, counts over 30 million users in Kenya alone, more than half of the country's population. Pix has become the dominant payment platform in Brazil. In China, the combined users of Alipay and Tencent (platforms used mainly in that country, though not only) account for far more than China's population. Cellphone payment apps prove particularly suitable for developing countries with large areas, sparse populations, and less firmly established fixed-line communication infrastructures.

One application merits a specific mention due to its breadth and functionality: the Single European Payments Area, or SEPA. This infrastructure, with an annexed legal regime, was launched in 2008 by the European Union with the principal aim of integrating payments across eurozone countries. It covers thirty-six countries, well beyond the eurozone (today comprising twenty countries). In the eurozone, SEPA ensures that cross-border payments are indistinguishable in cost and speed from domestic ones. A credit transfer facility allows the transmission of deposit funds with next-day settlement at zero cost for the user. Instant settlement is also available at a small cost. The success of SEPA in the eurozone is demonstrated by the fact that the use of personal checks has virtually disappeared in Europe – with the partial exception of France. By contrast, in the United States, where banks charge high fees for deposit transfers both across and within states and multiple separate payment platforms exist, the use of personal checks is still common.

Credit transfers in SEPA are large on average, in the order of 7,000 euros. But this average comprises payments between enterprises of maybe hundreds of thousands of euros and much smaller regular payments such as rent or utility bills. By contrast, card payments, domestic and cross-border, average less than 50 euros. There is thus a distinct specialization between card payments, growing fast in number but relatively small, and SEPA transfers, dwarfing other payment channels by the aggregate amount.

An important feature of all payment platforms discussed so far is that all transactions are eventually settled, in a final way, through entries in the books of a central bank. Whether we transfer funds by online banking instructions; using a credit or debit card linked to bank accounts; via PayPal, which links to bank accounts or payment cards; or using smartphone apps and e-wallets containing credit card data, in all these cases, at the end of the line there is a central bank which writes the transaction on its electronic books and has the exclusive legal authority to ensure the finality of the payment and the convertibility with a tangible instrument – the banknote – whose acceptance as legal tender is guaranteed by law. To paraphrase the observation we make later with regard to the Gold Standard, we are now in a paper standard, with a mountain of digital money on top of a small banknote amount.

Central banks combine the power to ensure the finality of payment almost everywhere with the authority to oversee the payment system in order to ensure its proper functioning.

As we will discuss more extensively in Chapter 7, modern payment systems are thus structured on layers. There is a "guardian and enforcer," the central bank. There is a "money custodian," the banking sector which maintains most of the monetary instruments digitally written in their electronic ledgers with transactions settled among them on the balance sheet of the central bank. The banking sector is surrounded by a network of "retailers and innovators" offering payment applications tailored to the needs and preferences of the community of users. There is then the universe of final users. Borderlines may be blurred at times, for example, some banks also offer payment applications, but in principle, the three elements are distinct and complementary. The central bank ensures stability and adherence to a set of rules designed for the collective interest. Banks, and today especially the nonbank tech industry, promote innovation, growth, and efficiency. The banking and financial sector provides the essential link between money and credit; the transformation of savings into investments which they promote is the ultimate engine of economic growth.

To ensure the efficiency and stability of this composite system, preserving public–private partnerships is essential. Efficient and trustable money requires two facets, one private and one collective. The first uses technology to ensure that the system works well, satisfying efficiency requirements: ease of use, prompt identification, storability, and transferability. Technology advances require innovation, entrepreneurship, and investment, which stem from private initiatives. However, private action alone cannot guarantee money's collective benefits, which largely reside in its finality and stability. Finality of payments was easy in ancient times when the delivery of a purse of coins was sufficient to settle an obligation. Even then, the real value could not be trusted if the mint was controlled by cash-hungry rulers. In modern times, increasingly sophisticated means of payment and stores of value make finality more elusive, and the preservation of monetary value has not become simpler. No less than in the past, stable and reliable money requires rules and oversight by dedicated public institutions.

NOTES

1. France was a cradle of popular movements throughout the nineteenth century. Revolutions erupted in 1830–32 (immortalized in Victor Hugo, *Les Misérables*, 1862), in 1848, and again in 1871 (the *Commune de Paris*, celebrated by Vladimir Lenin in *The State and Revolution*, 1917). In all cases, the French uprisings inspired popular movements elsewhere in the continent.

2. We draw here from R. Triffin, "The Myths and Realities of the So-Called Gold Standard," originally published in 1964 and reprinted in Barry Eichengreen and Marc Flandreau, *Gold Standard in Theory & History* (Routledge, 1997).

3. Angela Redish, "The Evolution of the Gold Standard in England," *The Journal of Economic History* 50, no. 4 (December 1, 1990): 789–805.

4. Wikipedia Contributors, "Timeline of Historic Inventions," *Wikipedia*, September 14, 2023.

5. Henry Adams, "The Rule of Phase Applied to History," in Henry Adams and Brooks Adams (eds.), *The Degradation of the Democratic Dogma* (Macmillan, 1909).

6. Arthur J. Rolnick and Warren Weber, "Banking Instability and Regulation in the US Free Banking Era," *Quarterly Review* 931 (1985): 1–9.

7. We owe much of our understanding of the dollar system in the nineteenth century to exchanges with Jeffry Frieden and to his essay "Lessons for the Euro from Early US Monetary and Financial History," Bruegel, June 30, 2006. Jeff is not responsible if our understanding of that period is still incomplete or not precise enough.

8. Data and explanations are provided by Kenneth D. Garbade and William L. Silber, "The Payment System and Domestic Exchange Rates: Technological versus Institutional Change," *Journal of Monetary Economics* 5, no. 1(January 1, 1979): 1–22. A Gold Settlement Fund was also created, which eliminated gold transfer costs.

9. For a graphical exposition of the US payment system in this period, and of the reform after the creation of the Federal Reserve, see the Online Appendix to this book available at Ignazio Angeloni's blog (ignazioangeloni.home.blog).

10. Charles M. Kahn and Wiliam Roberds, "The Economics of Payments Finality," *Federal Reserve Bank of Atlanta Economic Review* 87 (2002): 1–12.

11. On Fedwire's finality and the system's historical developments see Federal Reserve, "Fedwire Funds Transfer System: Assessment of Compliance with the Core Principles for Systemically Important Payment Systems," July 2014; and Anton Badev, Lauren Clark, Daniel Ebanks, Jeffrey Marquardt, and David Mills, "Fedwire Funds Service: Payments, Balances, and Available Liquidity," *Finance and Economics Discussion Series*, no. 2021-070, November 5, 2021, 1–51.

12. The Fedwire system and the Fed's role in securing the management and settlement of bank checks were partly modeled on the example of the German Reichsbank, which, since 1876, had offered check cashing services free of charge. The Reichsbank example was studied by the monetary commission which prepared the constitution of the Fed. See National Monetary Commission, *The Reichsbank: 1876–1900* (Government Printing Office, 1910), 96. Available from FRASER, The Federal Reserve Archival System for Economic Research.

13. See Badev et al., "Fedwire Funds Service"; Ben Norman, Rachel Shaw, and George Speight, "The History of Interbank Settlement Arrangements: Exploring Central Banks' Role in the Payment System," Bank of England Working Papers 412, 2011.

14. Not every commercial bank in the United States participated in the leased wire system; only the banks designated as "national" (the large ones) were obliged to do so. The smaller state-chartered banks were, however, allowed to join, and they increasingly did so as they saw the advantages. Extensive information is available in the Annual Reports of the Federal Reserve and the Comptroller of the Currency for 1919, both available from FRASER.

15. Gottfried Leibbrandt and Natasha De Teran, *The Pay Off: How Changing the Way We Pay Changes Everything* (Elliott & Thompson, 2021) argue that the success of payment cards depends partly on how easily they combined with subsequent technologies.

16. "Mastercard Brand History," Mastercard website.

17. See Wikipedia contributors, "Visa Inc.," *Wikipedia*, November 23, 2023.

18. Sachin Banker, Derek Dunfield, Alex Huang, and Drazen Prelec, "Neural Mechanisms of Credit Card Spending," *Scientific Reports* 11, no. 1 (February 18, 2021).

19. Some credit card companies do not allow merchants to recover the cost from customers via so-called credit card surcharges, and in several US states, credit card surcharges are forbidden. In the European Union, surcharges for credit and debit cards are effectively banned; see European Commission, "Payment Services Directive: Frequently Asked Questions," January 12, 2018; see https://ec.europa.eu/commission/presscorner/detail/fr/memo_15_5793.

20. The chip-equipped "smart card" is due to a French Egyptian inventor, Roland Moreno, as early as 1974. The brilliance of the idea was not immediately appreciated, though; it took several decades before the chip became ubiquitous.

21. In 2009 Paul Volcker, the former Fed chairman credited for defeating the Great Inflation of the 1970s, defined ATMs as "the only useful invention banks have made in the last 20 years." This statement is rather extreme, but certainly, ATMs are one of the most enduring innovations ever.

22. The gold link was definitively abandoned on August 15, 1971, when US President Richard Nixon ended the Fed's obligation to convert the US dollar into gold, and the system of fixed exchange rates, holding monies linked to one another, collapsed. Since then, the value of money in all its forms and denominations depends solely on the authority and trustworthiness of central banks.

4   **What Money Is and Does for Us**

> Money is only a tool. It will take you wherever you wish, but will not replace you as a driver.
>
> Ayn Rand

Readers who endured 5,000 years of monetary chronicles deserve now an explanation of why history is so important for this book.

Economists use theories, or models, in the attempt to approximate reality. They typically regard their models as independent of history: Model results hold because they logically descend from axioms of general validity. Once built, and after passing certain logical and statistical tests, a model can be employed in a variety of ways: to make predictions, to measure the impact of certain events, or to rerun history by conducting "what if?" experiments. Axioms cannot be tested: They are assumed because they make sense. And the logic used to make deductions also makes sense. Unfortunately, what "makes sense" to economists does not always fit what happens in the real world. That's where history helps.

Once upon a time, economists used to be practitioner historians as well: An example is Adam Smith, the "father of modern economics," whom we already mentioned as a proponent of an early theory of money which, by the way, drew on his reading of history. At one point in the nineteenth century, however, economists took a turn; perhaps influenced by the wave of optimism pervading the "belle époque," they started believing that economic "laws" could be derived by deduction from behavioral axioms, obtaining economic models capable of explaining everything: from individual choices to laws of production, from pricing to the determination of wages, from scarcity to abundance. Including the laws governing money.

An early master of this intellectual revolution was the Englishman William Stanley Jevons (1835–82). With two contemporaries, the Austrian Carl Menger and the French Léon Walras, he is credited for inventing the "marginalist" approach to economics – the concept according to which prices and quantities of goods and services produced depend not on the utility and cost of all of them but of only the last unit produced. One can actually derive this conclusion from a set of simple and apparently sensible premises. More important to us is that, in a book he did not consider his best, Jevons developed a theory of what purpose money is supposed to serve[1] – a remarkably enduring theory, which arrived to us almost unchanged and can be found in all textbooks on which today's economics students are trained.

Jevons himself was very attentive to the lessons of history, but with his successors in the twentieth century the "axiomatic" approach became predominant. Not all economists were happy about this, though. Some of the most illustrious ones resisted the tendency or expressed dissatisfaction with it. John Maynard Keynes, for example, arguably the most influential economist ever, was keenly aware of the lessons of history. Milton Friedman, a close second, coauthored a monumental monetary history of the United States.[2] Robert Solow, a Nobel laureate himself and a mentor of many others, wrote in 1985 about how history should complement economic theory:

> Economic theory can only gain from being taught something about the range of possibilities in human societies. Few things should be more interesting to a civilized economic theorist than the opportunity to observe the interplay between social institutions and economic behavior over time and place. ... economic history can offer the economist a sense of the variety and flexibility of social arrangements and thus, in particular, a shot at understanding a little better the interaction of economic behavior and other social institutions. That strikes me as a meaningful division of labor.[3]

With Solow, we think that theory and history work best when they are combined. Here we proceed in steps. First, following Jevons and his heirs, we explain the dominant "textbook" ideas of what money is and what purpose(s) it serves, which mainly descend from casual observation and simple logic. We look at some spectacular historical examples in which money failed, or succeeded, in performing its functions beneficially for society. With these theories and examples in mind, we discuss the requirements money must fulfil in order to do its job properly. Such requirements draw on Jevons' work but try to go a bit beyond. Finally, parting from Jevons altogether, we discuss other characteristics of money that may contribute to understanding what money is and is supposed to do, in our contemporary world and going forward.

BASIC FUNCTIONS

Economics students learn early in their training that money serves three purposes: as means of payment, unit of account, and store of value.

As a means of payment, money is exclusively used in exchange of goods and services. For that, it must be universally accepted. A seller must always be content to receive money in transacting goods or services with the other party. Acceptance must be universal because the variety of goods and services money can purchase is potentially unlimited. "Limited purpose" vouchers, exchangeable only for certain products, are not money. The use of money should be convenient and unencumbered in the full range of transactions it can support.

To be a unit of account, money must offer a convenient accounting framework to measure the value of each product against money itself as well as the relative values of more than one product against another. The accounting framework should be clear and easy to memorize and employ. Specifically, it should be equally suitable for products that have very different values, from the most expensive to the cheapest ones.

To be a store of value, money must offer an effective means – though not necessarily the only one – to carry value across space and store it over time. Purchases and sales are not only distributed across sometimes far places but they also do not happen simultaneously: A time interval normally separates the time in which we sell something (e.g., our work in exchange for a salary) and the time in which we buy something else (e.g., our daily grocery). Between the two moments, it must be possible to conveniently and safely keep money in store, ready for use at a later time.

Jevons explained these three functions in detail and also considered another one: that of a "standard of value." This referred to the fact that money measures not only the value of products at a given time but also that of future obligations. A standard of value gives certainty of values across time, including how debts can be extinguished. This function can be subsumed into the other ones, in fact being an extension of them.

The store of value function also encompasses speculative and precautionary motives. Demand for currency can surge at times because the confidence in other stores of wealth deteriorates – perhaps because of a financial crisis. But this is transient. In addition, holding money can be profitable in times of rising interest rates, when the market value of long-term fixed-income securities tends to fall: This is the "speculative" motive of money demand theorized by James Tobin and others, to which we will return in Chapter 6. Conversely, the other two motives (unit of account and means of payment) transcend financial structures, times, locations, and economic cycles.

Usually, the distinctive characteristic of money is to fulfil all three functions at the same time. Other instruments can fulfil some of them but not others. For example, people store wealth also using precious objects, real estate, or other valuable items, unsuitable for daily transactions. In some cases the unit of account is not used for payments; for example, the International Monetary Fund calculates its internal accounts in Special Drawing Rights, a conventional unit that virtually nobody uses as a means of payment. The peculiarity of money is that it is equally suited, or at least sufficiently suited, to perform all three purposes.

Sometimes, however, the way money performs these functions is temporarily modified or suspended, as a result of crises, political decisions, or monetary reforms; in other circumstances, the monetary functions may be disjointed and performed separately. Occasionally, money's ability to perform its functions is destroyed by dramatic events. These instances are interesting because, like scientific "experiments," they help reveal something about how and why money's nature and effectiveness in performing its functions can be altered. Europe's recent history contains some of these "natural experiments"; let's take a look at them.[4]

MONETARY DRAMA: THE WEIMAR REPUBLIC IN 1923

Berlin, German finance ministry, early hours of Monday, November 20, 1923. Sitting in his temporary office, a basement cubicle formerly used as broom closet, the newly appointed "national currency commissioner" Hjalmar Schacht knows three things for certain. First, the preceding Monday Gustav Stresemann, the new chancellor of the Weimar Republic, has assigned him that vaguely sounding title with one mandate only: stopping the catastrophic fall of the republic's currency, the Reichsmark. In October alone, the currency has lost 1,000 times its purchasing power.[5] Second, people's confidence in the government's ability to deal with the situation has reached such a low point that only a "shock therapy," undertaken by a reputed leader and clearly visible and understood by all, can have a chance of success. Third, on that very day, the Reichsmark reaches a powerful symbolic level: a million of a millionth (one divided by one followed by twelve zeroes) of its prewar Gold Standard value. The opportunity to act then should not be missed. It wasn't.[6]

The German hyperinflation had its roots five years earlier: in November 1918, with the abdication of the emperor followed two days later by post–World War I armistice signed with the French at Compiègne. The "original sin" of stipulating the defeat in the war had left the young republic with an undeserved reputational weakness, making its task of putting Germany back on its feet all the more difficult.

The country's economy was collapsing and wartime inflation was still raging. While tens of thousands of exhausted and frustrated soldiers returned from the battlefields, the political leaders faced a fragile situation on all fronts: social, political, and economic. The main concern was social unrest: communists in the north, where Karl Liebknecht and Rosa Luxemburg had lost their lives attempting a Bolshevik revolution; fascists in the south, where paramilitary gangs roamed freely and a young Adolf Hitler was blowing on the fire. As so often in history, political stability was temporarily preserved by swollen government deficits and the money printing press.

Weimar's rulers had tried to sooth discontent on multiple fronts. On the left side of the political spectrum, by means of generous social programs. Toward the industrialists and financiers, already leaning toward the Nazi camp, by ensuring generous finance to investors and speculators. Vis-à-vis the victorious Allies, by accepting onerous war reparations, to be paid in hard currency purchased by selling domestic currency on the London and New York exchange markets. The combination of these forces could only result in a growing spiral of external depreciation and domestic inflation, filling a budget gap that regular taxation was unable to finance. While inflation allowed meddling through for a while, the unsustainability of the situation became increasingly clear in the early 1920s, in a dramatic impoverishment of the middle class and the disappearance of first necessity goods from the stores, hidden and hijacked by commodity speculators.

Schacht, a former banker, fluent in English and at ease in the financiers circles of Britain and America and, above all, a practical man, was the right pair of hands to deal with the situation. His recipe was in three parts: resurrect the Rentenmark, a monetary instrument backed by arable land created months earlier but as yet little used; cut twelve zeroes from the debauched Reichsmark, returning to it a value which in the popular psychology symbolized stability; and stop completely the monetary financing of the deficit, while in the meantime negotiating with the Allies a lightening of the war reparation. The effects of the package surpassed all expectations: Prices stopped growing and the goods returned to the shop shelves. One year later, Germans were allowed to convert their old Reichsmarks into new money, effectively ending the parallel circulation. Negotiations on the war reparations eventually led to the Dawes Plan (1924), which ended the stalemate initiated five years earlier with the Treaty of Versailles.

Extreme in every possible way, and for this reason much-studied by historians and economists, the German hyperinflation and the successful stabilization of the currency contain lessons relevant for inflation more generally. Ending major inflations is a complex and risky exercise, an art more than a science, requiring a combination of technical skills, resolve, and successful psychology. The "magic" of Schacht's experiment was to change the unit of account – the earlier one was no longer usable – in a "confidence building" way: a fixed conversion rate that to the German mind was reminiscent of stability. That helped ensure the result, price stability and economic recovery, in spite of the fact that the continuity of the three monetary functions was effectively broken.

MONETARY RESURRECTION: GERMANY 1948

The summer of 1948 was unusually warm, but Europeans did not enjoy the sun. The bleak landscape of bombed-out cities, ruined factories, and fallen bridges did not invite tourism. The inhabitants of West Berlin were locked into their city by Stalin's blockade and depended on an airlift for essential supplies. In the whole of West Germany, money was useless because most goods were rationed. Many were without a job and everybody had to scrounge for the necessities of life. City dwellers went to the countryside to barter for the little food farmers still hoarded, unwilling to sell it at official prices for worthless money. Officially, the currency inherited from the Nazi regime, the Reichsmark introduced in 1924 after the hyper-inflation, was still valid. However, given that all prices had been fixed at low levels, nobody was willing to sell anything in exchange for that money.

The German economy went from bad to worse for three years following the surrender to the Allied forces on May 7, 1945. The country seemed unable to restart without external help. This changed in 1948 when the US administration led by Harry Truman launched the massive economic program called the Marshall Plan. Crucially, this included the launch of a new money, the Deutschmark (D-Mark).

On June 20, 1948, the new currency was introduced and the old Reichsmark became de facto worthless. The new cash had been surreptitiously printed in the United States and shipped in unmarked boxes to Germany. Every German citizen received forty of the new D-Mark to get the new currency going and to allow the people to survive until they received their first salaries in the new currency.

The impact of the reform was spectacular. Prices stabilized and goods became available: Merchants previously unwilling to sell their goods for a defunct currency suddenly put them out in their shop windows, creating the impression of an overnight miracle. Success has many fathers: Both the US military administration and the German authorities claimed paternity. In reality, both had realized that the economy could not recover under the old monetary regime since money had become worthless overissuance during and after the war.[7]

Critical to success were speed and effective logistics. A gradual approach would have taken a long time to bear fruit. Another reason was that the unit of account was not changed. By and large, rents, salaries, and other current payments were converted 1:1 from the defunct Reichsmark to the new D-Mark. This ensured continuity in the price level: Consumers were not suddenly confronted with higher prices. The reform thus did not induce a stepwise increase in the price level even after price controls were lifted. The prices of different goods were now determined by relative scarcity, some moving up and some down. Preserving the unit of account proved essential to maintaining money's purchasing power. This combination of a stable unit of account and making money useful in everyday life helped the success of a reform that contributed to no small extent to Germany's rebirth and postwar economic miracle.

MONEY TAKEOVER: EAST GERMANY 1989–1990

Over the next forty years, the D-Mark established itself not only as a reliable domestic currency but as the leading European currency and one of the most sought-after in the entire international monetary system. That success, however, led to new challenges. What destiny had in store was, in essence, a giant monetary takeover. Or better said, a political takeover by means of money.

After World War II, Germany was divided into two: an economically prosperous Western part, the Bundesrepublik, and a poorer Eastern part, euphemistically called the German Democratic Republic (GDR). Life in the GDR was more boring than unbearable, at least for the vast majority of the population unwilling to get involved in politics or espionage.[8] The GDR had its own currency, the Ostmark; it was worth little, but there wasn't much to buy anyway. Anything people wanted was in short supply. Shelves of the few stores were empty or contained shoddy goods nobody wanted. The Ostmark's role as a means of payment was rather formal; the real currency in the GDR was the D-Mark, the only way to access West German products. Having access to D-Marks, often through relatives living in the West, was the key to prosperity. However, in the black market, they were expensive and buying them was dangerous. Eastern Germans dreamt about living in a D-Mark world.

The economic gap between East and West Germany continued to widen in the 1970s and 1980s, but politically, the status quo seemed destined for eternity. East Germany was, after all, the most prosperous country behind the Iron Curtain, with advanced technology in certain sectors (precision mechanics), its own-produced cars (the Trabant, affectionately nicknamed Trabby, a small family car), and even some microchips that were only a generation behind those of the Western world.[9]

But below the lid, the kettle was boiling. The beginning of the end was a series of peaceful demonstrations in the summer of 1989 asking for freedom, especially to travel. When the demonstrations grew exponentially, the Soviet leader Mikhail Gorbachev refused to order the army to suppress the revolt (much to the frustration of a junior secret service officer called Vladimir Putin) the regime all of a sudden found itself without support and uncertain about what to do. It felt it had no choice but to mediate and make concessions.

In the end, what precipitated the demise of the communist regime, and the historical fall of the Berlin Wall, was a misunderstanding.

On November 9, 1989, a gray day in Berlin, the routine evening press conference by the spokesperson of the Politbüro of the ruling Socialist party, Günther Schabowski, was ending. It has been an eventful day. The Politbüro had agreed on new rules to make foreign travel easier, partially in the hope that troublemakers would leave the country. The new rules were supposed to be implemented the next day, but that detail was not mentioned in the handwritten note Schabowski was looking at.[10] When a journalist asks him whether the new freedom to travel entered into force immediately, Schabowski stuttered at first, then confirmed.

Broadcasted on radio and television, the news that free travel was possible spread like wildfire. Oblivious to the rain, thousands of citizens left their homes and massed at the city's transit points to the West, waving their passports and asking to cross to the other side. Lacking orders, the guards let them pass. History happened on that very moment: After 10,316 days, over 100,000 attempted escapes (only 5,000 of which were successful), and over 600 persons killed or otherwise dead for attempting to cross,[11] the dreaded Berlin Wall was no more, soon to be destroyed by the joyful crowd with axes, hammers, and bare hands.

Once the feasts were over, the discussion turned to economics: The key problem was the deteriorating living conditions in the GDR. The majority of its population did not want a reformed socialism – they wanted the most successful economy of Western Europe and, above all, its money, as vividly captured by the popular slogan: "Kommt die D-Mark, bleiben wir. Kommt sie nicht, geh'n wir zu ihr" ("If the D-Mark comes, we stay; if it doesn't come, we go to it").[12]

This was not an empty slogan. In the early months of 1990, hundreds of thousands moved from the collapsing GDR to West Germany. The West German authorities needed to do something, and quickly if they wanted to stop this mass migration. Once the abysmal state of the Eastern economy became apparent, the consensus among economists was that it needed a period of adaptation with separate currencies to catch up at least partially before the two economies could be united. The massive exodus scuppered these plans. By early 1990 the West German government agreed to take over the entire GDR and provide the coveted D-Mark to its people.[13] The changeover took place on July 1, 1990, eight months after the fall of the wall. More than a monetary union, it was a monetary takeover. The formal takeover came later, with the GDR disappearing on October 3 inside the old West Germany. For very senior East German citizens, this was the third time they had to change money after the 1923–24 reform and the introduction of the Ostmark by the Soviets in 1948.

Most regular payments like salaries, pensions, and rents were converted 1:1 from Ostmark to D-Mark. This gave Eastern Germans a huge boost in purchasing power since the black market exchange rate had been closer to 4:1. The 1:1 also applied to cash, but, as in 1948, bank accounts above a certain amount, equivalent to 4,000 euros today, were converted 2:1. This was still generous relative to the black market rate. The 1:1 rate was a political decision, a powerful symbol expressing the will of unity of all Germans after the wound of postwar separation. It had nothing to do with the relative condition of the two economies.

The 1:1 rate had real consequences. One of them, highly symbolic, was the little Trabant. With equal monies, prices, and costs between the two countries, the little subcompact with a plastic body and a two-stroke engine had no chance against the mighty Volkswagen, not to speak of premium brands like Mercedes and BMW. The finance minister of the short-lived transition East German government remarked that it made no sense to continue producing Trabants because the needs of museums and collectors of curiosities had already been amply satisfied.

A similar fate awaited other parts of the Eastern economy. With some exceptions, its companies could not compete and entire industries went bankrupt.[14] It eventually took three decades and hundreds of billions of taxpayer D-Marks to deal with the legacy of a planned economy. The West itself paid a price in the form of a temporary inflation burst. But on impact the currency reform was an instant success. With the D-Mark, East Germans had fully functional money again.[15] Banks started to operate normally, providing credit to the many new shops and enterprises that sprang up in the hitherto neglected services sector. The Eastern industrial sector, flagship and pride of the earlier regime, took much longer to recover.

A NEW MONEY IS BORN: EUROPE 1999

Arguably one of the biggest monetary reforms in history, the adoption of the euro on January 4, 1999, by eleven independent nations continues to attract the attention of economists and historians. The transition was prepared for years, broken into logistical steps, and executed by a legion of central bankers and government officials from the EU member countries. The introduction of the new currency came in two steps: in 1999 the launch of a new accounting unit (the euro), including the takeover of monetary policy powers by the European Central Bank (ECB); in 2002 the circulation of new euro-denominated banknotes and coins. This meant that for three years the euro would only exist as a new unit of account and (partly) as a store of value, not as a means of retail payments. Meanwhile, the legacy national currencies would continue to be used for day-to-day small purchases. The three functions of money were temporarily delinked, not only over time but also across different population segments and economic purposes.

Interestingly, the first step – the euro-changeover of 1999 – was almost a nonevent. It did not produce any significant changes in prices, financial markets, or economic activity. This is remarkable considering that the transition was computationally complex, involving sometimes small units and many decimals. For example, one Italian lira was converted into 0.0005164569 euros. The permanence, for the time being, of the national banknotes and coins in retail markets helped to "anchor" individual perceptions of value. The changes of the unit of account were largely performed by computers, which converted bills, ledgers, balance sheets, and so on automatically, undisturbed by numerical complications.

The key to this outcome was the fact that in retail markets nothing had changed for merchants and consumers; the same banknotes were used, hence the same unit of account. Three years later, when people began paying in the new banknotes and coins, the experience was very different.

THE BIGGEST CURRENCY REFORM EVER: EUROPE 2002

"Deux kilos de lichées, s'il vous plait," "Ça fait 75 euro centimes." This exchange just after midnight of January 1, 2002, in a market stall on the small French island of La Réunion in the Southern Indian Ocean ushered the biggest monetary policy experiment in modern history. Thousands of European officials and private retailers had worked hard for years to prepare for this day. Billions of euro notes and coins had been printed and minted, to be distributed in the early hours and days of 2002. Tens of thousands of automated teller machines had to be reconfigured to provide 300 million people with the new currency.

To economists, this change looked like a nonevent. But in fact, merging twelve national currencies (Greece had joined the euro in the meantime) had real implications, and the experience says a lot about what money is and does. What money did people use during the "schizophrenic" period from 1999 to 2001? The euro or their national currencies? A German would answer: The D-Mark, of course. My salary has not changed, it is still paid in D-Mark, and I am using the same good old banknotes as before. French, Italian, and all other eurozone citizens thought the same: Nothing had changed for them as well in January 1999.

By contrast, financial market participants had internalized the arrival of a new currency immediately. From January 1999, they used the euro in their contracts. Bonds and shares were bought and sold against the euro. Bank accounts were kept in euros. Ubiquitous computers allowed the banks to calculate the exchange rates up to the sixth decimal (one-millionth of a euro). The individual customers did not notice this because households still received their information in the national currency (and close to the end of the transition period in both euro and the national currency).

In this sense there existed during this transitional period a "digital euro" alongside the national currencies. It had nothing to do with the digital euro the ECB is now contemplating (see Chapter 10), though technology plays a key part in both. Without the complete digitalization of the "scriptural" money, it would have been impossible to manage the temporary coexistence of one euro with many national currencies.

In 2002, households and retail merchants received new sheets of paper and had to adjust to a new unit of account. Italians were used to prices in thousands of lira even for small items like a cup of coffee. Now they suddenly had to think in much smaller numbers. For Germans, the new prices in euro were about one-half of those in D-Mark they were used to. Of course, their wages were also approximately one-half. Changing the currency used every day by retailers had also tangible consequences because it changed their unit of account.

For many consumers, it appeared that the arrival of the euro made life more expensive. Prices of some small, frequently bought goods were suddenly much higher than they should have been had they been faithfully converted into euro-adjusted goods. Merchants invariably round prices, or sometimes post "attractive" prices, just one cent below the rounded number. Typical examples of rounding at the time were coffee sold in bars, newspapers, and sometimes T-shirts. The temptation to round up the price, say, of a coffee from 1.13 euros to 1.20 euros was strong. This generated the impression of an inflationary effect of the euro. In Germany, some talked, only half-jokingly, about a "Teuro," a play of words on the German word for expensive, which is *"teuer."*[16]

In reality, these were isolated instances; the average price level recorded by the statisticians did not go up significantly. Later research revealed that, across all the eleven countries that participated in the euro from the start, one could observe a very small, temporary, increase in the price level. For most big-ticket items of household expenditure, like rent, cars, furniture, and utilities, the new prices had been correctly converted into euros at the official conversion rates.[17] Yet the popular perception of a "Teuro" proved immune to scientific research. A similar phenomenon occurred in most countries that joined the euro area later, though without a similar dual currency phase.[18]

This shows that the three-year interval in which new and old units of account had coexisted had not been sufficient to firmly take root in the perceptions of consumers – and merchants.

The temporary rise in inflation experienced by Germany in 1990 had not been caused by the currency reform but by the macro-economic imbalances induced by the huge expenditure required by reunification. By contrast, in 2002 the new unit of account was too new to be fully incorporated into consumer sentiments although it had been used in the financial sector since 1999. Hence, one-off price increases could happen – an indication of the fact that money can be "debased," or in other words lose value, if the unit of account and means of payment functions are separated.

MONEY'S REQUIREMENTS: THE CONVENTIONAL VIEW

In Chapter 2, discussing the early monetary instruments of the ancient populations, we noted certain practical requirements: in particular, the fact that money should be easily recognized by everybody, conveniently transferable across space as well as over time, and practically divisible to match the different values, large and small, existing in the economy.

Jevons' analysis of those requirements was largely adopted by later economists. But some of the requirements he added were actually wrong. For example, later history has demonstrated that the first one he cites – that money must possess inherent value – isn't really needed. Jevon's articulate argument is worth reproducing extensively:

> Since money has to be exchanged for valuable goods, it should itself possess value, and it must therefore have utility as the basis of value. Money, when once in full currency, is only received in order to be passed on, so that if all people could be induced to take worthless bits of material at a fixed rate of valuation, it might seem that money does not really require to have substantial value. Something like this does frequently happen in the history of currencies, and apparently valueless shells, bits of leather, or scraps of paper, are actually received in exchange for costly commodities. This strange phenomenon is, however, in most cases capable of easy explanation, and if we were acquainted with the history of every kind of money the like explanation would no doubt be possible in other cases. The essential point is that people should be induced to receive money, and pass it on freely at steady ratios of exchange for other objects; but there must always be some sufficient reason first inducing people to accept the money. The force of habit, convention, or legal enactment may do much to maintain money in circulation when once it is afloat, but it is doubtful whether the most powerful government could oblige its subjects to accept and circulate as money a worthless substance which they had no other motive for receiving.

His conclusion is then:

> In order that money may perform some of its functions
> efficiently, especially those of a medium of exchange and a store
> of value, to be carried about, it is important that it should be
> made of a substance valued highly in all parts of the world, and, if
> possible, almost equally esteemed by all peoples.[19]

Modern "fiat" monies made of paper or cheap metals are not convertible into any inherently valued material, yet they are generally accepted because people know or at least hope that they can be traded for valuable goods later. They are backed by a promise by central banks to maintain their value over time, relative to valued goods and services. If this promise is institutionally protected and believed, it performs the same function as Jevons' inherent value. This argument is interesting to us because one critique raised against cryptocurrencies is that they have no inherent value – they are just bits and bytes stored in a computer. In Chapters 8 and 9 we will argue that this is not their main problem but rather that they require considerable technical knowledge and that the blockchain technology on which they are based does not lend itself to be scaled up to serve for millions or billions of retail transactions.

Other requirements cited by Jevons are all practically important:

1. *Portability.* This is the property of being easily transported, which as we noted constitutes one of the advantages of coinage relative to bars of precious metals and of paper over coins. The notion includes security as well; today's equivalent of portability can be identified in the effectiveness and efficiency of electronic and digital money transfer systems.
2. *Indestructibility.* This element was important in the transition from perishable materials – like barley for the Mesopotamians – to more durable means.
3. *Homogeneity.* This means that one piece of money should be identical to another. Again, barley and other seeds do not satisfy this requirement, nor do other archaic instruments like shells.

4. *Divisibility.* This is the property of being divided into subunits. Seeds are perfect in this respect, whereas bars of precious metals may not be so in practice. But digital money is perfectly divisible.
5. *Stability in value.* This property has been key in the whole history of money and continues to be so. The dire consequences of debasement, which we discuss in various parts of this book, clearly indicate that it is a critical requirement. Monies that lose value tend to be rejected and replaced.
6. *Cognizability.* As we mentioned, money must be easily recognized and distinguishable from other instruments. The lion head impressed on the Lydian coins provided an assurance of the proper metal alloy. Even today, central banks devote much time and resources to ensure that banknotes are distinct and their identity immediately apparent, by means of different sizes and colors as well as design.

Modern money, in its many forms, banknotes, bank accounts, credit cards and apps, must fulfil these requirements as well. It remains to be seen whether technology can generate competitive alternatives.

BEYOND MONEY'S CONVENTIONAL ROLE

The textbook characterization of the three functions remains broadly valid today but is becoming increasingly incomplete as a result of financial and technological innovation. Additional elements need to be brought into the picture.

We already mentioned the Keynesian "liquidity value": Other things equal, money is more valuable than other assets because it is exchangeable immediately at any time, without losses, for goods, services, and other assets. Modern electronic and digital technologies increase this liquidity value because they lower the cost and effort of enacting payments. At the same time, however, financial innovation softens the "availability constraint"; for example, several payment platforms, such as PayPal and Klarna, offer a variety of convenient (though not necessarily cheap) online "buy-now-pay-later" modalities. To the extent that this happens, money tends to lose its advantage in liquidity value because credit becomes more accessible and illiquid assets can more easily be liquidated, without selling them, by using them as collateral. Spending patterns may change as a result, as we have already seen when discussing the psychological effects of credit cards.

Money's liquidity value helps fulfil basic human aspirations because it is immediately usable to procure things people desire. As such it contributes to long-standing human aspirations: self-control, the ability to seize opportunities as they arise, flexibility, and freedom of choice. These are real and enduring benefits and technology is capable of promoting them.

But there are also dangers. Money may cease to be an "instrument of the buyer," available to and controlled by those who own money and decide to spend it, and become an "instrument of the seller," akin to a subtle marketing device. Spending patterns reveal information on habits that can be exploited to incite further spending or even overspending. Sellers can be small retailers but also large, powerful, and hidden subjects distorting people's behavior to their own advantage. These dangers increase with the complexity of technology and the integration between payment and information technologies. Money in the twenty-first century must be *informationally safe*: The information generated by a purchase must be protected as part of the individual's private sphere. With traditional payment means, like banknotes and coins, the privacy of exchange is inherently granted. This is not the case for other payment technologies used today. Moreover, money increasingly depends on technology in order to function. Banknotes and coins once in circulation do not rely on other infrastructures, whereas electronic and digital means, both online and offline, rely on the hardware and software that support them. Today's domestic and international monetary systems run on the internet, which, like all infrastructures, is vulnerable to failure as a consequence of accidents and intentional attacks. Modern monetary systems must therefore be *technologically robust*, with in-built features and emergency backups that reduce their vulnerability.

MONEY AND THE STATE

The relationship between money and the state has fluctuated in history; the state is never totally absent, but it is not often the monopolist of it, nor always the primary actor behind its development.

The role of the state in ensuring the stability of money became paramount at the start of coinage. In Europe, coinage was mostly based on silver or gold (for larger transactions). China, in contrast, stuck with its copper coins (with a square hole inside) for two millennia. Another hallmark of Chinese monetary history is that the central state never relinquished tight control. This is particularly striking in the case of paper money, which arose from private sector initiative in Europe but was imposed from above in China. Part of the motivation to issue paper money might have been a genuine desire to provide an additional means of payment given the limitation of copper mentioned earlier.[20] But the experiment lasted only as long as the emperor was able to keep its expenditure under control.[21]

We recounted in Chapter 2 how, after its victory over its Mediterranean rival Carthage, the Roman Republic established a silver coin, the *denarius*, that became the monetary standard of the known world for four centuries. This association between fiscally strong states and a strong currency represents a regularity in history. Only when the third-century emperors reduced the silver content did the value of the *denarius* fall, and inflation started to increase. The decline of the *denarius* (and that of the Roman empire overall[22]) started after AD 211, when the emperor Septimus Severus on his deathbed told his sons: "Live in harmony; enrich the troops; ignore everyone else."[23]

His sons did not live in harmony (one killed the other), but the survivor, Caracalla, did enrich the troops, so much so that he had to debauch the currency. In the 1926 Hemingway novel *The Sun Also Rises*, Bill asks "How did you go bankrupt?" Mike answers, "Two ways. Gradually and then suddenly." This also applies to the Roman Empire. The decline was first gradual. It had taken two centuries until Septimus Severus for the price level to double, but it took only forty years to double again and then the intervals became shorter and shorter until the silver content of the *denarius* was so low that it was no longer recognizable as a silver coin and it took over 70,000 of them to buy one pound of gold.

The Romans were technically unable to produce hyperinflation, say, an inflation above 50 percent per month. One needs paper money and a twentieth-century printing press to achieve this. However, the rapid debasement of the currency led people to hoard the old coins with a higher silver content and use the new ones to spend or pay taxes. Prices rose ever more quickly as merchants became unwilling to sell for debased currency. At that point, money ceased to function, and one emperor even tried to fix prices by imperial edict.[24] But this attempt failed and ended up further reducing the usefulness of money, destroying commerce and forcing many communities to revert to autarchy. The reduction in economic activity further reduced tax revenues, inducing the emperor to either increase already oppressive taxes or debase the currency even further.

Those living in economies with relatively stable political systems do not need to fear this degree of inflation. Depending on history's cycles, the state can be either the guardian of the value of money or its nemesis when the polity is stressed.

GLOBALIZED MONEY

Another development of the last half century or about is that money became less connected to national sovereigns. In the aftermath of World War II, there were some seventy-six countries in the world; barring a few exceptions, each of them had its own money.[25] Today the number of countries, as measured by the membership of the United Nations, has grown to 197, and the number of currencies to 170.[26] Political fragmentation has increased alongside the number of currencies used by multiple nations. The frontrunners of this development are the euro, now used by twenty countries (without counting some smaller independent states such as the Vatican), and the US dollar, used by thirteen countries apart from the United States. In addition, the major currencies, like the dollar and the euro, circulate widely outside their own jurisdiction's borders, in parallel with the official local currency.

This is not an unprecedented phenomenon. In premodern times coins circulated widely, often outside of the state (kingdom, empire, or republic) that had minted them. We already alluded to Roman coins found in India as one extreme example. In effect, the *denarius* had become a sort of global reserve currency.

The internationalization of money has multiple facets and complex implications. Dysfunctionality of the domestic money represents one driver of the use of foreign money. We already mentioned how the US dollar had become the de facto unit of account and store value during the German hyperinflation.

Seigniorage, historically a major recurrent means of resource appropriation by national governments, becomes more difficult to extract when money goes global. Seigniorage extraction requires a "captive" money market, implying a demand for money not very sensitive to inflation. If money demand is not very "elastic" – a term economists use to mean that its demand does not depend much on its return – then seigniorage becomes a more effective source of revenue for governments and can even be, within boundaries, an efficient one from an optimal taxation perspective.[27] Otherwise, seigniorage tends to shrink the tax base. This effect is not very strong when people have no choice but to use the national currency. However, with globalized money, the tax base becomes more sensitive and volatile. This is not an unprecedented phenomenon. We already mentioned that "currency competition" among Greek city-states kept them from debasing their local coins.

In bank-based systems governments have an alternative to literally printing money. They can tax banks by requiring them to hold substantial reserves with zero interest at the central banks. Required reserves on which banks received no interest were widely used after the war when international financial transactions were largely prohibited. But when global financial markets reopened, banks could evade the reserve requirements by booking deposits offshore. The globalization of finance may therefore contribute to explaining why governments have largely given up taxing the banking system via nonremunerated required reserves and monetary aggregates have been on the rise in recent decades.

Another implication of globalization is that monetary management, especially with regard to the most important global currencies, like the US dollar, the euro, and the Chinese renminbi, has acquired geostrategic importance. The issuance of reserve currencies is regulated by countries, or in the case of the euro by an international union. Global currencies are used far beyond the boundaries of the countries or unions concerned. At the same time, domestic banking and financial sectors largely control the intermediation processes and the payment systems of those currencies, with two consequences.

First, national governance and regulation generate cross-border externalities: The consequences of policy or regulatory actions are no longer limited by national boundaries. In principle, this calls for international coordination; in practice, the geography of cross-border use of currencies, official and unofficial, is too extended and complex to be matched by the existing policy coordination arrangements, very limited in the area of finance. At the very least, however, the international dimension calls for monetary and payment systems with cross-border reach to be *more extensively regulated* so that their external effects are at least partly internalized.

Second, money is being used to promote geopolitical goals. An example we examine later in this book is the Society for Worldwide Financial Telecommunications, or SWIFT, the Belgium-based digital messaging system supporting cross-border payments. Political pressure can be applied to the administration of SWIFT to cut out certain users from accessing the network. This type of financial sanction via SWIFT was applied in a number of cases, most recently against Russia after its aggression on Ukraine. We will examine in more depth the role of SWIFT and the scope of the international use of currencies and their geostrategic implications. There are also milder and more nuanced forms of strategic use of currencies, for example, to encourage certain financial practices (disclosure, transparency) or promote national interests in various other ways. Whether the strategic use – sometimes called "weaponization" – of currencies is an acceptable instrument of foreign policy is a value judgment. From a positive perspective, it is likely that the jurisdictions enjoying such privilege will want to defend it by ensuring that the national infrastructures that govern money at home are *tightly ring-fenced*. We will discuss in Chapter 12 whether and when this weaponization can actually succeed.

ONE MONEY FOR THE WORLD?

The adoption of a common currency, the euro, by a group of diverse economies in Europe has revived the long-standing question of why one could not go further, adopting continental monies or even one single money for the entire world. The Romans did this successfully for the world they knew then.

The concept of world money is implicit in the call for global government repeatedly made by philosophers over at least the last eight centuries, from Dante to Kant.[28] A founding father of modern economics, John Stuart Mill, is reported to have said: "So much barbarism, however, still remains in the transactions of most civilized nations, that almost all independent countries choose to assert their nationality by having, to their inconvenience and that of their neighbors, a peculiar currency of their own."[29] More recently, a linkage among the world's currencies, if not a single global money, was advocated by the Stanford economist Ronald McKinnon, though that view was not shared in the economic profession.[30] Facebook's project, eventually failed, to privately create a global digital currency which we discuss later in this book harkened back to that same idea.

The main argument for one money for the world is simple. Mill calls it convenience; economists call it transaction costs. We discuss in Chapter 12 why international transfers, despite having accelerated with digitalization, have remained much more costly and slower than domestic transfers. The benefits of sharing a currency obviously depend on the intensity of trade and other economic relations. The savings in transaction costs loom large in an economically tightly interconnected area like Europe that shares one integrated market. The semiofficial motto of the euro project was "One Market, One Money."[31] However, this argument is much less strong for most other areas of the world where economic integration is much less intense.

The arguments for retaining separate currencies for nations pertain to the realms of economics, politics, and even, one should say, political psychology.

In each country, wages and prices are fixed in the national currency. Not having a separate currency creates a problem if a country experiences a shock and needs to export more to overcome unemployment. To export more, that country needs to become more competitive. This could be achieved either by reducing wages or by depreciating the exchange rate. The latter is far easier to implement because workers resist lowering their wages. In a nutshell, the argument for keeping a national currency is that it facilitates adjustments to adverse shocks. This argument does not depend on the form of money, whether digital or paper-based. It is based on the assumption that wage earners resist wage cuts but more easily accept – or less easily recognize – a cut in real wages via higher prices. Economists call an area in which the kind of shocks requiring an adjustment of the exchange is rare an "optimum currency area."[32]

However, the reason why national currencies survive is not just technical. People do not always behave like rationally calculating economic agents. No matter how far economies evolve, integrating among themselves and hence approaching "optimum currency area" conditions, the attractiveness of retaining monetary autonomy is hard to overcome, among politicians and their electorates. This partly depends on the fact that confusion between nominal and real variables (the so-called money illusion) is very persistent in the minds of people.

There are other reasons as well. Some argue that having national money is an essential part of a sovereign nation-state because, with a national currency, the central bank can bail out the government or banks in times of need.[33] This problem became apparent, for example, during the euro crisis in some countries like Spain, Ireland, and Greece, whose national central banks could not autonomously provide liquidity to rescue their banks. Eventually, a single money always requires deep institutional reforms and a high degree of political cohesion and will among the countries involved.

The future is open. It is a fact, however, that the long-lived dream of having a single global money is unlikely to materialize any time soon.

NOTES

1. William S. Jevons, *Money and the Mechanism of Exchange* (D. Appleton, 1875), vol. 17.

2. Milton Friedman and Anna J. Schwartz, *A Monetary History of the United States: 1867–1960* (Princeton University Press, 1961).

3. Robert M. Solow, "Economic History and Economics," *The American Economic Review* 75, no. 2 (1985): 328–31.

4. The Online Appendix to this book, available at Ignazio Angeloni's blog (ignazioangeloni.home.blog), contains a synoptic table that compares these monetary reforms through the lenses of the three functions of money: as means of payment, unit of account, and store of value.

5. Data reported by Costantino Bresciani-Turroni, *The Economics of Inflation* (Allen & Unwin, 1937).

6. Fascinating accounts of the German hyperinflation and the role of Schacht in the eventual stabilization of the Reichsmark are offered by Liaquat Ahamed, *Lords of Finance: The Bankers Who Broke the World* (Penguin, 2009) and Adam Fergusson, *When Money Dies: The Nightmare of the Weimar Collapse* (PublicAffairs, 1975).

7. For a detailed account of the reform see Thomas Mayer and Guenther Thurmann, "Radical Currency Reform: Germany 1948," *Finance & Development, March 1990* 27, no. 1 (January 1, 1990).

8. A hilarious portrait of the contrasting East–West German lifestyles during the Cold War is offered by the 1961 Billy Wilder movie *One, Two, Three*, in which a memorable James Cagney plays the role of Coca-Cola's chief executive officer in West Berlin.

9. And very expensive to produce: James W. Cortada, "Information Technologies in the German Democratic Republic (GDR), 1949–1989," *IEEE Annals of the History of Computing* 34, no. 2 (February 1, 2012): 34–48.

10. NDR (German Radio), "Schabowskis Zettel," November 9, 2022.

11. See the Berlin Wall Memorial website at "Victims of the Wall," Berlin.de.

12. Bundestag, "Geschichte, 21. Juni 1990: Ja zum Einzug der D-Mark in die DDR," Bundestag, 2021.

13. A dissenting voice in the West German Parliament, the Bundestag, characterized this as "Die DDR-Regierung wird zum Junior partner der Deutschen Bundesbank." See Bundestag, "Geschichte, 21. Juni 1990."

14. For an in-depth analysis see Gerlinde Sinn and Hans-Werner Sinn, *Kaltstart: Volkswirtschaftliche Aspekte Der Deutschen Vereinigung* (Mohr, 1992).

15. Daniel Gros and Alfred Steinherr, *Economic Transition in Central and Eastern Europe: Planting the Seeds* (Cambridge University Press, 2004).

16. Hans W. Brachinger "Euro or 'Teuro'? The Euro-Induced Perceived Inflation in Germany," University of Fribourg Department of Quantitative Economics Working Papers 5, July 17, 2006.

17. See, among the many analyses of the phenomenon, Ignazio Angeloni, Luc Aucremanne, and Matteo Ciccarelli, "Price Setting and Inflation Persistence: Did EMU Matter?," *Economic Policy* 21, no. 46 (April 1, 2006): 354–87.

18. Hubert Gabrisch and Martina Kämpfe, "The New EU Countries and Euro Adoption," *Intereconomics* 48, no. 3 (May 1, 2013): 180–86.

19. William Stanley Jevons, *Money and the Mechanism of Exchange* (D. Appleton, 1875), chapter V.

20. Hanhui Guan and Jie Mao, "The Silver Standard as a Discipline on Money Over-Issuance: The Mechanism of Paper Money in Yuan China," Economic History Society Working Papers 18013, 2018.

21. Hanhui Guan, Nuno Palma, and Meng Wu, "The Rise and Fall of Paper Money in Yuan China, 1260–1368," The University of Manchester Economics Discussion Paper Series 2207, 2022.

22. The classic reference is the nineteenth-century magnum opus Edward Gibbon, *The Decline and Fall of the Roman Empire*, vol. 1 (Bohn, 1883).

23. Jonathan Blum, "Inflation Is Tricky: Just Ask the Romans," Brookside Research, July 28, 2022.

24. See, for example, Alfred Wassink. "Inflation and Financial Policy under the Roman Empire to the Price Edict of 301 A.D.," *Historia: Zeitschrift für Alte Geschichte* 40, no. 4 (1991): 465–93.

25. This information is drawn from Alberto Alesina and Robert J. Barro, "Currency Unions," NBER Working Papers 7927, September 1, 2000.

26. Information can be found on Wikipedia: Wikipedia contributors, "List of Circulating Currencies," *Wikipedia*, August 11, 2023.

27. See Gregory Mankiw, Matthew Weinzierl, and Danny Yagan, "Optimal Taxation in Theory and Practice," *Journal of Economic Perspectives* 23, no. 4 (November 1, 2009): 147–74.

28. Dante Alighieri, *Monarchy* (1309); Immanuel Kant, *Perpetual Peace* (1795). Kant's views on the subject were, however, rather changeable and complex: An accessible summary of views is offered by "World Government," *Stanford Encyclopedia of Philosophy*, January 5, 2021.

29. John Stuart Mill, Principles of Political Economy (1848).

30. Ronald I. McKinnon, *An International Standard for Monetary Stabilization* (MIT Press, 1984). For a different view see, for example, Kenneth Rogoff, "Why Not a Global Currency?," *The American Economic Review* 91, no. 2 (May 1, 2001): 243–47.

31. Emerson, Michael. *One Market, One Money: An Evaluation of the Potential Benefits and Costs of Forming an Economic and Monetary Union* (Oxford University Press, 1992).

32. See Robert A. Mundell, "A Theory of Optimum Currency Areas," *The American Economic Review* 51, no. 4 (1961): 657–65.

33. Charles Goodhart, "The Two Concepts of Money: Implications for the Analysis of Optimal Currency Areas," *European Journal of Political Economy* 14, no. 3 (August 1, 1998): 407–32.

5   The Paradox of Cash

Today people who hold cash equivalents feel comfortable.
They shouldn't.

Warren Buffett

"Money, money, money!" aired a fashionable tune by the Swedish pop group ABBA in the 1970s. Group member Frida Lyngstad sang: "If I got me a wealthy man, I wouldn't have to work at all, I'd fool around and have a ball." The video, still popular online, features the four singers intermingled with cascades of coins and banknotes: US dollars, by the way, not Swedish krona.

Half a century on, this seems very outdated. The text does not meet today's gender parity standards. The imagery is antiquated as well; a remastered edition today would probably feature the four musicians, now all between seventy and eighty years of age, surrounded by cards and apps, and maybe some Bitcoin as well.

Three decades after invading the discos, the paths of ABBA and cash met again when the band leader Björn Ulvaeus, a popular figure in Sweden, initiated a campaign to ban cash altogether. The reason was personal. In 2008, burglars broke into his son's apartment. They did not find cash, only other valuable material; yet father and son thought that finding banknotes was what had motivated them in the first place. The campaign got traction. The Sveriges Riksbank, Sweden's central bank, studied ways of replacing krona banknotes with electronic means. On these premises, Sweden spearheaded a worldwide unique experiment: eliminating cash entirely. To some extent, it worked: The use of cash in small payments halved, from 40 to 20 percent (recently it has been rising again). Bank robberies declined as well, demonstrating, in the eyes of the believers, that eliminating a potential object of theft would eliminate theft altogether.

Not much time passed before the Riksbank concluded that, yes, cash and cash robberies had indeed declined, but meanwhile, other more sophisticated digital forms of robbery and fraud had increased.[1] The net effect on people's safety was uncertain. By then, however, Sweden's use of cash had become one of the lowest on the planet, cash holding amounting to only about 1 percent of GDP, compared to around 8–10 percent in other large developed economies. Sweden has become the poster child of those who predict that cash will soon disappear, as well as of those arguing that cash *should* disappear – the two crowds largely coincide.

Sweden is a peculiar case in terms of cash use because its central bank has periodically invalidated old banknotes giving people little time to exchange them for new ones.[2] But it is also just ahead of a global trend. Almost everywhere, digital payments are substituting the use of cash for retail transactions. Observing this makes many believe that cash is obsolete and should be on its way out. On the other hand, its supposed disappearance makes central banks nervous: Faced with the prospect of losing their signature product, banknotes, they feel pressured to find a replacement. Hence the effort to develop so-called central bank digital currencies, which we will discuss in Chapter 10. This causal circle, accentuated by the media, feeds into the "hype" surrounding digital monies which now pervades public debates, business strategies, and public policy circles.

Is this going too far?

No doubt, today's digital means of payment have changed the ways we make our daily expenses for the better. Most of them are indeed convenient and safe. Things like shopping or paying your bills, which years ago required trips to the bank or the shops at specific times of the day and interminable queuing waits, today can be done comfortably at home, round the clock, touching the screen of a smartphone. This is a real improvement. But concluding on this basis that cash should be on the way out does not necessarily follow.

An older payment technology should not disappear simply because newer ones exist. The right questions to be asked are: Is cash still appreciated by some users, for some purposes? Are these purposes legitimate? Does cash provide a useful complement to more modern technologies, in a diversified and well-functioning payment system? How do the costs and benefits of banknote production compare? And vice versa, are there compelling reasons *against* some (probably limited) use of cash?

In the following pages, we look into some of these and related questions. The first is factual: Is cash indeed disappearing? Another is normative: Are there reasons why it *should*? This latter question is relevant for policymakers, central banks, and other regulators, which have in their toolkits a variety of regulatory instruments that can boost or discourage certain means of payments as opposed to others.

Before coming to this, however, we step back for a moment and examine the basic rationales for holding cash (banknotes and, to a much lesser extent, coins in circulation) rather than other assets. This is a subject to which academic economists have devoted a good deal of study, many years ago.

THE ECONOMICS OF CASH HOLDINGS

The simplest theory to explain the demand for cash was proposed in 1952 by the Princeton economist William J. Baumol. A three-quarters century on, his theory is still admirably fresh and relevant.[3]

Baumol imagined an individual – a lady we think, though he wasn't specific about this – who needs to use cash to carry out a given amount of expenses over a period of time – say, a month. She has personal funds invested in a bank at an interest and she has to decide how much cash to take out of the bank and keep on hand every day. The more frequently she goes to the bank to withdraw cash, the more money she can keep in the bank, to earn an interest, and the lower her average cash holding. That person must therefore balance the nuisance of going to the bank often with the forgone interest from the bank. In this simple setting, Baumol showed that the average cash holding varies inversely with (the square root of) the interest rate and directly with (the square root of) her monthly expenses.

Does this stylized model make sense in today's profoundly changed monetary and payment world? More than it seems at first sight. To start with, though many retail transactions today are done with means different than cash, like debit or credit cards, there are still many situations in which the use of cash is either necessary or more convenient – we will return to this later. Second, the "nuisance" of going to the bank has declined after the introduction of ATMs (automated teller machines, or cash dispensers), which shortened the average distance between each consumer and the nearest source of cash and eliminated, in most cases, the need to stand in lengthy lines at the cashier. ATMs first appeared in the United States, Britain, and Australia in the late 1960s, and have grown constantly ever since: There is now an ATM every 500 persons (minors included) on average in the United States, every 1,000 in the euro-zone, and every 2,500 world over.[4] Still, there is always some residual cost of procuring cash, more so in remote areas where teller machines are less common.

A key factor discouraging people's desire to hold cash is, as Baumol correctly pointed out, the return they forego from other investments. Alternative returns, which economists call "opportunity costs," play a central role in all financial decisions. For many years, banks have paid little or no interest on their customers' deposits; in the euro area some even *charged* interest, or, in other words, applied a negative rate. However, this has changed recently with banks, sometimes reluctantly, paying interest again.

Cash, by nature, does not earn any interest. It is thus natural to assume that people take the interest that accrues on bank deposits, or any other assets, as a factor influencing their demand for cash. There are also other factors involved. As Baumol himself wrote, "We must also extend the meaning of the interest rate to include the value of protection against loss by fire, theft, etc., which we obtain when someone borrows our cash."[5] Those risks have not changed much, and probably still matter today when we decide how large a sum of cash we keep in our pocket or at home.

The role played by interest rates as determinants of cash-holding decisions is actually more complex than implied by Baumol's model. Economists have long realized that money, of which cash represents a minor but significant part, is held not only to carry out routine expenses but also as a form of financial investment. The first to theorize this motive was the Yale economist and Nobel prize recipient James Tobin. In a 1958 article,[6] he argued that money holdings were, in part, a "behavior towards risk." This motive is different from the "opportunity cost" we discussed earlier, which is measured by the *level* of alternative returns. It depends on the expectation of how interest rates will *change* in the future. A rise in the level of interest rates makes the price of bonds fall – as many investors painfully noticed when rates abruptly increased in 2022. In Tobin's argument, when interest rates are at historical lows and are expected to return to their higher long-term norms, investors tend to shift from bonds to money, which is not subject to any loss in value. The spirit of the argument is that money is not held only for expenses but also and perhaps even more as a component of a portfolio of financial investments This argument is, admittedly, more relevant for forms of money different from cash, like bank deposits.

These mechanisms help us interpret the recent increase in the demand for money, including cash, a phenomenon which has gone on at a global scale over the last quarter century alongside the decline in interest rates. Baumol's and Tobin's theories – one based on transactions, the other on portfolio choices – predict that when interest rates fall the demand for money will rise. This has indeed happened on a grand scale.

ALIVE AND WELL: USE OF CASH AROUND THE WORLD

Those who predict or look forward to the proximate demise of physical currency must come to terms with a fact: People hold cash in large amounts almost everywhere in the world. Cash holdings have actually increased sharply in recent times.

Central banks maintain and publish detailed statistics on banknotes and coins outstanding. The European Central Bank (ECB) is particularly interested in monitoring the demand for cash in its area of competence, having introduced brand new banknotes in 2022. Are they popular? Detailed tables and charts on its website provide the full picture.[7] In a nutshell: The ECB can be quite happy with the message the data convey. In the two decades or so of their existence, banknotes in euro have grown steadily in value, at the staggering average annual rate of about 10 percent, increasing eightfold from only 200 billion in 2002 when euro cash was first introduced to over 1,600 billion today. Over the same period, GDP of the eurozone and consumption have grown in monetary terms at about 3 percent every year on average, only doubling over the entire period. Cash holding per unit of output or consumption has thus risen by a factor of four, and the ratio of cash to GDP from roughly 3 percent to 12 percent. While this increase may be exaggerated by the fact that prior to the introduction of the new banknotes cash holdings had fallen to unusually low levels, the relative increase just mentioned is startling, especially considering that in the period many new technologically advanced payment instruments were introduced.

A similar trend, just a bit less pronounced, is observed in most other major countries. For example, the comparable figure for the US dollar is 6.5 percent. In the United States, currency holdings increased since 2000 from 570 billion to 2100 billion, an increase of over 350 percent. The US economy has also increased in size, but proportionally less, so that the ratio of cash to GDP increased from 5.6 percent to 9.4 percent. A value this high was last seen in the postwar years (1947–48). A similar phenomenon is observed in the United Kingdom: Cash denominated in British pounds rose over the same period by 5.2 percent per annum.[8]

One popular explanation is that cash is the favorite payment means for criminals of various sort: smugglers, money launderers, drug dealers, tax evaders, and other similar characters. As we argue in some detail later, this factor cannot provide most of the explanation. The increase in the demand for cash is steady year after year; crime rates do not display such a regular pattern. Moreover, coins increased steadily as well;[9] it is unlikely that criminals make an extensive use of coins.

Further evidence of why and how people hold and use cash comes from ATM withdrawals. It suggests a large difference across the Atlantic. ECB data show that over 1 trillion euros are withdrawn from cash machines each year.[10] Household expenditure in the eurozone runs at about 6 trillion euros; from this, one may be tempted to conclude that less than 20 percent of household purchases are done with cash. However, a large part of household expenditure goes to paying regular bills, rent, electricity, or consumer loans, most of which are done by bank transfers. Perhaps only one-half of household income is spent on purchases in shops, an estimate that matches the consumer survey results showing that about 50 percent of all consumer expenses are paid in cash. This indicates that the use of cash by consumers in the eurozone, while declining, remains very significant.

During the COVID-19 crisis, cash withdrawals accelerated, but the share of expenditure paid in cash is likely to have declined, replaced by online purchases. In that period, cash hoarding is likely to have become more important relative to its use for transaction purposes.

For the United States one finds lower numbers. The Federal Reserve estimates that total ATM withdrawals amounted to approximately 800 billion dollars in 2018, with a steady increase over time. Cash withdrawals in 2018 amounted to only about 6 percent of US personal consumption expenditure of around 14,000 billion dollars. Less than one-half of all consumer expenditure goes to regular shopping items like food, entertainment, or clothes, implying that the share of cash is much higher than 6 percent for person-to-person payments, but overall, this provides a first indication that cash usage is lower than in continental Europe. Federal Reserve studies for the

United States show that the share of cash payments has fallen to below 20 percent of all transactions and is rapidly declining, especially after the pandemic.[11]

The declining use of cash in the United States may also depend on the fact that the existing currency denominations have lost most of their original value. The 1-dollar bill, with the portrait of George Washington shown on its front side, is worth today no more than 4 percent of its original value, when first introduced a century and a half ago. Coins in the United States today are virtually valueless and hardly usable. The use of cash has become less practical than it used to be, hence less attractive.

Cash withdrawals give only an indirect picture of the importance of cash in everyday transactions. A more direct picture emerges from large-scale surveys in which representative samples of households report for a period of time their purchases and how they paid for them.

The move toward cashless and contactless payments is advanced in the smaller and more high-tech-inclined Northern European countries. Sweden is the best example.[12] Here cash has indeed become marginal, with only 10 percent of respondents in a survey in 2021 reporting that they had paid for their last purchase in cash.[13] The move has been gradual but strong. In 2010 that ratio was still 40 percent. The social distancing measures imposed during the COVID-19 epidemic accelerated this process over the last two years as the government recommended contactless payments (although scientists agree that it is highly unlikely that the coronavirus can be transmitted by banknotes or coins). Economists at the Swedish Riksbank have asked themselves whether their country is "ahead of the curve" or just a special case.[14] Looking at the international evidence, the latter seems to be the case.

Sweden, as well as its Scandinavian neighbors Denmark and Norway, is not representative of what happens in the rest of Europe, where cash remains by far the most popular option. In Germany, around 60 percent of all transactions are still done in cash (2021 data), but in terms of value, the share of cash transactions has already fallen to 38 percent because larger transactions are already done digitally, mostly via debit cards.[15] The social distancing requirements have accelerated the change here as well, with the share of cash payments falling considerably relative to the previous editions of this survey. In Southern Europe, digital payments are less common.

All in all, the euro area's average payment patterns are still largely based on cash. According to an ECB study,[16] in 2016 cash was used by households in almost four-fifths of all retail transactions, amounting in value to over one-half of the total spent. There are differences across member countries: The share of cash use over total payments was close to 70 percent in Spain and Italy, but much lower in France (where checks are still common) and Finland (both around 33 percent).

The picture on a global scale masks some significant differences, especially across emerging countries. Some of these countries are rapidly moving up the technology ladder. An International Monetary Fund study measuring the use of cash of half of the world's population documents that the use of cash for everyday transactions is declining almost everywhere.[17] China, for example, is leapfrogging the card stage with its urban class in the prosperous eastern part of the country having fully adopted the payment apps of the Chinese internet giants. However, in the less prosperous interior, about which less is known, cash is likely to continue to play a large role. It is only natural to expect large regional differences in a country with 1.4 billion inhabitants, with a very diverse pace of development across geographical areas in recent years.

THE PARADOX OF A "SECULAR" RESURGENCE OF CASH

Longer-term trends provide additional perspective on this puzzling phenomenon. During much of the nineteenth century, banknotes and coins were the main form of money available; bank deposits played a minor role, except toward the end of the period. One would thus expect that today, with all the modern payment methods and digital monies available, cash-to-GDP ratios should be much lower. But this is not the case. Secular data reconstructed for a number of countries show that the ratio of cash to GDP, after slowly declining until the 1920s, shot up during and after the Great Depression of the 1930s. With the banking failures that characterized that period, depositors were "flying to safety" by exchanging risky bank deposits for safer central bank liabilities as paper currency. This continued in the wartime period, after which a long phase of decline in cash-to-GDP ratios ensued. More puzzling, late in the century, when payment systems innovation was beginning, cash ratios were not lower than in the previous century. Furthermore, they started rising again, steadily and sharply, at the turn of the century, while payment innovation was experiencing rapid advance, which still continues today.

Already a century ago there were large differences in the intensity across countries. In the 1870s, the values range from over 15 percent of GDP in Germany down to 6–7 percent of GDP in the United States. Some of these differences have proven to be surprisingly persistent. The United States still has a lower cash-to-GDP ratio than most continental European countries, and German-speaking countries like Germany, Switzerland, and Austria still have a higher cash-to-GDP ratio. The United Kingdom is the exception here, switching position from a relatively high cash ratio in the mid 1900s to having one of the lowest among the major advanced countries today.

The resurgence of cash is common in most countries and in almost all advanced ones. But what about other forms of money? The data show that they have also increased globally. The World Bank publishes regularly the ratio of the broadest definition of money, called M3, which includes savings deposits, relative to global income.[18] This M3-to-GDP ratio has risen from about 60 percent in the 1980s to 100 percent around the turn of the century to close to 150 percent now. The conclusion is that people want to hold more and more money, both in physical and in digital form. In many advanced countries one finds that the ratio of digital to physical money (bank accounts relative to cash) has remained roughly constant at about eight–ten to one in favor of digital forms of money. The United States represents a somewhat special case in the sense that the use of demand deposits (also called M1) has declined more than elsewhere. The drivers of the demand for savings deposits (in M3) and demand deposits (M1) are different, however. A shift from demand deposits that usually do not pay interest to interest-yielding instruments included in M3 is due to the wider availability in the United States of interest-yielding substitutes of bank deposits. We discuss later in Chapter 9 the role of MMFs in the United States. In the euro area, where this type of innovation was less pronounced, all monetary components grew roughly at the same pace, as ratios to GDP.

The increase in recent times in the amount of currency in circulation (while its use for transactions is declining) is a global phenomenon. Statistics collected by the Bank for International Settlements (BIS) for the group of eleven most advanced economies (the former G10 plus Switzerland) show that in the last forty years,[19] the value of cash and coins per inhabitant has grown in all countries at annual rates comprised between 3 and 6 percent, with the only exception of Sweden, where it has decreased. Again, this appears to be an exception.

One explanation, as we mentioned, relies on low interest rates, which increase cash demanded for both transaction and portfolio purposes. In Baumol's model, for example, the elasticity of the demand for cash (the ratio between changes of cash and changes in the interest rate both in percent) is negative and equal to one-half. This implies that when interest rates approach zero, as has happened in recent decades as a result of what has been called "secular stagnation," cash demand rises by increasingly large amounts. Tobin's theory can also be shown to produce ever higher demands at rates approaching zero. Each of these theories, therefore, could in principle explain the puzzle.

This explanation, however, is unlikely to be sufficient. A factor that may have become more relevant recently for the major reserve currencies is the extent to which cash is held outside the national boundaries. If held abroad, by nonresidents or residents alike, money is normally held for different reasons than those which motivate domestic holdings.

Banks record exports and imports of euro banknotes. Cumulating these net flows since the start of the euro, one finds for 2019 that a total worth about 13 percent of the total value of the euro banknotes in circulation was held outside the eurozone. This seems low, and indeed it is probably a lower bound since it neglects all informal channels through which euro cash can be exported, like tourism, remittances, and currency smuggling. These other channels cannot be precisely measured. A survey of various approaches conducted by the ECB finds that the share held abroad could be as high as 50 percent.[20] The ECB concludes that foreign holdings represent the key to the paradox of banknotes. This conclusion does not answer the next question – why are foreign holdings so high? – fully, of course, but to some extent it does: It is unlikely that the reason depends on simple transaction needs. Illegal motives may play a role here.

A simple calculation supports this conclusion. The euro tends to be used mainly in the poorer and less stable countries close to Europe.[21] These are emerging and developing countries, whose economic size is small, even including Russia: The combined GDP of this group is 3,600 billion euros or about 30 percent of that of the euro area. The citizens of these countries would have to hold 20 percent of their national income in euros, in order to absorb close to one-half of the euro cash in circulation of over 1,600 billion. It is unlikely that euro cash holdings amount to 20 percent of GDP in these countries, whose citizens hold only about 4 percent of GDP in local currency.

Some euros might also be held in richer European countries which are not members of the euro area, such as Denmark or Switzerland. But the amounts are unlikely to be large since these countries have stable currencies and well-developed payment systems of their own. Their population has thus little need to hoard large amounts of euro banknotes.

The situation in the United States is different. The foreign countries where the dollar circulates have a combined GDP of about 80 percent of that of the United States (summing up Latin America, the Middle Eastern region, Africa, and developing Asia excluding China, one arrives at over 16 trillion dollars, compared to the 20 billion dollars for the United States). These countries together might absorb over one-half of all dollar bills if their dollar holdings amount to only 6 percent of their GDP. It follows that for the US dollar it is much more likely than for the euro that a very large share of cash is held abroad. It is also more likely that a large share of it is held for legitimate transaction or portfolio purposes. What is harder to explain based on these considerations, however, is a steady increase in cash holdings that systematically surpasses that of the dimension of the countries concerned.

Time to move on now and examine factors which, often ignored by economists, can explain the persistent demand for cash.

SMALL AND BIG SECRETS

A feature cash shares with no other payment means is its ability to keep a secret. Cash leaves no trace when it changes hands. Nor does it leave a trace of where, by whom, and why it is kept. Undoubtedly, this unique characteristic plays a role. But how much, and why? How much cash is kept, or used, for reasons which are intended to remain secret? We do not mean crime-related reasons only but also legitimate ones that people prefer to keep confidential. These questions are by nature unanswerable with any degree of precision: A secret is a secret. Only indirect and partial evidence is available.

Our collective imagination overflows with images of huge stashes of cash kept hidden for criminal purposes. Much of it comes from movies, which abound with scenes of drug traffickers, ransom seekers, tax evaders, and other disreputable characters flashing wads of (especially but not only) US dollars or opening suitcases filled with them. This is anecdotal evidence, though probably not too far from the truth. Anonymity makes cash ideal for all kinds of illicit transactions; what is difficult to measure is how much there is of it and how it is distributed across different activities.

All over the world, cash is used in the so-called gray economy: activities conducted informally, most often to avoid regulation or taxes. Cash is a sort of "oil" which lubricates the mechanisms of the gray economy. "Black economy" instead refers to outright unlawful criminal activities. A plumber who prefers payment in cash to avoid declaring his income is an example of the gray economy, whereas money from drug dealings is an example of a black economy transaction.

Establishing a link between cash usage on one side and the gray and black economies on the other is difficult. The Harvard economist Kenneth Rogoff, in a book titled *The Curse of Cash*,[22] which reveals the desire to get rid of cash altogether, discusses various "gray" and "black" motives for holding cash, including tax evasion, human trafficking, illegal immigration, and terrorism,[23] with very large estimates of the amounts involved. Maybe. But at least regarding tax evasion, we suspect that the amounts which are enabled or fostered by the use of cash are dwarfed by other modern and sophisticated forms of tax-dodging, such as those practiced by multinational corporations through tax loopholes.[24] The suspicion that the link between cash and tax evasion is overstated is reinforced by the low (though generally positive) correlation which is normally found across countries between cash usage and the incidence of the "shadow" economy – another way of calling the gray economy.[25]

Empirical studies on the shadow economy normally offer point-in-time estimates for advanced countries, usually in the range between 10 percent and 20 percent of GDP. With this low weight, it is difficult to explain high cash-to-GDP ratios with the shadow economy, particularly for countries like Japan or Switzerland for which the weight of the shadow economy is at the lower end of the range. The few studies which show the evolution of the shadow or gray economy over time find in general a decline of its importance since the early 2000s.[26] This makes it impossible to explain the increase in cash holdings with tax evasion or similar illicit activities.

The use of cash is also often associated with paying kickbacks or other forms of corruption. Corruption is important in itself, but from the point of view of explaining the holdings of cash, it does not seem to be a very important factor. Diverging international experiences of cash usage, for example, between Scandinavia and countries with similar law enforcement structures and performances, do not seem to be explained by the diffusion of corruption or the extent of the underground economy. At least, other important factors must be at play.[27]

The use of cash in the black economy (involving more dangerous and bloody criminal activity) can be gauged with an even lesser degree of precision than that of the gray one. Estimates of the size of the criminal economy vary, reportedly between 2 and 5 percent of GDP.[28] The lower bound, which would correspond to one-tenth of the gray economy, seems more appropriate for advanced countries. Given the small size of the black economy (perhaps one-fiftieth of that of the overall economy), it is difficult to argue that criminals account for a large share of the outstanding cash in circulation. Moreover, there is little indication that it has increased relative to GDP; crime trends point in the opposite direction.

A central problem with the argument that the use of cash is associated with the black economy is that the long-term trends of crime and cash holdings go in the opposite direction. Historians of crime have documented a long-standing declining trend in crime rates in the Western world. This trend persisted until the 1950s. However, the following three decades (roughly from the mid 1960s to the mid 1990s) saw a partial reversal, with crime rates increasing again.[29] That period was actually characterized, most clearly in the United States, with declining cash holdings relative to GDP. From the 1990s onward crime rates started to decline in the United States and in Europe, but cash holdings increased strongly, both in absolute terms and relative to GDP. Lower crime rates might actually encourage higher cash holdings. People will carry less money with them if they have to fear being mugged on a stroll through the park. One would also keep more money at home if one does not have to fear burglaries.

Criminals always face the problem of enjoying the gains from their activity without attracting attention. Hence the need to "launder" their money holdings so that they appear legitimate. The potential for money laundering is often assumed to constitute one major motive for large cash holdings. However, laundering large amounts of illegal/gray cash by putting it in bank accounts, playing in casinos, or buying luxury goods (yachts, autos, and the like) is becoming ever more difficult as anti–money laundering (AML) provisions become more stringent. But it still happens on a large scale as official reports from European and other law enforcement agencies document.[30]

The main money laundering operations uncovered in Europe over the last year did not involve cash operations but went through regional bank branches whose officers were willing to turn a blind eye to large amounts of suspicious transactions. For example, hundreds of billions of dollars of suspicious transactions from Russia transited through a single branch of a mid-sized Danish bank in the tiny state of Estonia.[31]

Lately, cash has probably ceased to be the favorite type of payment preferred by criminals: According to data published by the Drug Enforcement Administration, forfeitures of Bitcoins have recently exceeded those of cash.[32] All that being said, discouraging cash, or in extreme cases banning it altogether, would probably create new problems across a broad range of illegal activities. Many examples suggest that crooks find creative expedients around many obstacles. Even in exemplary Sweden, financial criminals found ways to overcome the progressive discouragement of the use of cash; as mentioned earlier, online theft has increased while bank robberies have declined.

Are large denomination banknotes the problem?

Short of restricting cash as a whole, an approach adopted by some central banks is to limit the supply of specific large denomination banknotes. Some of them are used by criminals more than others. The 100-dollar and 500-euro notes are obvious examples and corresponding targets for abolition.

The 100-dollar bill is probably the best-known banknote in the world: It features in countless movies, often involving drug traffickers. More than 11.5 billion of this piece of paper has been printed, enough to give every person on this globe one of them. Although much better known around the world, the 100-dollar bill has actually been eclipsed in sheer numbers by the 50-euro note, of which there are over 13.5 billion in circulation. This denomination cannot be withdrawn since it is massively used in normal transactions. One way to measure whether the denomination of a banknote is appropriate for daily use is to relate it to the income of those who use it. The 100-dollar bill represents more than most inhabitants of the emerging world might ever touch and is more than a month's wage in many countries. In the United States it represents only about 6 percent of an average monthly income. In China, the highest denomination bill is 100 yuan, which corresponds to a similar fraction of the average monthly income of 2,500 renminbi (about 4 percent) as the 100-dollar note in the United States. By contrast, the Swiss 1,000-franc note represents about one-half of the Swiss monthly income. The euro area's 500-euro note, which is still in circulation but no longer issued, is closer to the upper range represented by Switzerland. However, its circulation is declining from a peak of 610 million in 2016 to 370 billion as of the end of 2021.

The euro area and Switzerland, both of which have higher cash-to-GDP ratios than the United States, seem to vindicate the thesis that high-denomination bank notes facilitate cash hoarding. However, in Japan the highest denomination banknote, 10,000 yen, is similar in terms of the average wage to that of the United States. But Japan still has the highest ratio of cash to GDP (now 18 percent) among the G7 countries.

The lack of a clear link between the value of the largest denomination banknote and cash holdings as a share of GDP suggests that medium-value banknotes might be rather good substitutes for large ones. This applies in particular to legal holdings, where the volume of the stack of bank notes does not matter that much. It follows that abolishing high-denomination bank notes is unlikely to have a major impact on cash holdings. In 2016, the ECB decided to stop issuing the 500-euro note. The decision came into effect in 2019, but already in 2016 the number of 500-euro notes started to decline, whereas that of its closest substitute (the 200-euro note) started to increase. As of the end of 2021, the combined value of these two banknotes (200-euro notes and the remaining 500-euro notes in circulation) was similar to their combined share five years earlier, amounting to only about one-fifth of the total. Most of the increase in the euros in circulation over the last years was in the form of the 50-euro note, whose legitimate use is prevalent.

The biggest and most revealing experiment in curtailing the availability of large denomination notes occurred in India, a country of over a billion people. In late 2016 the Indian government announced that the existing two highest denomination bank notes (of 1,000 and 500 rupees, respectively) would be withdrawn from circulation and that the holders had to deposit them in a bank account to exchange them into new banknotes. The value of the banknotes had not been particularly large, amounting to about 1.6–3 percent of monthly wages, similar to the 100-dollar or the 200-euro note. The aim of demonetization was to boost electronic payments and reduce tax evasion.

The exchange did not go smoothly. Long queues at ATMs and other hurdles led to a fall in economic growth, as economic life was disrupted in many ways. Over 99 percent of the targeted cash was exchanged, and the use of electronic payments did increase, initially at the expense of cash – the cash-to-GDP ratio fell to about 9 percent from 12 percent. But over time the cash-to-GDP ratio returned to its previous level and it stands now close to 15 percent. The cost of this ultimately futile operation is difficult to estimate. The direct cost of printing billions of bank notes again was probably minor compared to the widespread disruptions to payments, which according to some estimates cost about 1–2 percent of lost output.

The 2016 demonetization was the third attempt in India to use a forced exchange of banknotes to reduce the underground economy.

None of these attempts succeeded in the long run, suggesting that excessive cash use is a symptom, not a cause, of an underlying problem with the rule of law and the functioning of the local administration.

IN TOUCH WE TRUST

So far we have disregarded the most obvious characteristics which set cash apart from any other commonly used monetary assets: banknotes and coins can be seen and touched. We can keep them close by – store them in a safe box, stick them under our mattress, or hide them in a sugar bowl on a kitchen shelf. Could it be that physical proximity, with the sense of comfort and reassurance that goes with it, is a factor behind the continuing popularity of cash?

Mainstream economics assumes not. Financial theorists, corporate treasurers, and prudential regulators do not reason in this way. They do distinguish between tangible and intangible assets but not in the way we mean here. They classify physical capital, equipment, and inventories as tangible corporate assets; in fact, they can be touched. Reputation, brand, and bad will are intangibles; indeed, they cannot. But the similarity ends here. What matters is marketability, not tactile perception, in spite of the name. Intangibles are harder to value and, hence, are treated differently by accountants and supervisors. Accordingly, securities are treated as tangibles, even if dematerialized – most securities today are. So are liquid assets, whatever form they take: cash, bank accounts, digital assets, or other.

Behavioral scientists, who look at reality from a different angle, have long recognized that sensorial perception of physical proximity contributes to trust building. Scholars of corporate management and organization consider, for example, that part of the value of in-person meetings – as opposed to virtual ones – resides not in the tasks they deliver but in the sense of community and trust that derives from participants being near one another and knowing each other personally. They concluded that virtual interaction is productive – indeed, efficient – only if preceded by, and intermingled with, opportunities of personal contact.[33]

The parallel between interpersonal dynamics and the attachment to a physical object like cash is not immediate. Sheets of paper and metal disks are not people; trust-building functions differently in that case. But psychological mechanisms of comparable nature are at play in both cases. Recent evidence from two different studies suggests that

> the sensory experience of touching a tangible object helps consumers to psychologically connect to a service, which, in turn, results in more positive behavioral intentions towards the service. (...) Study 1 showed a positive effect of touching an object on behavioral intentions towards a service provider via psychological connection. Notably, this effect was stable independent of whether participants received legal and/or perceived ownership of the object. Study 2 extended these findings by showing that the opportunity to touch a tangible service object only led to a stronger psychological connection and to more positive intentions when the object had a high aesthetic appeal. This finding supports the notion that providing tangible objects triggers a bodily-related, sensory reaction in contrast to a purely cognitive attribution of properties from the object to the service.[34]

Clearly, the fact that tangible objects are perceived as less risky, or "better" in any other sense, does not mean that they are. Tactile perceptions can be misleading, ultimately biasing the judgment of consumers/investors in the wrong way. A variety of cryptocurrencies, for example, Bitcoin and Ethereum, are being made available also in the form of physical tokens; perhaps, their creators thought this may enhance trust in them. Obviously, the fact that they can be touched does not mean that they are any less risky than their digital counterparts.

Interestingly, behavioral studies also give weight to the aesthetic appeal of the object in question. In this as in other realms, the power of beauty should not be underestimated. For professionals of the field, banknote design is an art, or at least a supreme form of craftsmanship. There are associations for the study and collection of banknotes like philatelic clubs for collectors of stamps – another endangered species. New banknote series are projects involving legions of professionals. Aesthetic and security considerations are linked: Beautiful banknotes tend to be more elaborate, hence safer. A prominent example involved the ECB. In preparation for the new euro banknotes, issued on January 1, 2002, the ECB launched an international competition among specialists from the twelve partic-ipating countries. The competing series can still be admired on the ECB website;[35] looking at them it is difficult to see them as much different or less than works of art. Unfortunately, in the opinion of the authors of this book, not the most beautiful ones were chosen. The ECB is now planning a new series.[36]

Trust and aesthetic appeal may have something to do with an episode that occurred recently, which reveals something about how cash can be hoarded in mass for reasons which have nothing to do with an immediate transaction or portfolio-management purpose. The evidence we refer to was provided by a natural disaster. The reader should be prepared for the biggest officially conducted "money laundering" operation in history.

AFTER THE FLOOD

One night in the summer of 2020 torrential rains fell on the Ahrtal region, the valley of the River Ahr (a tributary of the Rhein) in west-ern Germany. The intensity of the rainfall was so great it quickly exhausted the capacity of woods and prairies to soak up all the water falling from the sky. The local rivers became torrents acquiring speed and ever more destructive power as the water sped downhill. The locals in this sleepy area were going to bed when their houses were suddenly inundated by an unprecedented wave of mud and water. More than one hundred died and thousands lost their home. This disaster, due in large part to a failure of the local authorities to issue a timely warning, provided an unexpected window into the savings habits of the local population.

In the following weeks, hundreds of bags of banknotes and coins were deposited at the local offices of the German central bank, the Bundesbank, for cleaning. The mud and water which had entered thousands of homes had covered the cash people held at home with a sticky and smelly film, rendering it unusable. The Bundesbank, as the national agent for the ECB, provides a little-known service to anybody who holds a damaged banknote. As long as more than one-half of the banknote is still intact, the Bundesbank will exchange it for a clean new one. Most central banks in the world (Sweden is again the exception) have a similar policy of replacing damaged banknotes, which in normal times occurs rarely.

When this avalanche of dirty money arrived at the local office of the Bundesbank, the first task was to clean it so that it could be examined and the owners be issued new cash. The Bundesbank thus provided literally a money laundering service. Full service. The cash was put in large laundry machines, washed with special detergents, and then dried and ironed by hand.

The most interesting aspect of the story is the amount of cash that came to light in this episode. The disaster thus provided a natural experiment to shed light on a key mystery in monetary theory: Who holds all this cash?

The astonishing fact is that 1.5 million banknotes, worth more than 100 million euros were handed in for cleaning (about 60 million from private individuals and 40 million from banks whose vaults and ATMs had been flooded).[37] This is a very large number for the relatively small number of houses affected by the inundation. The number of damaged homes has been officially estimated at about 3,000. At an average occupancy of four, this makes about 12,000 persons (children included). About half of the cash came from bank vaults that had been flooded. But even excluding that part one arrives at cash holdings worth about 5,000 euros per capita (on average 20,000 euros per household).

There must thus have been many households with tens of thousands of euros in cash in their kitchens or cellars. One person even had the equivalent of 1 million euros to be cleaned. This money cannot have been earned in the black economy, which does not exist in this small law-abiding hill community. The 1 million must have been "clean" money, as the person who brought it to be laundered must have shown to the authorities that he or she could have saved this sum from legitimate income sources.

Is the Ahrtal special and thus not representative of attitudes elsewhere? It probably is to some extent. For a number of cultural and historical reasons, Germans tend to be conservative and risk-averse. In addition, the inhabitants of Ahrtal were not financially sophisticated. The income per capita of this quiet rural area is about one-third below the German average. Its inhabitants are thus not particularly well-off. Moreover, the composition of the cash returned is rather close to the euro area average. The average value of the dirty bank notes from the Ahrtal was about 63 euros (99.6 million euros in 1.6 million bank notes), not far from the euro area average, which is about 55 euros (about 1,550 billion euros in 28 billion notes). However, there is a considerable difference between the average value handed in from private citizens (110 euros) and that for the banks (38 euros). It thus seems that banks hold smaller notes to distribute, but private individuals hoard larger denominations at home. This mitigates the suspicion that large denomination notes are held mainly by criminals for drug trafficking or other illicit operations.

In surveys, German households say that they tend to carry only around 100 euros in their wallets but keep almost 1,400 euros at home. This would make a total of 1,500 euros per person, but the cash which was laundered after the Ahrtal inundation suggests that the true number might be more than three times as high, that is, around 5,000 euros. This, even in a country like Germany, which is otherwise relatively sophisticated in its payment habits: The average number of payment cards per person in Germany is 2, whereas for the euro area it is 1.7. What the Ahrtal episode suggests is that actual cash holdings can be much larger than surveys or other evidence may suggest.

EXTINCTION OR SURVIVAL? CASH IN THE TWENTY-FIRST CENTURY

The main conclusion one can confidently draw from this review is that cash holdings around the world, far from disappearing, are persistently high and actually rising. Exceptions to this rule are minor. A persistent propensity to hold cash emerges in general, though to different extents, in different economic, institutional, and technological environments.

In the past cash was the only "legal tender," meaning that everybody must accept it. Reality is now different. Cash is no longer accepted for large transactions (usually those above 10,000 euros or dollars) and in some countries some merchants no longer accept cash for small transactions because they have no place to store it.

Cash is unique because it embodies four characteristics that are valuable from the point of view of contributing to a complete and resilient payment system. Cash is:

1. Simple: using it requires no technology or complication whatsoever.
2. Definitive: instantly settles any financial obligation.
3. Private and personal: leaves no trace when it changes hands.
4. Self-sufficient: does not depend on any other infrastructure functioning.

Secrecy, while arguably beneficial within proper limits, lends itself to a multiplicity of illegal uses which challenge law enforcement authorities at the national and global levels. To contrast such illegal uses, specific restrictions and controls on the use of cash can help: among them, restrictions or bans on certain banknote denominations and legal limits on the use of cash for large-value payments. International cooperation among law enforcers and financial authorities helps enforce these or other similar restrictions.

However, the arguments we presented suggest that restrictions and controls should not go as far as discouraging the use of cash in a generalized and indiscriminate way. The reason is that in meeting those challenges the other three characteristics must be preserved.

The first two characteristics (*simplicity* and *finality*) make cash particularly effective for small retail payments, especially by unsophisticated people. However, today these two characteristics tend to be obviated by the efficiency, reliability, and increasing simplicity of the new digital techniques. By contrast, the fourth characteristic (*resilience*) remains important even – maybe we should say particularly – at a time in which most payments migrate to online platforms. Digital infrastructures are vulnerable and their continuing performance cannot always be taken for granted. This is also one of the reasons why in Sweden the central bank has reversed its position and issued an appeal that "[p]olitical decisions [are] needed urgently so that everyone can pay."[38]

A resilient and diversified financial ecosystem must include simpler payment technologies, even imperfect ones, able to fill the gap in emergencies. Financial resilience is a constant policy priority, unlikely to be overcome by technical progress.

NOTES

1. Sveriges Riksbank, "Crimes Linked to Cash Have Fallen," Sveriges Riksbank, November 7, 2019.
2. Hanna Armelius, Carl Andreas Claussen, and André Reslow, "Withering Cash: Is Sweden Ahead of the Curve or Just Special?," Sveriges Riksbank Working Paper Series 393, 2020.
3. William J. Baumol, "The Transactions Demand for Cash: An Inventory Theoretic Approach," *Quarterly Journal of Economics* 66, no. 4 (November 1, 1952): 545.
4. "Automated Teller Machines (ATMs) (per 100,000 Adults)," *World Bank Open Data*, https://data.worldbank.org/indicator/FB.ATM.TOTL.P5?locations=VN%EF%BC%88%E9%96%B2%E8%A6%A7%E6%97%A5%EF%BC%9A2022.
5. Baumol, "The Transactions Demand for Cash," 545.
6. James Tobin, "Liquidity Preference as Behavior towards Risk," *The Review of Economic Studies* 25 (1958): 65–86.

7. European Central Bank, "Circulation," August 7, 2023; European Central Bank, "Banknotes and Coins Production," December 15, 2022.

8. Data for several countries and for the world as a whole are reported by Clemens Jobst and Helmut Stix, "Doomed to Disappear? The Surprising Return of Cash across Time and across Countries," CEPR Discussion Paper 12327, September 2017.

9. Data for the eurozone are included in the websites mentioned earlier.

10. See, for example, Henk Esselink and Lola Hernández, "The Use of Cash by Households in the Euro Area," ECB Occasional Papers Series 201, November 24, 2017. Data for Germany are provided by a regular survey on payment behavior conducted by the Bundesbank; see Bundesbank, "Payment Behaviour in Germany in 2020: Making Payments in the Year of the Coronavirus Pandemic," 2020. Euro area data by country can be found in the online ECB Statistical Data Warehouse.

11. "Federal Reserve Payments Study (FRPS)" and Laura Kim and Shaun O'Brien, "2021 Findings from the Diary of Consumer Payment Choice," San Francisco Fed, May 5, 2021.

12. For an in-depth analysis of the Swedish case and a comparison with Canada, see Armelius et al., "Withering Cash," and Walter Engert, Ben Fung, and Björn Segendorff, "A Tale of Two Countries: Cash Demand in Canada and Sweden," Sveriges Riksbank Working Paper Series 376, 2019.

13. See Sveriges Riksbank, "Cash Is Losing Ground," Sveriges Riksbank, October 29, 2020.

14. See Engert et al., "A Tale of Two Countries."

15. See Bundesbank, "Payment Behaviour in Germany in 2020."

16. Esselink and Hernández, "The Use of Cash by Households in the Euro Area," ECB Occasional Paper Series n. 201, November 2017.

17. Tanai Khiaonarong and David Humphrey, *Measurement and Use of Cash by Half the World's Population* (IMF, 2023).

18. See "Broad Money (% of GDP)," *World Bank*.

19. Data based on BIS tables.

20. Laure Lalouette et al., "Foreign Demand for Euro Banknotes," ECB Occasional Papers Series 253, January 2021.

21. Data can be found in the IMF World Economic Outlook Database for emerging and developing Europe.

22. Kenneth S. Rogoff, *The Curse of Cash: How Large-Denomination Bills Aid Crime and Tax Evasion and Constrain Monetary Policy* (Princeton University Press, 2017).

23. Rogoff, *The Curse of Cash*. See also Kenneth S. Rogoff, "Costs and Benefits to Phasing Out Paper Currency," *NBER Macroeconomics Annual* 29, no. 1 (May 2014): 445–56.

24. Alan Rappeport, "Tax Cheats Cost the U.S. $1 Trillion per Year, I.R.S. Chief Says," New York Times, October 13, 2021; and William G. Gale and Aaron Krupkin, "How Big Is the Problem of Tax Evasion?," Brookings, April 9, 2019.

25. See Friedrich Schneider, "Restricting or Abolishing Cash," SUERF Policy Note 90, August 2019.

26. See Friedrich Schneider, "Estimating the Size of the Shadow Economies of Highly-Developed Countries: Selected New Results," *CESifo DICE Report* 14, no. 4 (2016): 44–53; see also Ben Kemalson, Koralai Kirabaeva, Leandro Medina, Borislava Mircheva, and Jason Weiss, "Explaining the Shadow Economy in Europe: Size, Causes and Policy Options," IMF Working Papers, December 13, 2019.

27. For example, see the comparison between Canada and Sweden in Engert et al., "A Tale of Two Countries."

28. See, for example, Friedrich Schneider and Ursula Windischbauer, "Money Laundering: Some Facts," *European Journal of Law and Economics* 26, no. 3 (October 21, 2008): 387–404.

29. For a historical overview, see Manuel Eisner, "Modernity Strikes Back: A Historical Perspective on the Latest Increase in Interpersonal Violence 1960–1990," *International Journal of Conflict and Violence* 2, no. 2 (November 2008): 288–316.

30. See this report from Europe: Eurojust, "Eurojust Report on Money Laundering."

31. See Wikipedia contributors, "Danske Bank Money Laundering Scandal," *Wikipedia*, November 23, 2023.

32. US Drug Enforcement Administration Website, "DEA Asset Forfeiture," DEA.

33. Jun Zheng, Elizabeth Veinott, Nathan Bos, Judith Olson, and Gary Olson, "Trust without Touch: Jumpstarting Long-Distance Trust with Initial Social Activities," Proceedings of the SIGCHI Conference on Human Factors in Computing Systems, January 1, 2002.

34. Nora Nägele, Benjamin von Walter, Philipp Scharfenberger, and Daniel Wentzel, "'Touching' Services: Tangible Objects Create an Emotional Connection to Services Even before Their First Use," *Business Research* 13, no. 2 (May 2, 2020): 741–66.

35. European Central Bank, "Euro Banknote Design Exhibition."
36. European Central Bank, "ECB to Redesign Euro Banknotes by 2024," December 6, 2021.
37. Deutsche Bundesbank, "Bearbeitung von Flutgeld durch die Deutsche Bundesbank – Hochwasserkatastrophe Juli 2021," February 9, 2022.
38. Sveriges Riksbank, "Political Decisions Needed Urgently So That Everyone Can Pay," Sveriges Riksbank, October 27, 2023.

6 Banks as Creators and Stores of Money

If you owe your bank a hundred pounds, you have a problem.
But if you owe a million, it has.

John M. Keynes

In the heart of the US coastal town of New Haven, two blocks away from Yale University, lies a simple two-story building, hardly noticeable amid impressive residences on both sides of the street. Unbeknown to many bystanders, that unassuming construction hosts a prestigious institution embodying much of the best tradition of economic scholarship of the twentieth century. Of the ninety-plus people who as of today have received a Nobel prize in economics (for the record, all men, except three), nearly one-third were one way or another associated with it.[1]

The Cowles Foundation was not always a foundation, nor was it always at Yale. It was established in 1932 as a "Commission" by the businessman Alfred Cowles. After the Great Crash of 1929, which as everybody else he had failed to foresee, Cowles wanted to understand whether the stock market was predictable at all. He concluded it probably was not, but hoped that further study, perhaps by his newly established creature, may succeed. In 1939, the Commission moved from Colorado Springs to Chicago, whose university hosted the most highly reputed economics faculty in the world, including such heavy-weights as Milton Friedman, Theodore Schultz, Gary Becker, and George Stigler, all later recipients of Nobel prizes.

From then on, the Commission became the epicenter of one of the biggest controversies in the history of economics, the one between "monetarists" and "Keynesians." Discussions raged mainly on the nature and meaning of money. Today's young economists have vaguely heard of it, if at all. They would be surprised to know how relevant some of those discussions still are.

Before we start, one warning to the reader. This story is interesting and helps understand modern monetary developments, including digitalization. But it requires an extra pinch of theoretical salt relative to what we have dispensed so far. Readers opting for a superficial pass may move directly to the concluding section. To the other ones: Join us on a fascinating trip to Econland.

BANKS AS CREATORS OF MONEY
AND THE KEYNESIAN–MONETARIST DISPUTE

In a nutshell – the original sources can be consulted online[2] – the controversy was as follows.

The "monetarists" believed in self-adjusting markets and in a natural tendency of the economy to return to full employment. They regarded the quantity of money as determined by the central bank. The central bank controls the printing press and receives deposits from banks (funds freely convertible into cash, hence equivalent to it), so it can push "high-powered money" (the sum of cash plus bank reserves) into the economic system at will. Once in circulation, money cannot go out – international capital flows were largely disregarded. If people and banks do not want to hold it, they get rid of it by purchasing goods or real estate. A fashionable image at the time was that of a "hot potato": People pass it on lest it burns their hands. The economy adjusts to this purchasing pressure by increasing prices – remember, the economy is stable at full employment – until the value of money in real terms (meaning, deflated by prices) returns to its initial level. Result: After some adjustments, prices have risen in proportion to the quantity of money supplied by the central bank.

In its essence, the "quantity theory" was nothing new: It mirrored ideas proposed by the eighteenth-century philosopher David Hume.[3] What was new in the 1950s, however, as we saw in Chapter 3, was the phenomenal rise of retail banking, as a result of the postwar economic recovery and the financial and technological innovation spearheaded, in the United States, by Bank of America. Bank deposits were transferred by the millions of checks written every day, which banks were learning to handle with the help of digital computers. A central monetarist tenet, that the mass of payment means in circulation could be proxied by "high-powered" money alone, was no longer tenable. Money, whatever that name meant, should include deposits at commercial banks as well.

The monetarists had a prompt answer to this objection: the so-called money multiplier. Normally, if you ask an economist to name a theory that is both true and not obvious, the answer is the law of comparative advantage: the prediction that it is efficient even for countries that are inefficient in all productions to produce something, namely the product in which they are relatively less inefficient. The monetarist "money multiplier" comes a close second: It says that money can be created at will by bankers, apparently out of nothing. The mechanism goes as follows. If a person enters a bank and deposits cash, the banker can lend some of it out. A fraction is kept as a reserve, because of legal limits or for reasons of prudence. The sum lent out is redeposited at that or another bank, hence increasing the overall amount of money in circulation. The process continues until all the initial cash rests with the banking sector in the form of reserves. At that point, bank deposits have increased by a factor equal to the inverse of the reserve ratio: If that ratio is, for example, 5 percent, bank deposits increase by a factor of twenty. The overall amount of money is still controlled by the central bank but that control is magnified by the money multiplier. The monetarist view is salvaged and actually becomes more powerful.

The "Keynesian" economists at the Commission did not share the monetarist's faith in self-adjusting markets or in any tendency to full employment. Following the writings of the celebrated Cambridge economist Jonn Maynard Keynes, especially his *General Theory of Employment, Interest and Money*,[4] they believed that market economies were prone to underutilization of labor resources and that it was the responsibility of governments, through economic policies, to attain better economic and social outcomes. Nor did they share the monetarist reasoning as regards the money supply process and its impact. First, they claimed, the money multiplier was not stable: It changed depending on how much reserves the banks wanted to keep in excess of the legal limit, a choice which in their view is as volatile as all financial markets are. Torrents of ink and thousands of hours of data crunching have gone into testing statistically whether this multiplier was stable, especially relative to another multiplier, that of public expenditures popularized by Keynes. As often happens, the results were not conclusive; few people changed their minds as a result of that research. Second, and more importantly, the Keynesians pointed out that the banks can control the supply of credit but not the demand for deposits: People in the street are free to decide whether to deposit their cash at a bank or keep it, in their pocket or at home. The monetary multiplier could not be relied upon, and the link between the stock of money and the central bank balance sheet was not watertight.

Amid bitter internal disputes, the continued permanence of the Commission at the University of Chicago was no longer deemed appropriate. In 1955, it moved to Yale and morphed into a foundation. This coincided with a turn in its ideological imprint. The chair was taken by the most prominent economist of that faculty, James Tobin, a Keynesian of strict observance and himself a later Nobel laureate. In his new position, Tobin proceeded to lay down a systematic exposition of his views on the monetary mechanism and its implications.[5]

Tobin did not deny the "miracle" of money creation by banks, or that a meaningful definition of money must include bank deposits. But he saw deposits are just one in an array of financial assets available to wealth holders, who chose among them based on risk and return considerations. The use of deposits for making payments was just a particular service provided by that instrument, hence a component of its return. Portfolio choices depended on the whole spectrum of yields in the financial markets, determined by demands and supplies of all assets. The money multiplier then becomes no more than an accounting ratio between two loosely related variables, commercial bank deposits and central bank money. The money stock which exists in the economy is willingly held by investors. The "hot potato" is not hot at all: People are more than happy to keep the money they hold. The whole monetarist construction, including the proportionality between money and prices, collapses.

The two views led to radically different predictions and prescriptions regarding the functioning of the economy and economic policy. Taken at face value, monetarists emphasize a constant link between money and prices and reliable mechanisms through which money is determined by the supply of the central bank. In its purest form, monetarism is a simple one-directional model, running from monetary policy to prices. The Keynesians, in the version articulated by Tobin, see money as just one among many portfolio assets, all determined by the demand side in an all-encompassing economic equilibrium. Money has no particular link with or implication for prices.

Expressed in these terms, the differences could not be more radical and irreconcilable. But a reconciliation was actually coming, right at the time Tobin was writing, from another scholar associated with the Cowles Foundation.

The Italian-born Franco Modigliani had left his country in 1938, fleeing Mussolini's anti-Jewish laws. In the early 1960s, he joined the Massachusetts Institute of Technology and started to collaborate with the foundation. In 1963 he proposed a "synthesis" of the two approaches.[6] His model echoed the monetarist approach in collapsing the entire financial sector into a single asset, money, and treating the rest as redundant. But it was Keynesian in seeing money as determined not just by the central bank but by the conjunction of demand and supply, depending on interest rates, and in embodying no explicit link between money and prices. The model predicted a constant ratio between money and prices (so-called money neutrality) over long spans of time after all adjustments had taken place. In the shorter run, however, output employment and prices were determined, Keynesian-style, by interest rates. Modigliani's model was so successful that it quickly became a benchmark of economic analysis. The US Federal Reserve Board used it as a basis to construct its large-scale econometric model in the 1970s, followed by many other central banks.

For all its intellectual merits, however, Modigliani's synthesis would probably not have had the impact it had in the central bank boardrooms, where monetary policy decisions are made, if not for the contribution of another heavyweight economist: Benjamin Friedman, today the William Joseph Maier professor of political economy at Harvard. As we write, Ben Friedman – not to be confused with his partial homonymous Milton – is best known for his analyses of the links between morals, religion, and economic history.[7] In the 1970s, a prominent participant in the Keynesian–monetarist debate, he demonstrated in a seminal article that the monetarist prescriptions regarding monetary policy hinged on very restrictive and empirically implausible conditions regarding the stability of money markets.[8] He showed that central banks should make their decisions keeping their eye not only on money but on multiple variables, each weighted by the information value it possesses with regard to the final goals of economic policy. Econometric models based on Modigliani's theory are one source from which those informational weights can be estimated.

STAGE EXTRAS OR LEADING ACTORS?

Today, banks create through the "money multiplier" most of the instruments we call money. Banks are the largest and most important entities in the global financial sector, playing a decisive role in the processes connecting savings to investment. But why is it so? Is that role coincidental or fundamental? Can it be done without? Can they one day be replaced by digital instruments produced by other subjects – fintech companies, technology firms, or cryptocurrency miners?

The monetarist and Keynesian views just described shared one feature: Banks did not matter in a fundamental way. For the die-hard monetarist, the banker is not a human being but a robot, automatically lending out funds deposited into it until the money multiplier is extended in full. For Keynesians like Tobin, it is just another intermediary, a portfolio manager with no particular distinction but for the fact that it provides transaction and clearing services. Even in Modigliani's compromise model, the existence of banks and their role in the functioning of the economy are posited, not demonstrated or explained. Banks are just a fact one takes note of, without particular justification.

The logical conclusion, or a dead-end if one prefers, was reached in 1980 by Eugene Fama, another would-be Nobel recipient from Chicago. He analyzed more deeply the role of banking, concluding there was none: In a fictional world where means of payments and stores of value were performed by other institutions, money's unit of account value could be fixed just as well by imposed legal requirements on spaceship owners, instead of banks.[9] A profoundly disturbing conclusion: Banks, by miles the most important institutions of global finance, were found to have no justification at all.

As the 1970s drew to a close, things were ready for a radically new vision. The "revolution" consisted of reversing the logical order: Rather than banks using deposits as input to extend credit, they were from then on seen as using profitable assets (credit on the asset side) as input to offer liquidity to depositors (their liability side). The credit mechanism was moving to center stage. With this switch in perspective, which still dominates the economics of banking today, banks cease to be stage extras in the economic show to become leading characters in the saving–investment process. It becomes clearer what their function in the economy and the rationale for regulating them are. They also acquire a more meaningful role in the transmission to the economy of the effects of monetary policy.

The new perspective rests on two conceptual blocs: the economics of information and the theory of banking regulation.

The first insight, due largely to the Princeton economist Joseph Stiglitz (it is becoming monotonous by now to say that he received a Nobel too), is that participants in credit markets do not have the same information: Borrowers know more about their own characteristics – specifically, whether they will be able and willing to reimburse the credit they get – than lenders.[10] Information is "asymmetric" – borrowers have more of it than lenders. When putting money in the bank, depositors have no way of knowing the characteristics of those to whom the bank will lend their funds. The bank solves that problem for them by collecting the information necessary to screen and select the quality of borrowers. By specializing in the production of that particular intelligence, banks contribute to eliminating, or at least mitigating, the cognitive imperfection which hampers the functioning of credit markets. In possessing their unique information, banks are irreplaceable – at least until another technology is found to perform the same function (more on this later).

The insight behind the second breakthrough consisted of noting that banks intermediate funds not only across groups of people (between savers and investors, or consumers and producers) but also across time. They receive liquid funds (deposits) and apply them to long-term uses (credit going to finance longer-duration investments). Depositors value liquidity – the ability to get their funds back or spend them at any time. Borrowers, on the other hand, whether they are firms building up their capital or households getting a mortgage, need time before they can reimburse what they have borrowed.

Banks provide the link between short and long because size allows them to diversify many unrelated flows and risks. By doing this, the banks contribute to economic growth, thereby performing an essential social function. This comes at a cost, though: The maturity mismatch makes banks, even solvent ones, vulnerable to losses of confidence. Banks that lose confidence can be attacked by nervous depositors, who may run to take their money out before it is too late. In the last two centuries, since banks morphed into "deposit banks," there are plenty of examples of bank runs: Those that happened during the Great Financial Crisis of 2008–09 are the latest examples. Modern banking theorists, the best known of which collected their prize in Stockholm in 2022, have proved that even solvent banks (those whose assets exceed or equal their liabilities) are not immune to runs, that is, sudden massive withdrawals of funds.[11] In fact, rational depositors have an incentive to withdraw their deposit from solvent banks if they think that others will do it anyway.

Because of the key function they perform, banks need protection from the risk inherent in these double equilibria – the coexistence of good states in which they survive and bad ones in which they fail. The risk of a "bad equilibrium" is especially damaging because banks lend to one another: The failure of one can lead to chains of other failures and put the whole system at risk. Accordingly, banks worldwide are granted by governments certain safeguards and are subject to controls. The most important is the direct contact with and assistance from the central bank, which includes special finance in emergencies. The lending of "last resort" – meaning, when the bank is denied credit in the market – is critical to prevent runs on their deposits. Another instrument to prevent bank runs is deposit insurance, pioneered on a large scale in the United States after the devastating banking crisis of 1933. Deposit insurance is usually funded by the banking system but regulated and organized by governments. The basic idea behind deposit insurance is that small savers would leave their money in the bank even if there are rumors about its state of health because they know that their savings are protected.

The need for a safety net provided by the central bank and regulation, ultimately backed up by governments using taxpayer resources, depends directly on the fact that banks create depositor liquidity out of illiquid assets and on the fact that liquidity creation is essential for the proper working not only of the monetary system but of the economy as a whole.[12]

CAN BANKS BE REPLACED?

To move forward, let's first connect some of the arguments made so far.

In essence, a payment is a transfer of wealth. Wealth cannot be used to "pay" for something, because it is not liquid. Suppose I own a house and you own a company, and I need to pay you. I cannot give you a room, or a door belonging to my house. Besides, you probably would not be interested. Nor can I deliver a piece of machinery or equipment that you need in your company: I don't have it. Payment, therefore, requires a liquid asset to be transferred and act as a numeraire to measure values. In one word, money. Short of it, people cannot pay and the economy comes to a gridlock.

Money can be upheld by mandatory legal provisions – like banknotes, which everybody is obliged to accept. Their nominal value is granted by the government. The real (or purchasing) value depends on the central bank's ability to maintain a stable purchasing power over time. By contrast, bank money – money created by banks through credit–deposit multiplication – is not supported by direct legal constraints. Yet today this is by far the most important component of money, everywhere in the world – we show data in the next section. Banks create money by transforming (part of) their illiquid assets into deposits. As we have seen, providing this "transformation service" to the economy is inherently costly and risky: It exposes banks to confidence crises and runs on their deposits. Banks are normally private companies, but they border the public domain because of this essential function they perform in the public interest. They are regulated accordingly.

The 2008–09 financial crisis and the digital revolution have challenged this established way of thinking, bringing up some fundamental questions. Will banks become obsolete? Can they be replaced by other arrangements? Should banks be regulated further, perhaps separating the monetary function from the rest of the business? Or alternatively, is deregulation the answer – a transition toward fully private money, entirely new products like those in the crypto world?

In some respects, these questions are not new. They tend to come up in the aftermath of banking crises. After the Great Depression of the 1930s, which featured multiple bank failures, a group of economists in the United States proposed a system – the "Chicago Plan" – which would eliminate fractional banking in the

United States by requiring banks to hold 100 percent of demand deposits in the form of reserves. This plan would effectively sever the deposit and payment function from the provision of credit; the latter would be extended by different institutions, banned from issuing demand deposits but otherwise essentially unregulated. The concept behind this was that by separating the credit function, the monetary function would be better protected. The idea was influential but was eventually shelved: A milder version was passed, separating commercial and investment banking (Glass–Steagall Act of 1933). Yet as an intellectual argument, the narrow banking proposal never died and periodically resurfaces.

Three objections can be raised against such a system. First, separation would not eliminate risk but shift it away from deposit banks toward the "unregulated" sector.[13] While banned from issuing deposits, this sector would be able to adopt alternative forms of financing, equally risky from the point of view of the stability of the financial system as a whole. The Great Financial Crisis of 2008–09, in which asset managers drove the US financial sector to the brink of collapse by offloading massive investment repos – repurchase operations through which investment banks financed themselves by rolling over temporary sales of securities – is a case in point.[14] While the classic theory of bank crises focuses on deposit runs, in modern financial sectors a "run" can occur on a variety of funding instruments. Future innovation will undoubtedly result in new channels through which maturity-transforming balance sheets can be destabilized. Maturity transformation in itself can hardly be eliminated, because it is the most important service provided by finance. The spectacular demise of the crypto exchange FTX in 2022 provided yet another illustration of this general problem.

Second, separation would likely exacerbate cyclical fluctuations in the supply of credit. In cyclical downturns, when risk perceptions increase and investors move to safer assets, money tends to shift away from the unregulated and toward the regulated sector. The supply of long-term credit would consequently shrink, exacerbating the downturn. In a fractional system, movements can occur more easily within the balance sheet of banks. A flight toward safer investments can still occur, of course, as a result of investment decisions by banks. But that shift is likely to be milder and more gradual than would be the case if separation were rigidly built into the structure of the financial sector.

Third, even "narrow" banks (as 100 percent reserve banks are often called) can be risky. Evidence of this surfaced recently, during the Great Financial Crisis of 2008–09 and subsequently. MMFs, financial intermediaries issuing liabilities similar to deposits in certain respects (withdrawable on demand and supposedly at fixed one-to-one value, though not covered by insurance), were massively attacked in the United States during that crisis; we will tell their story in Chapter 9. The shift occurred largely toward other funds invested in government paper. This case suggests that, in order to be risk-free, "narrow" banking constructions should not only eschew long-term investment but also short-term investments, which are also at risk in a recession. Even government paper can be risky, as sovereigns are not immune from default.

Bottomline: Segregated money-issuing banks would be really safe only if they invested only in ... money. Unfortunately, transforming a financial instrument into itself is not a promising business proposition.

At the opposite extreme, the temptation may be to lift regulation altogether, privatizing money. What in the past was called free banking today resurfaces under different clothes as crypto finance. We will discuss in Chapters 8 and 9 how cryptocurrencies and stablecoins complement each other, trying to give rise to an experimental monetary system without banks. Stablecoins are in essence narrow banks which offer monetary instruments and services on their liability side (hence "coins") and invest in supposedly stable assets or adopt other arrangements assumed to keep their value stable (hence "stable"). They are mainly used to transact in cryptocurrencies. A critical feature is that they are as yet unregulated, but an unregulated narrow bank is a paradox; without rules, it is unlikely to remain narrow and is likely to become riskier over time. A presumption that is confirmed by recent cases of contagion and failure.

The multiproduct, or "universal," bank, combining credit selection and liquidity transformation, in partnership with the central bank as the guardian of payments and last-resort lending, subject to regulation and supervision, is admittedly a land in between: a compromise. As such, it possesses the virtue Churchill attributed to democracy: It is the worst possible arrangement, after all the others. This does not exclude change, even a radical one. For example, a revolution of sorts is happening on the credit side: Borrower screening is increasingly taking advantage of big data and artificial intelligence to produce automatic scores. On the funding side, payment services are combined with frontier technologies – digital apps and wallets – offered by high-tech industries. Some banks have begun experimenting with blockchains, though their value added is still an open question. Human judgment is critical in guiding all these processes. The universal banking model requires regulation and constant supervision. There too, human judgment is needed. Regulation and supervision are prone to failure and capture by the industry,[15] but they are unlikely to ever be effectively replaced by market discipline alone, smart institutional architectures, or technology.

GLOBAL TRENDS IN BANK MONEY

In most advanced countries, it is taken for granted that everybody has a bank account and thus access to digital means of payment. In Europe, the United States, and Japan, the vast majority of the adult population has a bank account, though in Southern Europe and certain areas of the United States, the use of banks is less widespread. For example, whereas in the United States 93 percent of the adult population has an account, among the poorer four-tenths that proportion falls to 85 percent, and among those without completed secondary education it is only 65 percent. This "underbanked" part of the population gives rise to the phenomenon of "financial exclusion": This is a form of inequality, specifically in the use of financial services.[16]

Where there is financial exclusion, cash is predominantly used; normally, people without a bank account also do not have access to digital money, which usually requires a bank account. There are exceptions to this, in some developing countries; for example, in some African countries a system called M-Pesa is used, where people transact and store money using cellphones. In the United States, those with an income below 25,000 dollars use cash for more than a third of their transactions whereas cash use falls to 11 percent for those with an annual income above 150,000 dollars. The use of credit cards shows the opposite pattern: The highest-income group uses credit cards for almost one-half of all purchases (44 percent) whereas that proportion falls to 12 percent for the poorest.[17]

Financial exclusion is diminishing almost everywhere in the world, though in low-income countries it is still rather high. Only one-third of the adult population in low-income countries (as defined by the World Bank, with gross national income per capita of less than 1,085 dollars in 2021) has a bank account. For lower-middle-income countries (income between 1,086 dollars and 4,255 dollars) this percentage is higher but still far below the levels in advanced countries.

Economists have long debated which monetary instruments are used mainly for transactions or as stores of value. For example, are savings accounts with a notice period of several months available for spending? If not, they should be considered only a store of value.

Central banks classify the money supply according to different aggregates, denoted with the symbols M0, M1, M2, and M3, indicating progressively larger and more encompassing definitions of monetary means. The broader aggregates include many products at the boundary between payment means and savings instruments, from the viewpoint of the holder. Some of them may also perform a sort of "dual use" function; for example, a checkable mutual fund, popular in the United States, provides both a store of value and a means of payment.

M0 is also called "base money" or "outside money" because it represents a claim on the central bank. This is composed of banknotes and the reserves commercial banks hold with the central bank.[18] Base money is made up of two very different elements: cash and reserves of commercial banks with the central bank, which take the form of entries on the digital ledgers of the central bank and often run in billions (euros or dollars or whatever the national currency is). Many central banks still oblige banks to hold reserves, though in most advanced countries required reserves no longer play an important role in monetary policy. Some less-advanced large economies, like China, keep higher reserve ratios and use them actively as instruments of monetary control.[19]

An important change came after the Great Financial Crisis of 2008–09, when central banks in a number of countries, especially in continental Europe, lowered interest rates sharply. As inflation remained stubbornly low and policy rates went down to zero or later even negative levels, central banks deployed what are called "unconventional" policy instruments, buying massive amounts of government and other bonds financed by offering banks to deposit their excess funds at the central bank. Commercial banks were not forced to acquire these additional reserves; they did so willingly when the price was right, that is, when the yield on bonds dropped to such a low level that the bank preferred to hold reserves at the central bank at zero (or even negative) interest rather than a long-term government bond. Total reserves at the central bank rose dramatically as central banks increased their bond purchasing programs in the face of a long period of low inflation.

The size and meaning of "M0" as the monetary base changed radically in the 2010s, when central banks started engaging in massive asset purchases. With negative rates, bank reserves turned from a source of tax into one of subsidy. As long as the interest rate of the European Central Bank (ECB) on reserves was zero, banks would be happy to hold them. Between 2014 and 2022, when the ECB's policy rates were negative, required reserves became de facto a profitable parking lot for banks to put their liquidity without facing negative rates. The ECB had to even limit the amount banks could put into the "required" reserve account (at a zero rate), forcing them to put all the excess reserves into another account at negative rates.

Today, banks keep again – as in the precrisis normal – a minimum of required reserves, and central banks have to incentivize them to continue to hold the vast reserves created through bond purchases by paying the banks a high rate on the excess reserves, that is, the reserves above the required level.

A few figures can illustrate the radical changes that occurred in the composition of M0 over the last decade and a half. At the beginning of 2008, the total monetary base of the United States amounted to about 830 billion dollars, of which only 15 billion dollars or less than 2 percent were reserve balances. In December 2021, the monetary base had increased almost eightfold to 6,400 billion dollars, two-thirds of which, about 4,200 billion dollars, were reserve balances. Reserve balances had thus increased by more than fifteen times. The balance sheet of the ECB shows a similar trend: In 2008 the monetary base amounted to about 1,300 billion euros, of which roughly one-third were reserves, and by the end of 2021 the total monetary base had increased to about 5,800 billion euros, of which 4,300 billion euros, or almost four-fifths, were reserves.

M0 just constitutes the base on which all the bank money that we use every day is built. The definition of money the reader will most easily recognize is M1. It is normally defined as cash plus all bank deposits which could be used immediately for transactions (i.e., demand deposits). There is also M2, rarely used nowadays as a money definition, which comprises besides sight deposits also those with a fixed time period. M3 adds savings deposits and other similar instruments to the previous categories. The purpose of savings deposits, as the name suggests, is to serve as a store of value. They cannot be used immediately to make purchases. Consumers first have to withdraw funds either in cash or transfer them to a bank deposit to spend them. Moreover, they are subject to restrictions on withdrawals or other transactions over given time periods. These restrictions vary from bank to bank and country to country. It is thus difficult to compare the "moneyness" of savings accounts across countries.

In the predigital age, when savings deposits came in the form of savings booklets, any withdrawal involved a personal trip to the bank and a new entry in the book. Today, in Europe and the United States the distinction between savings and other types of accounts is becoming less relevant as users, especially those with online banking, can switch between them digitally at low cost. The main difference between a sight and a savings deposit for a bank is that its supervisor requires higher balances of cash against the former because in a crisis savings deposits could not be liquidated as quickly. For investors, the difference between different types of bank deposits becomes relevant when interest rates increase, rendering the yield on savings deposits interesting.

If money is defined as an instrument with immediate purchasing power, one should also count open overdrafts or unused credit card limits as money. A line of credit for an enterprise also represents funds that are immediately available to purchase inputs or pay workers. However, these items are usually not added to monetary statistics, mostly because little systematic information is available about them. These limiting cases illustrate the complexity of the term "money" and suggest that there is no single best way to measure it.

INCREASING MONEY HOLDING ALL OVER THE WORLD

Not only is it difficult to decide what are the most relevant monetary aggregates but one also has to be careful in cross-country comparisons given that each country has different regulations on bank deposits and instruments that could be considered close substitutes to bank deposits. However, global financial institutions like the World Bank have tried to construct aggregates that can be compared across countries and over time.[20] These data show a clear upward trend in all principal monetary aggregates over the last fifty years: People all over the world have gradually come to hold more and more money.

As we mentioned in Chapter 5, in 1960, when the digitalization of money started, the global ratio of money (M3) to GDP was about 50 percent. But by 1990 this had almost doubled to close to 100 percent. Since then money has increased again, to over 150 percent today.

The global average hides great differences across countries. High-saving Asian economies show ratios of M3 to GDP over 200 percent (China) and close to 300 percent for Japan. Across the Atlantic, the values are much lower. For example, both the United States and the euro area have now reached ratios of M3 to GDP close to 120 percent, much below that of Japan and China today. But even in Europe and the United States money holdings have doubled relative to GDP over the last half century. Interestingly, the United States had one of the highest ratios of M3 to GDP in the 1960s and early 1970s, which might explain the intensity of the controversy over the role of banks and money at the time.

The trend toward more money holding, both absolute and relative to income, is clear. But what motivates this increase? In Chapter 5 we found that illicit transactions and the gray economy are unlikely to be the main drivers. As regards both cash and the broader forms of money, the lower interest rates and the expansionary monetary policies pursued by central banks provide part of the answer.

Tobin's theory of money predicts that when interest rates are low, as they have been most of the time in recent decades, investors prefer to hold money than bonds because the latter fall in value when central banks increase rates. This is indeed what happened in 2021–22. Those who held long-term government bonds at the time made large losses, but holders of savings accounts saw only their return finally increase.

But other factors might also have contributed. One that might come into play when interest rates stay low for long periods is "rational inattention."[21] The theory of rational inattention is economists speak for the fact that nobody can absorb all the information about the economy that arrives constantly. One must therefore decide what is important and deserves attention. Central bankers have used this concept to explain why people react differently in periods of high and volatile inflation than during periods of constant prices. The explanation is simply that when prices are stable, people no longer pay attention to them. But when suddenly prices start to increase and eat into the purchasing power of household budgets, people start paying attention. This common-sense reaction had not been anticipated by central banks. They were then surprised by the strong reaction of households to the return of inflation in 2022.[22]

Applied to savings patterns, this theory would predict that during long periods of low rates, households would just leave their money in bank accounts. Other forms of safe investment would not promise higher returns anyway. When returns do not move much over a long period, people get distracted and no longer pay attention to their investments.

A different but related issue is the propensity of people to hold physical currency, as opposed to using money and near-money instruments offered by banks not included in the broader monetary aggregates. Here one finds interesting differences between the United States and the eurozone.[23] Up to the 1900s or early 2000s, the ratio of physical currency to broad monetary aggregates declined gradually. This expresses the secular expansion of bank intermediation observed, during the postwar era, in most developed economies. A specific contributing factor in the United States is likely to have been the development of quasi-money substitutes, with a high degree of liquidity but earning higher interest, such as MMFs, included in M3, because they are similar to the new instruments called stablecoins.

In the early 2000s, something changed. In the United States, the ratio of cash to broad money increased again. In the euro area, the turnaround was even stronger because the changeover to euro cash in 2002 analyzed earlier had caused a dramatic drop in cash in circulation, in the expectation that the old banknotes would go out of circulation. The actual changeover was then followed by a few years

of an even stronger pick-up in cash in circulation. The boom in financial markets that preceded the Great Financial Crisis of 2008–09 first
favored bank deposits, but this was temporary. After the crisis there
was again a strong increase in the cash-to-money ratios, both in the
United States and in the euro area, reflecting the massive scale-down
of bank intermediation in both areas. Moreover, the decline in interest rates reduced the opportunity cost of holding cash, enhancing its
use as a saving and precautionary instrument. The cash usage relative to bank deposits stabilized just before the COVID pandemic at a
similar, but slightly higher, level than the one observed in the 1970s
and 1980s.

What is striking is the relative stability of the ratios over the
very long run, in spite of major changes in monetary institutions
(a new currency in Europe, banking legislation changes in the United
States), in monetary technology (toward a dominance of digitalization), let alone business cycles. In the early 2020s, the ratios seem to
have topped up in both areas but at different levels, with cash holdings at about 14 percent of M3 in the United States and 9–10 percent
in the euro area. One reason for this difference is the large circulation
of dollars outside the United States, including in countries that have
"dollarized" their monetary systems. It should be noted, however,
that the ratio in the euro area is now higher than it was before the
creation of the euro: It was about 7–8 percent of cash relative to M3
in the late 1990s. This indicates a higher preference for holding euros
today, relative to the preceding constituent national currencies.[24]

THE CHANGING ROLE OF BANKS

We have shown that in "fractional" reserve systems, that is, when
banks hold reserves against their deposit liabilities, a multiplier effect
arises in that any infusion of central bank money leads to a more
than one-to-one increase in deposits. Contrary to monetarists' belief,
however, the money multiplier was never quite stable but moved
over long periods in a sufficiently gradual and seemingly predictable

way to allow central banks, at least in theory, to control the money supply via its control of the monetary base. However, this in the end turned out to be an illusion.

During the 1960s and 1970s, when the monetary controversy was in full swing, the money multiplier in the United States rose from about six to almost twelve. This means that in 1960, 1 dollar of monetary base led to 6 dollars of deposit money (M3), but by 1980 this had increased to 11 dollars of M3 per dollar of monetary base. From the mid 1980s the path of the money multiplier became more erratic. First, it fell quickly but then stabilized for over a decade at the level of the 1970s. The biggest change came after the Great Financial Crisis of 2008–09 when people realized that bank deposits were not as safe as they had assumed, thus reducing their demand for them. At the same time central banks, including the Federal Reserve, began to flood the banking system with reserves, rendering the old idea of stable reserve ratios obsolete. In a few years, the ratio of broad money to base money fell from above eight to below four.

A similar evolution can be observed for the euro area. The fall in the money multiplier was even stronger as the newly created ECB imposed very small reserve requirements, allowing banks to create more than 10 euros in M3 for every euro of ECB base money. By 2022 this had fallen to close to three as the ECB engaged in even more bond purchases than the Federal Reserve, leading to an even greater increase in (mostly excess) reserves.

Banks thus remain the central providers of money, but their role has changed. Central banks have become much more active, also using new instruments. Even the most fervent monetarists no longer believe that it makes sense to try to manage the money supply directly via the balance sheet of the central bank. However, the role of banks remains central even though they can no longer be relied upon to create a certain amount of deposits from a given monetary base

SUMMING UP: WHAT MODEL FOR BANKING?

Banks provide the fundamental nexus between the payment system and the saving–investment process. The payment system provides, with bank accounts as the main instrument, the backbone for daily transfers of wealth. Credit intermediation leads, over time, to the creation of wealth through economic growth. Combining the two functions in one institution requires special regulation of the banking sector and a safety net to protect it. The question arises: Could/should the two functions be separated? Can one design the financial system in a radically different way, with payment providers incorporating the depository function while remaining separate from the intermediation of savings? Separating the two functions seems the implicit assumption of those who would like fintech to supplant the role of banks. How would the credit market and the saving–investment nexus work in that world?

Addressing these questions goes beyond our ambition. It would require another Cowles Commission sifting through mountains of evidence and new theories. We can only offer our instinct, which is that delinking the two functions should not be attempted. We see three reasons for that.

The first is that the distinction between money and other forms of wealth is tenuous, at best. Between pure transaction balances and illiquid assets like stocks and housing, there is a whole range of quasi-monetary forms of wealth, a gray area where boundaries cannot be easily drawn. Wealth is a continuum whose composition changes continuously with the spectrum of returns, risk perceptions, and tastes. The more the financial sector progresses, the more it resembles a real-world analog of the theories of the economist James Tobin, mentioned earlier. This world does not admit a sharp distinction between depository institutions, specializing in payment services, and pure intermediaries focused on credit and asset allocation.

The second reason is that the credit function is complex, requiring specialized skills, experience, and information. It cannot be developed quickly or improvised, let alone rendered completely automatic – although information technology and artificial intelligence coupled with big data can sharpen human judgment. Payment system providers do not possess that expertise; if they developed it, they would end up duplicating banks and adopting their business models. Were a significant share of today's bank deposits redirected toward payment providers, that part of the saving–investment process would be at risk. This argument also applies, by the way, to the case of a sizeable migration of bank deposits toward digital currencies created by central banks (see Chapter 10).

The third reason is that there are synergies among banking functions, on both sides of the banks' balance sheets. Payments, asset allocation, credit screening and monitoring, business advisory and financial support in all its forms, and insurance are increasingly part of a single menu of services that banks offer to personal and corporate clients. The oft-criticized universal banking model has never been seriously challenged or has found valid and concrete alternatives.

NOTES

1. Their names are listed in "Nobel Laureates with Connections to Cowles," *Cowles Foundation for Research in Economics*.
2. Interested readers should see, on the Keynesian side, Franco Modigliani, "The Monetarist Controversy or, Should We Forsake Stabilization Policies?," *The American Economic Review* 67, no. 2 (1977): 1–19; Paul Davidson, "Why Money Matters: Lessons from a Half-Century of Monetary Theory," *Journal of Post Keynesian Economics* 1, no. 1 (September 1, 1978): 46–70; On the monetarist side, Milton Friedman, "Discussion, on the Monetarist Controversy," Federal Reserve Bank of San Francisco Economic Review Supplement, 1977; and David Laidler, "The Legacy of the Monetarist Controversy," Federal Reserve Bank of St. Louis Review, March 1990, 49–64.
3. David Hume, *Essays Moral, Political, and Literary* (1875), pt. 2, essay 3, "On Money."
4. John Maynard Keynes, *The General Theory of Employment, Interest and Money* (Palgrave Macmillan, 1936).

5. The clearest statement can be found in James Tobin, "Commercial Banks as Creators of 'Money'," Cowles Foundation Discussion Paper 159, 1963.

6. Franco Modigliani, "The Monetary Mechanism and Its Interaction with Real Phenomena," *The Review of Economics and Statistics* 45, no. 1 (February 1, 1963): 79. Modigliani's model draws on John Hicks' interpretation of Keynes' theory, as presented in John Hicks, "Mr. Keynes and the 'Classics': A Suggested Interpretation," *Econometrica* 5, no. 2 (April 1, 1937): 147.

7. See, for example, Benjamin M. Friedman, *The Moral Consequences of Economic Growth* (Knopf, 2005); and Benjamin M. Friedman, *Religion and the Rise of Capitalism* (Knopf, 2021).

8. Benjamin M. Friedman, "Targets, Instruments, and Indicators of Monetary Policy," *Journal of Monetary Economics* 1, no. 4 (October 1, 1976): 443–73.

9. Eugene F. Fama, "Banking in the Theory of Finance," *Journal of Monetary Economics* 6, no. 1 (January 1, 1980): 39–57.

10. Joseph E. Stiglitz and Andrew Weiss, "Credit Rationing in Markets with Imperfect Information," *The American Economic Review* 71, no. 3 (1981): 393–410.

11. Douglas W. Diamond and Philip H. Dybvig, "Bank Runs, Deposit Insurance, and Liquidity," *Journal of Political Economy* 91, no. 3 (June 1, 1983): 401.

12. Douglas W. Diamond and Philip H. Dybvig, "Banking Theory, Deposit Insurance, and Bank Regulation," *The Journal of Business* 59, no. 1 (January 1, 1986): 55.

13. This is the central argument against 100 percent banking made by Diamond and Dybvig, "Banking Theory, Deposit Insurance, and Bank Regulation."

14. Gary Gorton and Andrew Metrick, "Securitized Banking and the Run on Repo," *Journal of Financial Economics* 104, no. 3 (June 1, 2012): 425–51.

15. George J. Stigler, "The Theory of Economic Regulation," *The Bell Journal of Economics and Management Science* 2, no. 1 (January 1, 1971): 3.

16. Data on financial inclusion are published in: "The Global Findex Database 2021," *World Bank*.

17. See the 2022 findings from the Diary of Consumer Payment Choices of the Federal Reserve Bank of San Francisco: Emily Cubides and Shaun O'Brien, "2022 Findings from the Diary of Consumer Payment Choice," *San Francisco Fed*, May 5, 2022.

18. Modern central banks deal only with commercial banks: Nobody else can hold a digital claim on the central bank. This might change if central banks issue a digital currency (central bank digital currencies), which we discuss in Chapter 10.

19. When interest rates are high, reserve requirements amount to a tax on banks and thus indirectly also on bank deposits. This tax in the past has been substantial. To make a concrete example, if banks have to hold an amount equal to one-fifth of their deposits in a non-interest-bearing account at the central (meaning the required reserve ratio is 20 percent) but interest rates are 10 percent, the banks implicitly lose 2 percentage points on all their deposits. They can then pay their depositors only 8 percent. The central bank invests the funds it obtains under the required reserve regime usually in government debt. This implies that implicitly the government obtains some financing at zero interest. The practice of using high reserve requirements to finance the government (also called financial repression) was abandoned after the 1970s as inflation fell and financial markets were liberalized.

20. See "Global Financial Development: DataBank," *World Bank*.

21. The concept was pioneered by the economist Sims, another Nobel prize winner; see Christopher A. Sims, "Implications of Rational Inattention," *Journal of Monetary Economics* 50, no. 3 (April 1, 2003): 665–90. For a recent review see Bartosz Maćkowiak, Filip Matějka, and Mirko Wiederholt, "Rational Inattention: A Review," *Journal of Economic Literature* 61, no. 1 (March 1, 2023): 226–73.

22. See Bartosz Maćkowiak, Filip Matějka, and Mirko Wiederholt, "The Rational Inattention Filter," ECB Working Papers 2007, 2017.

23. Data for the United States and eurozone countries are available respectively from the Federal Reserve Bank of St. Louis and the ECB.

24. The Online Appendix to this book, available at Ignazio Angeloni's blog (ignazioangeloni.home.blog), contains these charts for the United States and the euro area, over the last fifty years.

7   Cards and Apps from Above and Below

Up and down, and in the end it's only round 'n round.

Roger Waters and Richard Wright

The oldest international financial institution in the world sits quietly in the heart of the (equally quiet) Swiss city of Basel, its upward-pointing round shape attracting occasional wry smiles from bystanders. Unknown to all except a restricted circle of insiders, its influence in the world of finance is much greater than its fame. So is its relevance for the future of money, especially in digital form. This is where our journey into the bewildering world of payment apps, cards, and digital wallets begins.

In spite of its name, the Bank for International Settlements (BIS) is neither a bank nor has it ever settled a payment, except among the sixty-three central banks that today subscribe to its capital. Founded in 1930 with just eight members with the mission of organizing ("settling") what remained of Germany's World War I reparations, it soon found itself out of business after the Great Depression (1931), and the rise to German chancellor of Adolf Hitler (1933) made any such payments obsolete. In retrospect, that was the institution's fortune, because it forced it to find a new mission.

Over the course of its history, the BIS has made reinventing itself an art. A crucial asset was its location, few kilometers from the French and German borders and meters away from the train station. In the 1930s, railroads were the only long-distance transportation means in continental Europe. Central bank governors and their senior staff travelled on luxury rail cars from their European capitals to attend routine gatherings at the BIS. There, the "lords of finance" found a friendly environment to exchange views and co-organize their activities. The neutrality of the terrain was crucial at a time in which political relations in Europe were souring, eventually leading to the outbreak of World War II.[1]

It seems unlikely that it would fall onto the BIS, a global institution located in a neutral country that always refused to take part in Europe's political projects, to be the cradle of negotiations eventually leading to the European Central Bank and Europe's currency, the euro. Yet this is precisely what happened. After the war, the Allied victors wanted the BIS to be disbanded, not least because it seemed to have acquiesced to certain monetary demands of the Nazis. But the advantage of the location prevailed. The BIS was given a new mission: reorganizing Europe's cross-border payments and currency convertibility in the new postwar monetary order founded at Bretton Woods in 1944. The "European Payment Union" morphed in 1964 into a "committee" of European Central Bank governors, the embryo of the future European Central Bank.[2] Once again, the monetary masters chose to stay in Basel – the EU Commission thought they should meet in Brussels instead – for reasons of logistical convenience. Basel ended up hosting the negotiations for the establishment of the European Monetary System, the rules governing European currencies before the monetary union.

Until the European Central Bank governors established new headquarters for their meetings in Frankfurt (1993), the mission of the BIS proceeded along two paths: one European and one global. The latter progressively grew and eventually fully absorbed the institution's agenda. In 1974, the BIS became the center of global banking oversight rules with the establishment of the Basel Committee on Banking Supervision and later (1988) with the so-called Basel Accord, setting prudential standards for banking supervisors worldwide. The Accord was further extended twice, in 2004 and 2017. Additional committee structures were established over the years, to debate and coordinate central bank action in the areas of financial markets and payments.

The mission of the BIS expanded further after the Global Financial Crisis (2008–09), increasingly addressing financial stability issues. The Financial Stability Board, a global forum of central bankers and financial regulators created in 2009 among economically advanced and emerging countries, established its headquarters at the BIS. At the same time, the institution gained a reputation as a center for economic research, often on frontier issues less covered by mainstream academia.

Nowadays, the BIS is increasingly engaged in research on the evolution of the global monetary system in the digital age. An "Innovation Hub" was established in 2019 to foster analyses and support central bank involvement in innovative financial technologies. This turn in the BIS's ever-evolving mission coincided with the time crypto assets were booming and central bankers conceived the idea of issuing their own digital monies. Once again, the BIS emerged as the venue of choice for central bankers to exchange views and coordinate their activities on these new issues. New challenge, same place.

A FITTING METAPHOR

Today one of the major research centers on monetary digitalization, the BIS has developed a "vision" of how the monetary and payment ecosystem should look in the digital era. This vision was explained in 2022 in a dedicated chapter of the BIS flagship publication, its Annual Economic Report.[3] In the rest of this section, we elaborate on the BIS argument exposed there.

To convey its message, the BIS uses a fitting metaphor: a tree, whose roots, trunk, branches, twigs, and leaves complement each other, giving the plant what it needs to live, grow, and strive – solidity, resilience, and vitality.

In the BIS's language, from the aforementioned Annual Report:

> The metaphor for the future monetary system is a tree whose
> solid trunk is the central bank [...]. As well as exemplifying the
> solid support provided by central bank money, the tree metaphor
> expresses the principle of the monetary system being rooted

(figuratively speaking) in payment finality through ultimate settlement on the central bank's balance sheet.

The monetary system based on central bank money supports a diverse and multi-layered vibrant ecosystem of participants and functions in which competing private sector PSPs [i.e., payment service providers] can give full play to their creativity and ingenuity to serve users better. Underlying these benefits is the virtuous circle set off by network effects arising from the data architecture, consisting of digital identity and APIs [i.e., application programming interfaces], that enables interoperability both domestically and across borders.[4]

The metaphor fits in several ways. The trunk expresses the solidity and stability required for the upper structures to lean and develop. Likewise, the central bank settlement infrastructure provides certainty to all payments in the monetary system. One may add here that the roots, at the base of the trunk, provide not only that stability but also the sap that transmits vital nourishment to the upper structure. In the central bank analogue, this is the money-creating function: the unique prerogative of the central bank to create fiat payment instruments. At a certain height, the trunk splits into major branches, metaphorically representing banks and other major financial institutions which both provide settlement services to retail payment system users and use the central bank to settle payments among themselves. The branches ultimately support the complex of smaller branches, twigs, and leaves, representing the universe of smaller participants in the payment system. Unlike the underlying structure, this part is flexible and ever-changing. It provides life to the plant through its exposure to the "light and air" of market exposure. It can be subject to lesser rules – it can move, unlike the immobile part of the plant below. However, its flexibility is only made possible by the fact that it is solidly planted on the underlying structure.

Images of this metaphorical tree appear in several BIS publications (e.g., in the aforementioned annual report, page 92). The central bank is at the base of the tree. It is connected to the population of private payment service providers, on top as the tree's canopy. The connection is made of "application programming interfaces," interconnected computer software that allows swift interaction among operators. Above the base, the trunk supports the whole tree structure. The branches departing from the trunk can be thought of as banks, connected to the central bank through centralized settlement accounts. Banks stand between the central bank and the multiplicity of private sector payment providers. Connected to the banks is the universe of payment service providers, the tree's canopy. The latter is a flexible and ever-changing entity, exposed to competitive forces, that provides efficiency and technological innovation.

Let's keep this image in mind, while descending into today's multifaceted and bewildering world of checks, apps, and online platforms.

PERSONAL CHECKS AND THEIR SURPRISING ENDURANCE IN THE UNITED STATES

Until twenty years ago or so, noncash retail payments were still made largely with personal checks. In 2000, about 42 billion of them were written in the United States, one every two days for each adult citizen. Comparable data for Europe are not available, but their diffusion was probably similar. Then and now, checks are issued and settled by banks. In the tree's metaphor, one may think of a single, huge, leaf, attached through multiple twigs to many branches. Hardly a structure that would allow a healthy plant to develop.

We saw in Chapter 3 how checks provided essential support and stimulus to the post–World War II economic expansion by allowing the mobilization of bank deposits, the main financial instrument then available to individuals and small businesses. The resilience of personal checks owed much to their inefficiency. Banks, the issuers and handlers of checks, had a vested interest in their survival. Even after the check-handling process had been largely automatized with the introduction of mainframe computers, they still required a work-force for nonstandard functions – design and production, cashiers, and transportation. Staff and managers' interests converged in support of a comfortable status quo. The need for checks to return physically to the issuing bank (in the United States, a legal requirement until 2004) created a lag between the moment in which payments were credited to the account of the payee and the one in which they were debited to that of the payor. The resulting accounting expansion of deposits (the so-called float) allowed banks to inflate their balance sheets, with convenient window-dressing practices. The shortcomings of this system were exposed in the United States on September 11, 2001, when the grounding of planes following the terrorist attacks brought the check-handling processes to a halt. From then on, a process was set in motion whereby checks were eventually transformed into digital images by the receiving banks and sent to the issuing one, while the paper document was destroyed ("truncated"). The float collapsed.[5]

By today's standards, checks are inefficient and unsafe. For starters, payments made with them are not legally final, though they may enjoy certain guarantees. Second, small sheets of handwritten, low-quality paper are highly perishable, especially if negotiable because after being "endorsed" they may circulate extensively. They are also prone to fraud. Last but not least, they are slow: The paper document has to be brought to a bank and processed. Even after the "truncation," there is no match in terms of efficiency with modern digital payments.

For this reason, checks have essentially disappeared in the eurozone, except to some extent in France, where their use persists, though declining. The average eurozone inhabitant today signs one check every three months. By contrast, checks are still popular in the United States: Each citizen signs three checks per week on average. Surveys show that this instrument is favored by elderly and less educated individuals, suggesting an underlying resistance to change. A Federal Reserve staff study dated 2008 concludes as follows:

(The) ongoing reliance on checks is unique among developed countries and creates some inefficiency in the U.S. payment system (...) the social cost of a typical grocery store check payment (is) $1.21 versus $0.78 for the cheapest electronic alternative (payment with a debit card). Much of the difference derives from checks' higher processing cost, which in turn stems from the cost of physically moving and storing paper. Recent moves toward "electronifying" check processing—most notably the Check Clearing for the 21st Century Act of 2003—have reduced these costs, but the check clearing system still processes many checks in paper form.[6]

CARDS, APPS, AND ONLINE PLATFORMS: BANK PAYMENTS RUN BY OTHERS

In retrospect, the failure of bankers to grasp the potential of digital technology in the payments industry early on, during the 1990s and part of the 2000s, was a tragic mistake for them. The payment system is slipping through their hands, passing to the tech sector, which dominates payments today. Another reason is the advent of the smartphone and the speed of its diffusion. Only four years separate the launch of the first generation of iPhone (2007) from the first payment app (2011).[7] At that time, the competitive battle with big tech for payment's innovation frontier was already lost by the banking sector. Controlling both hardware and software, big tech was only a step away from controlling the direction and the pace of innovation of the whole payment sector. Which is what happened.

Survey studies by the Federal Reserve reveal that the number of card payments in the United States climbed to 160 billion dollars per year in 2021 (the last year where comparable data are available), from less than 24 billion in 2000.[8] Payments with personal checks collapsed from 42 billion to 11 billion. Transfers directly via banks by money orders, the main remaining item, also grew but less spectacularly and are comparatively less important. These data conceal the component of retail payments executed via smartphone apps and wallets, for the reason that these payments indirectly use payment cards and bank accounts as part of their settlement processes. The European landscape is comparable, though with some differences to which we will return.

When loading their smartphone wallets with payment apps, users specify the preferred mode(s) of payment. To make an example familiar to us: Your authors' combined e-wallets contain between five and ten debit and credit cards, issued by banks in multiple countries but all belonging to US card networks. Smartphone apps and e-wallets connect to banks and online platforms. A particular mode of payment is chosen each time depending on the location, circumstances, nature of the transfer, acceptance by the payee, availability of funds at that particular moment, or simply chance. The system works well: efficient, user-friendly, and secure.

The picture differs if payment values are considered, rather than the number of payments. The Federal Reserve surveys show that direct bank transfers top the list, with a combined amount of over 90 trillion dollars in 2021, against 18 trillion in 2000. This is due to the fact that most of these payments refer to regular transfers related to incomes, rents, and salaries, whose amount is on average larger than single retail purchases. A typical rent payment would be at least several hundred dollars or euros and most salaries would be even higher. By contrast, the typical retail card payment is an order of magnitude lower, around 50 dollars/euros but nowadays often even less. Again, the patterns are broadly common to Europe.

When values are factored in, the role of checks declines but less spectacularly: from 40 trillion to 27 trillion. The role of cards increased, but their overall incidence in the total value of payments executed in the US economy is quite low. This pattern, which is probably like that experienced in other parts of the world, is due to the fact that card and app payments are mainly used for retail payments (where most payments are small), rather than in the wholesale segment.

Looking "from above," the payment ecosystem appears incredibly diverse. Technical features differ from one means to the other; each competitor tries to find its niche and attract users by means of a new design, attractive payment options, ease of use, complementarity with other software installed on the device, and more. Like the leaves of a tree, payment cards and apps never look exactly alike. However, when we look at them "from below," they share a key common feature: They all eventually settle via an account at a bank somewhere. Just as many leaves are attached to the same branch, and all of them to some branch, all payments are solidly attached to a settlement mechanism that has at its base the payment sector, and below that the central bank and, for international transactions, the community of the world's (mainly Western) central banks. This ensures the solidity and vitality of the system. Like the crown could not survive without the trunk, the payment system cannot survive without its base in the banking (including central banking) sector.

Cards and apps perform the functions historically performed by checks and earlier on by handwritten money order and letters of exchange. They signal a transfer from one owner to another. The key features are ease, security, and speed. In ancient Mesopotamia, authenticity was witnessed by the impression of cylindrical seals on wet clay, combined with the authority of the priests. In cooler climates, wax seals did the job, and for checks, the signature, combined with bank control procedures, was the key element. With cards and apps, the key security element has become a personal identification number (PIN), a biometric recognition, a fingerprint, or the iris of an eye. Cards and apps are essentially messaging systems. They do not by themselves execute transfers; they help certify the authenticity of the message. As the reader has surely grasped, the fundamental purpose – ensuring clarity and safety to the payments function – is unchanged. Only the technology evolves, to fulfil that purpose better.

Assembling a comprehensive list of cards and apps available today is virtually impossible; not only are they many, but the list and the ranking of importance change over time. As we write, the global payment card circuit is topped by Mastercard and Visa, followed at a distance by American Express – all US-based companies. Certain cards, like Discover Card, circulate mainly in certain countries; others, like the three just mentioned, are global.

Cards come in two varieties: credit cards, allowing the holder to spend more than she has in her bank account, with the balance settled in a monthly billing cycle, and debit cards, settling immediately or with a short delay on the payor's account. Debit cards are prevalent in Europe whereas credit cards dominate in the United States, where they usually offer the advantage of various reward and retention programs, encouraging customers to remain loyal and use them as much as possible. Most debit cards and part of credit cards are issued by banks, with different conditions on overdraft, payment terms, and so on. But most cards carry the brand of one of the dominant networks. A separate category is represented by prepaid offline cards, mainly used by younger users, whose money balance is digitally stored in the card's chip.

Technological companies offer payment apps often in combination with other products and services. Apple Pay, for example, is automatically made available to Apple phones and tablets, and so is Samsung Pay. Google Pay is part of the portfolio of services offered by Google. PayPal originated in online stores, mainly Amazon initially; now it is virtually everywhere and can be accessed via any smartphone, also for customer-to-customer transfers. Alongside these industry "giants," there is a myriad of smaller and more specific products. The Swedish Klarna specializes in buy-now-pay-later, an online form of consumer credit. Xoom and Venmo, part of PayPal's group, are popular for small transfers, both domestically and internationally. For person-to-person transfers across borders, especially in Europe, the Lithuanian-born Revolut is a rising star. One common characteristic of all these systems is that they ultimately settle on a bank account and a central bank.

Compared to China, the United States and Europe are lagging years in terms of mobile payments. Already ten to fifteen years ago, when China was much poorer, it had hundreds of millions of smart-phone users, most of whom had a bank account. One reason for the instant success of mobile payments in China was that the leading companies chose a relatively low-tech solution, namely QR codes that could be read also by basic cellphones that most Chinese owned at the time.[9] By contrast, Western competitors, like Google and Apple opted for a more demanding technology (near-field communication) that requires more expensive smartphones available in the West.

The Chinese authorities gave subsidiaries of the two dominant internet giants (Alibaba and Tencent, with over 1 billion custom-ers combined) a (restricted) banking license that allows them to offer almost the full range of banking services. For example, Ant Financial, a subsidiary of Alibaba, also allowed its users to deposit funds on its account, making it soon the largest money market mutual fund globally.

The result of all this is that China is the absolute leader in mobile payments with a mobile payments penetration rate close to 90 percent, double that of the United States and even further ahead compared to most EU countries.[10] Statistics on payment patterns in China have become scarcer recently as the Chinese authorities consider more and more data relevant for national security. Press reports suggest that on "singles day" alone (the Chinese alternative to Valentine's day) online sales totaled the equivalent of over 150 bil-lion US dollars, several times more than those of Black Friday in the United States.[11]

THE COST OF DIGITAL PAYMENTS

Mobile payments are expanding everywhere because they are more convenient for consumers. But how much do digital payments cost? Are they cheaper than traditional payment methods? Who bears that cost, and how?

What makes these questions difficult to answer is the fact that payment costs are partly hidden in the price of the goods and ser-vices we buy. Consumers do not see those costs, because they are "explicitly" borne by retailers. But to the extent that retailers adjust their sales prices, consumers "implicitly" bear part of them.

It has been estimated that of the total cost of payments at a global level, amounting to some 1.5 trillion to 2 trillion dollars per year, about half is borne by businesses and the rest by the consumer.[12] The direct cost of a credit card payment to retailers is often estimated to be in the order of 3 percent but can vary depending on the type of card and jurisdiction. In Europe, charges tend to be lower, due to the fact that part of the costs is translated by banks to their customers through other channels.[13]

The cost explicitly borne by the retailer is usually split in three parts, one going to the customer's bank (the issuer of the card), one going to the merchant's bank, and the third to the card's network. The split between the three can vary considerably. More importantly, these fees do not necessarily reflect the real cost of the payment, since banks and other payment service providers get compensation also in different ways – for example, by interest margins between lending and funding costs or by overcharging certain services like the use of cards to get cash at an automated teller machine. For these reasons, measuring the true cost of payments and determining who bears the cost are not easy. One thing, however, is certain: Sooner or later, directly, or indirectly, through one channel or another, end users eventually shoulder most if not all the cost of the payments they make.

To be true, cash payments are not costless either, though they may appear so. The merchant has to keep the cash somewhere, probably needs insurance, cash needs to be brought to the bank to deposit in a bank account, and so on. The "all in" cost is thus definitely not zero. The use of cash for payments is declining everywhere, increasingly so for low-value transactions as well. The advantage of cash for the consumer is that it does not need a system, or a technology, except that incorporated in the banknote or the coin itself – design and security features. By contrast, cards and apps require that both sides of the transaction be connected to the same system. A debit card is especially useful when merchants have point-of-sales terminals with which they can read the card and reach the bank network. Similarly, peer-to-peer systems like PayPal work only if both sides have a PayPal account (which is very easy to obtain, anyway).

New payment systems involve significant initial investments – the so-called set-up costs. But once this has been borne, transactions are very cheap. This generates "economies of scale" in the payments industry, meaning that average costs decline with scale. In addition, payment technologies become more attractive the more people use them – the so-called network externalities. Once most people get used to a certain type of payment method, it becomes difficult to introduce a new one because it requires changing people's habits. Merchants are hesitant to add to their systems a new one that will, at least initially, be used little. This hurdle can eventually be overcome only by major innovations, which can deliver significantly lower costs or more convenience for consumers or merchants.

As computing and telecommunication costs fall, scale economies and network effects are enhanced. During most of the twentieth century, computing power and fixed-line telecommunication costs fell dramatically: Moore's law says that the computing power of a chip roughly doubles every eighteen months. Over the last two decades, the biggest progress has been in mobile telecommunication, which now leads to the substitution of cards with apps installed on the ubiquitous smartphone. At present, we are still in the phase where no single global standard of mobile payments has emerged. Advanced digital payments associated with mobile devices are most widely used in small countries with very high standards of education and digital knowledge (examples are Sweden and Switzerland) and in the big cities in China, where the economies of scale are massive and growth has been so quick that most of the new middle class has gone directly from cash to mobile apps without any intermediate stage.

Metcalfe's law suggests that the value of a transaction system increases with the square of the share of the population which uses it. This is why the competition in the fintech industry is so fierce: It is a "winner takes all" market in which those who occupy a niche first can then reap considerable profits. This creates a consumer protection problem: Once the winner has overcome the competition and borne the set-up costs, it is tempted to abuse this monopoly position. This has long been a concrete problem in the payment card industry, which is dominated by two incumbents,[14] Visa and Mastercard. The latter was created in the 1960s by a small group of large US banks and had a monopoly until a rival group of banks created a competitor. These two bank-based incumbents dominate the market, leaving only a niche to others, like American Express, which concentrates on the travel segment. The card business is thus an integral part of a bank-based business model. In principle, entry into the app-based business should be easy, but economies of scale again explain why the first movers tend to become the largest and usually buy up nimble upstarts, as PayPal has done, for example, with Venmo.

It is impossible to determine the cost of any individual transaction in the digital payment industry, but one can compare the average cost across different systems. One way to provide an estimate is to compare the revenues of the company providing the service with the number and value of transactions processed. This approach yields an order of magnitude for the average cost, both per transaction and as a proportion of the value transacted.

Data on the three globally dominant payment service providers (PayPal, Mastercard, Visa) obtained from their respective annual reports show that they are rather similar in terms of overall revenues: In 2022, all earned between 20 billion and 30 billion dollars. The main difference is in the number of users or cards, a metric on which Visa, with nearly 4 billion cards, is larger than Mastercard (2.7 billion) and almost ten times larger than PayPal, which has only 400 million users. Important differences among these payment vehicles regard the nature of their transactions, the volumes of payments, and their costs. PayPal's average value per transaction (over 60 dollars) is higher than Mastercard and much higher than Visa, which is now increasingly used for extremely small payments like subway fares.

The revenue per transaction for the two credit card companies is only about 10 cents, which amounts to 0.3 percent of the average transaction value for Mastercard but about 1 percent for Visa with its much smaller transactions.

The power of economies of scale emerges clearly from the data. The biggest card company earns less than 20 cents of a dollar per transaction, only 0.23 percent of the value of the average transaction, worth about 60 dollars. The cost of credit card payments is usually much higher than 0.23 percent because banks, especially in the United States, charge additional fees for processing the payments on their networks. Card owners do not perceive any cost for an individual payment, but they may have an upfront cost for obtaining the card. This fixed cost can amount to twenty to fifty euros or dollars depending on the features of the card, especially the maximum credit amount. Debit cards are usually much cheaper because no credit assessment is necessary. The upfront fee goes not to the credit card companies but to the bank that issues the card. Despite their name, credit card companies do not issue any cards, only provide a brand name and a standardized messaging service to connect merchants to the banks.

By contrast, PayPal, the globally leading app, earns about 1.3 dollars per transaction, which amounts to about 2 percent of the average transaction value, which is, like for credit cards, around 60 dollars. PayPal requires higher revenues per transaction because it operates outside the banking system. Its service appears free to consumers; its revenues come exclusively from merchants. Merchants agree to pay because the platform greatly facilitates their online sales. PayPal also provides a "peer-to-peer" function, whereby you can send money to your friend for free but only in the same currency (Revolut offers multicurrency portfolios and instant exchange and payment services). This service can be provided for free because peer-to-peer transactions are small relative to online sales and providing this service increases the customer base, another factor that convinces merchants to accept payments via PayPal. In sum, the key metric of business return in digital payments is not the direct cost but the marketing value determined by consumers who rely increasingly on their smartphones to organize their lives.

The numbers presented here do not comprise the full cost for credit card payments because Visa and Mastercard only provide a brand and standardization of the payment instruments on both sides (standardized cards for the consumer and point-of-sales terminals for merchants). The banks over which the payment is executed are the ones that shoulder most of the cost of a credit card transaction and obtain most of the revenues.

Transaction services constitute for banks an important source of income, which they are loath to lose. They seem to treat businesses and individuals very differently. The global consulting company McKinsey estimates that banks make hundreds of billions on transaction fees, with a profit margin on domestic transfers to and from consumers at a generous 22 percent but only 2 percent on transfers to and from business. This is why banks collect almost twice as much in transaction fees from consumers than from businesses although the transaction volumes are ten times higher for the business sector.[15] The margin on cross-border transfers is even larger than that for consumers. The underlying reason is that cross-border transactions are irregular, are less frequent, and involve more costs for AML procedures.

The average cost banks charge on retail transfers is about 0.3 percent of the transaction value, which does not seem large. But the total take of banks is about ten times larger than that of the credit card companies, whose charges are thus only a fraction of the total cost that ultimately has to be borne by consumers even if this is not directly visible. The 2023 McKinsey Global Payments Report shows that banks obtain hundreds of billions from the transactions or connection fees they charge to credit card companies, costs that ultimately are all borne by card users.[16]

The revenues of credit card companies have grown rapidly over the last two decades as the use of cards has replaced checks and cash. As one would expect, apps (PayPal and others) grow more quickly than credit cards. The credit card industry has achieved near-saturation levels in advanced countries, whereas the customer base for online mobile payment is still small and growing more quickly. But the difference in growth is not that large because credit cards have also become easier to use with contactless features – without or within smartphone wallets. Apps are likely to eventually overtake and crowd out cards, enhancing the illusion of free instant payments. Consumers increasingly pay with the one item they never lose sight of, namely their cellphone.

China represents a special case as its newly affluent middle class in the big cities has gone straight to the use of homegrown apps. Illustrating the economies of scale explained earlier, the two first movers, Alipay and WeChat, totally dominate the market. These economies of scale ultimately constitute the reason why the attempt of the otherwise almighty Chinese government to create a competitor in the form of the e-yuan has failed, as we document in Chapter 10.

BRANCHES, TRUNK, AND ROOTS

In the metaphor we described earlier, the main branches supporting smaller twigs and leaves represent deposit banks, which perform the upper part of the payment settlement function. Being the inter-mediate component of the system, banks connect the multivariate universe of fintech to the "base," the final settlement in central bank money. All payments enacted through the aforementioned digital means settle eventually in this way, in the bank and cen-tral bank accounts. This is what gives solidity and reliability to the payment system.

The fact that most payment innovation happens outside the banking sector is sometimes attributed to banks being overburdened by regulation. This is a bit unfair. Regulation is justified by the role banks play as financial intermediaries. Banks sit on a rather uncom-fortable fence: They both provide means of payment on their liability side and offer credit on their asset side. This transformation entails risks for depositors, other stakeholders, and the broader economy. This requires specific regulation over and above the one attached to the fintech sector, which performs only the payment function.

Virtually all noncash payments in the economy today settle on commercial bank books. Some see this as a limitation, but the advantages are overwhelming: Bank regulation ensures – except for occasional supervisory mistakes – that the money banks issue is backed by sound assets. This is what distinguishes money issued by banks from, for example, non-reserve-backed crypto assets. Referring again to our botanical image, like leaves live only if attached to the plant, money survives only if attached to a sound depository institution.

REVOLUTION OR EVOLUTION?

All together, we come to a picture in which the changes in the way people pay that occurred in the last twenty years look less fundamental than they appear at first sight. For sure, less "revolutionary" than how they are portrayed in many public statements on the subject, often originating from industry insiders. Practitioners concentrate on the surface – the crown of the tree – where changes are evident. But if one looks at the full structure of the payment "tree," monetary digitalization is less impressive. The underlying need – transferring wealth cheaply and safely – is fundamentally unchanged. Its performance is improved by technology but needs protecting from hazardous innovations which may put it at risk.

Below the crown comprised of the myriad of cards, apps, platforms, and online and offline payment facilities, there is a double layer of depository institutions and central banks guaranteeing the soundness of the system. The accounting systems where their transactions are recorded function largely in a centralized manner. Centralization confers efficiency and safety to the system.

End of the story? Not really. In the last decade and a half something fundamentally new has appeared in the monetary firmament, a new star promising to revolutionize payments by way of a new concept and a new technology: cryptographic proof combined with distributed ledgers and blockchains. Let's now turn to cryptocurrencies and find out whether they can indeed provide an alternative to traditional money.

NOTES

1. Some of the early BIS meetings and the topics discussed there are vividly described in the fascinating book Liaquat Ahamed, *Lords of Finance: The Bankers Who Broke the World* (Penguin, 2009).
2. Harold James, *Making the European Monetary Union* (Harvard University Press, 2012)
3. BIS, *Annual Economic Report*, 2022, chapter 3.
4. BIS, *Annual Economic Report*, 2022, chapter 3.
5. The demise of checks and the role of September 11, 2001, are recounted in detail by David B. Humphrey and Robert M. Hunt, "Getting Rid of Paper: Savings from Check 21," Federal Reserve Bank of Philadelphia Working Papers 12, January 1, 2012.
6. Stephen Quinn and William Roberds, "The Evolution of the Check as a Means of Payment: A Historical Survey," *Federal Reserve Bank of Atlanta Economic Review* 4 (2008): 1–28.
7. Probably by Western Union: "The Western Union Company: Western Union Celebrates 160 Years of Innovation," *Western Union*, May 19, 2011.
8. Federal Reserve Payment Study of the Fed Board of Governors, "2022 Accessible Version of Trends in Noncash Payments." Comparable data prior to 2000 do not exist; estimates by Geoffrey R. Gerdes and Jack K. Walton, "The Use of Checks and Other Noncash Payments in the United States," *Federal Reserve Bulletin* 88 (2002): 360–74, suggest that a peak in the use of checks may have been reached during the 1990s.
9. "China: A Digital Payments Revolution," CGAP, September 1, 2019.
10. Statista, "Adoption of Mobile Contactless/Tap to Pay in 23 Countries Worldwide in 2019 and 2021," September 18, 2023.
11. See Casey Hall, "China's Singles Day Festival Wraps Up with $156B in Estimated Sales, Alibaba and JD.Com Reporting Growth amid Low Expectations," *Fortune*, November 12, 2023, or Yuchuan Wang, "JD. Com's Record-Breaking 2022 Singles' Day Grand Promotion Reflects Robust Consumption Vitality," JD Corporate Blog, November 11, 2022.

12. See Gottfried Leibbrandt and De Terán Natasha, *The Pay Off: How Changing the Way We Pay Changes Everything* (Elliott & Thompson, 2022).

13. See "The Cost of Payments Methods in the Retail Sector," *Deutsche Bundesbank Monthly Report*, June 2019.

14. In Europe, for example, this has led to a long battle between the competition arm of the EU Commission and the major US-owned credit cards networks, such as Mastercard and Visa. Eventually, the networks have agreed to cut the fees they charge to retailers (so-called interchange fees), which affect consumers because they are partly translated to retail prices.

15. "Rethinking Correspondent Banking," McKinsey & Company, June 1, 2016,

16. 2023 McKinsey Global Payments Report, September 18, 2023.

8 Promises and Failures of Crypto

> What problem does this technology solve?
> What does it do that other, much cheaper and
> easier-to-use technologies can't do just as well or better?
> I still haven't heard a clear answer.
>
> Paul Krugman

Laszlo Hanyecz, a computer programmer, had an outlandish idea. On Tuesday, May 18, 2010, he wrote on Bitcoin.org forum: "I'll pay 10,000 Bitcoins for a couple of pizzas. like maybe 2 large ones so I have some left over for the next day. I like having leftover pizza to nibble on later ... If you're interested please let me know and we can work out a deal."

By Friday he must have been hungry since nobody had yet taken up his offer. However, by Saturday, May 22, he finally got two large pizzas from Papa John's delivered to his home and he proudly announced his exploit to the world. Since then, May 22 is "pizza day" for the Bitcoin community.[1]

The origins of Bitcoin (otherwise referred to as BTC) in the marketplace are as humble as that. The rest is history; it took some years before the instrument outgrew its small niche of digital-savvy enthusiasts. The number of users and the price grew by leaps and bounds until Bitcoin became a household name. The immense public interest in cryptocurrencies can be gauged from the fact that since 2017 Bitcoin has been a more popular search term on Google in the United States than even Kim Kardashian or Taylor Swift.

Cryptocurrencies – a term people use to refer to both cryptocurrencies proper, such as Bitcoin, which are the object of this chapter, and related assets like stablecoins, discussed in Chapter 9 – provoke strong emotions and reactions. For some, they are the harbingers of a new era of money which is organized by a community of free thinkers not bound by government regulations which stifle innovation. Bitcoin in particular has been advertised as inflation-proof because its supply has an absolute limit. For the sceptics cryptocurrencies represent Ponzi schemes, which make unrealistic promises to take advantage of badly informed investors.

We prefer to take a less ideological approach: We look at the structures underpinning cryptocurrencies to ascertain to what extent they can fulfil the classical attributes of money, that is, as a means of transactions, store of value, and unit of account, plus the other functions we discussed in Chapter 4.

The cryptocurrency universe has grown by leaps and bounds over the last few years. There exist now thousands of different cryptocurrencies. But many of the newer creations are of little importance. We will concentrate on Bitcoin as the best-known example, with by far the biggest market capitalization, subject to enormous fluctuations. It peaked at over 1 trillion (1,000 billion) dollars in 2021, was down to less than one-third by the end of 2022 and then recovered to over 1 trillion. But there are others, like Ethereum, with a market capitalization of 200 billion to 400 billion dollars, about one-fourth of that of Bitcoin, whose market share remains over 50 percent.

The multibillion market capitalization is impressive if one considers that a few years ago these "currencies" did not exist at all. In fact, their macroeconomic relevance is still limited. Even at its peak, Bitcoin's market capitalization was equivalent only to the value of currency in circulation in Japan, which is worth close to 1,000 billion dollars. This is a small amount relative to global cash holdings or other global monetary aggregates. The second most important cryptocurrency, Ethereum, looks even smaller compared to wider financial markets to which it should be compared since its main appeal is that it is more than a cryptocurrency because it can incorporate "smart contracts."

We will prepare for the journey into cryptoland by explaining the key innovations of cryptocurrencies, namely blockchain, or distributed ledger, and mining. Armed with a basic understanding of how cryptocurrencies work we will then go back to the origin in what now appears the distant past, the publication of the idea for a peer-to-peer payment system in 2008. We then explore a number of key aspects of Bitcoin, as the main protagonist of cryptoland: How much does it cost to transact, is it secure, what services can it deliver, and why do criminals prefer to use this instrument in ransomware?

The reader is warned that understanding crypto requires some patience and attention to detail.

CRYPTO ESSENTIALS: BLOCKCHAIN, MINERS, AND DISTRIBUTED LEDGERS

To most laymen, a cryptocurrency may represent simply a way to get rich quickly; at least so it seemed when cryptocurrencies went only up in value. Fear of missing out was surely a motive for many to invest in crypto and "hodl" them.[2]

The hype was punctured when prices crashed in 2022. Remarkably, even during this turbulent period the underlying infrastructure continued to work without problems. One needs to understand how cryptocurrencies work if one wants to gauge its future beyond the second "crypto winter" of 2022.

Blockchain and Distributed Ledgers

Every cryptocurrency is based on a "blockchain." This term describes the fact that individual transactions in the cryptocurrency are bunched together in blocks each of which can contain up to hundreds or thousands of individual transactions. These blocks are then chained together via cryptographic mechanisms. This chain of (blocks of) transactions is open-ended and the record of past transactions cannot be altered.

The reason why the record of past transactions (the blockchain) cannot be changed is that this record is held as a distributed ledger.

This ledger is simply the list of all transactions in the cryptocurrency that have ever taken place. The peculiarity of cryptocurrencies is that this list of transactions is not held by only one institution. It is public, that is, anybody willing to download hundreds of gigabytes can see all transactions from the beginning of the blockchain in 2009, which we illustrate in the section on the origins of Bitcoin.

The Bitcoin blockchain had about 500 gigabytes of data by the end of 2023 and it will continue to grow without limit, unless new technologies are adopted. Its most recent version can be downloaded at https://Bitcoin.org/en/download. Given the size of this dataset, which is text only and thus corresponds to more than 10,000 times this book stored in a PDF format, a strong background in digital technologies is required to extract useful information.[3]

Given that the blockchain is public, one might assume that there is no privacy. However, this is not the case. Anonymity is ensured because the blockchain records only "pseudonyms," that is, the equivalent of account numbers, not the identity or personal data of the holders of these accounts. These accounts are called wallets. But a wallet is just whatever holds the crucial information, namely the personal key, which allows one to interact with the blockchain.

In the traditional bank-based money system all transactions are recorded by some intermediary. The resulting ledger of past transactions is centralized and ultrasecret. The traditional system works on the basis of trust in these intermediaries (banks, credit card companies, central banks, etc.). In particular, the public must trust these intermediaries not to tamper with the record of past transactions to favor themselves or somebody else. This does not seem to be a problem. Few would suspect that their bank secretly changes the account balance or the credit card company to make unauthorized transfers. Besides, most of us check our bank statements regularly, for possible mistakes; this is another "distributed" way of ensuring the integrity of the ledger.

One should distinguish between trust that the intermediaries will not commit fraud and trust in the safety of bank accounts. The latter can be endangered even if the banker is entirely honest. Banks may make large losses on their investments, or rumors may spread that they have made them. Banking crises are a recurring feature of the existing monetary system. They have become rarer thanks to a stringent set of regulations enforced by zealous supervisors. The Great Financial Crisis of 2008–09 provided the background for the creation of Bitcoin, and historical experience suggests that this will not be the last one. This is a problem that cryptocurrencies were designed to avoid.

Miners

The central problem all cryptocurrencies need to resolve is how to verify new transactions. They need a decision-making mechanism which, without a central institution, ensures that nobody creates Bitcoins for herself and that no one can spend them twice. The solution is to enlist the "wisdom of crowds." A large number of people, acting independently verify that every new transaction is compatible with the existing record and that all transfer orders come from wallets (or accounts) with a sufficient balance. The underlying idea is that a large number of people will discover any malicious intent if they act independently. Any single verifier might have a malicious intent (e.g., to create some Bitcoins for herself), but any single attempt to cheat will fail because the transaction will be rejected by all the others.

There are two ways to do that: "Proof of Work" and "Proof of Stake." Proof of Work underpins the most popular cryptocurrency, Bitcoin. Proof of Stake (to be explained later) has been adopted by the second most important, Ethereum.

Both systems utilize the same underlying cryptographic mechanism whereby the miners have to find a "hash," that is, a string of numbers which encrypts the transactions in a special way, namely such that anybody who knows this hash can easily verify the outcome. But finding the right hash can be made very difficult. This technology was not invented for cryptocurrencies; it had been proposed early on as a defense against spam email and denial of service attacks.[4] Bitcoin combines that technology with the idea of a peer-to-peer transfer system.

Miners (anybody with the necessary hardware to execute hash operations sufficiently quickly) are paid for their effort with a reward, which consists of a certain amount of the newly created cryptocurrency awarded to the first one to find the correct hash. This creates an incentive to participate in the verification mechanism without which it would not work – and a race among miners to be the first, attracting a large number of people to join the race. One academic study found that in 2019 there were over 6,000 miners operating in 139 countries.[5] This suggests that there should be enough independent sources of verification of transactions.

In the following, we will concentrate on the dominant cryptocurrency, Bitcoin. It is better known than the generic term 'cryptocurrency': Bitcoin appears twice as often in Google Trends and seven times more often as the next most valuable cryptocurrency, Ethereum.

This cursory summary of the underlying technology clearly suggests that for most people it will always remain a black box. Nondigital natives thus need the services of exchanges and other intermediaries which offer easy-to-use interfaces to deal in Bitcoin or other cryptocurrencies. Experience has shown that the problems with crypto that emerged in the scandals of 2022 had little to do with the technology itself but rather with the fraud and self-dealing of these intermediaries, especially the crypto exchanges which allow one to buy or sell cryptocurrencies for "real" money.

Since January 2024 investors have another avenue to deal in Bitcoins, but only indirectly. There now exist a number of officially approved Exchange Traded Funds (ETFs) from large financial institutions that are linked 1:1 to its price. By buying shares in these funds one does not buy the underlying instrument. The transaction is not recorded on the blockchain, only the value of the ETF will mirror exactly the price of Bitcoin.

THE ORIGINS OF BITCOIN

The early history of Bitcoin is extraordinary. The basic idea was launched in 2008 in a nine-page note entitled "A Peer-to-Peer Electronic Cash System," signed by a person (or collective) who called himself or herself "Satoshi Nakamoto."[6] The paper was not even published, it was just sent to the mailing list of this mysterious person or collective.

It took the idea only fifteen years to span a multibillion industry and a brand name that is as widely known as the ubiquitous US dollar. The inventor or author of the paper who started this movement remains unknown. Despite many speculations, nobody has been able to link a real person to the pseudonym Satoshi under which the idea was proposed and then developed. This is surprising because the inventor would certainly gain immense fame if he or she (or the group) were to out themselves. Even stranger is the fact that the pseudonym Satoshi Nakamoto stopped contributing to the development of Bitcoin in 2011.

It is worth reading carefully the first paragraph of Satoshi's paper: "Commerce on the Internet has come to rely almost exclusively on financial institutions serving as trusted third parties to process electronic payments."[7]

The opening line motivates the endeavor with the needs of commerce on the internet. But Bitcoins are almost never used for commerce in the internet (or online shopping as we would call it today). Moreover, the existing payment modalities, usually card companies and banks as "trusted third parties," seem to work well as described in Chapters 3 and 6.

So, what is the problem? Satoshi continues arguing irreversibility is the main issue:

> While the system (of commerce on the Internet) works well enough for most transactions, it still suffers from the inherent weaknesses of the trust-based model. Completely non-reversible transactions are not really possible, since financial institutions cannot avoid mediating disputes. The cost of mediation increases

transaction costs, limiting the minimum practical transaction size and cutting off the possibility for small casual transactions, and there is a broader cost in the loss of ability to make non-reversible payments for non-reversible services. With the possibility of reversal, the need for trust spreads …

What is needed is an electronic payment system based on cryptographic proof instead of trust, allowing any two willing parties to transact directly with each other without the need for a trusted third party. Transactions that are computationally impractical to reverse would protect sellers from fraud, and routine escrow mechanisms could easily be implemented to protect buyers.[8]

After expounding the general idea, Satoshi needed the help of experienced programmers to create the entire program on which the system was to run. This took some time. But once the program had been debugged it was ready to use. By early 2009 the ledger was up and running. The first entry on the ledger dates January 9, 2009, when Satoshi awarded himself the first 50 Bitcoins. This historic entry is shown here as a "coinbase" transaction.[9]

Hash
0e3e2357e806b6cdb1f70b54c3a3a17b6714ee1f0e68bebb44a74b1efd
512098
Time stamp 2009–01–09 03:54

Input	Output
COINBASE	*12c6DSiU4Rq3P4ZxziKxzrL5LmMBrzjrJX*
(Newly Generated Coins)	*50.00000000 BTC*

This entry just means that the wallet "12c6DSi U4Rq3P4ZxziKxzrL5LmMBrzjrJX" received 50 Bitcoins because its owner solved the puzzle to "mine" this first block (which contained just one transaction).

The first transaction from one person to another came when three days later (January 12, 2009, block 170) Satoshi sent ten of his newly minted Bitcoins to Hal Finney, the programmer who had invented the Proof of Work method and had then helped him to write and debug the source code.[10]

| 50.00000000 BTC |
| *Hash* |
| *f4184fc596403b9d638783cf57adfe4c75c605f6356fbc91338530e9831e* |
| *9e16* |
| *Time stamp: 2009–01–12 04:30* |

Input	Output
12cbQLTFMXRnSzktFkuoG3e HoMeFtpTu3S	*1Q2TWHE3GMdB6BZKafqwxXtWAW gFt5Jvm3*
50.00000000 BTC	*10.00000000 BTC*
	12cbQLTFMXRnSzktFkuoG3eHoMeF tpTu3S
	40.00000000 BTC

This first transaction illustrates one seldom-mentioned feature of how the instrument works. One can infer the initial holding of the sending wallet when one receives some Bitcoins from a known source. This is a consequence of the fact that the holdings of the sending wallet (left-hand side of the message) are also recorded on the ledger. For example, in the case of the first transaction mentioned here, Satoshi had announced to Hall Finney that he would receive 10 Bitcoins from him. Hall Finney could then check on the Bitcoin ledger the entry which had awarded him 10 Bitcoins. But the record from this transaction also contains the address of the wallet from which these Bitcoins had come. This implies that Hall Finney could find out how many Bitcoins Satoshi had in the wallet from which he sent BTC 10 (it was 50). Moreover, from that point on he could follow all further transactions of this wallet of Satoshi – and Satoshi could do the same for Hall Finney's original receiving wallet (the first one on the right-hand side of the message). Other people could of course also see all the transactions of these two wallets. But unless either Satoshi or Hall Finney had told them, they could not know who the owners were. It is this "pseudo-anonymity" of Bitcoin that many users value, but it is also a veil that can be lifted by law enforcement agencies as we recount later.

If the sender and receiver value privacy, they have an incentive to change wallets after almost every transaction. One way to change wallet is for the owner of Bitcoins to create a new wallet and then transfer the balance to another one controlled by the same person. For example, the Bitcoin ledger shows that there were further transfers from the wallet from which Satoshi sent the first 10 Bitcoins to Hall Finney. But Hall Finney could not know whether these transfers went to wallets that were also controlled by Satoshi or were genuine transfers to other, third, parties.

For the first year, most entries on the ledger are boring as they record only the BTC 50 rewards for the few miners of the day. All these initial rewards had no economic value as the algorithm was known only to a few "geeks" who supported the idea of creating a currency that would work without (in reality almost without) human intervention.

The attentive reader will notice that the sending wallet, the one ending with Tu3S, appears also on the right-hand side. This illustrates a peculiarity: The input must always equal the entire holding of the sending wallet. When sending BTC 10 from a wallet containing BTC 50, Satoshi thus had to indicate where the balance (also called "change") should go. In this case he wanted the rest to remain in the sending wallet. This is why the output specifies BTC 40 for the sending wallet. This peculiarity becomes important if one wants to correctly interpret the data on the value of transactions. In this early transaction, the usual statistics would indicate a turnover of BTC 50 when in reality only BTC 10 changed owner. The measured transaction volume is thus likely to vastly exaggerate the true one. Moreover, the need to indicate the address for the "change" increases the size of all messages and thus contributes to the low throughput of the entire system.

Bitcoin's original intention was to create a means of payment used also for small transactions. It must thus have been disappointing to its inventor that, for the first year of its existence, Bitcoin was mined and exchanged only within a small group of aficionados. Some people posted indicative values early on their websites, but these were based on the estimated cost of the (then small) power required for the mining, which, at the time, could be done by a simple personal computer at home.[11] It therefore took some time (over a year) before somebody actually was able to use it to pay for something real. The first case was famously Laszlo Hanyecz who, as described earlier, proudly announced on May 22, 2010, that he had been able to order his dinner by exchanging BTC 10,000 for two pizzas. Today this amount would be worth hundreds of millions of dollars or euros.

Looking closer at this iconic episode, the celebrations over Pizza Day seem exaggerated. First of all, it took Laszlo some time (four days) to find somebody willing to take his Bitcoin, which at the time was known only to computer aficionados. Second, Laszlo did not really "buy" the pizzas from Papa John's pizzeria. He just found somebody else (nineteen-year-old Jeremy Sturdivant) who perhaps sold Laszlo's 10,000 Bitcoins for 40 dollars and in exchange ordered the pizzas to be delivered to Laszlo. Nobody knows how much he paid for the order. It probably was much less than 40 dollars. For sure, he did not pay in Bitcoin.

Today the situation is not that different. Granted, only a fraction of a Bitcoin would be required for the value of two pizzas. But even today it remains difficult to order an ordinary pizza paying with Bitcoin; besides, the transaction would cost far more than the pizza, as explained later. No pizzeria advertises its price list in Bitcoin as it would have to change its prices almost by the minute. Any holder of the instrument would thus need to do something similar to what Laszlo had to do then: Find somebody else to exchange Bitcoins for real money, which could then be used to buy pizzas.

Anybody trying to use Bitcoin for shopping would have to first establish a digital wallet. This would be very difficult for anybody unfamiliar with basic programming. Today many websites provide simple user-friendly interfaces to buy Bitcoin via a credit card transfer or a normal bank account. But this is costly and defeats the original purpose of crypto, namely dispensing with intermediaries.

There are even automated teller machines (ATMs) to buy Bitcoin with normal cash. Their number has risen exponentially to about 40,000 by the end of 2022,[12] a big number but only about one-hundredth of the over 3 million of ATMs. Moreover, the transaction fees for buying Bitcoin at an ATM are high, in the 12–20 percent range.[13] Dealing with normal cash is much cheaper.

The key question is then whether the merchant has a Bitcoin wallet. If yes, the transfer from the buyer to the seller would be relatively straightforward, but subject to the time delay and costs described more in detail later.

These continuing difficulties in using this instrument in ordinary life did not dent its popularity. The modest initial purpose was superseded by a different narrative, that of Bitcoin as a libertarian ideal of a currency without any control by governments or other potentially hostile actors.

We do not want to enter into this hype and the ideological discussions about freedom from government control; we expound our tentative ideas on this in Chapter 11. A constructive discussion about the pros and cons of cryptocurrencies needs to start with a closer look at the substance of how cryptocurrencies work in practice and whether they could perform the key functions of money.

THE FUNCTIONING OF A DISTRIBUTED LEDGER

The main selling point of cryptocurrencies in general is that they can work without "trusted intermediaries." Relying on banks for transfers and credit card companies is not perceived as a problem for most of us. We suspect that most readers are not even aware of the, sometimes complicated, transactions among banks, card companies, and other intermediaries which are triggered when we put in a card number to pay for a movie ticket or the latest must-have gadget sold on the internet.

But for the original tightly knit Bitcoin community, avoiding intermediaries was one important motivation. Moreover, creating a system that is secure without intermediaries represents an intellectual challenge. The innovation proposed by Satoshi Nakamoto thus needs to be taken seriously.

As mentioned earlier, distributed ledger and blockchain are often used interchangeably. But the second describes better the essential elements of Bitcoin, namely a chain of blocks (of transactions) linked one to another from the first one. The full chain thus contains all transactions from the first to the last one. The full chain of all transactions is publicly available – for anyone able to download a file of 500 gigabytes (as of end of 2023). Given that the full chain, with all past transactions, is widely available it is practically impossible to tamper with. Anybody who claims to have found a different version of the blockchain would immediately be contradicted by all the others.

But how does one decide what transactions are to be added to the blockchain? For Bitcoin it is the "node," or rather the miner who wins the race to solve the mathematical problem, the hash, which validates the current block of transactions and adds it to the long chain of past blocks. As mentioned earlier, this is called Proof of Work, under which each node essentially competes with its computing power. The greater the computing power, the more likely that a node succeeds in hashing the current block thus obtaining a reward in the currency of the system (a number of Bitcoins). The other nodes signify acceptance of the result if they resume working on the next block. If more than one-half of the other miners accept the block, it is taken as approved and work on the next block can begin.

BITCOIN'S TRANSACTION STRUCTURE

How movements of Bitcoin are recorded on the blockchain is peculiar, as illustrated earlier by the example of the first transaction on the Bitcoin. When Satoshi had a wallet containing BTC 50 and wanted to send BTC 10 to his friend and helper Hall Finney, he had to send the remaining BTC 40 somewhere else, either to his own wallet or to somebody else. If he had not done so, he would have lost the "change." Satoshi was of course aware of this as he encoded it himself.

Very often the transaction path gets even more complicated. Many people use automated programs to generate new wallets to empty the current wallet when they make a transfer and send the change to a new wallet that they "own" (owning in the blockchain world means having access to the private key). This technique is particularly popular with anybody who wants to dispose of illicit gains using Bitcoin. The first step is to put funds into a Bitcoin wallet and then make a series of small transactions from this wallet to numerous new wallets, a step which can be repeated several times. As will be discussed later there now exist organizations which have automated this process and offer "tumbler" services which promise to make Bitcoins untraceable. Makarov and Schoar show that up to 90 percent of all transactions are of this type,[14] which implies that the economically relevant transaction volume on Bitcoin is much smaller than appears at first sight.

The transaction data analyzed here for March 30, 2022 (a typical, normal day), confirms this pattern. Ordering transactions by size one finds 120 transactions valued at over 1,322 billion dollars (then about 20,000 Bitcoins). However, the amounts exchanged in these transactions were much smaller than appears because, in reality, the wallet from which these transactions originated belonged probably to an exchange that made these transactions on behalf of its clients. The balance of this wallet diminished over the course of the day, but only little (by about 40 million dollars) considering its starting level, with the average change (which indicates the real transaction value) of about 33,000 dollars (40 million divided by 120). This example shows how the blockchain records extremely large amounts for transactions while the value actually transferred is an order of magnitude smaller. This renders it even more difficult to gauge the usefulness of Bitcoin as a means of transaction.

These peculiarities of the recording of transactions have important implications on whether Bitcoin could be used as a vehicle for many daily transactions.

The code implies that each block could contain up to 4,000 transactions. Given that blocks arrive in intervals of approximately ten minutes, the rate of transactions is thus often given as about seven (4,000/600 = 6.66) per second. But in reality, the average block contains mostly less than 2,000 transactions (in 2021 the average was 1,660), implying that the average speed of the entire Bitcoin system in reality is only around 3.5 transactions per second (1,660/600).

In comparison, major card companies handle thousands of transactions per second. Moreover, the upper end of the range of 3.5–7 transactions per second represents the maximum speed of Bitcoin, whereas other payment networks have not only much higher average transactions per second but also even higher peak values (i.e., on Fridays for retail payment networks). The Visa network processes on average about 1,700 transactions per second, hundreds of times more than Bitcoin, but claims to be able to process up to 65,000 transactions per second, 10,000 times more than Bitcoin.[15] In China Alibaba has reported a peak of over 500,000 transactions per second on a single day,[16] equivalent to roughly 100,000 times the throughput possible for Bitcoin.

There are also physical limits to the speed at which blockchain transactions can be recorded. Electronic messages travel in fiber optic cables at about two-thirds of the speed of light in vacuum (only 200,000 kilometers per second). This implies that a signal traveling between two nodes at opposite positions of the globe would need about one-tenth of a second – often more, because the signal might be routed via a satellite or might be held up for fractions of a second in some server. It thus takes necessarily some time before the thousands of transactions in a block can be packed in one block that is then received and validated by thousands of miners.

On top of this, one has to take into account the cumbersome way in which "change" is recorded on the blockchain, which doubles the number of any true transactions that have to go through the system at any time. The blockchain technology is thus not competitive with existing card payment and even bank transfer systems.

At first sight, the low rate of transactions per second could easily be improved by increasing the block size or by reducing the time interval between the recording of new blocks. However, these two approaches do not resolve the problem in practice.

Reducing the interval of time between the recording of two blocks increases the risk that new blocks will be rejected because not enough nodes have already received the news that there is a new block. Some researchers have argued that reducing the time interval could even lower transaction speed because of the increased frequency of rejected blocks.[17] Increasing the size of each block (fixed at one megabyte) would also reduce transmission speeds, thus leading to similar problems of not all nodes working on the same information.

This conundrum illustrates the so-called scalability problem of the Proof of Work approach to validating transactions. The bigger the number of participants, the more difficult it becomes to ensure that everybody is working on the same blockchain (which itself is getting bigger and bigger, surpassing 500 gigabytes as of end of 2023). There have been many technical proposals to increase the transaction throughput of Bitcoin's blockchain, for example, by reducing the amount of information from each transaction. But all the technical tweaking cannot escape the fundamental tension between the costs that an increasing number of nodes creates and the desire to substitute trusted intermediaries with the wisdom of crowds.[18]

Why 21 Million Bitcoin?

One big selling point of Bitcoin is that the total amount ever to be mined is fixed at 21 million. However, the Bitcoin documentation does not say anywhere that only 21 million can be mined. Instead, this limit can be derived from the rule that the reward for each block starts at BTC 50 per block and then halves every 210,000 blocks (it takes about four years to reach 210,000 blocks since only

144 are mined each day). The total number of blocks is thus equal to 210,000 times the sum of (50 + 25 + 12.5 + 6.25 + ...). The sum of the sequence starting with 50 but then halving periodically is equal to 100. This implies that the total number of Bitcoins ever mined will be 210,000 times 100, or 21 million.

This calculation only leads to the question of why the halving should take place every 210,000 blocks. In the end, one can only conclude that the limit on the total number of Bitcoins does not really matter and was chosen in a totally arbitrary manner.

BITCOIN AS A MEDIUM OF EXCHANGE

In Chapter 7 we documented how much the digitalization of payment systems has reduced the unit cost of making a payment via a card or an app. We have shown earlier that there are inherent limitations on how many transactions can be made each hour or day. But this limited number should at least be cheap and quick given that cryptocurrencies are totally digital and do not require expensive point-of-sales terminals.

However, this is not the case. Transactions on the major cryptocurrencies are slow and expensive. The blockchain technology has some inherent limitations which lead to this result.

Speed

On the blockchain, transactions are added and validated in bunches or blocks, not one by one because it would be too expensive to validate every single transaction. The Bitcoin blockchain is programmed to allow one new block, on average, every ten minutes (or about 600 seconds). This implies immediately that a Bitcoin transaction cannot be quicker than ten minutes. It can last longer if there is a queue of transactions waiting to be validated. Ten minutes is certainly quicker than the day it might take for a bank transfer to arrive in another bank account, as is the case today for small transfers within the European Single Euro Payments Area system – unless one uses the instant settlement modality offered at a small cost in online applications of most banks. PayPal and similar peer-to-peer transfer systems already allow instantaneous transactions.

Moreover, the person making a transfer of Bitcoin cannot be certain ex ante when exactly it will go through because miners can choose which transactions they want to validate. If there is a queue of transactions waiting to be validated (called mempool), miners will validate first those promising a higher fee (per byte). There is thus no certainty of when a transaction submitted to the blockchain will be validated. If the sender offers a high fee, there is virtual certainty that the transaction will be included in the next block, which should not be more than ten minutes away. Offering a high fee might not be a problem for larger transactions, but for smaller ones the fee could eat up a sizeable part of the amount to be transmitted.[19] Moreover, it is difficult to know beforehand what amount of fee will ensure that the transactions will go through with the next block.

The fact that a Bitcoin transaction can only be validated (and thus made irreversible) with a variable delay makes it difficult to use Bitcoin for everyday shopping. Customers will not be willing to wait for ten minutes at the cashier of the supermarket or their preferred boutique for the transaction to be validated. The same applies to online shopping: If the customer wants to pay in Bitcoin she would have to wait for several minutes for the validation. Moreover, most merchants require up to six rounds of validation before considering a Bitcoin payment final, implying that it might take up to an hour before the purchase goes through.[20] By contrast, with the existing cards and apps, the validation is instantaneous.

This problem of speed cannot really be solved as long as transactions are processed in "blocks" which follow each other with a certain time lag. There are of course some types of transactions, typically larger ones, like buying a car, for which speed is not essential. But one has to ask whether it makes sense to create a separate payment system for these larger and necessarily less frequent type of transactions.

Ethereum, a rival of Bitcoin, has managed this problem by making the blocks smaller, which enables the system to reduce the time span between two blocks to about fifteen seconds. It is thus possible to increase the transaction speed of cryptocurrencies, but there remains an inherent limit from the bunching of transactions in blocks.

Even aside from speed, cryptocurrencies like Bitcoin face the problem of high costs per transaction.

Fees and Other Costs

There are two costs – one is visible to the consumer, the other not. The visible cost consists of the fees. The part that is not visible consists of the rewards to miners for validation – and it is much larger.

The system of transaction fees of Bitcoin is ingenious and self-regulating. But for the simple consumer it introduces an unwarranted source of uncertainty. At first sight, it seems to give consumers more choice since when initiating a transfer on the Bitcoin blockchain one can indicate what fee to offer to miners for the validation. However, more choice also means more uncertainty. It is as if somebody making a credit card purchase could choose what fee should be paid to the credit card company and that the authorization would then take longer the lower the fee offered, but the precise outcome is uncertain. Having to make this choice for every purchase would make the process much more cumbersome, especially when dealing with many small routing transactions.

Moreover, a higher fee does not automatically guarantee a quicker validation because this depends mainly on the size of the mempool and partially on the strategy of the miners, that is, whether they only take into account the transaction fee offered when deciding about the priority to give to different transactions. The size of the mempool varies over time. The fees demanded by miners thus also vary over time in a manner that is difficult to predict for the uninitiated. In 2021 it was often above 20 dollars. But during most of 2022 and 2023, the average fee was around 2 dollars (per transaction), with the median even lower, at 70 cents. However, when Bitcoin trading surged with the anticipation of the approval by the

US Securities Exchange Commission of Bitcoin ETF, the transaction fee increased to over 10 dollars.[21]

Mining Rewards

There is another, hidden, cost element that is much larger. It derives from the fact that each block must be validated by miners, who at present receive BTC 6.25 per block. Each block can theoretically contain up to 4,000 transactions. But this figure constitutes only an upper limit. In reality, as mentioned above, the block size fluctuated in 2022 around 1,600. This implies that the miners receive a reward equal to 6.25/1,600 or about 1/250 of one Bitcoin per transaction.[22]

These calculations can be verified on a normal laptop. Your authors downloaded all transactions for one randomly chosen day (March 30, 2022). The Bitcoin network validated that day over 288,000 transactions in about 150 different blocks (thus a little less than 2,000 transactions per block). Miners received that day BTC 975 (6.25 per block), which were worth 45 million dollars (at 46,995 dollars/Bitcoin, the price of that day). Dividing this sum by the 288,000 transactions yields 159.6 dollars per transaction. This seems to be a typical figure. The website of Bitcoin shows that the average reward to miners per transaction has fluctuated with the price of Bitcoin around 150 to 200 dollars over the last years.[23]

The miners' rewards do not constitute a cost to society. When a miner receives a Bitcoin and sells it on an exchange, she receives only a transfer from the buyer. However, the real resources (mostly energy) that the miners expended to obtain their reward represent a cost that cannot be neglected. As discussed later, a very conservative estimate suggests that miners have to spend about one-half of their reward in electricity to power and cool their hardware. This implies that the social cost of each transaction would be on average about 1/500 of the value of one Bitcoin.

The cost of such a small fraction (2/1,000) of one Bitcoin could be regarded as negligible when the price was low. But this is no longer the case today. Our rule of thumb suggests that if miners expect an average price of 40,000 dollars/Bitcoin, they should be willing to spend about 80 dollars (=2/1,000 of 40,000) on their efforts. As this calculation is conservative, they would still make a small profit if the price goes to 30,000 dollars/Bitcoin because in this case the block reward would still be 195,000 dollars (6.5 × 30,000) more than enough to cover their costs of 160,000 dollars.

This implies that under these circumstances (i.e., when the price of Bitcoin expected by miners is around 30,000–40,000 dollars) for any transaction below 80 dollars the implicit expenditure of miners would be higher than the value of the transaction itself. Making many small transactions with Bitcoin is thus extremely costly, certainly much costlier than today's card and bank-based systems in advanced countries. As the price of Bitcoin tumbled in 2022, these costs had to come down, even pushing some miners into bankruptcy, with the subsequent recovery of the price new miners entered the market.[24]

Somewhat surprisingly, the data from the blockchain show that many small transactions do take place. The median size of transactions drawn from the random day chosen as mentioned earlier was only 625 dollars, meaning that for that day half of all transactions were below this value. The transaction size which occurred most often (technically the mode) was even lower, 48 dollars, and lower than our estimate of the true transaction cost.

The explanation is simple: Those making a transfer of Bitcoin do not see the full cost. The blockchain records only the transfer, minus the relatively small transaction fee mentioned earlier, which is usually proportional to the size of the message incorporating the transfer, rather than the value of the transfer itself. The rewards for the miners are paid by those who are willing to buy the new Bitcoins allocated to the successful miner. In this narrow sense, Bitcoin relies on a Ponzi scheme: The blockchain can grow only if the miners are rewarded for their efforts by the funds flowing in from new investors.

Gold is also held because people speculate about its future price. However, by contrast to Bitcoin, gold has some intrinsic value, as jewelry and in some high-tech applications (a typical smartphone contains about 3 percent of a gram in gold, worth a bit less than 2 dollars). About 10 percent of gold production goes to these industrial uses and another half ends up as jewelry, leaving only about a third for investment and speculative purposes.[25]

A key feature of Bitcoin is thus that most of the cost of executing transactions is not borne by those initiating them. At first sight, this feature is similar for credit card payments. The major card companies have made the use of their cards free for the consumer but then charge the merchant significant fees, as explained in Chapter 7. These fees then pay for the point-of-sales terminals and the entire system of verification set up by the credit card companies. However, the "hidden" fees for credit cards pale in comparison to the hidden social cost of transfers with Bitcoin.

The fees applied by credit card companies might be too high due to the market power these companies have (the market is dominated by only a handful of them). But they appear very low if compared to the transaction costs of Bitcoin. Credit card fees, even at the upper range of 2–3 percent (see Chapter 7) would amount to only 70 cents to a dollar when applied to the average credit card purchase of 35 dollars, less than a hundredth of the cost of a transaction on the Bitcoin blockchain. A further difference between Bitcoin as a transfer system and a credit card system is that in the case of Bitcoin most of the cost arises in the form of energy to run and cool special chips whereas credit card systems involve many other cost items, including the cost of terminals and software to detect fraud. This is why in terms of pure energy expenditure Bitcoin performs even worse than the 100:1 ratio calculated here.[26]

The cost of Bitcoin transfers is thus much too high to be competitive with existing payment systems. As a result, many other cryptocurrencies have been created, which promise lower cost and higher speed. However, these alternatives have so far remained of limited importance. One reason for this could be the workings of Metcalfe's law, according to which the value of a network increases with the square of the number of its users.[27] Some research has shown that Metcalfe's law seems to have a strong influence on the market capitalization of different cryptocurrencies.[28] One explanation why Bitcoin remains the most important cryptocurrency could thus be a legacy/network effect. It remains on top because everybody knows it already and can assume that others know it as well.

THE PRIVATE AND SOCIAL COST OF MINING

As mentioned already, cryptocurrencies receive much criticism because of the energy requirements of mining.

The overall size of the Bitcoin mining industry can be estimated from the rules governing the Bitcoin blockchain. As mentioned earlier, over 900 Bitcoins are mined every day. (One block every ten minutes implies a daily total of $24 \times 6 = 144$ blocks. The reward for each block is currently 6.25 Bitcoins, a total of $144 \times 6.25 = 900$ Bitcoins per day.[29]) This is an approximation because each day might have a slightly different number of blocks, as the time interval between the validation of new blocks is not exactly fixed at ten minutes but can vary widely around this value (between one minute and over twenty minutes).

With between 900 and 1,000 blocks mined each day, the rewards for miners can be substantial. At a price of a Bitcoin of around 60,000 dollars (as in 2024), the total rewards earned by all miners each day are worth about 54 million to 60 million per day or close to 20 billion dollars per year. No wonder Bitcoin mining has become a serious industrial activity. In 2022 the Bitcoin price temporarily dropped to about 15,000 dollars, which still left about 5 billion dollars annually.

The rewards to miners are of course not the same as the cost of mining. If mining were a competitive industry, one would expect that miners would be ready to spend this amount to mine Bitcoin. In this case, the reward would be equal to the cost (plus a small profit margin). But given the high concentration of the mining industry and the risk involved due to the high variability of the price, documented by Makarov and Schoar,[30] it seems more realistic to assume that miners demand a substantial profit rate to cover the risks and their fixed costs.

A very conservative estimate of the costs involved suggests a very generous profit rate of 100 percent. The overall rewards of 12 billion would then be split between 6 billion dollars in running costs and 6 billion dollars for buying equipment plus a substantial profit. Most of the running costs are for power (mainly cooling the processors). If one assumes that miners pay only 5 cents per kilowatt-hour (households in Europe pay usually more than 20 cents), it follows that they have bought about 120 terawatt-hours per year of electricity, more than the entire power consumption of a small country, such as Norway or Denmark.[31] Other estimates based on the hardware requirements for Bitcoin mining arrive at a similar order of magnitude.[32]

This calculation assumes of course that miners have to pay at least a modest price for the electricity they consume. But this is not always the case. For example, during the rainy season, the dams in some regions of China produce more power than can be used locally, and the energy goes wasted. This is one of the reasons why for some time China became the most important place for Bitcoin mining, but with strong seasonal variations. The Chinese authorities banned Bitcoin mining in 2021, but this does not mean mining stopped. The miners simply packed up and installed their equipment elsewhere. For example, in Siberia where the residents of some regions benefit from ultralow electricity prices, many have taken up Bitcoin mining.

Among climate activists, Bitcoin has acquired a dirty reputation because of its high power consumption.[33] Enthusiasts argue that miners use electricity that would otherwise be wasted and that in some cases the mining activity has useful side benefits. For example, during the winter in Siberia, the heat produced by the mining machines is actually welcome in some households (who pay only the equivalent of one cent per kilowatt-hour).[34]

Taking a look at the costs involved in two potential "competitors" to Bitcoin as an asset might help to gain a perspective on the overall waste of resources from Bitcoin mining of around 10 billion to 12 billion dollars.

First, cash. The original ambition of Satoshi was to create a peer-to-peer "electronic cash" system. One should thus compare the cost of running Bitcoin to the cost of supplying the economy with currency. The Federal Reserve, which provides the world's leading currency, spends about 1 billion per annum to replace worn-out banknotes. This is less than one-tenth of the amount spent on Bitcoin mining.

Second, gold. This is another asset that does not yield any interest and dividend with gold holders speculating on rising prices. Gold production amounts to about 3,000 tons per annum, worth about 200 billion dollars, at 2,000 dollars per ounce or 62 million dollars per (metric) ton. The cost of gold mining is estimated to be about 1,000 dollars per ounce,[35] or about one-half of the price (early 2022) of 2,000 dollars per ounce. Gold mining thus seems to operate on similar margins as Bitcoin mining. This leads to an estimate of annual mining costs of gold of 100 billion dollars, eight to ten times more than Bitcoin. Real-world mining is also very energy-intensive but maybe somewhat less than Bitcoin mining since the workers (the real-world miners) are part of the cost. But even if gold mining were only about one-half as energy-intensive as Bitcoin mining, worldwide gold production would require about four to five times more energy than Bitcoin mining.

But if one compares the annual mining cost to the value of the asset, the advantage of Bitcoin disappears. The market value of the 19 million Bitcoins created so far amounted at its peak to 1,200 billion dollars (at a price of 60,000 dollars/bitcoin). The market value of all the gold mined so far (estimated at about 200,000 tons[36]) amounts to about 12,000 billion dollars,[37] ten times larger than Bitcoin at its peak and thirty times the Bitcoin market cap as of the end of 2022.

The real question is not so much the emissions of greenhouse gases associated with mining but whether the costs of mining can be justified by some tangible social benefits (as opposed to the private gain of having one Bitcoin).[38] Finding these benefits is exceedingly difficult for Bitcoin, as for any cryptocurrency, because the number of transactions and their speed have inherent limitations. By contrast, cash is used daily in countless transactions, and gold is used in industry and even as jewelry it yields some benefits. Moreover, gold is much more durable than the stored bits which make up a Bitcoin. Gold has survived thousands of years. Bitcoin is unlikely to survive, at least in its present form, thousands of years of rapid technological progress. Other, more efficient, technologies than blockchain are likely to arise in the long run.

Some argue that Bitcoin energy consumption is "only" equivalent to that of US data centers or US household tumble dryers. However, data centers deliver a measurable service and tumble dryers deliver, well, dry clothes. It remains difficult to find a tangible benefit of Bitcoin; perhaps one should compare Bitcoin trading more to gambling, another activity whose social value is difficult to measure.

The high energy consumption engendered by both the mining of gold and Bitcoin is a function of their high prices. The price of gold had been fixed at 35 dollars per ounce for a long time. Mining companies would expend far less energy and other expenses if the price were still at that level (instead of the 2,000 dollars/ounce of today). The same applies to Bitcoin. There would be no mining farms if its price were still only a few dollars per Bitcoin.

In this sense, both gold and Bitcoin have become victims of their own success.

ETHEREUM: PROOF OF STAKE TO SAVE ENERGY

Ethereum, the second most important cryptocurrency, has undergone a profound remake in 2022. Up to that point, it faced cost and energy waste problems similar to Bitcoin. Its cost structure was similar in that there was both a reward for validating a block (2 ether, worth between 6,000 and 7,000 dollars at 2021 values) plus a "gas" fee per transaction which influences the order by which miners prioritize transactions. As for Bitcoin the block reward was not visible to the user, and it was also of a similar order of magnitude, with a cost per transaction of around 90–100 dollars, leading miners to expend a lot of energy on Ethereum mining.

The part of the transaction cost which users can see, because they have to pay it directly, is also higher for Ethereum. But this cost varies greatly over time, depending on network use and on the priority the user gives to its transactions. High-priority transactions pay a higher "gas fee" than normal ones.

In September 2022, Ethereum underwent a profound change, called the "merge," under which the blockchain transitioned to a new confirmation mechanism called "Proof of Stake." Under Proof of Work, miners compete in solving a complicated mathematical problem, which requires a lot of energy. Under Proof of Stake, there are no miners but only "validators" who acquire their status by depositing a certain amount of the cryptocurrency (32 ether in this case). This deposit is called a "stake," and it freezes this amount of the Ethereum cryptocurrency (ether, symbol ETH) for one year. The validators have to be able to run the necessary software and be available to perform the validation when called upon. Validators are called upon randomly and are penalized if they do not react immediately. Being a validator for the Ethereum blockchain represents thus a considerable commitment. Blocks are then approved if they have received repeated positive attestations from validators representing at least two-thirds of the total staked Ethereum.

By eliminating the need for miners, Ethereum cut the energy needed to run the network by over 99 percent. One important criticism of cryptocurrencies was thus addressed. However, the overall transaction costs remain high because gas fees remain, and the validators are allocated rewards proportional to the stake they have put up. These rewards are determined through a complex formula which rewards different types of activity at different rates depending also on the overall amount staked. The rewards also depend on the total amount staked, falling if more people stake their ETH holdings. As of the end of 2022, the interest rate on staking was about 7 percent. It then went down to a little over 3 percent in 2024.[39]

Since staking requires hardware and considerable expertise, most staking takes place via intermediaries, which accept deposits of ETH from the public and then pool them in larger stakes. These larger pools benefit from economies of scale. This has led to considerable concentration in ETH staking, with the five largest staking pools accounting for 66 percent of the total. If these five institutions were to band together, they could control the network and manipulate individual transactions.

To guard against this eventuality (highly unlikely since these institutions would use their stakes and reputation) and as a last defense the Ethereum Proof of Stake also contains this proviso: "the community can resort to social recovery of an honest chain if a 51% attack were to overcome the crypto-economic defenses."[40] This means that on the Ethereum any transaction could be reversed; no transaction can be considered really final because "the community" could always decide to invalidate it. This is the opposite of what the whole crypto-idea was supposed to achieve, namely a record of transactions which could never be changed.

The switch of Ethereum to Proof of Stake has not made this cryptocurrency more user-friendly for time-sensitive transactions since it has increased the time needed for a transaction to be confirmed. A new block is mined every few seconds, but the Beacon chain takes up to ninety-six iterations to confirm a transaction, which amounts to approximately fifteen minutes.[41] This makes Ethereum unsuitable for transactions that require real-time reactions, as everyday shopping. For the proponents of Ethereum, the lengthy confirmation time was not a problem since the purpose of Ethereum was never to become a means of transactions but rather to allow financial contracts to be executed on a blockchain, because it can contain not only information about transactions but also other programming pieces.

Ethereum thus came from the start with a more ambitious aim than providing a new form of money, namely to provide an alternative to many traditional finance instruments.[42]

Programmable Money

The distributed ledger of Bitcoin was designed to contain all transactions, and only data about the transactions, making sure that transactions are irreversible once they have been executed. Some blockchains have been designed in a way that additional code can be inserted which makes the transfer conditional upon the occurrence of certain events. The Ethereum blockchain has this facility.

The simple innovation of allowing for the insertion of additional code in a transaction is called a "smart contract" or sometimes "programmable money." The purported advantage of smart contracts is that the contract itself cannot be changed and that execution is automatic and irreversible. Programmable money has become one of the most frequently mentioned use cases for cryptocurrencies as it has become apparent that, given their high transaction costs and extremely unstable value, cryptocurrency cannot be used in normal online shopping.

However, smart contracts seem of little utility for ordinary transactions. Online shopping involves in most cases parties who know each other. The consumer knows Amazon, and Amazon knows the consumer, has usually her credit card details, and must know her address to deliver the merchandise. The potential to conclude contracts between parties that do not know each other is thus of little practical importance.

Smart contracts are thus mostly self-referential:[43] They are only useful to make transactions with crypto assets, mainly with stablecoins.

Smart contracts would face serious practical problems were one to try to use them in real-world cases, whether online shopping or other online business. A contract must contain provisions for many contingencies, many "what happens if." These contingencies must be clearly spelt out in the contract, but this cannot be done in plain

English, or "natural language" as computer experts call it. It must be done in some programming language. This implies that only specialists versed in bespoke computer programming languages will be able to read smart contracts. Few managers and even fewer normal consumers have this background.

An even more serious obstacle is that a smart contract cannot refer to anything outside the blockchain world. For example, a smart contract cannot be used for the purchase or sale of real-world goods. For any practical application a smart contract thus needs "validators," independent instances which could give the input needed for the execution of the smart contract. For example, a freight delivery company could certify that the merchandise has been delivered, triggering automatic payment in the form of a transfer of Bitcoin. But what happens if the delivery person made a mistake and left the new pair of jogging shoes at the wrong address? What happens if the receiver thinks the shoes do not correspond to the online advertisement? That would make the contract more complex and would require the intervention of additional validators.

A smart contract which needs the intervention of real-world validators is unlikely to be superior to a normal contract.

Some have argued that smart contracts could be useful for the case of many small payments, such as fractionated electricity bills. But this case can easily be dealt with by either bunching payments or, as often done in Europe, by authorizing the electricity company to withdraw the amounts due from the bank account of the client. This requires of course that the consumer trusts the company not to abuse this power. In reality, this is not a problem since utilities are regulated and tightly supervised. The trusted third party is in this case the state in the form of consumer protection agencies.

Smart contracts will remain a niche product for financial or speculative transactions within the crypto world but is of little importance for the wider economy or ordinary citizens. Crypto is unlikely to radically transform finance, but it could provide a catalyst for change in some niche areas.[44]

ARE CRYPTOCURRENCIES SECURE?

The best short answer would be "it depends." Experience so far has shown that blockchain technology itself works well, but the wider sector remains vulnerable. This is hardly surprising. Any new technology has to mature; only time will tell whether the initial imperfections can be ironed out.

From time to time, one reads about reports that hundreds of millions worth of cryptocurrencies have been stolen or misappropriated.[45] How is this possible given the "crypto(graphic)" basis of distributed ledger technology?

There are two ways this can happen. The "old fashioned" way of fraud and theft or the uniquely crypto way of mounting a 51 percent attack. Let us start with the latter.

Fifty-One Percent Attack

The selling point of the distributed ledger technology is that it relies on the active participation of many validators or miners who cannot collude because they work all on their own. The condition that miners act independently of each other is critical for the safety of the validation process. In the Proof of Work approach, a new block is accepted if more than one-half of the validators accept it. It thus becomes very difficult for a malicious external agent to subvert the process when there are thousands of active miners. To subvert the blockchain and steal existing balances the attacker would have to control more than one-half of the mining capacity (not necessarily more than one-half of the number of miners). This is called a "51 percent attack." For large established cryptocurrencies like Bitcoin it seems at present very costly (but not impossible) to assemble the mining capacity to dominate the blockchain. Moreover, it would be exceedingly difficult to cash out on the theoretically hundreds of billions of dollars which such an attack would yield as law enforcement authorities all over the world would be hunting for the perpetrator and few would accept Bitcoins once news about the attack spreads.

The payoff from such an attack would thus most probably be much lower than the cost of organizing it.

However, the cost of organizing an attack on smaller cryptocurrencies is much smaller, as the latter promise only lower rewards and thus have much less mining power invested in their validation process. To make matters worse, it is now possible to rent the capacity to mine since the mining operations are very similar across different cryptocurrencies. There exists even a website which provides a measure of the cost of a 51 percent attack for many smaller cryptocurrencies (i.e., the cost of renting one hour of computing power stronger than one-half of the total employed in mining a particular cryptocurrency).[46]

The explosion of global mining capacity has greatly reduced the cost of a 51 percent attack on smaller networks also because a group of miners could just repurpose their mining capacity from Bitcoin to another cryptocurrency. Such attacks are not just a theoretical possibility. There have been indeed a number of such attacks on smaller cryptocurrencies such as Bitcoin SV, Bitcoin Gold, and Ethereum Classic; see Makarov and Schoar for more details.[47]

Some scholars have even argued that the potential of a 51 percent attack limits the economic importance a cryptocurrency like Bitcoin can ever attain.[48] This line of thought starts from the observation that the cost of an attack is a flow, that is, the computing power necessary only once to gain control over all the Bitcoins ever mined. But if a group of malicious miners takes over the entire blockchain they might have gained very little because the value of Bitcoin would crash immediately once it becomes known. Moreover, as noted earlier, experience has shown that it would be close to impossible to cash in on any attack that results in very large gains.

The dangers created for new and thus necessarily smaller entrants by the massive mining power concentrated on the industry leaders Bitcoin and Ethereum could thus stifle competition. However, this has not happened so far. The danger of a 51 percent attack has not deterred the enthusiasm for the new crypto variants that are being born almost daily, at least as long as crypto prices are going up.

The few 51 percent attacks that have taken place seem small in number compared to the thousands of cryptocurrencies that already exist. But it remains to be seen whether well-organized criminal actors may be able to exploit other opportunities one day. The key deterrent is likely to be the problem of how to dispose of any gains from attacking a minor cryptocurrency. An attacker might be able to transfer to itself a high number of, say, Bitcoin Gold, but the value would be low, and the attacker would have to find quickly an exchange to transfer these units of Bitcoin Gold into something else that can be used in the real world. Achieving this without leaving a trace is likely to remain difficult. But this could change with the proliferation of exchanges in jurisdictions which do not require identification of customers (the so-called Know Your Customer or KYC requirements).

Old-Fashioned Fraud and Theft

In practice the most serious problems for individual users have arisen not so much from 51 percent attacks on the working of the blockchain mechanism itself but from the so-called on- and off-ramp transactions, that is in the exchanges which allow people to convert crypto holdings into traditional currencies through an exchange. It is one of the ironies of the blockchain revolution that for those not familiar with programming it is too complicated to access directly the blockchain mechanism. Most of us thus need intermediaries who create an easy-to-use interface to make blockchain transactions or to buy and sell Bitcoins. The opaque nature of cryptocurrencies thus increases de facto the need for intermediaries which the consumer can trust – although the original purpose of Bitcoin was the aim of obviating the need for trusted intermediaries.

To make secure transactions in normal currencies, one needs to trust established financial institutions like banks or credit card companies, most of which are heavily regulated and have a track record stretching over decades. But many of the intermediaries in the cryptocurrency world are new and the "get rich quick" mentality pervasive in this market means consumer protection is less of a priority. There have indeed been a number of documented cases of large-scale theft of tokens from a number of exchanges.

For example, over several years more than BTC 750,000 were stolen from customers of the MT Gox exchange located in Japan. The theft was made possible by sloppy security provisions of the exchange itself. When it was discovered in 2014, the value of the stolen Bitcoins was calculated at 470 million dollars, and this is the value usually reported. Part of the Bitcoins stolen were recovered, but the bankruptcy proceedings took several years, and customers are still waiting for the refund, which could be significant given that the price of Bitcoin has increased so much.[49] The net loss to customers of BTC 550,000 would be worth around 2 billion dollars at the early 2024 price of around 40,000 dollars.

The use of credit cards also involves a risk as the card number or the personal identification number (PIN) could be lost, stolen, or hacked. But most cards offer protection against these risks and allow customers to cancel fraudulent transactions even after they have been booked. By contrast, Bitcoin or Ethereum transactions are irreversible and there is no insurance against losing one's private key or the hacking of one's wallet.[50]

Given the deliberately opaque nature of cryptocurrencies, it is naturally difficult to document the extent of fraud, but a June 2022 Report of the US Federal Trade Commission's Consumer Protection Unit found that crypto accounted for one-fourth of all reported fraud, more than any other payment method.[51]

Fraud and theft are of course happening also on a vast scale using credit and debit cards. Some specialists have found that credit card losses are more frequent given the much larger user base of cards (more than 1 billion globally), many more than the existing wallet of Bitcoin or Ethereum.[52] Given that only a fraction of all instances are reported, it is next to impossible to estimate the amounts occasioned by fraud or hacking.[53]

The Cost of Forgetting Your Key

To the losses resulting from fraud or hacking, one would need to add those resulting from human error, for example, when someone loses access to her private key. This key is a string of dozens of alphanumeric symbols. The example of the first Bitcoin transaction showed one example. This Bitcoin "pin" is too long to keep in memory like the four-digit PIN for a credit card or bank account. Many of those who earned Bitcoins in the early days tended to store the key on their devices but then forgot that fact when they upgraded or changed their laptop. They then scrambled to get hold of their private key when they realized years later that they would be millionaires if only they could recover their key from some old, long-forgotten, and discarded device. A British engineer threw out the hard drive of his personal computer during the spring cleaning of 2013. Unfortunately, the private key for his Bitcoin wallet containing BTC 7,500 was stored on this drive. At the time, the value of the loss amounted to over half a million dollars. Today these Bitcoins would be worth over 100 million dollars. Years of excavating the landfill where the local council brought the rubbish did not yield any results, forcing him to acknowledge that this fortune was lost forever.

A widely circulating estimate that about 20 percent of all Bitcoins are lost is based on the guess that wallets which have not seen any activity over at least five years should be considered lost. Technically speaking, inactive wallets are those containing "Unspent Transactions Output or UTC" unchanged for more than five years.[54] The total amount held in these wallets amounts to about four million Bitcoins, or about one-fifth of the over 19 million Bitcoins mined as of 2022. This would amount to a loss worth 240 billion dollars at the Bitcoin price of 60,000 $.

Such losses cannot occur with "conventional" digital money. In the end, one can visit the bank in person even if one loses the PIN or there are other ways to access online banking. Cash can of course also be lost, and in this respect might be considered similar to cryptocurrencies. But the loss rates for cash are much smaller. Some evidence is provided by the changeover to the euro cash in 2002, described in Chapter 3. One year before the changeover, about 260 billion in deutschmark banknotes (and coins) were in circulation, worth about 135 billion euros. At the end of 2002, one year after the introduction of euro cash, only about 10 billion euros remained and today only 7 billion deutschmarks in banknotes, or less than 3 percent of the total, remain unaccounted for.[55]

Another way to lose Bitcoins is by getting the receiving address wrong. Since the transaction is irreversible, the funds are lost unless the person at the receiving end (whose identity might be unknown) agrees to send them back.

CRYPTO AND THE UNDERGROUND ECONOMY

The anonymity cryptocurrencies afford makes them naturally attractive for illicit transactions. Bitcoin is the most often used cryptocurrency demanded for ransomware payments. The main reason for this seems to be practical: The criminals who launch the ransomware attack want a quick payment. But few victims have some cryptocurrency wallet ready to use to pay the ransom within the next few hours. However, for most of them, it would be possible to access Bitcoins rather quickly because that is the one cryptocurrency the corporate treasurer might already be familiar with.

This combination of speed and wide availability thus constitutes the main reason why most ransomware payments are in Bitcoin, although some other cryptocurrencies such as Monero offer more anonymity. The open nature of the Bitcoin blockchain which records all transactions would in principle allow the police to follow the Bitcoins paid as ransom. But, as mentioned above, there exist platforms, called "tumblers," which can make it impossible for law enforcement to follow the trail of transactions, which ultimately allows the criminal to cash out.[56] The tumblers achieve this by mixing the contents of many wallets so that it becomes impossible to say whether the Bitcoin transferred to a particular new wallet came from the ransom payments or something else.

Monero (whose symbol is XMR) sells itself as a "secure, private and untraceable cryptocurrency." It is of course the last qualification that makes it attractive for criminals. The software which makes Monero untraceable is even more complicated than that of Bitcoin. In essence, in the Monero system, every transaction is anonymous and thus one cannot follow the transactions of any individual wallet online. A report to the US Treasury on ransomware payments noted that a large majority demanded payment in Bitcoin but some also required payments in Monero. In a number of cases, the victims were given a choice of Monero or Bitcoin, with a discount for the former, presumably reflecting the additional cost of "laundering" Bitcoin via the tumblers.[57]

The de facto anonymity of cryptocurrencies thus raises the same issues as large denomination banknotes. Cash is convenient for "offline" illicit activity and cryptocurrencies constitute the best vehicle for illicit online activities. As for cash, cryptocurrencies can be used for a wide variety of underground activities, ranging from the criminal to the gray economy where tax evasion might be the main motive. Moreover, there are some countries in the world where privacy is indispensable for any political activity. For example, the organization of Alexei Navalny, the imprisoned Russian opposition politician who died in a Russian forced labor colony, had to solicit financial support in Bitcoin because any bank transfer would have been traced by the Russian authorities. We come back to this relationship between money and freedom in Chapter 11.

In many cases, US federal investigators have been able to trace back initiators of Bitcoin transactions. This was particularly the case for large transactions from the most important ransomware attacks.[58]

The simple reason is that it is not worth investing large amounts of time of skilled experts and computing capacity to follow the trail of a few thousand dollars' worth of crypto. Investigative work remains usually secret. But in 2023 the US federal police, the Federal Bureau of Investigation (FBI), announced officially that it had been able to recover cryptocurrency funds stolen by North Korea.[59]

There is one key difference between cash and crypto: Payment in cryptocurrency constitutes the only possibility to get paid for international ransom. With cash it would be impossible for a tech-savvy criminal, say, in Europe, to extort money from, say, a regional hospital in the United States. And a bank transfer would be easy to trace. Another difference is in the scale of the transactions which are possible. With cash, it is difficult to make transactions much beyond a million dollars or euros because the bulk of the stash of banknotes then becomes unwieldy. Moreover, it is nowadays very difficult to dispose of large amounts of cash without arousing suspicion. In many countries, large cash withdrawals and payments are illegal or otherwise need to be explained and traced. By contrast, for crypto, there is no upper limit on the size of the transactions and also on the size of the amounts which could be cashed in quickly for other uses. Even hundreds of millions of Bitcoins, laundered via tumblers, can be converted quickly into usable bank account balances via the existing exchange services.

The mixing of Bitcoins to achieve anonymity is essentially the same process as laundering cash, but contrary to cash, there exists no process to limit this activity. Tumbling is generally rather cheap, although the quickest tumblers and those promising the highest degree of anonymity might charge a few percentage points.[60] But this is a cost the perpetrators can bear.

However, the tumbling services and the privacy protection of Monero are never perfect. Especially when very large sums or many people are involved, it is usually possible for law enforcement agencies to follow the trail. Two recent cases illustrate how this cat-and-mouse game does not always see the mouse escaping. In one case, a Manhattan couple tried to launder billions' worth of Bitcoin by recycling them through many different wallets. Given the sheer number of wallets, they had to store their private keys electronically, and once the FBI obtained access to that information it could unravel the entire trail.[61] Another example was the success of a joint effort of the FBI and the German federal police to shut down what was believed to have been the largest darknet marketplace, called Hydra.[62] That operation also led to the freezing of a large number of Bitcoins.

As for cash, it is difficult to ascertain what motivates the mass of Bitcoin transactions. The entire history of Bitcoin transactions is available to everybody on the Bitcoin ledger. One can thus easily know the time and amount of each Bitcoin transaction. But only the wallet involved (or "pseudonyms") of the two sides of each transaction are public, and the reason for the transfer is not recorded anywhere. However, researchers working with the Harvard economist Ken Rogoff, the crusader against cash we mentioned in Chapter 4, came up with a clever idea: They obtained the transaction data on the most important peer-to-peer cryptocurrency exchange on which one can trade Bitcoins for hundreds of currencies.[63] The researchers filtered the millions of trades they could see for those where the same amount of Bitcoin was first used to buy some fiat currency (e.g., dollars) and then sold immediately again for fiat currency. For these transactions, Bitcoin represented a vehicle currency. They found that about 7 percent of all transactions (but only 3.5 percent in value) on this Bitcoin exchange could be characterized this way. At first sight, these percentages might appear low (although they are certainly much higher than for cash), but they must be seen against the large-scale speculative trading which took place during that period. Moreover, a criminal cashing out his gains in many small withdrawals of Bitcoin would not be caught by the methodology.

SCALABILITY

Blockchain technology promised to create a secure decentralized transaction system that would work without a trusted intermediary. The question is whether these two attributes can be maintained when the system increases in size. The calculations presented in the previous sections and experience have shown that blockchains cannot easily be scaled up, because the more participants and validators there are, the bigger the chain of blocks of transactions becomes and the more information must be exchanged among more participants, all of whom in principle should have a copy of the entire block-chain.[64] This problem is behind the very large energy consumption documented earlier.

Another way to formulate this problem is to say that it is not possible to have a system based on a distributed ledger that is decentralized, is secure, and still can have an unlimited number of participants. Vitalik Buterin, one of the cofounders of Ethereum, has called this the "scalability" or blockchain trilemma.[65]

There have been of course many technical proposals to deal with the scalability problem. Most approaches to increase the throughput of the blockchain rely on add-ons, for example, aggregators which bundle many transactions into one. However, these add-ons go against the spirit of a cryptocurrency as a decentralized mechanism that can work without trusted intermediaries.

The key argument that the validation mechanism of cryptocurrencies is secure is that the computational capacity to find the hash for the next block is widely distributed over the entire globe, ensuring that no single node could take over the network. However, this argument is not as strong as it appears. Miners have an incentive to join so-called mining pools when the difficulty increases because the income stream from the pool will be steadier than that of a single miner. This is why already today some big mining pools constitute a substantial share of the total hashing power for Bitcoin. In June 2022, only five mining pools accounted for over one-half of the mining capacity dedicated to Bitcoin. These five could thus in principle organize a "51 percent" attack.

This tendency for mining power to concentrate applies both to the Proof of Work and to the Proof of Stake validation approach. When the difficulty increases, miners prefer to pool resources to reduce their risk.

We already described the treat to smaller cryptocurrencies. It might be hard to accumulate enough computational capacity to dominate Bitcoin or Ethereum. But even a small share of the huge Bitcoin hashing community would be enough to dominate smaller or newer coins. This is not just a theoretical possibility; it has happened. In 2018 such an attack on Bitcoin Gold resulted in over 18 million dollars' worth of the currency being double spent.[66]

INVESTING IN CRYPTO?

This book is not intended to provide investment advice. But investing is part of the store of value function of money. Some have argued that digital assets, including cryptocurrencies, should be considered an acceptable complement to traditional investment strategies, which concentrate on equities and bonds.

What makes cryptocurrencies stand apart from other investment types is their extremely high volatility. The annualized standard deviation of the dollar/Bitcoin exchange rate since 2014 has been 93 percent, compared to 8 percent and 12 percent for the dollar/euro or the dollar/Mexican peso exchange rate pairs. Moreover, cryptocurrencies do not seem to move much together as one asset class. The "exchange rate" between Bitcoin and Ethereum has been almost as volatile as the price of either Bitcoin or Ethereum.

Investors might also be willing to hold an asset which yields no monetary return if that asset appreciates in price during difficult times. The Princeton economist Markus Brunnermeier calls this the "friend in need" attribute of so-called safe-haven assets, which appreciate if the market crashes.[67] However, there was little evidence of Bitcoin being a safe-haven asset when the market crashed in early 2020 at the start of the COVID-19 pandemic or in 2022 when all markets went down. Cryptocurrencies do not perform better than other risky assets, like stocks, during periods of financial market stress.

Bitcoin enthusiasts often point out that the overall supply has been capped (at 21 million) and that this should therefore make Bitcoin a good inflation hedge. Bitcoin was created at the start of a period of low and stable inflation, which makes it difficult to check whether this assertion is true in the long run. The years 2021–22 do not suggest that crypto is a good inflation hedge. Their price tumbled while inflation went to record highs.

The one factor which seems to drive crypto adoption is the price itself. Research by the Bank for International Settlements, the central bank for central banks globally that we met in Chapter 7, shows that retail investors flock to cryptocurrencies when the price of Bitcoin increases.[68] Speculative buying (and selling) happens also in other asset markets. But other assets have at least some intrinsic value which limits the volatility of prices. Shares promise dividends, bonds provide interest payments, and even gold has considerable uses in multiple industries. This would change, of course, if Bitcoin could become the currency of a country with widespread everyday use. This was tried in one case, and the result was not good, as we document now.

A REAL-WORLD TEST: BITCOIN IN EL SALVADOR

The small Central American State El Salvador, with a population of only 6 million and a national income of about 30 billion dollars, made headlines in 2021 when its parliament adopted a law which made Bitcoin legal tender. This was supposed to show how a cryptocurrency could solve real-world problems. The reasons given for this step were two: to reduce the cost of remittances from Costa Rican citizens living in the United States and to attract "cryptocurrency tourism" by building a "Bitcoin city" in which miners could draw on volcanic energy to mine Bitcoins tax-free.[69]

The legal tender status of Bitcoin had anyway little meaning since it just meant that merchants and the government had to accept Bitcoin instead of dollars, but only at the price of Bitcoins of that day or moment. El Salvador had adopted the US dollar as its national currency already in 2001; it thus did not have a national currency whose legal tender status could be affected by Bitcoin. The real-world impact of the law was rather limited, as most businesses reported never having made a single transaction in Bitcoin.[70]

El Salvador's crypto plan involved much more than just giving Bitcoin some ill-defined legal tender status and supporting Bitcoin mining. It also involved the creation of an entirely new payment system via an app called Chivo, to allow anybody, even those without a bank account, to transact both in Bitcoin and in dollars. To encourage uptake, the government gave every citizen an opening balance worth 30 dollars on Chivo. This might appear a modest sum, but in that country, it represented more than 10 percent of a monthly wage. Moreover, the government promised not to charge fees for transactions on Chivo. Most Salvadorans cashed in on the adoption gift and then forgot about the new app.[71]

Only a very small proportion of all transactions on the "Chivo" system is in Bitcoin (and it seems that the few that are in Bitcoin originate abroad).[72] This should not be surprising. One could hardly expect the average El Salvadorian to follow Bitcoin prices by the minute and then translate the price of a tortilla into a fraction of a Bitcoin to know whether she can afford it. This is another example of the key importance of a stable unit of account.

One must carefully distinguish between the headlines "El Salvador adopts Bitcoin" and reality, which is much more prosaic, with almost no Bitcoin use in daily transactions. More consequential, and disastrous for the country, was the president's decision to invest part of its reserves in Bitcoin. This was a very risky investment, undertaken against the firm advice by the International Monetary Fund. That decision led to substantial losses for the country when the Bitcoin price crashed in early 2022. It is of course still possible that Bitcoin and other cryptocurrencies recover, but the risks of such an investment strategy for a national treasury were shown by this episode to be unacceptably high.

CONCLUSIONS

When looking at cryptocurrencies as "money," one needs to step back from the hype of how technology can transform and democratize money. Our detailed analytical look at how cryptocurrencies work and what they can achieve clearly suggests that cryptocurrencies fulfil at most two of the three basic functions only partially at best.

Crypto assets certainly do not constitute useful units of account because they are not sufficiently stable in terms of their purchasing power of the goods and services a firm needs or a family buys every day. A cryptocurrency subject to wild price changes does not fulfil this criterion. We will investigate in Chapter 9 whether stablecoins could fulfil this role.

As a means of payment, crypto also has a problem because it could never handle the tens or hundreds of thousands of retail transactions per second of existing systems, and for most daily transactions its costs are much higher and the speed slower than those of today's payment systems. These instruments will never be used on a wide scale for daily transactions. In this sense they do not constitute "money" – at least for legitimate transactions.

A key drawback of all cryptocurrencies is that ordinary people need ready-made, user-friendly interfaces to access the mysterious blockchain. But this negates the key motive of a cryptocurrency, namely, to eliminate the need for trusted intermediaries. A functioning crypto world in fact needs a number of intermediaries. The intermediaries needed are different from the banks and card companies that run the fiat currency world, and they seem to be much less worthy of trust, as multiple scandals have shown, with the collapse of FTX in 2023 representing the biggest example.[73] Partially this is because the crypto intermediaries (exchanges, wallet holders, etc.) are new and have so far not been regulated. The early days of free banking were also full of fraud and failures. But this has changed, with regulators all over the world catching up.[74]

Some research suggests that not all Bitcoin transactions are pure speculative buying and selling. A considerable fraction seems to originate from domestic and cross-border transfers. Most of this is likely to be capital flight, sanctions evasion, or money laundering, since the average size of transactions is tens of thousands of dollars, much too high for worker remittances. This type of "gray" and "black" business could generate an important demand for Bitcoin.

The key use case for Bitcoin is thus that it offers a quick and anonymous (or at least very difficult to trace) route for global transfers on a much larger scale and without the limitations of cash, which is difficult to transport in bulk for larger sums and over long distances.

It is unlikely that Bitcoin and its peers will find a use case as a store of value. Cryptocurrencies do not yield any interest or dividends, and their prices tend to be extremely unstable so far. It is true that what matters for financial markets is not so much its variability than the extent to which it is correlated with other prices. Bitcoin might be valuable to investors if it represented a hedge against extreme events, like inflation, deflation, or market crashes. Unfortunately, there is little evidence that this is the case so far. Crypto prices have tended to follow the wider financial market. When the market crashed in early 2020, or when inflation increased in 2022, Bitcoin prices declined. This means that cryptocurrencies are unlikely to ever represent more than a marginal addition to the portfolio for some adventurous investors. In this limited sense, Bitcoin might have some similarity with gold, which also does not yield any financial dividend (in the form of jewelry it yields a nonmonetary amenity) and whose price is also highly variable, but at least gold provides some diversification benefits.

Bitcoin was born as "a peer-to-peer electronic cash system" but is rarely used as such. It has become a mixture of a speculative asset, the preferred currency for ransomware, and more in general a channel for evading AML regulations. In democratic societies these uses of Bitcoin represent a problem. However, Bitcoin can also help to finance opposition in dictatorships. As mentioned already, the movement led by Alexei Navalny in Russia relied on donations in Bitcoin because ordinary Russians would be taking great risks if they were to make a bank transfer to the accounts of its organization.[75] The autocratic turn in China and the Russian war on Ukraine have given some credence to the libertarian position expressed by the Russian-born Canadian founder of Ethereum,

Vitalik Buterin: "We live in a dangerous world, and protecting free-dom is serious business."[76]

The use of Bitcoin by people living under dictatorships is proba-bly dwarfed by its use for payments of cyber ransoms and other illicit transactions. But this odd mixture of use cases might sustain crypto-currencies for some time and prevent the price of Bitcoin from fall-ing too far. But the longer-term future is more uncertain. The source code of Bitcoin outlines in principle its future until 2140, but it is unlikely that it will be smooth sailing until then. Advances in infor-mation technology are so quick that the cryptographic mechanism underpinning crypto is unlikely to survive a century.

With the availability of ETFs, Bitcoin has become officially an investable asset. But those buying a Bitcoin ETF do not become owners of the cryptocurrency; they only participate in price changes up and down. They are essentially speculating that there will be enough demand for the transaction services of Bitcoin to sustain its value and pay for all the energy wasted on mining. This can go on for a long time, but it is unlikely to last forever. But for the time being crypto can enjoy what Yale's economist Bob Shiller, a Nobel Prize winner, called "the old allure of new money."[77]

NOTES

1. Moneycontrol News, "Bitcoin Pizza Day 2021: Some Interesting Facts about This Special Cryptocurrency Day," *Moneycontrol*, May 22, 2021.
2. A term apparently originated from a typo in an early Bitcoin chat; "hodl" stands for "hold." See Andy Rosen, "What Does HODL Mean? How a Typo Became a Crypto Meme," NerdWallet, February 1, 2023.
3. See Dorit Ron and Adi Shamir, "Quantitative Analysis of the Full Bitcoin Transaction Graph," Lecture Notes in Computer Science, 2013, 6–24.
4. For a concrete example see Blessing Adesiji, "How Preventing Spam Emails Led to Proof-of-Work: Coinmonks," Medium, January 4, 2022; for an earlier contribution: Debin Liu and L. Jean Camp, "Proof of Work Can Work," Workshop on the Economics of Information Security, 2006; Adam Back, "Hashcash: A Denial of Service Counter-Measure," 2002, discusses proof of work as a defense against denial of service attacks.

5. Wei Sun, Haitao Jin, Fengjun Jin, Lingming Kon, Yihao Peng, and Zhengjun Dai, "Spatial Analysis of Global Bitcoin Mining," *Scientific Reports* 12, no. 1 (June 23, 2022).

6. Satoshi Nakamoto, "Bitcoin: A Peer-to-Peer Electronic Cash System," *Decentralized Business Review* 21260, 2008.

7. Introduction to Satoshi Nakamoto 2008, https://bitcoin.org/bitcoin.pdf.

8. Introduction to Satoshi Nakamoto 2008, https://bitcoin.org/bitcoin.pdf.

9. Block 1, "Blockchain.com Explorer | BCH | ETH | BCH."

10. Block 170, "Blockchain.com Explorer | BCH | ETH | BCH."

11. Ronan Manly, "Dawn of Bitcoin Price Discovery 2009–2011: The Very Early Bitcoin Exchanges," Bullionstar, January 28, 2021.

12. See Statista, "Monthly Number of Bitcoin ATMs Worldwide 2015–2022," November 15, 2022.

13. See https://blog.coinsource.net/Bitcoin-atm-fees/.

14. Igor Makarov and Antoinette Schoar, "Cryptocurrencies and Decentralized Finance (DeFi)," BIS Working Papers 1061, December 2022.

15. See Daren Fonda, "Solana Could Be the Visa of Crypto Networks. Not So Fast, Says Visa," Barron's, January 13, 2022. This claim is disputed.

16. Tiffany Lung, "Alibaba Smashes Singles Day Sales Records, A Saving Grace for Retail in COVID-19 Times," Forbes, November 11, 2020.

17. Johannes Göbel and A. E. Krzesinski, "Increased Block Size and Bitcoin Blockchain Dynamics," 27th International Telecommunication Networks and Applications Conference (ITNAC), November 1, 2017.

18. For a list of hundreds of proposals, see Bitcoin, "GitHub – Bitcoin/Bips: Bitcoin Improvement Proposals," GitHub; a prominent example is the so-called Segregated Witness (Consensus Layer), Bitcoin, "Bips/Bip-0141.Mediawiki at Master · Bitcoin/Bips," GitHub.

19. David Easley, Maureen O'Hara, and Soumya Basu, "From Mining to Markets: The Evolution of Bitcoin Transaction Fees," *Journal of Financial Economics* 134, no. 1 (October 1, 2019): 91–109.

20. Jordan Tuwiner, "How Long Do Bitcoin Transactions Take?," Updated October 29, 2023.

21. See Joe Hall, "Bitcoin Transaction Fees Briefly Doubled yet Remain Exceptionally Low," Cointelegraph, March 9, 2022.

22. For a financial view on mining, see Euny Hong, "How Does Bitcoin Mining Work?," Investopedia, May 5, 2022.

23. See "Blockchain.Com | Charts: Cost per Transaction," n.d.

24. See Aoyon Ashraf and Eliza Gkritsi, "Bitcoin Miner Core Scientific Files for Bankruptcy, Expects Support from Some Debt Holders," CoinDesk, December 21, 2022.

25. Statista, "Global Gold Demand Share by Sector 2022," May 30, 2023.

26. See, for example, Statista, "Energy Consumption of a Bitcoin (BTC) and VISA Transaction as of May 1, 2023," May 9, 2023.

27. See Bob Metcalfe, "Metcalfe's Law after 40 Years of Ethernet," *IEEE Computer* 46, no. 12 (December 1, 2013): 26–31.

28. See Timothy Peterson, "Metcalfe's Law as a Model for Bitcoin's Value," *Alternative Investment Analyst Review* 7, no. 2 (January 22, 2018): 9–18; Ken Alabi, "Digital Blockchain Networks Appear to Be Following Metcalfe's Law," *Electronic Commerce Research and Applications* 24 (July 1, 2017): 23–29; Zach Pandl and Isabella Rosenberg, "Cryptocurrency Valuation and Network Size," Goldman Sachs Economics Research, July 19, 2021.

29. The reward of 6.5 BTC/block has been applied until 20 April 2024, at which time the creation of new Bitcoins and the reward for the miners have been cut in half. This "halving" had little or no impact on the price of Bitcoin (as did previous halvings).

30. Igor Makarov and Antoinette Schoar, "Blockchain Analysis of the Bitcoin Market," *NBER Working Papers* 29396, October 1, 2021; see also Makarov and Schoar, "Cryptocurrencies and Decentralized Finance (DeFi)."

31. Nic Carter, "How Much Energy Does Bitcoin Actually Consume?," *Harvard Business Review*, May 6, 2021.

32. See Oscar Gonzalez, "Bitcoin Mining: How Much Electricity It Takes and Why People Are Worried," CNET, July 18, 2022.

33. Jeremy Hinsdale, "Cryptocurrency's Dirty Secret: Energy Consumption," State of the Planet, May 22, 2023.

34. Dmytro Kharkov, "Crypto Mining Drives Electricity Consumption in Siberia," Crypto.News, May 4, 2022.

35. According to the World Gold Council: Adam Webb, "Gold Mining AISC Remained Flat in Q4'21, but Significantly Higher in 2021," World Gold Council, March 29, 2022.

36. World Gold Council, "Above-Ground Stocks," World Gold Council, February 8, 2023.

37. See "Market Cap of Gold (Precious Metal)."
38. This is why the comparative analysis of energy per "value" created in Max Krause and Thabet Tolaymat, "Quantification of Energy and Carbon Costs for Mining Cryptocurrencies," *Nature Sustainability* 1, no. 11 (November 5, 2018): 711–18, is misleading.
39. Milk Road, "Ethereum Staking Rewards: Top ETH Staking Platforms," July 20, 2023.
40. Ethereum, "Proof-of-Stake (POS) | Ethereum.Org," ethereum.org.
41. See BlockNative, "The Ethereum Merge: A Proof-of-Stake Upgrade Guide."
42. Paul Apostolicas and Jaya Nayar, "Explaining Ethereum: Interview with Vitalik Buterin," *Harvard International Review* 42, no. 4 (September 20, 2021): 50–57.
43. Sirio Aramonte, Sebastian Doerr, Wenqian Huang, and Andreas Schrimpf, "DeFi Lending: Intermediation without Information?," *BIS Bulletin* 57 (June 14, 2022).
44. Michael Casey, Jonah Crane, Gary Gensler, Simon Johnson, and Neha Narula, *The Impact of Blockchain Technology on Finance: A Catalyst for Change, Geneva Reports on the World Economy* 21 (CEPR Press, 2018).
45. Florian Zandt, "The Biggest Crypto Heists," Statista Daily Data, March 31, 2022.
46. "Cost of a 51% Attack for Different Cryptocurrencies | Crypto51."
47. Makarov and Schoar, "Cryptocurrencies and Decentralized Finance (DeFi)."
48. Eric Budish, "The Economic Limits of Bitcoin and the Blockchain," *NBER Working Papers* 25407, June 1, 2018.
49. For details on the Mt. Gox saga see here: Jordan Tuwiner, "Mt Gox Hack Explained," Buy Bitcoin Worldwide, September 14, 2023.
50. Klaus Grobys, "When the Blockchain Does Not Block: On Hackings and Uncertainty in the Cryptocurrency Market," *Quantitative Finance* 21, no. 8 (February 5, 2021): 1267–79.
51. See Emma Fletcher, "Reports Show Scammers Cashing In on Crypto Craze," Federal Trade Commission, August 11, 2022.
52. See the "Annual Fraud Statistics" released by the Nilson Report. Nilson Report, "Card Fraud Losses Reach $27.85 Billion – Nilson Report," January 23, 2023.

53. Ben Charoenwong and Mario Luca Bernardi, "A Decade of Cryptocurrency 'Hacks': 2011–2021," Social Science Research Network, January 1, 2021.

54. See Dhruv Bansal, "Bitcoin Data Science (Pt. 2): The Geology of Lost Coins," Crypto Words (now WORDS), May 29, 2018.

55. Bundesbank, "Der DM-Bargeldumlauf – von der Währungsreform zur Europäischen Währungsunion," Monatsberichtsaufsatz, March 2002. For recent data see: "Informationen der Deutschen Bundesbank zum ausstehenden DM-Bargeld."

56. Sesha Kethineni and Ying Cao, "The Rise in Popularity of Cryptocurrency and Associated Criminal Activity," *International Criminal Justice Review* 30, no. 3 (February 6, 2019): 325–44.

57. US Treasury, "Ransomware Trends in Bank Secrecy Act Data between January 2021 and June 2021 | FinCEN.Gov," October 15, 2021.

58. Andrew R. Chow, "'Crypto Is Anything but Private.' An Author Examines Crime on the Blockchain," Time, December 8, 2022. For more details see Andy Greenberg, *Tracers in the Dark: The Global Hunt for the Crime Lords of Cryptocurrency* (Doubleday, 2022).

59. "FBI Identifies Cryptocurrency Funds Stolen by DPRK," Federal Bureau of Investigation, August 28, 2023.

60. See Barbara Thompson, "6 BEST Bitcoin Mixers & Tumblers (2023 List)," Guru99, September 9, 2023.

61. US Department of Justice, "Two Arrested for Alleged Conspiracy to Launder $4.5 Billion in Stolen Cryptocurrency," February 8, 2022.

62. For the German part see Bundeskriminalamt, "Illegaler Darknet-Marktplatz 'Hydra Market' abgeschaltet," April 5, 2022. For the US official communication from the Department of Justice see "Justice Department Investigation Leads to Shutdown of Largest Online Darknet Marketplace," April 5, 2022.

63. Clemens Graf Von Luckner, Carmen Reinhart, and Kenneth Rogoff, "Decrypting New Age International Capital Flows," *Journal of Monetary Economics* 138 (September 1, 2023): 104–22.

64. Makarov and Schoar, "Cryptocurrencies and Decentralized Finance (DeFi)."

65. Dong Ku David, "The Blockchain Trilemma," 2018; or Harry Halpin, "Deconstructing the Decentralization Trilemma," January 1, 2020; or this blog post: Vitalik Buterin, "Why Sharding Is Great: Demystifying the Technical Properties," April 7, 2021.

66. Inyoung Hwang, "What Is a 51% Attack?," SoFi, June 22, 2023.
67. Joseph Abadi and Markus K. Brunnermeier, "Blockchain Economics," *NBER Working Papers* 25407, December 1, 2018.
68. Raphael Auer, Giulio Cornelli, Sebastian Doerr, Jon Frost, and Leonardo Gambacorta, "Crypto Trading and Bitcoin Prices: Evidence from a New Database of Retail Adoption," BIS Working Papers 1049, November 14, 2022.
69. Nelson Renteria, "El Salvador Plans First 'Bitcoin City', Backed by Bitcoin Bonds," Reuters, November 22, 2021.
70. Anna-Cat Brigida and Leo Schwartz, "Six Months In, El Salvador's Bitcoin Gamble Is Crumbling," Rest of World, March 17, 2022.
71. Fernando Álvarez, David Argente, and Diana Van Patten, "Are Cryptocurrencies Currencies? Bitcoin as Legal Tender in El Salvador," *NBER Working Papers* 29968, April 1, 2022.
72. Western Hemisphere Dept., *El Salvador: 2021 Article IV Consultation-Press Release; Staff Report; and Statement by the Executive Director for El Salvador* (International Monetary Fund, 2022).
73. Wikipedia contributors, "Bankruptcy of FTX," *Wikipedia*, November 12, 2023.
74. The European Union is the first major economic area to have prepared new legislation; see Dirk Andreas Zetzsche, Filippo Annunziata, Douglas W. Arner, and Ross P. Buckley, "The Markets in Crypto-Assets Regulation (MiCA) and the EU Digital Finance Strategy," *Capital Markets Law Journal* 16, no. 2 (April 1, 2021): 203–25. In the United States existing regulations to protect investors are being used.
75. Kollen Post, "What Russian Journalists Can Learn from Navalny's Bitcoin Wallet," Cointelegraph, February 25, 2021.
76. Vitalik Buterin, "In Defense of Bitcoin Maximalism," April 1, 2022.
77. Robert J. Shiller, "The Old Allure of New Money," Project Syndicate, July 30, 2018.

9   Stablecoins or Troublecoins?

> The use of stablecoins … may facilitate those seeking to sidestep
> a host of public policy goals connected to our traditional banking
> and financial system.
>
> Gary Gensler

We showed in Chapter 8 that cryptocurrencies such as Bitcoin fluctuate so much in price that they cannot fulfil the traditional functions
of money. Their volatility depends on the delicate instantaneous
equilibrium between the demand by users and the supply provided by
miners. Resourceful fintech entrepreneurs came up with a solution: a
cryptocurrency whose value is stable, named "stablecoin."

Stablecoins quickly became the new rising star of the crypto-
asset universe. The total amount of financial instruments that bear
this name grew very quickly from virtually zero in 2019 to close to
200 billion dollars at some point in 2022.[1] By the end of 2023 this
was back down to about 120 billion dollars – still impressive for such
a new instrument, although this level remains small in comparison
to the money supply of the United States, which stands at over 15
trillion dollars or over hundred times larger. A more appropriate comparison might be between the largest stablecoin (Tether, or in short
USDT) and individual MMFs, the closest relative to stablecoins in
noncrypto finance. On this account, one finds that Tether can hold
its own relative to most large European MMFs but is much smaller
than the largest MMFs in the United States.[2]

Their (initial) explosive growth places stablecoins among
the most remarkable innovations in recent financial history. What
explains this phenomenon? What are their potential and their risks?
What will their future be?

In a nutshell, stablecoins are meant to offer investors both elements embodied in their name: "stability" and "coin." Something as usable as a coin and equally stable, in digital form. The standard of stability adopted by most stablecoins is the US dollar: Ideally, one stablecoin should always be exactly equal to 1 dollar. The problem for the promoters is that a "stablecoin" already exists: the US dollar itself. Attracting investors is a daunting challenge which requires winning the competition of both the Federal Reserve, the official issuer of US dollars, and the banking sector, which for decades has been offering dollar deposits in digital form. Two formidable well-established competitors. Can there be room for something new, promising to deliver essentially the same?

Actually, there are many contestants. At the peak, in 2022 (dates are important because the phenomenon changes rapidly), there existed some 200 different stablecoins, most of them based on the US dollar, and less than 2 percent linked to the euro. Their total capitalization was highly concentrated. The first two, Tether and USD Coin, accounted usually for over two-thirds of the total. The rest consisted of a galaxy of small or minuscule entities. This pattern has persisted, with the number of smaller stablecoins evolving, with old stars dying and new ones constantly being born. All of them running after the same Holy Grail: a stable value while being "crypto." Not all succeeding though, as we shall see.

For the uninitiated it is difficult to distinguish between the different stablecoin offerings. Digging closer, the main difference among them, besides their size, is the "financial engineering" they rely on, that is, the mechanisms which are supposed to ensure their stability vis-à-vis the dollar. This is essential because it determines the likelihood of their stability being effectively guaranteed under a variety of circumstances, including adverse ones. Let's look at this feature, before examining what their record of stability has been and examining other aspects which help understand what their future may be.

NEITHER VERY STABLE NOR REALLY A COIN:
AN AWKWARD TRADE-OFF

Stablecoins are crypto assets whose value is "pegged" to (in other words, managed so as to equal) a reference asset. An overwhelming majority, including the two biggest ones, is pegged to the US dollar. But the peg can be to any currency, a currency basket, or another asset or index. Given their dominance, we will refer mainly to US dollar-pegged stablecoins, though our considerations apply to the whole asset class.

There exist two main approaches to guarantee stability with the US dollar.[3] Most stablecoins are "collateralized," meaning, backed by a portfolio of reserve assets supposed to match the total value of the stablecoins issued against them. In other words, if N stablecoins of 1 dollar have been issued, the total asset value must always be equal to (at least) N dollars. Seen in this way, a stablecoin is just another financial intermediary whose balance sheet comprises monetary means on the liability side backed by a portfolio of assets on the asset side.

Since in principle stablecoins can be redeemed on demand at any moment, the assets backing them must be very stable in value and also very liquid, that is, sellable at any moment without loss. Therefore, they have to consist of some combination of physical cash (stablecoins have no access to the central bank deposits or financing), bank deposits, short-term Treasury paper, and other forms of supersafe short-term paper, like top-rated commercial paper or repos. The more the stablecoins' portfolio differs from this restricted range of assets, the more unlikely it becomes that the stability and redeemability of the stablecoins can be assured at all times and in all circumstances. In fact, even some of the assets in the list we just mentioned are not always liquid and their value not always totally stable. For example, the market price of Treasury bills fluctuates with changes in interest rates, though usually not by much. In some cases, their market becomes illiquid, as witnessed in some financial crises. Private issuances such as commercial paper and repos have been subject to confidence crises and runs during the Great Financial Crisis of 2008–09. And banks, of course, may fail, and in that case their deposits are not guaranteed beyond a certain threshold.

In reality, most stablecoins do not allow unlimited withdrawals upon demand. For example, Tether limits redemption to business hours and has a high minimum threshold for redemptions. Other issuers only promise unlimited redemptions in kind.[4] There is thus a gulf between the small print and the mirage of a stable asset that can be redeemed at any time without a loss.

As the alert reader must have grasped, stablecoins look very much like banks of a special type. They are similar to banks in the fact that they have largely redeemable and transferable monetary means as liabilities and in the fact that these liabilities are backed by a diversified portfolio of assets. They are different primarily for two reasons: because they are not subject to bank regulation nor do they benefit from the safety net enjoyed by banks and because of the technology which is used to hold and exchange them.

The second feature is technological: Their balance sheets are not kept and exchanged in a centralized ledger, like those of banks and other intermediaries, but in distributed ones. Payment messages rely on cryptography and are processed in blockchains like those of cryptocurrencies. Stablecoins are run on crypto exchanges, such as Ethereum or Binance (or, until November 2022, the ill-fated FTX, masterminded and managed by the now convicted financier Sam Bankman-Fried), which also support trades in cryptocurrencies. For example, USDT can be run on the Bitcoin ledger or on the Ethereum chain. The coincidence of trading platforms creates operational complementarity, which makes stablecoins the payment instruments of choice for investors and traders in the crypto world. The link between stablecoins and cryptocurrencies is one of convenience, not of necessity; conventional monetary instruments can also be used to buy and sell cryptocurrencies, though in fact often they aren't because it would be more cumbersome and costly.

It is important to distinguish the technological aspect, consisting of the distributed ledger and the associated blockchain technology, from the financial one, the balance sheet structure and the nature of the instruments stablecoins offer and hold. The second aspect determines the financial risks that technology cannot eliminate.[5] The first aspect, technology, can add, or possibly remove or alleviate, certain other risks relating to the exchange infrastructure: robustness and finality of payments, transparency, anti-fraud security, and the like.[6]

From a financial standpoint, reserve-backed stablecoins sit on an inherently awkward trade-off. The commitment to mirror a conventional currency and the virtual absence of regulation and safety net force them to maintain very restrictive investment policies: Only very safe and very liquid assets can be held, lest putting confidence at risk. But with this balance sheet structure, they come close to transforming an asset into itself – a dollar into a dollar – which cannot be a meaningful and profitable business proposition – the same conundrum faced by narrow banks, which we discussed in Chapter 6. Escaping this trade-off involves a constant temptation to put the stability of the "coin" at risk by investing in higher-return and more risky assets. It can also be an inducement to maintain a certain ambiguity and opacity in their portfolio composition, facilitated by the lack of stringent rules. Lack of transparency increases investor uncertainty. The reserve-based Tether has repeatedly been subject to investigations and fines by market and accounting supervisors for its lack of proper disclosure.

There are also stablecoins whose quest for stability hinges not on reserves but on algorithms: computerized procedures that exploit market mechanisms to ensure the stability of the price. They can be of various forms. Some of them (so-called rebase) rely on computer algorithms that create ("mint") or destroy ("burn") stablecoins automatically depending on whether the market quote of the instrument is above or below the reference asset. In this way, the supply of instruments adjusts in a way to peg the value, assuming demand does not change drastically in the meantime. Others rely on arbitrage to obtain the same result, for example, allowing traders to mint or burn the native currency, hence earning an arbitrage revenue.

More complex algorithmic instruments are based on the interaction of several crypto assets, some having the ancillary function to stabilize the value of others by means of algorithmic trades involving different instruments. An example that gained prominence in 2022 was Terra USD, an algorithmic stablecoin created in 2019 by one Do Kwon (a pseudonym) based on the interaction between the main instrument (Terra, meaning earth in Latin) and Luna (moon). The scheme was supposed to work as follows. Whenever the value of Terra exceeded the reference (the US dollar and other currencies as well), arbitrage trades set in, involving the destruction of Luna and the creation of Terra. And vice versa, when the price of Terra was low. In theory, Terra was supposed to be pricey whenever Luna was cheap and vice versa; in either case, an automatic market mechanism would intervene to rebalance both instruments. Terra USD grew very popular until it became the largest algorithmic stablecoin in existence, with a market capitalization close to 3 billion dollars (large but still much smaller than the main collateralized stablecoins, Tether and USD Coin). All this seemed to work for a while, until prices of both Terra and Luna collapsed in May 2022, due to a sudden loss of confidence in the whole crypto market. A case of contagion, whose victim, not atypically, was the instrument judged to be more complex and hazardous. The value of both Terra and Luna dropped to near zero. The collapse of this particular instrument, in itself a small fraction of the overall stablecoin class, in turn, hit hard the whole crypto market, accelerating a massive fall in prices that, already in motion since 2021, would gain momentum after the fall of FTX in November 2022.

Mixed algorithmic–collateralized models also exist, combining both approaches. They try to import the confidence effect stemming from collateralization while at the same time using automatic mechanisms or market incentives to fine-tune the peg. Examples of this class are, however, relatively new and not very significant in terms of market capitalization.

The jury on stablecoins is still out as their record of success so far is mixed, with some spectacular failures and also successes, in the sense that most instruments so far seem to be able to hold the peg. The complementarity with cryptocurrencies suggests that their destiny, and specifically the role they may play in tomorrow's finance, is closely intertwined.

It is worth looking at how some of them have performed recently. The four largest stablecoins by market cap at the time of writing – the reader should be aware that the ranking may change – are, respectively, Tether USD, USD Coin, Dai USD, and True USD. All of them are collateralized. Their market price hovers in all cases around the 1:1 parity to the US dollar, but they display different volatilities and occasionally abrupt spikes upward or downward. Tether, the largest one, seems to have suffered more than others from contagion after the collapse of Terra USD in May 2022. By contrast, the US regional banking crisis of March 2023 pushed Tether's price up, while it had the opposite effect on others. Contagion and safe-haven effects therefore seem to alternate, depending on circumstances and perceptions. While prices are remarkably stable for all of them, they are far from an exact parity to the reference currency. Dai USD (backed by crypto assets) seems to fluctuate comparatively more than others (backed by traditional assets). USD Coin displayed the lowest volatility so far. While some volatility is not necessarily a problem, it is clear that stability being the signature feature of stablecoins, any significant and repeated departures from the peg can generate a loss of confidence.

In many respects, stablecoins are reminiscent of another instrument that came to prominence half a century ago, and again recently during the Great Financial Crisis of 2008–09: the MMFs already mentioned. It is therefore worth taking a look at this precedent.

A LESSON FROM THE ANCESTORS: MONEY MARKET FUNDS

Stability is the Holy Grail of finance: Financial engineering – the activity of inventing new financial instruments – constantly aims at offering investors more "stability," or, in other words, less risk. Stability is an elusive concept though; stable with respect to what? An asset can be stable relative to another one and yet it may lose or gain value with respect to a third one. Moreover, stability is not the sole relevant concept. Another key feature is a financial asset's "return": its inherent ability to create more wealth. There is normally a trade-off between stability and return: Safer assets yield a lower return, an implication of the fact that people tend, on average, to be risk-averse. The challenge of any new financial instrument, therefore, and of the "engineers" who invent it, is to offer a better combination of stability and return. Ideally, more of both.

Half a century ago, the search for better risk–return combinations produced one of the biggest revolutions in the postwar history of global finance: MMFs. Money market funds are an interesting benchmark to assess stablecoins because of the things they have in common. To start with, the fact that they have a similar origin: Both arose from the will to challenge banks (including central banks) in their core business, the supply of money.

In the United States, where MMFs first appeared, competing with banks was easier in the 1970s than it is now. Federal legislation limited the interest rate banks could pay on deposits. Legislation inherited from the Great Depression prohibited paying interest on small deposits withdrawable on demand. Remuneration on time and large denomination deposits or certificates of deposits was permitted but capped at a low level. Regulation Q (the name of the law in question) effectively prevented banks from competing with one another and with other financial institutions by offering higher returns. The rationale of the law was precisely to limit banking competition, which after the bank failures of the 1930s was deemed detrimental to financial stability. Few other countries had limits on the interest rates banks could pay on deposits. This is the main reason why MMFs have remained mainly a US phenomenon. In Europe, MMFs play only a marginal role.

Until the late 1960s, legal limits on bank interests did not create problems because the general level of interest rates was low and stable. Not so thereafter. At the end of the 1960s, inflation and interest rates started to rise in the US economy – in fact, all over the world. Capping bank interest rates created an opportunity for financial engineering: New instruments could offer the same liquidity as bank deposits and also pay interest to investors, exploiting the higher market returns. Mutual funds (pools of savings invested in bonds and stocks) already existed, but their shares weren't liquid enough – they could not be withdrawn at any time without loss. Virtually unregulated at the start, MMFs could offer their customers (formally shareholders) a redemption option at par, combined with a small remuneration, effectively bypassing Regulation Q. Another example, with many others in history, where a legal restriction spurs innovation whose purpose is to bypass the restriction itself.

By the early 1980s, when Regulation Q started being phased out, MMFs had grown significantly. As a result of banks' intense lobbying, Regulation Q was eventually repealed in 1986. This, however, did not stop the march of MMFs. Today, the total value of MMF shares in the United States is of the order of 4.7 trillion dollars, though since the early 2000s MMFs have grown less than the rest of the financial sector.

In the United States, MMFs benefit from a special regulatory regime in that they can carry their assets at "amortized cost," instead of their market value. In other words, they do not have to report in their regular accounts the changes in the market value of their assets. This allows US MMFs to promise that 1 dollar deposited at an MMF is always worth 1 dollar at any time – regardless of how the market values its portfolio. This made it possible to allow users to write checks on their MMFs, which thus became equivalent to demand deposits – but yield interest.

Money market funds have been less successful outside the United States, but they still constitute a significant component of the financial landscape in many countries. In Europe, the major hosts of this type of intermediation are France, with close to 400 billion euros, and Luxemburg and Ireland (the latter two are tax havens), with 400 billion euros and 600 billion euros, respectively. European regulation is less favorable to MMFs, which are thus not as widely used as a means of payment by households as they are in the United States. In Europe, most holders of MMFs are corporates that want to get a slightly higher return on their cash balances.

From the 1990s, MMFs have grown in Japan as well, and from 2000 in China, where they have reached the equivalent of 1.4 trillion dollars, benefitting from linkages with major e-retail platforms like Alipay that de facto now offer banking services as well.

A Cautionary Tale: The Reserve Primary Fund

The first MMF in existence, the Reserve Primary Fund (RPF), exemplifies the potential and drawbacks of the entire asset class. Two American businessmen, Bruce Bent and Henry Brown, established RPF in 1971. Career bankers first and financial consultants next, the two knew full well what investors wanted and how to create financial instruments to satisfy their demands. The new fund they created offered investors cash-like liquidity with a small interest on top, hence outperforming regular bank deposits. Bent characterized the fund's strategy as "boring"[7]: No risk should be accepted. The share's net asset value (NAV, the cost of a share) should always be at least equal to 1 dollar, the guaranteed redemption value – here is where the analogy with stablecoins begins to appear. To attain this rock-solid stability performance, the fund's portfolio should be supersafe: Essentially, the only admissible assets should be remunerated bank deposits and short-dated Treasury paper. Even commercial paper, normally regarded as a low-to-medium-risk investment, was considered anathema. The interest earned on their portfolio allowed RPF to remunerate the shares.

This conservative strategy was maintained for a long time: In 2006, its portfolio still consisted of bank certificates of deposits for 77 percent, repos for 19 percent, floating rate notes for 3 percent, and only 1 percent of asset-backed securities. At that point, however, RPF started to get heat from its competitors. While still calling themselves MMFs, many of them followed more aggressive, risky, and lucrative approaches. RPF saw no alternative but to follow the crowd. While not changing rhetoric, RPF quietly changed its strategy, entering heavily into the higher-yielding commercial paper and corporate bond segments. In 2008, on the verge of the Great Financial Crisis, its portfolio included large shares of asset-backed commercial paper and long-term corporate notes and bonds. What had been anathema before had become the rule. The boring strategy of the beginning had become more exciting but also riskier. For some time, the new strategy paid off: Its assets under management grew to a peak of nearly 65 billion dollars, just days before Lehman's failure. At that point, RPF was one of the highest-yielding MMFs in the industry, and one of the fastest growing. But the edge of the precipice was just one step ahead.

The MMF industry had already shown cracks: A year earlier (August 2007), three French funds sponsored by BNP Paribas, France's largest bank, had suspended redemptions following massive outflows. The alarm was not heeded. Far from pulling the breaks, RPF doubled down by increasing its exposure to higher-yielding asset-backed commercial paper. When the US investment bank Lehman Brothers collapsed (September 15, 2008) the fund was exposed to Lehman by a small amount, no more than 1.2 percent of its asset portfolio,[8] but big enough to spark a confidence crisis and massive requests for redemptions. The next day, RPF "broke the buck": NAV fell below 1 dollar per share. Redemptions were suspended: Investors who had moved earlier in anticipation had been able to liquidate their shares at par; those who had waited received far less and much later, pending the outcome of long judicial procedures.[9]

Reserve Primary Fund's failure modality, including the breaking of the buck, was a relatively isolated case even during the financial crisis. But the MMFs crisis was general: Many funds suffered outflows and could survive only because of support from other sponsoring institutions, usually banks, which purchased their assets at inflated prices or otherwise shouldered their losses. After the crisis, over 200 cases of MMF support by sponsors were recorded.

At that point, it was clear that the MMF industry needed rules. Regulation should be of a special kind because the MMF business model stands in the middle of two different financial businesses: mutual funds, which specialize in asset transformation (converting assets of given types into assets of different types), and banks, which specialize in liquidity provision to depositors. Liquidity transformation involves specific risks calling for capital requirements, lender-of-last-resort provision, and supervision. The MMFs had none of them. The authorities in charge – in all countries, market regulators like the Securities and Exchange Commission instead of bank supervisors – had no familiarity with banking regulation and lacked the necessary instruments to mitigate liquidity risks. The problem was aggravated by the popularity of MMF: Due to its size, the industry had become a critical node of the financial sector. On the asset side, MMFs were and still are key providers of short-term finance to many financial and nonfinancial entities, including banks. On the liability side, they are essential to liquidity management for many corporates. Only about one-fifth, or 1 trillion dollars of the total 5 trillion dollars, of MMF assets outstanding in the United States today are owned by retail investors. To corporate holders one can apply the principle "caveat emptor": They should be able to discern the risk involved. But there is another reason to worry. Most MMFs have "sponsor," usually a well-known large financial institution, to increase their reputation. The sponsor does not give a formal promise to guarantee a NAV of at least 1 dollar because such a formal guarantee would constitute balance sheet risk and require setting aside costly capital to underpin the guarantee. Instead, the sponsor just gives the impression that the MMF has a strong "parent" which could save in times of trouble. However, these informal promises become worthless in a financial crisis, when the sponsors themselves are in trouble and cannot save others. This led to a vicious circle with MMFs on the brink of breaking the buck and the banks no longer being able to honor their sponsorship, which in turn made the banks less trustworthy in the eyes of depositors and investors.[10]

The big financial crisis of 2007 suddenly revealed that in reality the stability of the banking system was linked to that of MMFs because banks sponsored them. For the regulatory community, dealing with MMFs is a tricky affair, with a potential systemic impact. And, needless to say, the sector's regulators face intense opposition from corporate and financial lobbies.

As a result of all this, MMF regulation was never completed and remains a thorny open issue to this day. The Financial Stability Board, a global body of financial regulators with considerable influence but without binding powers, has recently tried to restart the process, by issuing reform proposals and launching a public consultation.[11] Where this attempt will end up is anybody's guess.

Retail investors were much more important when MMFs were invented. In the early 1980, retail investors held three-fourths of the total. This proportion declined gradually as interest rates started a long decline from the late 1980s onward. MMFs continued to expand, but the share held by the retail sector fell to less than one-fourth as bank accounts became competitive in terms of interest rates and other services offered.

While the total of US MMF shares held by retail investors has plateaued in recent years, the corporate component has risen further, in spite of the lower interest rate levels, because for corporate treasuries even small interest differentials can be decisive. This gradual pattern changed abruptly when the US federal government sent out trillions in checks during the COVID-19 crisis. The sudden influx of liquidity was mainly parked in banks so that the relative importance of MMFs has at least temporarily declined. It remains to be seen whether over the next years investors will reduce their liquidity or switch them in a search for yield in MMFs.

With higher interest rates MMFs have become more competitive, having been faster than banks in responding to the rise of market interest rates. But experience suggests that along with the remuneration the risks may have risen as well.[12]

GENERAL LESSONS FROM MONEY MARKET FUNDS FOR STABLECOINS

We noted that an important element of MMFs is that they are usually "sponsored" by a large financial institution (a bank or investment fund). This widespread sponsorship practice constituted an important propagation channel for the crisis.

Luckily from the viewpoint of systemic financial stability, stablecoins at least so far have no sponsors. Any problems they might experience are thus unlikely to spread to the overall financial system. This element proved decisive after the demise of FTX, the ill-fated crypto exchange mentioned in Chapter 8, whose contagion remained strictly confined to the crypto industry. That difference aside, however, in order to understand the commonalities between the MMF crisis of 2008–09 and the potential issues facing stablecoins, one must examine the inherent fragility of MMFs in some detail.

Like banks, MMFs perform a function called "liquidity transformation" – in plain language, they promise investors cash-like benefits that most of their assets do not possess. As soon as confidence wanes and investors start doubting that redeemability can continue to be guaranteed, shareholders have an incentive to "run": liquidate their investment as soon as possible, before others do so. The first who run are better off because the others are more likely to suffer losses. This is a powerful incentive to run at the minimum perceived risk. This makes the whole construct highly unstable. As we have seen, RPF shareholders who "ran" on September 15, 2008, ended up better off than those who waited until the next day. This dynamic is inherent in the first-come-first-serve mechanism:

It does not depend on whether the asset pool is fundamentally solvent or not.[13]

There are three possible approaches to mitigate risks from the MMFs' liquidity transformation. The first is transparency and market discipline. This involves making investors aware, in a timely way, of impending redeemability risks by disclosing mark-to-market portfolio valuations. As mentioned, in the United States MMFs are generally allowed to calculate their assets at amortized cost, not at the market value implied by the interest rates of the moment. Using market values instead, or at least disclosing them – an approach sometimes called "floating rate NAV" – would rely on market self-regulation: Investors would be discouraged from investing in a fund whose market value makes redeemability unlikely. But market discipline may not work, particularly when investors think that MMFs are supported by sponsors or public authorities wary of reputational or systemic risks. Despite the insistence of some regulators, floating rate NAV proposals have never been implemented systematically – only partial versions have been adopted in the United States and Europe.

The second approach is the "prudential" one, like the one adopted by bank supervisors. It consists of imposing capital, liquidity, and other requirements on balance sheets to strengthen their security buffers to reduce the risk that the fund may "break the buck," and, last but not least, to exercise supervision on them to ensure that they do not break the rules. This approach brings MMFs closer to the banking sector, eliminating part of the light touch regulatory treatment which is at the basis of much of their success. So far, regulators on both sides of the Atlantic have been reluctant to pursue this option. European regulators have enacted, in 2019, a milder version that brings portfolio accounting closer to mark-to-market practices. This approach also relies on market discipline.

Finally, a third approach, which we can call "sand in the wheels," involves limiting or delaying redeemability to reduce the risk of redemption runs or of unequal treatment between first and late movers. Alternatively, variable pricing can be applied to redemptions depending on risk. This approach goes at the heart of the MMF business model because, in essence, it reduces their ability to perform liquidity transformation and brings them closer to traditional mutual funds. Like the other approaches, this one has never been applied in full either, though the EU regulators have introduced variable pricing linked to the portfolio composition of the fund.

The aforementioned approaches can be combined in various ways. Yet the post–Great Financial Crisis experience of implementation is not encouraging: In spite of some initiatives in the United States and Europe, risks embedded in the sector remain, as demonstrated by the renewed tensions in the early phases of the COVID pandemic.[14] The road toward a satisfactory regulatory treatment of the MMF industry is still long and now intersects that of dealing with the risks of a nascent industry, that of stablecoins.

Banks, Crypto, and Asset Management: The Land In Between

Stablecoins share certain features of MMFs while differing in other important respects.

Like MMFs, most stablecoins guarantee a stable redemption value to subscribers. They operate on a first-come-first-serve basis: Redemptions are executed in the order in which requests are received, therefore guaranteeing better treatment to firstcomers. As we have seen, this feature generates an incentive to "run" as soon as the slightest doubt exists, regardless of the composition of the portfolio – crypto, traditional, or mixed – or whatever mechanism is used to guarantee redeemability – collateralized, algorithmic, or other.

The most important feature putting stablecoins apart from MMFs is that the stablecoin "tokens" are exchanged on distributed ledgers, not on centralized ones. This creates a natural complementarity with cryptocurrencies, which makes them attractive to support cryptocurrency transactions. An investor in Bitcoin who wants to temporarily cash in gains but be ready immediately for another investment in the crypto space could of course exchange the Bitcoins for dollars in a bank account via an exchange and then use the dollars on the bank account to buy again. But these "off-ramp" and "on-ramp" operations would incur substantial exchange fees and the bank might credit the account only with a delay of one to two business days. A stablecoin allows the investor to stay in the crypto space with an asset whose value is stable and without incurring these costs and the funds would remain quickly available for investment. Stablecoins are thus important facilitators of crypto investments.

Most stablecoins do not have their own ledger. Instead, they piggyback on existing blockchains, often on more than one blockchain at once. For example, USDT is now available on nine different protocols. This was made possible by the parent company, Tether, which minted coins on all these blockchains and guaranteed their value.

The fact that stablecoins have always a parent company that issues them has two implications. One is that transactions are in practice reversible. The issuer of the stablecoin USDT, Tether Inc., can always cancel the USDT it has issued. Reversibility is a plus for a means of payment because it makes it possible to correct mistakes. But this means that stablecoins are far from the initial motivation of cryptocurrencies – irreversibility of transactions. Reversibility also explains why stablecoins are never demanded as ransom. The parent company could just invalidate any stablecoins paid out in ransom.

The second implication is that each transaction costs as much as a transaction on the blockchain on which it is executed and recorded because each stablecoin transaction needs to be recorded on its distributed ledger.

From a retail standpoint, an obstacle is that most exchanges accept a stablecoin transaction only after it has been validated several times. For example, Kraken – a crypto exchange named after the giant sea monster – requires an additional twenty blocks before it finalizes a USDT transaction. This implies that a typical stablecoin transaction takes around five to ten minutes. Stablecoins thus cannot be used in everyday shopping, which requires real-time validation. This time loss for repeated verification pales in comparison to the days that an "off-ramp" operation might require. This aspect thus does not constitute an important disadvantage for investors that simply want to get into, or out of, a cryptocurrency investment.

These technical and practical aspects suggest that stablecoins are much more attractive to large investors than to retailers. This is borne out by data on holdings of stablecoins by investment size. For Tether one finds that over 80 percent of the total is held in wallets worth over 1 million dollars and only about 2 percent by investors holding less than 10,000 dollars.[15] Given a total capitalization of Tether of around 120 billion dollars, this means that the amount of retail funds at stake (from all over the world!) is just a couple of billion dollars.

As we mentioned already, a key attraction of stablecoins is that they allow cryptocurrency holders to maintain their investment in the same environment, without exchanging into fiat currency, mostly dollars, which is usually costly and time-consuming. This is of course valuable only as long as the investor is confident that the 1:1 peg will be kept. Investor confidence can be random (economists speak of "sunspots" to refer to random events which may cause euphoria or crises without much fundamental motivation) but does not have to be: Loss of trust is more likely to occur if the underlying financial structure (the underlying "engineering" of the stablecoin) is less solid. No wonder Terra–Luna, with its astronomical engineering, was one of the first to collapse.

Solidity varies depending on the stablecoin type. A taxonomy proposed by the European Central Bank distinguishes four types within the stablecoin population.[16]

The largest category is given by the so-called tokenized stablecoins, those backed by a low-risk portfolio. These are the safest and most common members of the stablecoin community – Tether alone represents a large share of the entire capitalization of the sector. Tokenized stablecoins very much resemble the original spirit of the MMF industry, except that they are traded on decentralized platforms. Since business models can evolve rapidly as a result of competition or other forces, tokenized stablecoins may evolve toward another category, the so-called off-chain stablecoins, invested in riskier assets such as commodities or longer-term and less liquid assets, without market participants being fully and timely aware of the change.

"On-chain" stablecoins have a similar structure, except that the parity of the share is backed by crypto assets. One member of this category already mentioned is Dai. The on-chain option is popular among investors wishing to avoid any centralized intermediation, even in the form of an issuer or custodian of the backup asset. The stability performance of these instruments is lower than that of tokenized stablecoins, as reflected by higher volatility around the 1:1 parity.

Finally, the most volatile category is represented by the "algorithmic" stablecoins, where the parity is supposedly guaranteed by an automatic trading strategy. This was the case with Terra, which we already discussed. Not surprisingly, this category is characterized by the highest levels of volatility and has experienced several failures – with stablecoins losing the peg and collapsing at zero value, as Terra did.

There is another key difference between MMFs and stablecoins. MMFs evolved as a way to pay interest while providing some limited transaction services. Stablecoins provide a transaction service for holders of other, more volatile, crypto assets, but they do not pay interest, at least not directly as MMFs do. Stablecoin holders can "stake" their tokens on specialized platforms that promise to pay an attractive return. In practice, this works like a term deposit at a bank. The investor forfeits control over her stablecoin balances in exchange for the promised return. The staking business is not regulated and thus looks like banking in the Far West. Many different platforms advertise yields much higher than what banks or even MMFs would offer; even double-digit rates are not a rarity.[17] This is a market where caveat emptor reigns. There is no supervision to defend consumer interests since staking has formally nothing to do with banking or other retail financial services. Stablecoins thus provide interest only through an additional and rather risky route whereas the return on MMFs, while modest, arrives without any additional effort and little risk.

These considerations authorize skepticism on the future of stablecoins as an asset class. But the MMF experience suggests otherwise. Over the last fifty years, as we have seen, MMFs have come to occupy a well-established niche between two different intermediaries – mutual funds and banks – each of which could not offer the specific blend of services MMFs provide. In particular, MMFs are more responsive to market developments and to investor demands than banks can be, in light of the latter's heavier regulatory structure. In spite of their incomplete regulatory framework, MMFs have an established position in the financial markets. Stablecoins may grow toward a similar role in the future, occupying a territory in between the banking sector, the asset management industry, and the universe of crypto assets. The chance of this happening however depends on two conditions.

First, that crypto assets and the associated blockchain technologies become more solidly established within mainstream finance. This implies, inter alia, that transactions become as quick and convenient as everyday transactions in "normal" money. The second condition is the development of an adequate regulatory framework. As of now, this does not exist. Stablecoins are even less regulated than MMFs.

Systematic discussions on regulatory options have started, nationally and among global supervisory bodies and standard setters. The Financial Stability Board issued several recommendations, but recently it concluded that "overall, the implementation of the FSB [Financial Stability Board] high-level recommendations across jurisdictions is still at an early stage."[18] One advantage is that stablecoin regulation can avail itself of the experiences and debates conducted with regard to MMFs. In particular, the three-pronged approach we discussed (market discipline, prudential requirements, and "sand in the wheels") can be applied to stablecoins as well, with proper adaptation. This will need to be complemented by proper supervision of the technological soundness of blockchain structures, without losing any potential benefits from decentralization. Finally, transparency is an essential concurring element: Accounting and disclosures should follow criteria already adopted in the rest of the financial sector.

The regulatory agenda for stablecoins, and generally for crypto markets, is long and will not be easy. It should be undertaken as a matter of urgency before crypto markets grow further in size and their interconnection with mainstream finance enhances systemic risks. Current unsound market practices in the sector abound and risk becoming entrenched. Sound regulation is in the interest of crypto-asset holders themselves, no less than of the financial markets as a whole.

CAN STABLECOINS SOLVE THE PROBLEM OF REMITTANCES?

A potential use for stablecoins that has attracted attention recently is that of facilitating the cross-border transfer of international workers.[19] The term "remittances" means transfers from people working abroad, usually in rich economies like the United States, Europe, or some Middle Eastern countries to their families back home. They are small-size payments individually, but their number is large and therefore the total flows are considerable, representing an essential lifeline for some poorer countries. Central American countries like El Salvador and Honduras depend on remittances for more than 25 percent of their national income. For some Central Asian and low-income African countries, this dependency can reach even 30–40 percent. This is of a similar order of magnitude as the importance of oil rents to countries like Kuwait and Iraq. Remittances can become especially important for recipient countries in times of crisis.[20]

The World Bank estimates that in 2022 workers sent over 600 billion dollars back home. This amount is poised to increase alongside migration flows; it has already grown fivefold since 2000. But remittances are still dwarfed by trade in goods and services, which increased from about 8 billion dollars in 2000 to close to 30 billion in 2022. Remittances have thus grown more quickly than trade, but trade volumes still remain more important in their level, by a factor of forty.

Traditionally, the cost of sending small amounts across borders, especially toward less-developed areas, has been very large. In 2022, the average cost of remittances globally stood close to 6 percent, a very high level but declining relative to 9 percent ten years earlier.[21] Early analyses documented these costs and their causes, identifying determinants such as the type of intermediary involved, the degree of competition, and the technological infrastructure supporting the payment.[22] International organizations such as the World Bank, the International Monetary Fund, the Financial Stability Board, and the Bank for International Settlements have long recognized the problem and taken some initiatives. The United Nations has included the cost of remittances in its Sustainable Development Goals, adopting a target for the average cost at 3 percent and a maximum cost of 5 percent, both to be attained by 2030.[23] The World Bank publishes detailed statistics on a country-by-country basis to monitor progress.[24] In spite of these efforts, progress in this area is excruciatingly slow.

Part of the problem resides in the fact that immigrants from the Global South into advanced countries often work in the gray economy and get paid in cash. They might not even have a bank account because their immigration status remains irregular. This cash has to be put into some digital form at some money exchange office if it is to be sent back home.

Western Union, a telegraph company 150 years ago, today specializes in this area, taking cash at one end and paying out digitally at the other. Ninety percent of its 10,000 employees are outside the United Sates, often in recipient countries. Its business is now declining. Ten years ago, its revenues were of a similar magnitude as a major card company (Mastercard) or PayPal (around 5 billion to 6 billion dollars); now they have declined to around 3 billion to 4 billion dollars whereas those of PayPal have increased to close to 30 billion dollars. These contrasting trends partly result from the spread of bank accounts in poorer countries. Cheaper telecommunications and digital technologies facilitated financial inclusion, enhancing many people's ability to save, invest, and make financial transfers. According to the Global Financial Development Database of the World Bank, access to bank accounts in the poorest countries approximately tripled from a low of about 13 percent in 2011 to 35 percent in 2017.[25] Progress has continued, so that today even in the poorest countries, like Nigeria, close to one-half of adults have a bank account. Even lower-middle-income countries are still far from the over 90 percent coverage of bank accounts in advanced countries, but they are making rapid progress. India has already reached 80 percent.

Recent studies have analyzed the costs of sending remittances, concluding that they are declining but rather persistent, because so are the underlying inefficiencies. Remittances come in varying amounts. Migrant workers do not have high incomes and want to send regular support to their families at home. But sending too small an amount is not useful because the fixed cost might eat up a larger proportion of the sum sent. Research by the World Bank indicates that the average cost of sending 200 dollars (a typical value for a single remittance) cross-border is close to 7 percent. It reaches above 10 percent when a nonbank money transfer operator (MTO) is used, and it falls below 6 percent if a bank is involved. The global average cost of sending 200 dollars was thus about 14 dollars in 2022, more than an hour's wage for many senders. But this represents a decline of about 7 dollars from the 23 dollars in 2009 when the global average cost was first recorded. Given that prices have increased by about a third in the meantime, this implies that the cost of sending 200 dollars has almost halved in real terms.[26]

Foreign exchange conversion also plays a part. A hospital nurse in Miami is paid in dollars, but her mother in Mexico needs pesos; the housekeeper from the Philippines in Rome is paid in euros (often cash), but her family back home needs (Philippine) pesos. As for the fee, the exchange cost also partly accrues to the intermediary; the worker has little or no control over both.

Part of the ongoing reduction in the cost of sending remittances is due to digitalization. Digital-only MTOs, like PayPal or the much smaller MoneyGram, provide remittance services at lower costs, getting close to the Sustainable Development Goal of 3 percent. World Bank analysis showed that average costs are lower where these digital-only MTOs are present, and their competition forces other operators to lower prices as well.[27] While digitalization helps, bringing costs and speed down to the level consumers in advanced economies are enjoying for domestic payments seems, at present, a still distant goal.

Reducing the cost and increasing the speed of remittances are usually seen as worthy ambitions. Unfortunately, there is a snag. Remittances can also be used to conceal the payment for criminal activity. This has been documented for the flow of money from the United States to Mexico. Drug dealers apparently pay poor migrants in the United States to make many transfers just below the reporting threshold of 1,000 dollars to their relatives back home who then collect the money and deliver it to the criminal gangs. Both the workers and their relatives are usually poor and thus happy to accept the small percentage of the sums they are helping to "launder."[28]

Improving the transmission of remittances was mentioned as a possible beneficial impact of cryptocurrencies. When Libra, the stablecoin project launched by Facebook in 2019, was initially announced, providing smooth and cheap money transfers to cross-border workers featured among the goals.[29] MoneyGram, a big MTO, even proposed moving its remittance transfer services to the cryptocurrency domain.[30]

Compared to cryptocurrencies sensu stricto, stablecoins have the advantage of being, most of the time, more stable: The transfer needs of low-income workers would never be compatible with the high volatility and risk which characterized Bitcoin and its peers. Even there, however, transaction costs remain a crucial obstacle. Imagine an undocumented worker in the United States who wants to send a few hundred dollars to her family living in Guatemala. The most straightforward way would be to ask an MTO to deliver the dollars directly to the family in their small village. This transfer would of course be rather costly, maybe in the order of 5–10 percent of the total. But would a stablecoin, say USDT, provide an alternative? The worker would have to open an account with Tether via some exchange, which requires having a US bank account and a minimum deposit. Opening the account and making the "on-ramp" transfer already involves substantial costs. The family back home would need either local cash (quetzal) or quetzal-denominated funds in a local bank account. This means that the USDT would need to be exchanged back into fiat currency before her family (which might have only limited internet access) can use the funds. In most cases, an established payment provider, like PayPal, would be a better alternative. It is in fact much easier for relatives back home, with limited technology, to establish a PayPal account.

The technical and practical obstacles, let alone the potential risks, to using stablecoins to reduce the cost of remittances remain very high today. Large investors can be expected to be able to withstand losses, but the savings of the poor, ensuring the survival of their families, must be safeguarded fully. Moreover, stablecoins would make it even harder to follow drug-related flows, as described earlier.

STABLECOINS: CRYPTO WINE IN A NEW BOTTLE

Stablecoins represent an attempt to combine the purported advantages of crypto with a stable value. The outcome has only a very limited usefulness. The costs of making transactions in stablecoins are so high that they cannot be used for regular purchases. The main use of stablecoins is for investors in the universe. For them, stablecoins represent a convenient parking place if they want to get into or out of a cryptocurrency. Parking their crypto receipts in stablecoins allows them to avoid the high cost and inconvenience of the off- and on-ramp transactions that would otherwise be necessary.

Almost all stablecoins are denominated in US dollars, but this does not mean that they should be attractive only to the population of the United States. In contrast to bank accounts, stablecoins are not linked to any particular location or any particular bank. They can thus be transferred instantaneously across the globe. It was thus hoped that stablecoins could present a solution to the high cost of remittances. However, that hope has faded as it became apparent that the potential recipients of stablecoins in poor countries are ill-equipped to deal with this high-tech financial instrument. They need either good old cash or funds in a local bank account. For some underground activities, stablecoins are ideal because of the high degree of anonymity they provide. More and more reports suggest that established stablecoins like Tether are used for online gambling or other scams.[31] Not surprisingly, stablecoins are even more useful than cash for some gray and black activities.

As of today, stablecoins thus share the main characteristic of most crypto instruments. They are interesting more for their novelty and tech wizardry than their usefulness for everyday legitimate payment needs. The challenge for fintech entrepreneurs is to invent the "killer app" that makes stablecoins so useful that users prefer them to today's vast array of alternatives. Our journey through the crypto world has shown that innovations can arise unexpectedly and quickly. Stablecoins should thus not be written off prematurely, but they need to improve radically before they can succeed outside the shadowy crypto universe.

NOTES

1. Shaun Paul Lee, "Stablecoins Statistics: 2023 Report," *CoinGecko*, July 13, 2023. Note that contrary to cryptocurrencies discussed in Chapter 8, the market capitalization of stablecoins increases only if their usage increases.
2. Mitsutoshi Adachi, Alexandra Born, Isabella Gschossmann, and Anton van der Kraaij, "The Expanding Functions and Uses of Stablecoins," *ECB Financial Stability Review*, November 2021.
3. Richard K. Lyons and Ganesh Viswanath-Natraj, "What Keeps Stablecoins Stable?," *Journal of International Money and Finance* 131 (March 1, 2023).
4. Mitsu Adachi et al., "Stablecoins' Role in Crypto and Beyond: Functions, Risks and Policy," *ECB Macroprudential Bulletin*, vol. 18, 2022.

5. Lael Brainard, "Crypto-Assets and Decentralized Finance through a Financial Stability Lens," Bank of England Conference, London, July 8, 2022.

6. I. Angeloni, "Digital Finance in the Global Context: Challenges and Perspectives," in Thorsten Beck, Leonardo Giani, and Giuseppe Sciascia (eds.), *Digital Finance in the EU: Drivers, Risks, Opportunities* (European University Institute), 2024.

7. *The Economist*, "The Long Road Back to Boring," May 12, 2011, www.economist.com/finance-and-economics/2011/05/12/the-long-road-back-to-boring.

8. Diana Henriques, "Money Market Fund Warns of Losses," *New York Times*, September 17, 2008.

9. See SEC, "Litigation Release No. 21025/May 5, 2009," US Securities and Exchange Commission, May 5, 2009, for this and other details regarding the failure of the Reserve Primary Fund and its aftermath.

10. For a discussion of this issue and regulatory proposals, see Jill E. Fisch, "The Broken Buck Stops Here: Embracing Sponsor Support in Money Market Fund Reform," All Faculty Scholarship 1324, 2015.

11. Financial Stability Board (FSB), "Policy Proposals to Enhance Money Market Fund Resilience: Final Report," October 11, 2021.

12. Jeff Sommer, "The Fabulous Yields, and Lurking Risks, of Money Market Funds," *New York Times*, April 21, 2023.

13. This point was first explained by Douglas W. Diamond and Philip H. Dybvig, "Bank Runs, Deposit Insurance, and Liquidity," *Journal of Political Economy* 91, no. 3 (June 1, 1983): 401–19 – a paper that earned its authors the 2022 Nobel prize.

14. IOSCO, "Money Market Funds during the March-April Episode," Thematic Note, November 2020.

15. See Chart 4 in Brainard, "Crypto-Assets and Decentralized Finance."

16. ECB, "Stablecoins: No Coins, but Are They Stable?," Focus, November 2019.

17. See "Latest Stablecoin Staking Rewards of November 2023 | BitCompare," Bitcompare or "StableCoin Staking and DEFI Lending Rates | Staking Rewards," Staking Rewards.

18. Financial Stability Board (FSB), "Regulation, Supervision and Oversight of 'Global Stablecoin' Arrangements: Progress Report on the Implementation of the FSB High-Level Recommendations," October 7, 2021.

19. For example, the argument is presented in Brandon Zemp, "The Power of Stablecoins:– Enabling Fast and Efficient Cross-Border Transactions," *Forbes*, April 5, 2023.

20. Yorbol Yakshilikov, "The Unexpected Rise in Remittances to Central America and Mexico during the Pandemic," *IMF Country Focus*, September 21, 2021.

21. See World Bank, "Remittance Prices Worldwide | MAKING MARKETS MORE TRANSPARENT."

22. Thorsten Beck and Maria Soledad Martinez Peria, "What Explains the Price of Remittances? An Examination across 119 Country Corridors," *The World Bank Economic Review* 25, no. 1 (January 1, 2011): 105–31.

23. See United Nations, "International Day of Family Remittances: *BACKGROUND*," 2022.

24. See again World Bank, "Remittance Prices Worldwide."

25. See World Bank Group, "Global Financial Development Database," *World Bank*, March 29, 2023.

26. Oya P. Ardic, Hemant Baijal, Patrizia Baudino, Nana Yaa Boakye-Adjei, Jonathan Fishman, and Richard Audu Maikai, "The Journey So Far: Making Cross-Border Remittances Work for Financial Inclusion," *Bank for International Settlements (BIS) Financial Stability Institute Insights* 43, June 15, 2022.

27. Oya P. Ardic and Harish Natarajan, "Lessons Learned from Monitoring the Costs of International Remittances and Global Efforts to Lower Costs," *Journal of Payments Strategy & Systems* 16, no. 3 (October 2022): 292–303.

28. See "How Mexican Narcos Use Remittances to Wire U.S. Drug Profits Home," *Reuters*, August 18, 2023.

29. Joseph Dana, "Libra Shows Global Remittance Ripe for Change," *Asia Times*, February 18, 2020.

30. "New MoneyGram Survey Reveals Strong Remittance Consumer Sentiment, Driven by Needs Abroad and Digital Adoption," *MoneyGram*, December 16, 2021.

31. Scott Chipolina, "Tether Crypto Token Increasingly Favoured by Money Launderers, UN Warns," *Financial Times*, January 15, 2024.

10 Central Bank Digital Currencies

You say you want a revolution, well, you know, we all want to see the plan.

John Lennon and Paul McCartney

The surge of cryptocurrencies and stablecoins over recent years has induced central banks to start thinking about creating their own digital offerings. Central bank digital currencies, often called by their abbreviation, CBDCs, have become the latest "must have" for central banks all over the world. Often referred to as digital cash, they are in fact payment means issued by the central bank in digital form.

The whole idea of CBDCs started in 2019 after world finance was hit by a striking piece of news: Facebook was preparing to launch its own money, Libra, offered freely to its billions of customers all over the world. Central banks saw this as a serious threat: Their currencies risked being relegated to a secondary role if Facebook users, over 2 billion globally and a large fraction of the young population in many countries, were to adopt Libra for their everyday transactions. Clunky cash, the signature product of central banks for centuries, may be supplanted. To make things worse, at that same time, cryptocurrencies of various sorts were booming all over, in value and popularity. Another digital threat to the central banks' established role and prerogatives.

Something had to be done, or so it seemed. Many central bankers thought that issuing their own digital monies should be the natural response.

Eventually, Libra did not go anywhere. Its name was first changed to Diem, after which the project was downsized and later sold to a consortium, which in the end abandoned it completely.

Popular accounts of the demise of Libra allege that regulators and supervisors effectively doomed the project.[1] The real problem was elsewhere: a mesh of improvisation and naïveté resulting in design errors and, down the road, financial risk potentially of a major proportion. A story worth reminding because it holds lessons.

Similarly, although the Bank for International Settlements (BIS) showed in a recent survey that almost all central banks are studying the possibility of introducing CBDCs in their home country,[2] less than a handful have actually gone ahead and done it, of which none are the largest Western central banks. Most of them think they may do so in the future. Meanwhile, they stay on the fence, conducting studies. A website, www.cbdctracker.org, tracks the progress of each of them, from research to proof of concept, pilot, and then to full-scale launch.

A post-Kantian utopia planted in the digital reality of the twenty-first century, Libra supposedly would become a universal money. What its inventors overlooked was that real-world prices are quoted in national currencies which fluctuate against one another. Libra could not possibly be fixed against all currencies at the same time; consumers, therefore, could not easily use Libra because they would have had to deal with a different exchange rate every day, or even every minute. A planetary currency has been a philosopher's toy concept for centuries, as we saw in Chapter 4,[3] but in order to see the light – it never did, in fact – it would need to be preceded by worldwide monetary reforms. Libra's fanciful inventors thought the whole process could be jumped over.

The initial idea was quickly supplanted by a variant with different "national" Libras, denominated in dollars, euro, and so on. At that point, however, the charm of "universal currency" was gone. Besides, currency-specific digital payment systems already existed in 2019, and they exist in even greater numbers today. Few of us feel the urge to open yet another account and remember the associated security measures. A major problem of Libra/Diem was the lack of an overwhelming user case. As we will see, CBDCs face the same problem.

If all this wasn't enough, Facebook's "monetary dream" was marred by two other problems: one financial and one reputational. Each would have sunk the project even if there had been demand from users.

Libra would have a bank-like structure, with a large liquid liability toward its users (in fact, money), guaranteed by a corresponding amount of assets. No matter how liquid the latter were, the new currency would always contain some financial risk because of the maturity and currency mismatch built into its balance sheet. Facebook users could in principle withdraw their Libras or use them to buy goods at any moment whereas Facebook might not be able to liquidate its assets as quickly as needed.

By necessity, therefore, it should be regulated and supervised. Initially overlooked by its libertarian designers, this fact immediately put Libra on a collision course with global prudential regulators.

The fatal blow, however, was reputational. Facebook, a custodian of vast amounts of private information, was since the beginning marred by privacy scandals, most prominently the unauthorized use of its personal data by the political consultant Cambridge Analytica to serve, among other things, the 2016 US presidential campaign of Donald Trump. Disclosed in 2018, the scandal made sure that when Libra was announced in 2019 nobody was willing to put a cent on Facebook as custodian of private transaction data.

Libra is dead, as it deserved to be. But its most important offspring, the CBDC, is thriving, at least as an idea. Let's see in more detail what it is, what purposes it may serve, and what risks it entails.

WHAT IS A CBDC, REALLY?

To many laypersons, a CBDC is a form of electronic cash vaguely linked to the mysterious world of crypto. After all, they both appeared in the public discourse more or less at the same time, a few years after the Great Financial Crisis of 2008–09. And both of them are, or pretend to be, novel monetary instruments in digital form. However, the association between the two is less than half correct.

Technically, a CBDC is a direct liability of the central bank toward a nonbank holder – an individual or a company. It is not a cryptocurrency because it is not recorded on a distributed ledger but rather on a centralized book maintained by the central bank. In theory, central banks could use distributed ledger technology (DLT) to keep their own accounts, but none of them have so far seriously considered this possibility. This is not surprising because the alleged advantage of distributed ledgers is that thousands of participants record the same information; a reputed central bank usually does not need "the wisdom of the crowd" to convince people that its accounts are correct. Large financial institutions have not found an important use case for blockchain technology either, at least so far. As we explained in Chapter 8, DLTs are inherently cumbersome and slow. The arguments for and against issuing a CBDC, therefore, are independent of the DLT technology which underlies crypto assets, both currencies and stablecoins.[4]

As usually presented, the argument for central banks to issue digital currency seems unassailable at first glance. It goes as follows. For centuries, central banks have been issuing paper money. But cash is now used less and less for everyday transactions. Paper banknotes no longer represent the cutting-edge technology they once were, and besides, everything goes digital these days. Therefore, central banks should follow the zeitgeist and issue cash in digital format.

This apparently straightforward reasoning does not consider three objections. First, digital monies already exist, efficiently and safely supplied by the market, as shown in Chapter 7. Second, physical cash has certain useful characteristics which make it desirable even in a digital world; this we showed in Chapter 5. We also showed there that the demand for cash is increasing world over, even though its use for certain types of transactions is declining. Finally, the CBDCs risk having unwarranted implications for the functioning of the financial market and for the effectiveness of central bank policies. This, with other things, is what we plan to show in this chapter.

The basic technology for issuing a CBDC, a web of interconnected computer terminals, is widely available. As we showed in Chapter 3, money and payments have been digital for decades, and increasingly so. Not only has the technology existed for a long time, but digital claims on the central bank in fact already exist: All licensed commercial banks maintain reserve accounts in digital form with the central bank. The balances on those accounts, small in the past, have ballooned in the last ten years or so after central banks started buying massive amounts of assets – the so-called Quantitative Easing policy. In the United States these balances at the Federal Reserve went from barely 2 billion dollars in 2007 to over 4,000 billion dollars in 2021. In the euro area, the deposits of commercial banks at the central bank reached over 4,000 billion euros in early 2022, or 40 percent of the euro area GDP. Commercial bank deposits at the Bank of Japan reached close to 100 percent of GDP.

These balances are now shrinking as part of the central banks' fight against inflation. But their mere existence suggests that CBDCs are not new. The difference is that, so far, only banks have been allowed to hold balances at the central bank, an exclusive privilege expressing the fact that central banks have evolved historically as the "banks of the banks." The real novelty, therefore, is not in the digital nature of CBDCs but rather the fact that that privilege would be extended outside the banking circle, potentially to all persons and nonfinancial entities in the economy. A revolution in the inner structure of the monetary system, as a result of which the central bank would cease to be the "bank of the banks" to become the "bank of everybody."

THE DEVIL IS IN THE DETAILS

Central banks are naturally and legitimately interested in digital currency. Managing money is, after all, their core business.[5] Though their primary task is to keep its value stable, they traditionally have been given ample responsibilities as superintendents and regulators of payment systems as well. However, getting directly into the arena to provide themselves digital payment instruments, in competition with the private sector, would be an entirely different ballgame. It would be akin to "nationalizing" a service in which private companies have so far played the central role, and successfully so.

Being risk-averse, central banks are proceeding with caution.[6] For several years they have been studying the issue, pondering options, and running pilots, but few have actually taken the decisive step. While all central banks are studying the subject, the ones overseeing the three major global currencies (the dollar, the euro, and China's renminbi yuan) have taken quite different positions, each following its own political priorities and constraints.

The US Federal Reserve remains rather cautious and guarded vis-à-vis the idea of issuing a digital dollar. It is convinced that the dollar will maintain its status as the preeminent global reserve currency without the need for a digital complement to the greenback.[7] However, this might be changing as the Biden administration has published a report on the concept and mandated the Federal Reserve to study the issue.[8]

In comparison, the European Central Bank (ECB) has been more explicit in its intention to create the basis for what it calls a "digital euro." According to the intention, it should not substitute but rather complement cash as a means for daily transactions. Among the many arguments put forth, not only by the ECB but by the European Union's executive arm, the European Commission, one frequently mentioned is the need to maintain "strategic autonomy": ensuring European independence in a payment industry for a long time dominated by US-based companies, payment card networks such as Mastercard and Visa recently followed by online platforms and applications like PayPal, Apple, and the like. The ECB plans a long period of technical preparation, accompanied by a legislative process at the EU level, meaning that at the earliest it will be 2027 or later before anybody can actually hold and use a digital euro.

By contrast, the People's Bank of China (PBOC) has moved ahead in concrete terms by actually launching a digital currency.

One reason was political: The government, or rather the Communist Party, wanted to break the duopoly of the two huge companies that dominate the market in China of digital payments (Alipay and the payment arm of WeChat have both over a billion subscribers and process billions of payments every day).

In spite of the obvious differences, there seems to be a common motive between the European and the Chinese approaches: using public intervention to counteract private market trends they do not feel comfortable with. The United States clearly has fewer reasons to be unhappy about those developments, because US companies play a leading role in them. A more proactive approach by the Chinese might also depend on them being less encumbered by a long central banking tradition. The PBOC has already rolled out an e-yuan for use by the general public on an experimental basis, albeit with disappointing results so far as we illustrate later.

If the payment system goes digital, as it clearly does, should necessarily central banks go for a CBDC? This question must be looked at from two sides: first, asking what *existing* problems would be *solved* by a CBDC, in today's world where myriads of private payment means are already available to make secure and quick noncash transfers; second, looking at the possible *new* problems which may be *created* if central banks start competing with the private sector in this area.

The answer partly depends on what one means by a CBDC – in other words, on what its "design" is. Here details are essential. Three design features recur prominently in the discussions.

First, reference is typically made to a "retail CBDC" for situations in which the central bank would allow only individuals to open an account with them. The retail version characterizes, for example, the plan for a digital euro and the existing Chinese e-yuan. "Wholesale CBDC" instead means a case in which the central bank opens that possibility to corporations. This latter option seems the one favored by the US Federal Reserve, whereas the retail alternative is the one chosen by China and seems to be preferred by the

ECB, at least so far. The target group makes a difference, because the modalities of use of the instrument, the size and frequency of transactions, and the economic sectors most directly affected are all likely to depend on which user categories dominate. Combinations between retail and wholesale models are of course possible.

The second design feature concerns possible limitations or benefits attached to the use of the instrument. The ECB has been particularly attentive to those aspects. In particular, the European approach envisages upper limits to the holdings of CBDCs, in order to constrain their use as portfolio assets. Such a "limited retail CBDC" would, according to the plan, constitute a digital equivalent of cash. Another feature that has been studied is remuneration, possibly indexed to market interest rates.[9]

The third aspect regards the way those accounts would be managed. Would the central bank create its own payment system or piggyback on existing ones? Would the central bank onboard consumers and directly take charge of all operational and control functions (know your customer, or KYC, anti-fraud and anti–money laundering, or AML)? The prevailing orientation so far is to use, for all these functions, the payment industry itself, namely banks and other payment service providers (PSPs).

POTENTIAL ADVANTAGES OF CBDCS

A recent survey by the International Monetary Fund (IMF) lists as many as seven different rationales for CBDCs:[10] financial inclusion; access to payments; making payments more efficient; ensuring resilience of payments; reducing illicit use of money; monetary sovereignty; and competition. This is actually a short list: Wikipedia's catalogue of advantages is longer and far outnumbers the purported risks. The lack of a "killer argument" may in part reflect underlying confusion on what the central purpose should be. Moreover, the emphasis on alternative objectives tends to differ across parts of the world; CBDCs seem sometimes invoked as a "fix-all" for very diverse situations and problems. If one goes deeper into the rationales, one discovers that a CBDC might not necessarily represent a solution; sometimes it may even be counterproductive.

A central concern frequently aired at the global level is the need to make the payment system, both domestic and cross-border, more efficient and cheaper, notably by stepping up market competition and technological innovation. The CBDC could make payments cheaper and quicker by eliminating intermediaries like banks or credit card companies. As we have discussed in Chapter 7, payment systems have become increasingly efficient, competitive, faster, and cheaper – though, possibly, not enough – in the last twenty years, as a result of a flurry of new technologies largely associated with the introduction and dissemination of handheld digital devices: tablets, smartphones, and the like. Innovation and diversification have grown exponentially. This process is still advancing and one cannot discern an endpoint. It owes almost entirely to market forces, unfolding at a speed and in directions largely unexpected by regulators. The fundamental question here is twofold. Is the payment system created by private sector initiatives diverging from socially desirable goals? What are the best instruments regulators have to ensure that those goals are achieved?

It is sometimes argued that central banks could reduce transaction costs for users by setting up their own low-cost payment system. The benefit, however, is unclear.[11] Were central banks to go beyond their traditional roles as regulators and overseers of payment systems and directly provide payment services in digital form to the public, they may actually discourage private initiative, investment, and innovation.[12] Design choices are critical here. For example, central banks would need to decide whether to take charge directly of the so-called front-end functions involved – onboarding and offboarding, initiating and validating transactions, reversing invalid transactions, centralized settlement, and security functions like Know Your Customer (KYC) and AML obligations – or entrust those functions to banks and other payment service providers (PSPs), which already perform those functions on their own account.

Central banks do not have enough branch offices or other infrastructure to perform millions, potentially hundreds of millions, of on-boarding procedures for retail clients. It is thus likely that central banks would have to outsource the front-end functions to the banking system and existing PSPs. This raises issues. The first is that banks and PSPs would have no interest in providing this service for free. Central banks would thus have to pay for this service or use their regulatory powers to force its provision, or more probably both. Moreover, the prospect of CBDCs being really innovative would diminish because banks and other PSPs would by necessity tend to replicate their existing procedures.

Any extra element of competition injected into the system in this way would not be properly balanced: not only because central banks, unlike banks, are riskless entities, therefore enjoying a competitive advantage, but also because they act as payment coregulators, together with consumer protection agencies and competition authorities.[13] Their becoming market participants would raise a conflict of interest. Even if central banks were able to raise the efficiency frontier of the payment industry – a big if, since they have no experience in this fast-moving and technologically sophisticated sector – the extra competition would not guarantee market efficiency. Within the European Union, there are also strict limits on state aid that ensure that competition remains fair and that governments do not give one actor (in this case the central bank) an unfair advantage.

In modern bank-based payment systems, transactions are final only once they have been settled in the books of the central bank (Chapter 3). Arguably, a CBDC would achieve finality more quickly, right after the CBDC transaction takes place. The question is how important instant finality is in practice. It may be if there is a danger that one of the intermediaries in the transaction chain (retailer, credit card company, or the commercial bank involved) may fail before the transaction has run through the entire chain. Already today, the option of instant settlement is offered by most eurozone banks online, in addition to deposit insurance. This makes the danger of a transaction failure negligible; the entire chain is very safe and timing is compressed to a minimum. Achieving quicker finality is no longer an important argument for retail transactions, as consumer surveys suggest.[14]

Financial inclusion is also occasionally mentioned as a benefit of issuing a CBDC, because a digital euro, dollar, or pound could allow those without a bank account to make electronic transfers. However, in advanced economies, the share of the unbanked is already very low, often below 5 percent. Many banks also offer free or very low-priced banking services; the cost of a bank account does not seem to be a key obstacle. The cost of a smartphone plus a contract with mobile data might in many cases be higher than that of a bank account. To the extent that banks and other PSPs were to take charge of administrative functions associated with CBDCs, any obstacles related to the cumbersome and time-consuming process of opening a bank account would remain. In advanced countries, it is thus unlikely that a CBDC would have a noticeable impact on financial inclusion. Likewise, in emerging economies, where the share of the unbanked is higher, it is difficult to see how this part of the population would gain from a CBDC because they would have to first set up an account with the central bank, whose offices might be even more difficult to reach than the local bank. In many less developed countries, such as in Nigeria whose example is discussed later, retail users have directly moved to smartphone-based applications, jumping over the steps in between.

One dimension of financial inclusion of great relevance for the global economy is that of workers' remittances. As we have noted in Chapter 9, cross-border workers face significant (though declining) delays and costs in making money transfers to their families back home. For example, Eurostat estimates that over 5 percent of workers in the European Union are non-EU citizens and that share is in all likelihood bound to rise significantly. Facilitating money transfers for those workers is a valuable service from an economic and social perspective. As mentioned earlier, it is also probably an unprofitable task, hence one which may not be efficiently provided by the private financial sector. An active role of central banks in this area could therefore be justified. A dedicated CBDC for immigrant workers, not extended to all citizens, could represent a solution. It would require a high degree of interoperability among the central banks involved, notably between the countries of origin and those of destination, with strong bilateral cooperation. This could be an alternative, or perhaps complementary, to other solutions, like facilitating or subsidizing private services by banks or PSPs.

Another goal aired frequently in Europe is that the CBDC could help maintain monetary sovereignty or, as sometimes expressed, Europe's "strategic monetary independence." This concept is not only eminently political but also hard to define.

Monetary sovereignty is part of sovereignty in other dimensions. It does not need to be national: The euro, for example, is a sovereign currency with a multi- or rather sovranational dimension. Monetary sovereignty refers to the prerogative of a polity to collectively and autonomously (hence the notion of sovereignty) decide the form, organization, and governance of its monetary instruments and functions. The way monetary sovereignty is enacted is a political decision. The implementation of monetary policy is today usually delegated, within limits, to an independent authority, the central bank. Central bank statutes define the ways and instruments through which the currency is regulated, thereby giving concrete meaning to the notion of sovereignty.

Some argue that a national CBDC may be needed to defend that sovereignty in case some other currency, a foreign CBDC or a privately issued instrument such as a cryptocurrency, might outcompete the official currency. This argument appeals in particular when thinking in geopolitical terms; as mentioned, for example, in the United States the concept seems to be more popular in the executive branch than in the Federal Reserve. Though the "political" role of CBDCs cannot be dismissed in principle, it seems overstated. National currencies are well established everywhere, entrenched as units of account and familiar to consumers who use them every day. The existence of physical cash, in combination with the variety of digital instruments used by central banks to finance the banking sectors and maintain reserve accounts, provides strong backing to official currencies and strengthens confidence in them. Such confidence may be eroded if money becomes somehow unstable, for example, in the cases mentioned in Chapter 13, but this has nothing to do with the presence or absence of CBDCs.

Strategic monetary independence is sometimes mentioned in Europe as the political objective of ensuring that payment systems on the continent are provided by European entities. As we mentioned in Chapter 7, US-based payment card networks, smartphone applications, and online platforms dominate the market. Whether this threatens European independence, and what could or should be done about it, is far less clear. From an efficiency standpoint what matters is that the relevant markets remain contested and competitive, something the European Commission has a mandate to ensure. The dominance of US companies in retail digital payments does not seem so far to have threatened EU autonomy from an economic or political standpoint. On the other hand, it is far from certain that a European CBDC would effectively contrast that dominance, in an area in which other recent initiatives more directed toward that goal have failed or stalled.[15]

Some central bankers have argued that a digital euro may be necessary to preserve a "monetary anchor" in the digital age. This concept essentially revolves around the notion that in an epoch in which payments increasingly take a digital form, the stability of money and the preservation of its value may be compromised unless central bank money takes itself a digital form.[16]

The economic literature has repeatedly addressed the issue of ensuring a proper "anchor" to money, both theoretically and empirically by means of international comparisons. What is meant by maintaining an "anchor" is to preserve its purchasing power over time. It was demonstrated that this depends on the way monetary policy is conducted, in other words, the monetary policy "regime," not on the specific form, physical or digital, cash takes.[17] There is no evidence that the digitalization of the payment industry may affect the monetary policy regime.

In less precise terms, one may interpret the term "monetary anchor" to refer to the sense of security that individuals derive from the possibility of converting their deposits at commercial banks into a safe asset, like central bank money, at par. The concern may derive from a perceived risk that ordinary people may lose the only direct contact they have with the central bank. Admittedly, psychological phenomena can be important even when they may not seem fully rational. If this is the intended meaning, however, no instrument performs such a function better than a tangible instrument like cash. Far from disappearing, cash remains very popular worldwide because of its practicality and privacy. The less frequent use for daily exchanges reduces its velocity of circulation but does not compromise monetary stability; the monetary system is controlled by the central bank through its supply of liquidity and reserves to banks. These reserves are, in essence, as already noted, a form of CBDC but held only by banks.

THE RISKS FOR MONETARY POLICY AND FINANCIAL STABILITY

We have examined arguments suggesting that CBDCs may help improve the efficiency of the payment system, as well as counterarguments indicating that such effects may in fact be less important or even counterproductive. We now examine the implications of CBDCs for two core areas of central bank responsibility: monetary policy and financial stability. For simplicity, we limit ourself to a verbal explanation; readers preferring a more detailed analytical exposition can find it in the Online Appendix to this book.[18]

The introduction of CBDCs moves asset held by households and firms to the new instrument. The raises questions such as what assets are displaced to make room for the new one, and what is the order of magnitude of such changes?

One possibility is that the introduction of CBDCs results in a decline of physical cash – essentially banknotes; all other assets on private portfolios – in particular, bank deposits – remain unchanged. If that happens, banks are not affected: There is simply an exchange of one type of cash (material) for another (digital) in the balance sheet of the central bank. This change has no effect either on monetary policy or on financial stability. The reason is that monetary policy transmits its effects through either interest rates or bank credit, or both, whereas financial stability depends largely on the state of the banking sector. If interest rate and bank balance sheets are unchanged, so are monetary policy transmission and financial stability.

However, this outcome is unlikely. Banknotes have unique characteristics – simplicity, absolute privacy, and tangibility – that the digital euro would not have and that people value highly. By contrast, CBDC accounts would be very similar to bank deposits especially if, as likely, the central bank would outsource all front-end functions to banks. Banks would offer CBDC accounts using their usual procedures. Banks would remain responsible for onboarding and offboarding, KYC and AML checks, as well as providing users the services normally associated with deposits – online banking, payment cards, apps, and so on. There will be strong synergies between opening a bank deposit and a digital euro deposit – same process, same information, and same forms to fill. The user would perceive no difference between them. It is therefore likely that CBDCs would displace at least part of the outstanding deposits, therefore resulting in a disintermediation of banks.

If that happens, the balance sheet of banks is affected: Banks lose deposits and suffer a funding gap that must be filled. The central bank would need to intervene to refinance the banks. If the displacement is limited, the structure of credit intermediation doesn't change much, but beyond a certain level, it must. Banks are squeezed and must resort to central bank financing. The net effect on the economy is likely to be contractionary, through a restriction in the supply of bank credit. When funding is squeezed, the signal is transmitted to the bank's loan officers to be more guarded in extending credit. Additional financing granted tends to become scarcer and dearer. The central bank would probably try to offset the contractionary effect by offering more generous financing to the banks. However, deposit funding and central bank funding are not equivalent. Central bank credit may be perceived as not sufficiently stable compared to the deposit base, which normally provides the backbone of retail banks' balance sheets. As a result, banks would not supply the same amount of credit as before, and at the same conditions. A contractionary effect on the economy is hard to avoid.

If CBDCs do not yield a return – a likely case if CBDCs are to resemble as much as possible digital cash[19] – a large and variable negative gap would exist between the return of CBDC, zero, and the interest earned by banks on their reserve accounts with the central bank; the latter is, as we write, equal to 4 percent in the eurozone and 5.40 percent in the United States. This would open up arbitrage opportunities: Banks would have the incentive to offer clients fixed-term swaps transforming CBDCs into their own deposits at the central bank, profiting from the margin. The greater would be the scope for such operations, the more the CBDC would be used as a whole-sale form of deposit, by large corporate treasuries and high-wealth individuals. Those operations risk interfering with the conduct of monetary policy.

Let's now examine the potential effects of CBDCs on financial stability. A banking crisis normally takes the form of a flight of deposits from a bank, considered to be weak, usually toward other banks, perceived to be stronger. These movements can be very quick. For example, during the run on the deposits of the Spanish lender Banco Popular Español, in 2017, it was estimated that some 40 billion euros' worth of deposits left the bank *in a matter of weeks,* mainly directed to neighboring banks which were perceived by depositors to be stronger. In March 2023, the US Silicon Valley Bank lost a roughly equivalent amount of deposits but *in a matter of a few days.*[20]

The existence of a riskless alternative to deposits such as the CBDC, accessible digitally in real time, would provide an easy channel through which a rapid run on deposits could take place. If limits are imposed on CBDC holding, the danger is reduced but not eliminated. It is important to note that while the weak bank's liquidity is squeezed, that of other banks – those which receive more deposits – is increased. The latter can therefore compensate in part the restriction stemming from the bank being attacked, by increasing their supply of credit. This beneficial compensating effect is not possible if the run happens through a CBDC, because the liquidity flows into the central bank, which does not extend credit to the private sector, effectively remaining clogged outside the intermediation circle. As a result, under a bank run the overall contractionary effect on the economy is likely to be stronger when CBDCs are present than when they are absent.

The financial stability risk inherent in a retail CBDC would be smaller than that of a wholesale CBDC, which would probably have no or higher limits on CBDC holdings. Moreover, household deposits are guaranteed by deposit insurance up to relatively large amounts (100,000 euros in the European Union and 250,000 dollars in the United States), whereas most wholesale deposits by corporations are not. Household deposits tend to be comparatively stable, except during full-blown crises. Most recent cases of bank runs involved large corporate deposits, only partially covered by deposit insurance.

To sum up, these examples illustrate a basic issue related to the introduction of CBDCs, namely, that a new channel is opened whereby liquidity can exit the credit circle and end up in the central bank balance sheet. A net contractionary effect is likely to occur. The extent of it is difficult to assess ex ante because it depends on many factors: the demand for CBDCs, their design features, and the way in which the central bank refinances the banks. The existence of this effect constitutes an additional reason why most central banks intend to put limits on the permissible balances of CBDC holdings.

THE PROOF OF THE PUDDING

Our discussion in the previous two sections was a bit more con-jectural than we would have liked: This was necessary, however, because very little evidence is available as yet on the effect of CBDCs on bank intermediation. Let's now put our feet back on the ground to examine the concrete experience of countries that have already intro-duced CBDCs on an experimental basis. This evidence is too specific and recent to constitute a reliable basis for a final judgment. Yet, as a popular motto goes, the real "proof of the pudding" is not in its recipe but in eating it. So, let's look at examples of CBDCs in action.

By coincidence, the two main real-world implementations of CBDC have occurred in one of the smallest economies in the world, the Bahamas, and in the largest, China. The national income of the Bahamas is about 11 billion dollars, about a thousandth of that of China. To these two examples, one should add Nigeria, the biggest economy in sub-Saharan Africa.

The Bahamas' Sand Dollars

The Commonwealth of the Bahamas has a population of 400,000 living on hundreds of small islands distributed over a large area in the Caribbean. The country does not have an income tax, which has made it a natural destination for rich individuals who want to enjoy their wealth in a balmy atmosphere. The Bahamas have been on and off various tax haven blacklists of the United States, the European Union, and the Organisation for Economic Cooperation and Development. Tourism is another mainstay of the economy of the country.

The prosperity of the Bahamas thus depends on being known as an interesting destination for more than one purpose. When the Libra project initiated global interest in CBDCs, the idea was born to put the Bahamas on the map by being the first to venture into this new territory. The local central bank thus became one of the pio-neers in the field, drawing concrete plans to issue a digital currency.

They aptly called it "sand dollar," the name of a symmetrically shaped sea urchin found in great numbers on those Caribbean islands' beautiful beaches.

Another special reason for trying this experiment was that this island nation is frequently subject to hurricanes that can devastate entire villages, including bank branches. One of the purposes of the Sand Dollar was to allow people access to banking even if a storm had knocked out communications or destroyed local bank offices. The Sand Dollar was introduced in 2021 and instantly achieved world-wide fame as the first CBDC in action. A related hope was also to make the islands look attractive as a location for innovative digital finance. A desire they may later have regretted, as it was probably also behind the attractive conditions granted to FTX, the infamous crypto exchange which eventually collapsed, dragging to ruin several global investors together with the financial reputation of the Bahamas.

Despite its global notoriety, the Sand Dollar has not been a success. As of the end of 2023, there were only about 1.7 million Sand Dollars in circulation – a negligible sum, even for a small economy. For comparison, the cash in circulation of Bahama banknotes was about 500 times larger, at close to 600 million Bahamian dollars.[21] The reason for this limited success seems to be that, like most others, Bahamians have access to all the modern payment systems, including global payment cards and apps. Many Bahamians have downloaded a Sand Dollar electronic wallet but apparently have not seen a need to use it because it is not very convenient to use for consumers. Merchants have also been slow to accept Sand Dollars because this meant that they had to open another account and because this complicated the working of the national automatic clearing house.

The Central Bank of the Bahamas had invested over 7 million Bahamian dollars into the preparation of the Sand Dollar. This investment seems to have failed. But the authorities have not given up. In early 2023 the Central Bank announced a big push to foster the use of the Sand Dollar, including plans for many promotional events and the announcement that it would give away over 1 million Sand Dollars to "early adopters."[22] As we write, it remains to be seen whether this new promotional activity will have more success than in the past.

China's E-yuan

China was the first country to engage in research on CBDCs. Already in 2014, the PBOC created a special research group, which was able to draw on the experience of its Chinese domestic payment providers WeChat and Alipay. The decision to go ahead was then taken in 2020. As with so many other reforms in the initial opening up of the Chinese economy in the 1980s and 1990s, trials were undertaken in different regions to test whether it would work. A large initial uptake was ensured through large-scale lotteries with substantial cash rewards for the first who downloaded the app, a promotion technique that was also used by PayPal at an early stage. The e-yuan does not pay interest, as it is meant to be a pure electronic substitute for cash.

The PBOC has adopted the mixed or two-tier model, under which commercial banks onboard customers and provide basic accounting. The first step in opening an e-yuan account is thus a visit to a bank (as of the end of 2022 seven major banks have been authorized to do this).

The Chinese authorities have been active in international fora in emphasizing that the e-yuan should be an electronic substitute for cash but that safeguards were needed to prevent money laundering and other illicit uses of the e-yuan. Their solution to the trade-off between private demand for anonymity and the public need for safeguards against massive illicit use is the so-called managed anonymity, which leaves the user the choice between the need to share private information and the amounts that can transit through the e-yuan account.[23]

There are four different accounts or e-yuan wallet types available with different types of identification required. The smallest, or level IV, wallet requires only a cellphone number. In official accounts, this is usually described as requiring no identification. But in China, a cellphone number is always linked to a personal ID card. De facto there might thus be little difference in terms of anonymity between the different levels.

At the other end of the spectrum there is level I, which requires the same full personal information as opening a regular bank account and is essentially equal to a (limited service) bank account since it does not have any restrictions on balance and transaction size. This is where a key limitation becomes important. The e-yuan does not pay interest, as it is meant to be a pure electronic substitute for cash. It is thus difficult to see why anybody should use the e-yuan (officially also referred to as the e-CNY) for larger amounts when normal bank deposits pay cash. In China, bank deposits are anyway safe because most of the banking system is state-owned.

As mentioned earlier, the different wallet types of the e-yuan come with different limitations on transaction size and holding limits. For example, the smallest wallet, the one which comes closest to the official purpose of being a substitute for cash in small everyday transactions, has a limit on the amount of a single transaction of 2,000 renminbi, the equivalent of about 250 dollars or a bit less in euro. This would be ample for small daily transactions. But the annual limits on turnover could be biting even for average incomes. For example, the average monthly wage in manufacturing is about 8,000 renminbi per month or 100,000 renminbi for the entire year. But the annual limit on this wallet is only 50,000 renminbi, or about 6,500 dollars, one-half of the average income of manufacturing workers in China and much less for urban professionals. It is thus clear that middle-class households cannot rely on the e-yuan for the majority of their expenses.

Moreover, this wallet also has a holding limit, of 10,000 renminbi, a bit larger than the average wage. In practice, this represents an important limitation since an automatic transfer of wages or salaries to this wallet would risk problems. Users of the e-yuan would thus have to monitor the balance on their wallet, both to avoid exceeding the holding limit and to avoid running out of funds on it. This process could of course be automatized. But it is difficult to see why an urban household would opt to make these complicated arrangements when a combination of a normal bank account with Alipay on the smartphone works perfectly well.

The ubiquitous Alipay and WeChat, which have leapfrogged standard credit and debit cards in China, also have transaction limits but no holding limits. Moreover, the transaction limits are usually aligned with the income or spending power of the user and thus constitute much less of a constraint.

The e-yuan wallets with more formal identification requirements have much larger holdings and transaction limits, but they cannot compete with bank accounts or balances on Alipay that promise interest.

The PBOC has been quite active in promoting the use of the e-yuan, including a special campaign during the 2022 Winter Olympics in Beijing, but it has not given much information on its success.[24] The little information published so far suggests that the e-yuan is not widely used. The PBOC has stated that by the end of 2022 over 260 million Chinese have downloaded the app and that there have been over 360 million transactions. These two numbers are interesting because they imply that the average user has made only 1.4 transactions in the course of an entire year, compared to billions of transactions on WeChat and Alipay. The e-yuan has thus, at least so far, failed to make substantial progress toward being widely used as a means of payment. A priori this is surprising given the efforts of the PBOC to foster its adoption and the generous usage limits. In reality, this meagre take-up is what one would expect given that most urban consumers in China already use the very efficient electronic payment services of the two Chinese e-commerce giants, WeChat and Alipay.

Starting in early 2023 the PBOC included the e-yuan in its balance sheet, incorporating it into its money base aggregate with cash. The total amount of e-yuan circulation as of the end of 2022 was less than 14 billion renminbi, worth less than 2 billion dollars – as in the Bahamas, a negligible fraction (0.13 percent) of the overall money supply.[25] This suggests, if anything, that the use of the e-CNY has declined. Meanwhile, the demand for cash has continued to increase at double-digit rates, and apparently, there is no substantial demand to use the e-yuan instead of normal bank accounts or the ubiquitous domestic payment systems Alipay and WeChat.

More generally one should ask what advantage one could expect from a digital payment instrument in a country where the banking system is mainly state-owned and thus de facto part of the public sector.

It is telling that in China the digital yuan comes as a top-down initiative. In Chapter 2 we described how China invented paper currency in the eleventh century also as a purely top-down instrument; paper currency was later abandoned when the government weakened. It remains to be seen whether the digital yuan will follow a similar pattern. For the time being the PBOC is continuing the roll-out, putting pressure on merchants to accept it and providing the e-yuan with other advantages. For example, it does not charge intermediaries any fees, and the use of the e-yuan is free for individual users.

Nigeria's E-Naira

Nigeria represents a good test case, especially as regards financial inclusion. A large fraction of its population has a cellphone (about 100 million people, out of a population of 200 million) but no bank account.[26] The rationale for introducing an e-Naira (naira is the name of Nigeria's currency) would thus seem promising, as a means to provide financial services to the unbanked, leveraging on the high level of digitalization of the population. Another hoped-for advantage is to combat "informality," a euphemism for corruption and tax evasion, since transactions in e-Naira are traceable.

The Nigerian CBDC project is different from that of the Bahamas and of China in that e-Naira transactions are processed on a variant of a distributed ledger system. Nigeria has a thriving high-tech sector providing a homegrown system to process transactions which allows users to choose different classes of wallets. As in China, different wallets come with different degrees of anonymity. Wallets with tight limitations on daily transactions require only a phone number whereas those with larger ones require full identification (KYC).

In spite of the apparent promise and careful technical preparation, the e-Naira was a flop. The total number of e-Naira wallets stagnates at less than 1 million. The IMF estimates that only less than 2 percent of each e-Naira wallet is used every week and that the total monetary amount of transactions in e-Naira represents only a negligible share of the money supply.[27] This is particularly surprising considering that over one-half of the Nigerian population has traded cryptocurrencies,[28] confirming that technology is not a barrier.

The Nigerian authorities tried various measures to foster the instrument, including paying social services into e-Naira wallets, but to little avail so far. Resistance to it has been especially strong among merchants who fear the traceability of e-Naira transactions given the notoriously high degree of tax evasion in this sector. In December 2022 the National Bank of Nigeria even took the step to limit withdrawals of cash from automated teller machines in order to foster the adoption of electronic means of payments. As in the case of India, this turned out to create more problems than it solved. After street protests, the measure had to be abandoned.

PAYING INTEREST ON CBDCS

As we have mentioned, the existing CBDCs (sand dollar, e-yuan, and e-Naira) do not pay interest. However, other central banks may consider paying interest on their CBDC to ensure a higher take-up. With interest rates on bank accounts increasing, this might become an important consideration in consumer choice. A special poll commissioned by De Nederlandsche bank (the Dutch central bank) showed that one-half of the respondents would consider opening an account in the digital euro, especially if it paid a higher rate than normal bank accounts. But Europe is not, so far, planning to pay interest on the digital euro.[29]

However, paying high interest rates to entice a wider take-up of the planned digital euro, or the existing e-yuan, would create more problems than it solves. Consumers might still not use the digital euro widely for transactions even if they hold substantial balances of it because it offers higher interest than a bank account. Consumers will tend to continue to use the systems they find most convenient and are familiar with. Besides, paying interest may open a Pandora's box of tricky issues. CBDCs would no longer look like an electronic form of cash but a substitute for a bank account, or even a fixed-term security, therefore more similar to a portfolio asset. Central banks would need to assess more carefully the risk of disintermediating the banking system.

Conversely, not paying interest on CBDCs would create issues should central banks need to go to negative interest rates again. Doing this today, with cash, is cumbersome. In this case, consumers might opt to hold the maximum amount allowed in digital euros to escape negative rates on their bank account. However, as mentioned earlier it would not imply that they would necessarily use the digital euro also for daily transactions.

Any interest paid on a CBDC would be an expense for the central bank, whose profits would decline. The central bank is part of the wider governmental sector, and central banks normally remit their profits to their national budget. This implies that any interest paid on a CBDC would constitute a public outlay. The cost of paying interest could be quite large if it makes the digital euro or other CBDC attractive. For example, the digital euro balance would amount to about 900 billion if all the over 300 million inhabitants of the euro area above fifteen years of age were to fill their wallets up to the purported limit of 3,000 euros. At 4 percent interest this would cost the ECB 35 billion euros per year. In China, the potential numbers would be much larger since some types of wallets have no holding limit. But since most of the banking system is state-owned, any transfer from bank accounts to the e-yuan would have only a small net impact on government finances.

Central banks might be able to entice a larger uptake of their digital currency by paying interest that is competitive with bank accounts. However, this would not imply that the digital currency would actually be used for transactions and may involve heavy losses for government finances.[30]

GOING WHOLESALE?

The objections to retail CBDCs and their limited success where they have been implemented may be one reason why some interest has recently emerged in the alternative option: that of opening access to the central bank balance sheet not to individuals but to the corporate sector, giving rise to a wholesale CBDC.[31] The rationales must be quite different here: no longer financial inclusion, nor transforming old-fashioned cash into its digital version. The objections to a wholesale CBDC, however, are not lesser than those raised to its retail counterpart, only different. Payment systems at the wholesale level, those for large value transactions, are already real time and cheap because they usually involve only a limited number of participants that trust each other. All major transfer systems, like Fedwire, or Target II in the euro area already use a CBDC because they settle in central bank money via digital platforms. Opening the central bank gates to large corporates, whose treasurers move billions every day, can only increase the financial stability concerns that we have discussed earlier in this chapter. Evidently, those concerns could not possibly be mitigated by imposing on large corporates the same narrow limits that are being considered for retail CBDC holders.

The case for a wholesale CBDC must therefore rest on different considerations. One such use case is based on the observation that it is possible to represent real-world assets, such as securities or commodities, as digital tokens on a blockchain or distributed ledger. This digitization might allow for increased efficiency, transparency, and accessibility in the trading and settlement of these assets. Moreover, tokenized assets can be divided into smaller units, enabling fractional ownership and potentially increasing liquidity. A wholesale CBDC that is tokenized and put on the same blockchain could facilitate buying and selling tokenized assets. The case for this type of wholesale CBDC is thus that it facilitates securities transactions. This is so far mainly an abstract idea, but the Innovation Hub of the BIS has undertaken a feasibility study under the project Helvetia which shows that it could be done.[32] That said, it will certainly take a long time before tokenization takes off in the marketplace.

Another use case of wholesale CBDC revolves around the problems persisting in the area of cross-border transactions that have remained slow and costly. We discussed the high cost of remittances in Chapter 9 where the "last mile" of the transfer, namely relatives living in countries with inefficient payment systems, experience high costs in receiving the funds. The purpose of a wholesale CBDC would be different. Representatives of the IMF and the BIS have argued that global trade would be facilitated if there existed wholesale CBDCs in the major economies that could communicate seamlessly among themselves. Proponents of this approach to wholesale CBDCs would argue that they could facilitate not just monetary transactions but all the financial transactions that accompany the movement of goods and services as they move along today's long and complicated supply chains.

In sum, while these may all be very interesting arguments, the reality is that no central bank has so far tried to put these ideas into practice. Retail CBDCs have already been experimented in a few cases, but their success has been disappointing so far.

CONCLUSIONS

Central bank interest in CBDCs started a few years ago in response to a perceived threat from private markets: on the one hand, Facebook's plan to launch a private money, called Libra, and on the other, the rise of cryptocurrencies and their promise, widely believed at some point, that they may replace traditional monies. With hindsight, both challenges appear to have been exaggerated. But the allure of having a national digital currency survived in central banking circles, seemingly fueled by a "fear of missing out" and of appearing technologically backward. There is a group dynamic in this process: a worry about being left behind if others go first, hence outcompeting the domestic currency, leading to a suboptimal outcome.

A key consideration is that the payment ecosystem is already crowded – in many respects, overcrowded – with payment means that largely duplicate one another. Payment habits are sticky, and onboarding new payment instruments is cumbersome for users and costly for banks. The marginal gain of additional instruments quickly declines toward zero. It is doubtful that consumers could be enticed to use another means for their daily transactions. The limited uptake in China and the Bahamas confirms these considerations. These experiences are interesting because they show two cases in which there was simply no demand for a CBDC – at least for daily small-scale transactions, in spite of the official efforts to generate one. The costs of making payments via checks (still common in the United States and France) or cards and apps might still be high, but they are not visible to consumers. If proposed elsewhere, therefore, CBDCs may encounter the same lack of demand as they have met in China or the Bahamas.

It remains difficult to establish a clear case for a retail CBDC as a substitute for cash or for any of the incumbent digital means of payment at the retail level. Routine retail transactions today are already cheap and convenient. The added safety of the central bank and the finality of its settlement, both inherent in the CBDC, do not seem very attractive, especially in countries with well-structured and reliable banking systems. Far from being regarded as an electronic substitute for cash, CBDCs may turn out to displace part of bank deposits, becoming a new – but not particularly innovative – store of value. Moreover, it is highly unlikely that many customers would hold an unremunerated CBDC when there are alternatives that promise substantial interest. Central banks might thus be forced to pay interest if they want to ensure a large take-up of their CBDC offering. But this would involve substantial fiscal costs against unclear advantages.

By contrast, the potential risks are clear. We have shown that CBDCs may complicate the conduct of monetary policy and the management of financial stability risks. A significant transfer of deposits from the banking sector to the central bank may have a contractionary impact on the economy whose entity and remedies are hard to assess.

In essence, retail CBDCs would mean public intervention in an area where well-functioning markets already exist. It is therefore useful to think in terms of if and when those markets may fail, therefore justifying public intervention to pursue a collective interest. Market failure can happen for many reasons, and a complex and technologically sophisticated payment system like the one we have today is potentially subject to failure, for technological and other reasons. Unlikely scenarios, perhaps, but not impossible ones, which may require public authorities to step in. A reasonable case can be made that having in place digital payment infrastructures housed by the central bank, potentially accessible by a very large user base, may help overcome rare adverse contingencies. The related operational and legal infrastructures require a long preparatory phase. Preparing in advance can therefore be useful, even though the eventual use may appear uncertain or even unlikely.

NOTES

1. See, for example, Hannah Murphy and Kiran Stacey, "Facebook Libra: The Inside Story of How the Company's Cryptocurrency Dream Died," Financial Times, March 10, 2022.
2. Anneke Kosse and Ilaria Mattei, "Gaining Momentum: Results of the 2021 BIS Survey on Central Bank Digital Currencies," BIS Papers 125, May 6, 2022.
3. More recently, the British economist John Maynard Keynes in 1944 proposed a new currency, the Bancor, as part of the post–World War II monetary arrangement. The Bancor as such never saw the light of day, but an embryo of it still survives today in the Special Drawing Right, the unit of account used by the International Monetary Fund.

4. An IMF survey notes: "The experiences so far suggest that there is no universal case for DLT as the primary engine of CBDC, and jurisdictions have different views on the potential merits of the technology. The Bahamas and the ECCB have DLT-based systems, and staff from both central banks cite the security of the technology as valuable for their needs." Gabriel Soderberg et al., "Behind the Scenes of Central Bank Digital Currency," *Fintech Notes* 2022, no. 004 (February 1, 2022): 1.

5. This section and the next one draw on a few earlier publications by the authors; in particular, Ignazio Angeloni, "Digital Euro: When in Doubt, Abstain (but Be Prepared)," European Parliament Think Tank, April 17, 2023; Ignazio Angeloni, "The Digital Euro: What We Know and What We Don't," London, May 9, 2023; Ignazio Angeloni and Daniel Gros, "Letter: Banknotes Have Characteristics a Digital Euro Can Never Acquire," *Financial Times*, May 10, 2023 and Ignazio Angeloni, "Digital Euro: A Precautionary Device, not a Deus ex machina," SUERF Policy Brief, May 2023.

6. Christian Barontini and Henry Holden, "Proceeding with Caution: A Survey on Central Bank Digital Currency," BIS Papers 101, January 8, 2019.

7. Christopher J. Waller, "CBDC: A Solution in Search of a Problem?," Washington, DC, August 5, 2021.

8. Alexander Macgillivray, Nik Marda, and Alondra Nelson, "Technical Possibilities for a U.S. Central Bank Digital Currency," *The White House*, September 17, 2022.

9. However, the legislative proposal on the digital euro issued by the European Commission in June 2023 rules out a remuneration.

10. Soderberg et al., "Behind the Scenes of Central Bank Digital Currency."

11. Peter Bofinger and Thomas Haas, "Central Bank Digital Currencies: Can Central Banks Succeed in the Marketplace for Digital Monies?," Centre for European Policy Studies, December 16, 2021.

12. For example, in the ECB Statute, to "promote the smooth operation of payment systems" is identified as a "basic task" of the central bank in Article 3. Moreover, Article 22 reads: "The ECB and national central banks may provide facilities, and the ECB may make regulations, to ensure efficient and sound clearing and payment systems within the Community and with other countries." The wording clearly suggests that the central bank is mandated to oversee the payment systems

promoted by the market, not to invent its own, unless this is strictly needed. Statute of the ECSB and of the ECB, www.ecb.europa.eu/pub/pdf/other/ecbinstitutionalprovisions2011en.pdf.

13. This is already done in practice, especially at the European level where the EU institutions have been instrumental in lowering fees for bank transfers. The latest example is the proposal by the European Commission obliging banks to provide by 2024 their customers with the possibility to make free real time peer-to-peer transfers.

14. See, for example, Kantar Public, "Study on New Digital Payment Methods," March 2022.

15. In 2020, a European Payments Initiative was launched under the aegis of the ECB with the objective of contrasting the US dominance in the sector of payment cards. The initiative has not made significant progress so far. By contrast, other ECB sponsored initiatives, for example, the Single European Payments Area catering for domestic and cross-border bank deposit transfers and TARGET2, the real-time gross settlement interbank payment system owned and operated by the ECB and its constituent national central banks, are highly successful and efficient.

16. See, for example, Fabio Panetta, "Central Bank Digital Currencies: A Monetary Anchor for Digital Innovation," Madrid, November 5, 2021; and Olli Rehn, "Beyond Crypto-Mania: Digital Euro as Monetary Anchor," University of California, Berkeley, August 23, 2022.

17. See, for example, Frederic S. Mishkin, "International Experiences with Different Monetary Policy," *Journal of Monetary Economics* 43, no. 3 (June 1, 1999): 579–605.

18. The Online Appendix is available at Ignazio Angeloni's blog (ignazioangeloni.home.blog).

19. Itai Agur, Lev Ratnovski, and Giovanni Dell'Ariccia, "Designing Central Bank Digital Currencies," *Journal of Monetary Economics* 125 (January 1, 2022): 62–79, examine cases in which the design of a CBDC possesses attributes similar to cash or to deposits.

20. It has been suggested that as a result of structural factors in the banking sector, relating to the way information is spread and the mix and concentration of the population of depositors, the speed of bank runs may have increased; see Federal Deposit Insurance Corporation, Review of the Federal Reserve's Supervision and Regulation of Silicon Valley Bank, April 28, 2023.

21. See the annual report of the Central Bank of Bahamas, statement of financial position. www.centralbankbahamas.com/viewPDF/ documents/2024-05-06-13-22-45-2023-CBOB-Annual-Report-and-Statement-of-Accounts.pdf.

22. Central Bank of the Bahamas, "Press Release: Public Update on the Bahamas Digital Currency: SandDollar," April 3, 2023.

23. Pangyue Cheng, "Decoding the Rise of Central Bank Digital Currency in China: Designs, Problems, and Prospects," *Journal of Banking Regulation* 24, no. 2 (February 21, 2022): 156–70.

24. See TRADING ECONOMICS, "China Average Yearly Wages in Manufacturing: 2023 Data – 2024 Forecast."

25. See The People's Bank of China, "Financial Statistics Report (May 2023)," June 13, 2023.

26. The World Bank estimated that only one-fifth of Nigerians have a bank account; see Michael King, "The Unbanked Four-Fifths: Informality and Barriers to Financial Services in Nigeria," *World Bank Blogs* (blog), September 24, 2023.

27. Jookyung Ree, "Nigeria's ENaira, One Year After," IMF, May 16, 2023.

28. Charlotte Principato, "Report: U.S. Public Opinion on Cryptocurrency," Morning Consult Pro, July 2022.

29. See DNB, "Digital Euro Appeals to Half of the Dutch Population," 2021, www.dnb.nl/en/general-news/news-2021/ digital-euro-appeals-to-half-of-the-dutch-population/.

30. Justus Meyer and Federica Teppa, "Euro Area Consumers' Payment Behaviour and Banking Digitalisation," *De Nederlandsche Bank Working Paper* 772, March 22, 2023.

31. Michelle W. Bowman, "Considerations for a Central Bank Digital Currency," Georgetown University, Washington DC, April 18, 2023.

32. "Project Helvetia: Settling tokenised assets in central bank money," BIS, December 2020.

11 Money and Freedom

All that makes existence valuable to any one, depends on the enforcement of restraints upon the actions of other people.

John Stuart Mill

The relationship between money and freedom is a subject we approach with some hesitation. It cannot be avoided. Money plays a unique role in the interval of time and space separating the act of *parting with* something we own from that of *acquiring* something else we need or desire. In that interval resides the "freedom of choice," which is at the core of any free economic system.[1]

While unavoidable, the subject is complex and elusive, with multiple dimensions difficult to pin down and connect. It gets dangerously close to the subjective domain, even the philosophical one. Readers will find in this chapter more speculative reasoning than elsewhere in the book. A degree of subjectivity is inherent because people attach different values to freedom, even different meanings; clear-cut definitions do not apply. In a rare statement on this subject by a world leader, in 1941 the US President Franklin D. Roosevelt listed four fundamental freedoms: of speech, of worship, from want, and from fear. Money has no direct relation with any of them, but it does relate to individual liberty, broadly intended, in many subtle ways.

Social scientists debate whether money gives happiness.[2] For sure, it is a key factor in giving control over one's life. Having sufficient money means, most often, that one's actions do not depend on the decisions of others or on unforeseen and uncontrollable external circumstances. Money broadens our span of choice considerably, though not unlimitedly. This notion applies in the private and professional spheres. It applies to individuals as well as collective organizations, including nations. If this isn't freedom, it is very close to it.

Defining money more precisely strengthens this conclusion and adds other elements useful to our discussion. We have already noted the distinction between money and wealth and between money and income – concepts often mixed up in popular discourse. Wealth lumps together all owned assets, as diverse as they may be: spendable items like bank accounts or cash, negotiable securities, other nonmarketable claims, tangibles like homes or land, and even intangibles like education and know-how. Money is more specific: It is the portion of wealth that can directly be used to purchase goods and services. Income is the accrual of wealth per unit of time, not necessarily in the form of money.

The distinction between money and other wealth is "liquidity": a catchword meaning general recognition and acceptance in the marketplace in exchange for goods and services at a given nominal value. "Nominal" means value in terms of the unit of account, whereas "real" value indicates the value in terms of goods and services. Once these definitions and distinctions are factored in, it is clear that money generates more control, or more "freedom," than any of the other components of wealth. Nonmonetary assets must first pass the intermediate step of converting into money, an act whose success may depend on uncontrollable circumstances. A home can depreciate, even collapse. Intangible wealth also depreciates and eventually vanishes altogether; even before that, it cannot easily be sold. Financial markets do not always function; even when they do, securities fluctuate in value. Money can be stolen, but until that happens, it is the readiest and most reliable means by which one can fulfil our material wishes.

If money contributes to our autonomy and self-determination, the next question is: How is this contribution affected by the rise of the new digital monetary forms? Modern technologies affect the personal sphere in many important ways, potentially distorting, limiting, or enhancing that freedom. Recent discussions have concentrated on two key areas: The freedom of keeping one's personal sphere confidential ("privacy") and the freedom of using the monetary instrument of our choice. Let's turn to them in sequence.

MONEY AND PRIVACY

Threats to privacy and related concerns have increased in recent years, alongside the rise of the digital age. Information technologies (IT) allow us to collect, store, maintain, and disseminate information on all dimensions of individual and collective life. There is no technological limit to this capacity. Economic barriers have also fallen: The cost of IT has collapsed and access to it has expanded. The pace of innovation and the complexities involved are such that our understanding of the phenomenon, let alone its regulation, struggles to keep up. Compounding the process, the diffusion of IT among criminal organizations has generated a widespread opinion that restrictions on privacy, when motivated by security, are desirable and even necessary. Indeed, to some extent they are. But where should the limits be set, and how can they be defended?

Privacy is a basic human need. All ancient civilizations were aware of it, though awareness translated into social practice to different extents and in different ways, depending on cultures.[3] In modern times, privacy has become a cornerstone of common law. In a landmark contribution at the end of the nineteenth century, Samuel Warren and Louis Brandeis, the American scholars credited for establishing privacy's legal principles, noted that its boundaries have increased over time, covering not only the physical domain but also the intellectual and spiritual ones:

> Thus, in very early times, the law gave a remedy only for physical interference with life and property, for trespasses vi et armis. Then the "right to life" served only to protect the subject from battery in its various forms; liberty meant freedom from actual restraint; and the right to property secured to the individual his lands and his cattle. Later, there came a recognition of man's

spiritual nature, of his feelings and his intellect. Gradually the scope of these legal rights broadened; and now the right to life has come to mean the right to enjoy life, -- the right to be let alone; the right to liberty secures the exercise of extensive civil privileges; and the term "property" has grown to comprise every form of possession -- intangible, as well as tangible.[4]

Today, privacy is a constitutional right almost everywhere in the world;[5] the fact that this happens also in countries like Afghanistan and Russia, however, suggests that such a right is not respected everywhere to the same degree.

The privacy of spending decisions is one factor explaining the attractiveness of cash.[6] Today's commercial applications of IT present direct and relevant intrusions into the personal sphere. Such applications are as subtle and unconscious as they are broad-ranging and impactful. Knowledge of customer habits and preferences that derive from purchase patterns permits powerful marketing applications. We are all exposed to occult marketing practices, especially when we shop online. Our awareness and consent are requested, and formally granted, but are limited in practice. When we purchase online and distractedly click on buttons accepting cookies, we tend to forget that the pop-ups and emails we subsequently receive, soliciting further purchases, are the direct consequence.

There is no doubt that such strategies succeed: We buy more, and often we buy what we are suggested to.

Online commercial applications, including the burgeoning sector of "web influencers," partly taking advantage of private information unbeknown to customers, potentially modify spending habits and influence tastes, lifestyles, even cultures, in many ways. The concerns about this occult influence are growing and are a powerful argument suggesting that payment systems should be organized in a way to protect privacy.

Seeing from another angle, however, there are also reasons why some disclosure of payment patterns may be desirable, under democratic control. Unlawful payments are facilitated by anonymity. Cash is often, though decreasingly, the payment means of choice for drug dealers, tax evaders, and other criminals. Crypto assets, which promise pseudo-anonymity of their distributed ledgers, are increasingly used for this purpose, especially for large-value transactions.

The link between payment anonymity and crime explains actions occasionally undertaken by governments to limit the circulation and usage of large-denomination banknotes. For example, in 2016 the European Central Bank discontinued the production of 500-euro notes (while not withdrawing those already in circulation), after gathering information that its popularity was based on its use in gray or illegal transactions. Some have gone further, proposing to eliminate cash altogether – an idea that as we noted in Chapter 4 has received some academic support.

We tend to disagree with the extreme versions of this line of thought. The international evidence linking the popularity of cash to the shadow or illegal economy is not unambiguous.[7] The link between anonymity and illegality is complex. People's perception of the boundaries of legality may not coincide with the same perception of the legislator, more evidently in undemocratic regimes but occasionally also in liberal democracies. Even when it does, there are legitimate situations where one may wish to conceal perfectly legal acts: for example, when they reveal aspects of the personal sphere like medical conditions, opinion, affiliation, sexual inclinations, and others. A well-diversified payment system should consider these legitimate desires.

If unconstrained, the digitalization of money can lead to unwarranted restrictions of privacy. We argued in Chapter 5 that this is one reason against the elimination of cash or overly extensive restrictions on its usage. Cash, the quintessential confidential payment means, acts as a safety valve: It guarantees to anyone that there exists a payment option that is universally accepted, irreversible, and confidential. Cash is easy, but also inefficient to use. It requires effort to procure, carry, and protect. This disincentive automatically limits

its use. Barring extreme circumstances like catastrophic failures of IT infrastructure, cash will always remain on the fringes within the broader payment system.

The expression "digital cash" does not make sense. No digital payment offers the same characteristics and privacy features as physical cash. Cryptocurrencies, in spite of the claims by their proponents, are not fully anonymous; Bitcoin payments have been identified by law enforcement agencies.[8] As we illustrated in Chapter 8, those transactions can be followed by tracing the internet protocol uniquely associated with any computer connected to the Web. The decentralization of the ledger is not, per se, a guarantee of anonymity or confidentiality. This conclusion applies to stablecoins as well.

Conventional centralized ledgers such as those maintained by banks and central banks contain, by nature, information on all individual payments. From a strictly legal standpoint, they should be kept confidential. But laws can be changed or broken. Technically there is no obstacle to their disclosure or use for commercial purposes. Luckily, banks have, so far at least, had no commercial interest in monetizing their knowledge of the billions of transactions they process.

Should we rely on governments, or central banks, if they commit to draw and defend the borderline of payment privacy in all circumstances? Not always. Governments are by nature partisan; commitments can be reneged on or tweaked. Even constitutional provisions are not always sufficient, as we have seen.

Central banks guarantee confidentiality as issuers of cash, but it is doubtful that any digital "equivalent" could offer the same protection. The statutory independence of central banks depends on their conducting monetary and banking functions; it is motivated by arguments that have little or no relation to the protection of privacy rights. The confidentiality of transactions in any Central Bank Digital Currency would thus not depend on the central bank itself but on the government.[9]

The anonymity and privacy protection ensured by cash's inherent characteristics have their limits. Societal concerns about anonymity, because of unlawful or criminal activity, must be taken into consideration and justify specific and limited restrictions – such as ceilings on the amount of cash payments or on banknote denomination. Beyond that, there are powerful reasons why some privacy of monetary transactions should be preserved, and cash is uniquely suited to provide this area of privacy.

FREE TO CHOOSE (THE MONEY)

We just discussed the freedom of *how* to use our money without interference from others. A different question is whether there should also be freedom of *which* money to use. This subject, to which we now turn, has also attracted discussion in connection with the rise of the new digital monies.

Digitalization has slashed costs and obstacles to setting up alternative payment systems, other than traditional ones monopolized by banks and central banks. Some platforms include instruments that are potentially akin to alternative monies, delinked from the official ones in both value and infrastructure. A new world of "private digital monies" seems to lie ahead.

The idea of private money is an old one. Historians of economic thought can trace it back thousands of years. We already alluded at the failed attempt to foist shoddy copper coins on the Athenian populace. This could not work in a direct democracy. In classical Athens the state only fixed the design and weight of the main coin, the drachma, but put its mint at the disposal of anybody wishing to transform silver into Athenian currency.[10]

Somewhat surprisingly, it is in ancient China that one finds the first documented discussion about private versus public money. The occasion was a debate held in 81 BC at the imperial court of the first Han dynasty to discuss the role of the state in the economy in general and in particular whether to allow private minting.[11] The so-called modernizers won the day, and the government kept its monopoly on minting. Later emperors sometimes pursued more liberal policies and allowed private minting. However, these were relatively brief periods during millennia of tight state control.

In modern European history the idea of free money was proposed by the so-called Austrian School of thought, which originated in the late nineteenth-century Austro-Hungarian empire under the intellectual leadership of Carl Menger von Wolfensgrün (1840–1921). Its philosophical root is in the subjectivist notion that social phenomena are the result of individual choices and actions. Building on the utilitarian visions of the British philosophers Jeremy Bentham and John Stuart Mill, in his *Principles of Economics*, published in 1971, Menger applied utilitarianism to economic theory, contributing to launching the so-called marginalist approach, which, as we mentioned in Chapter 4, is still very much alive today in the economics classrooms. In Britain, the marginalist approach would soon find a systematic formulation in the work by Alfred Marshall (1842–1924), whose similarly titled book, published in 1890, was a major inspiration to John Maynard Keynes and most other modern economists. Marginalists see economic value as rooted in the utility of an additional unit of goods procured to individuals, in contrast to earlier theories which measured value in terms of labor content. The passage from a notion of value based on supply (hence on labor) to one based on demand (manifestation of utility) was bound to provide a key intellectual foundation to the rising Western market-based economic systems.

The concept of private money was only a step ahead, though. The principles of the Austrian school logically extended to political individualism as well, but early exponents did not go far. On monetary matters, they tended to adhere to classical theories which regarded prices as determined by money supply. To maintain price stability, they relied on a strict linkage between money and gold – the Gold Standard that was prevailing at the time. Under that system, money is a strict monopoly of the state.

That changed late in the twentieth century when the main exponent of the school, the Austrian British Nobel laureate Friedrich von Hayek (1899–1992), published his book *The Denationalization of Money* in 1976. Hayek proposed a system in which private institutions would create their own monies and offer them to users, like all other goods. Monies would compete for acceptance in the marketplace. This was a complete reversal relative to early Austrian ideas, motivated by dissatisfaction with the disarray the international monetary system had fallen into following the abandonment of the gold anchor in 1971.[12] In the post-1971 regime, the supply of money was discretionary: Currencies fluctuated against one another and were delinked from gold – depreciating with respect to it. This system was, at least initially, accompanied by high inflation and instability of exchange rates among the major currencies. Hayek believed that market competition could be counted on to reestablish monetary stability and soundness. He thought that stable monies would be more easily accepted and would eventually prevail – a monetary equivalent of the notion of "survival of the fittest."

In Europe, a similar idea was proposed in the years preceding the launch of the euro. The followers of Hayek thought that instead of introducing a new common currency one should let currencies compete. At most they would accept the idea of what was called a "hard Ecu," an artificial currency with a constant purchasing power.[13] A group of economists published in 1975 a "manifesto" in *The Economist* arguing that currency competition constitutes a better avenue for European Monetary integration than the merger of existing currencies under the aegis of a European institution.[14] These ideas must be understood against the backdrop of the high and variable inflation rates in most of Europe during that period. Countries like Italy, France, and the United Kingdom were experiencing inflation rates in excess of 20 percent, with their central banks seemingly incapable of restoring price stability. Only Germany kept price increases within single digits. This was also a period of limited financial development, at least in Europe. It is thus not surprising that price stability was regarded as a higher priority than financial stability.

But even apart from the contingencies of the time, Hayek underestimated important obstacles and objections to his ideas. Some of them apply to today's privately issued digital monies as well.

First and foremost, private monies allow for the private appropriation of the returns from issuance, the so-called seigniorage. When appropriated by the state, seigniorage is a tax; when it accrues to private subjects, it is personal or corporate income. Income from seigniorage generates an incentive to issue more and more money. Overissuance may lead to instability – as the example of the United States in the free banking years indicates – and eventually perhaps to less attractive money. At some stage this may be sanctioned by market competition, but if ever, this happens later, after people realize what is happening and draw their consequences. It takes time for that. By contrast, seigniorage income accrues immediately. Most profit maximizers have a short horizon, weighing immediate gains more than potential future disadvantages. As a result, a regime of private money is prone to incentives leading to excessive money creation, inflation, depreciation, and financial instability, all of them feeding into and reinforcing one another.

Another consequence disregarded by monetary libertarians is that money creates "network externalities": Its attractiveness increases with the spread of its use. Money which is used by many is more attractive and accepted because it is more likely that it will be accepted by others. The more it is used, the more desirable it becomes. Network externalities are the enemy of competition: They generate economies of scale and lead to monopolies. Also due to this reason, a regime of private monies competing with one another is inherently unstable.

Historical experiences support these caveats. The United States before the post–Civil War reforms is an example, as we mentioned in Chapter 3. The tendency of state-chartered banks to overissue relative to the size of their capital and assets in that period led to repeated bank failures and financial instability.

Hayek's proposal was never implemented, but his idea survived and is still present today on the fringes of economic discussions. Its attraction is cyclical: It grows when monetary instability increases and tends to disappear in periods of stability. Fundamentally it arises from a lack of confidence in and refusal to accept the existence of "central parties," banks of central banks, with the responsibility of managing the currency and the payments system. The lack of trust in central authorities is what brings Hayek's ideas close to those of modern crypto advocates. Not by coincidence, Bitcoin was initially proposed in 2008, during the Great Financial Crisis of 2008–09; in its foundational document, the anonymous author of the proposal, the pseudo-named Satoshi Nakamoto, emphasizes the lack of trust in centralized parties as the reason for the proposal.

Today the communities of crypto supporters and of nostalgics of the Austrian School largely coincide. Looking deeper, however, there are differences between the two ideas. The Austrian school wanted to use competition to ensure the stability of money relative to a basket of commodities and thought that sound monies should be freely redeemable into official currencies. In the words of Hayek:

> It might be expedient that the issuing institution should from the outset announce precisely the collection of commodities in terms of which it would aim to keep the value of the 'ducat' constant. (…) Competition would certainly prove a more effective constraint, forcing the issuing institutions to keep the value of their currency constant (in terms of a stated collection of commodities), than would any obligation to redeem the currency in those commodities (or in gold).[15] ["Ducat" is the fictitious name given to the proposed currency.]

By contrast, Bitcoin and its analogues never had the ambition to represent more than streaks of bits in a computer. They are built on thin air, not on a linkage with other, hard, measures of value or purchasing capacity. If anything, reserve-backed stablecoins, with their strong and collateralized currency peg, are closer to that notion.

All in all, while conceding that their market is still evolving and could mutate into something different and more reliable, the experience so far with cryptocurrencies justifies skepticism as to the possibility of realizing the ideal that Hayek could not attain – monetary stability through currency competition. Until now, Bitcoin seems to have attracted investor attention more for its *unstable* value (mainly increasing) than for its *stability*. Investors have cyclically stormed in or rushed to the exit, exacerbating volatility. This is what one expects from a speculative asset, not a reliable currency.

MONETARY FREEDOM IN THE DIGITAL ERA

Digital payments magnify the threat to privacy, and digitalization augments the prospect of privatizing the monetary system. For this reason, the digital revolution alters the debate on monetary freedom, competition, and privacy. Free banking ideas have never become mainstream, but support for them never ceased, gaining traction especially when traditional banking was deemed to have failed after crises or inflations. Launching a fintech or a cryptocurrency is easier than starting a bank. The "supply" of private monies has increased and is potentially very large. The "demand" side is also potentially large: Digital money holdings are easily accessed and stored on a computer or a cellphone. However, history does not support the idea that private competition in money creation improves the quality of money.

Privacy and anonymity are components of freedom: If a payment cannot be traced, it cannot be controlled either. But they involve trade-offs sought legitimately by some; privacy can also facilitate illegal transactions. While some restrictions are legitimate, even necessary, in democratic societies, we have argued that a well-articulated payment system must contain at least one instrument, well recognizable and familiar to all, which offers foolproof privacy. Cash has these characteristics. The fact that it is physical and visible, hence logistically somewhat cumbersome, may not be a drawback after all, as it helps to discourage large-scale criminal usage.

The potential of crypto money to enhance freedom, competition, and privacy is limited. Small investors are free to enter the game, but whether all of them knowingly pursue their interests as opposed to being misguided is doubtful. Miners, the only subjects capable of validating transactions and producing money, possess computer power and skills unattainable by most, and typically act in the shadow.

All in all, it appears that the prospect of a stability-enhancing "free money," of the type advocated by Hayek, is lower in the digital era than it has ever been. The mixed system in which central banks provide the currency but the private sector distributes it and provides the technology, subject to oversight, though not without its problems, has worked well and stood the test of time. Digitalization brings the technological frontier forward, but the need for a proper balance between the private and the public spheres is as present as ever.

NOTES

1. Among the most forceful proponents of this idea was Ludwig von Mises; see his Ludwig Von Mises and Margit Von Mises, *Money, Method, and the Market Process: Essays by Ludwig Von Mises* (Springer, 1990). But the same concept is shared also by less conservative schools of thought than the one von Mises belonged to. By contrast, when an economy relies on command rather than on freedom, money tends to disappear. See Clifford G. Gaddy and Barry W. Ickes, "Russia's Virtual Economy," Foreign Affairs, September 1, 1998.

2. Daniel Kahneman and Angus Deaton, "High Income Improves Evaluation of Life but Not Emotional Well-Being," *Proceedings of the National Academy of Sciences of the United States of America* 107, no. 38 (September 7, 2010): 16489–93, find that more money does not increase happiness, in all its dimensions. For a different view see Mark R. Killingsworth, "Experienced Well-Being Rises with Income, Even above $75,000 per Year," *Proceedings of the National Academy of Sciences of the United States of America* 118, no. 4 (January 18, 2021). Recently, Paul G. Bain and Renata Bongiorno, "Evidence from 33 Countries Challenges the Assumption of Unlimited Wants," *Nature Sustainability* 5, no. 8 (June 16, 2022): 669–73, find that people's

desires are not unlimited: "Ideal life" means, for the average person, possessing ten million US dollars. One of your two authors asked this question to his twelve-year-old kid. His answer was: "It all depends on how the money is used."

3. Alessandro Acquisti, Laura Brandimarte, and Jeff Hancock, "How Privacy's Past May Shape Its Future," *Science* 375, no. 6578 (January 21, 2022): 270–72.

4. Samuel Warren and Louis D. Brandeis, "The Right to Privacy," *Harvard Law Review* 4, no. 5 (December 15, 1890): 193.

5. See "Constitute Project," the Constitute Project website.

6. Charles M. Kahn, James McAndrews, and William Roberds, "MONEY IS PRIVACY*," *International Economic Review* 46, no. 2 (May 1, 2005): 377–99. Experimental evidence supports this idea; see Emanuele Borgonovo, Stefano Caselli, Alessandra Cillo, Donato Masciandaro, and Giovanni Rabitti, "Money, Privacy, Anonymity: What Do Experiments Tell Us?," *Journal of Financial Stability* 56 (October 1, 2021).

7. Boriana Madzharova, "Traceable Payments and VAT Design: Effects on VAT Performance," *CESifo Economic Studies* 66, no. 3 (2020): 221–47, based on international data, finds that the relation between cash and VAT (value added tax) collection is nonlinear, declining first but rising for high levels of cash withdrawals at automated teller machines. Michele Giammatteo, Stefano Iezzi, and Roberta Zizza, "Pecunia Olet. Cash Usage and the Underground Economy," *Journal of Economic Behavior and Organization* 204 (December 1, 2022): 107–27, find a robust negative relation between cash usage and VAT collection across Italian provinces.

8. John Bohannon, "The Bitcoin Busts," *Science* 351, no. 6278 (March 11, 2016): 1144–46.

9. An argument made also by Charles M. Kahn, "The Threat of Privacy," *The Journal of Financial Market Infrastructures* 6, no. 2/3 (March 2017): 21–30.

10. Jeremy Trevett, "Coinage and Democracy at Athens," in Andrew Meadows and Kirsty Shipton (eds.), *Money and Its Uses in the Ancient Greek World* (Oxford University Press eBooks, 2001), 23–34.

11. Ming Wan, "Discourses on Salt and Iron: A First Century B.C. Chinese Debate over the Political Economy of Empire," *Journal of Chinese Political Science* 17, no. 2 (February 26, 2012): 143–63.

12. The so-called gold-exchange standard was the post–World War II version of the Gold Standard regime prevailing in the late nineteenth and early twentieth centuries. In that version, the US dollar was convertible into gold at a fixed price, and all other currencies pegged to the dollar.

13. John J. Phelan, "The Road Not Taken: A Comparison between the Hard ECU and the Euro," *Economic Affairs* 35, no. 3 (October 1, 2015): 397–415.

14. Giorgio Basevi et al., "The All Saints' Day Manifesto for European Monetary Union," in Michele Fratianni and Theo Peeters (eds.), *One Money for Europe* (Palgrave Macmillan, 1978), 37–51.

15. Friedrich August Hayek, *Denationalisation of Money: An Analysis of the Theory and Practice of Concurrent Currencies* (The Institute of Economic Affairs, 1976), 40.

There's just one thing I got to know
Can you tell me please, who won?

David Crosby, Paul Kantner, and Stephen Stills

A bucolic park near Brussels, Belgium, is an unlikely place to organize the global payment system. Yet that is where the head office of the Society for Worldwide Interbank Financial Telecommunication (SWIFT) is located: more precisely, in the village of La Hulpe, population 7,000. With its renowned park and small chateau, it is a favorite weekend spot for Brussels' inhabitants, blissfully unaware as they stroll by that the heart of global finance is beating nearby: SWIFT manages the over 40 million daily payments that keep global trade alive.

The story of how SWIFT became dominant provides a fascinating lesson on how digitalization, economics, and politics interact.

CORRESPONDENT BANKING: THE BACKBONE
OF INTERNATIONAL TRANSACTIONS

The starting point of the digitalization of international payments does not lie with SWIFT. This came much earlier. But its origin and rise must be seen against the backdrop of the longer-term history of international banking, illustrating that international payments were the first to rely on modern information systems while small (especially cross-border) payments remained the last bastions resisting full digitalization, hence remaining slow, cumbersome, and expensive.

International banking is as old as civilization. In ancient epochs, the meaning of "international" was of course different; the neighboring city-state, maybe only a day's march away, was already foreign when long-distance travel was hazardous. Given the difficulties in communication and the absence of enforcement mechanisms, finance at long distances was thus based on trust and relationships; merchants located in distant cities could rely on the occasional message from their distant partner, usually authenticated with some seal but also informally through social norms.[1]

Long-distance communication remained difficult and unreliable over most of history. Legend has it that the Rothschild brothers in London and Paris were able to make a fortune when carrier pigeons sent from their siblings in Brussels allowed them to be the first to know about the victory of the British at Waterloo (also close to Brussels). According to one account,[2] the one to Paris carried the message "sell" and the one to London "buy." The Paris and London branches acted on this piece of advice because of the extreme level of trust that existed within the family. The real breakthrough with the electrification of long-distance communications came two generations later, in the mid nineteenth century, with the telegraph and its wired communications, as we noted in Chapter 3. Telegraph cables soon crisscrossed the United States and Europe and connected them via undersea cables. Some scholars have called this the Victorian internet.[3]

The long-term relationships that underpinned long-distance finance in antiquity and medieval times evolved into standardized agreements, called correspondent banking. We already encountered this notion, or a rudimentary version of it, in Chapter 3, when describing the US monetary system before the creation of the Federal Reserve. Correspondent banking can be defined, in general terms, as "an arrangement under which one bank (correspondent) holds deposits owned by other banks (respondents) and provides payment and other services to those respondent banks."[4]

The principle is simple. Suppose you want to transfer a certain sum to somebody with a bank account in another country. You can ask your local bank to make a transfer to a bank it knows in the other country which then makes the transfer to the local foreign bank. If your local bank does not have a "correspondent" bank in the other country, two correspondent banks have to be involved. Your local bank sends the money to a national correspondent bank which then makes the transfer to the foreign correspondent bank which then makes the final transfer to the local bank account in the foreign country. If this sounds complicated, it is. But it is still simpler than trying to establish a complete network of bilateral relationships of every bank with every other. There are many thousand banks in Europe alone, implying hundreds of millions of potential bilateral relationships. Using correspondent banks as central intermediaries is thus much more efficient than the alternative.

The correspondent bank plays a role akin to that of a "central bank" but in international transactions. Its role is crucial as the trusted intermediary because before sending funds over the border one would like to know that this bank will effectively execute the transfer.

Correspondent banking has remained the prevalent modus operandi for millennia and it remains dominant today facilitating international trade and creating an obstacle to full digitalization.[5]

DIGITALIZING CORRESPONDENT BANKING

The correspondent banking model did not present particular problems as long as international transactions remained sparse and mainly related to international trade. But when after the 1960s major economies liberalized cross-border capital movements, the volume of payments started to grow rapidly. This expansion of international finance was facilitated by new technology, like the telex machine, which allowed sending "digital" messages, that is, messages in alphanumerical code. However, the explosion of international transactions posed two practical problems. First, every country not only has a different language but also has different ways to identify a bank. The clerk at the correspondent bank in New York thus had to know how to identify the recipient bank account in Germany, probably without knowing German but using the German system of bank identification.

The second practical problem was the security and authentication of the messages. Large money center banks acting as correspondent banks needed hundreds of staff to deal with these problems.[6]

Banker Eric Sepkes describes his experience of international payment practices in the London office of Citibank during the 1960s as follows:

> [On] a telex machine you had two sets of tables, like logarithmic tables... the telex sender would perform calculations based on the value, currency, and amount. They would then use tables to work out the keys and come up with a tested telex result... For every single telex that was sent you had to manually calculate what this telex test key was... When you received the tested telex you had to do the reverse calculation to make sure that the telex hadn't been tampered with during transmit and receive cycles. So you can imagine, there were hundreds – if not thousands – of these messages being sent every day from some of these banks. It was incredibly labour intensive, it was incredibly prone to human error... imagine the costs.[7]

The only solution to deal with this mess was standardization. This is exactly what First National City Bank proposed with its Machine-Readable Telegraphic Input (MARTI) system, operating from 1974. This system was quickly adopted by the international group of banks to which First National City Bank belonged. However, MARTI did not become globally dominant because its proponents made one capital mistake: They tried to impose it on all others, telling other banks in mid 1975: "We advise you to use MARTI from now on. If you don't use it, we will not execute your instructions. If your instructions are non-MARTI and come via telex, we will return the telex. If we receive them by mail, we will put them into an envelope and send it back to you."[8]

The MARTI ultimatum was unacceptable for most other banks because complying with it would have meant to become dependent on a competitor for all international transactions. The attempt of one group of banks to foist its system on all others greatly strengthened the SWIFT consortium, which had already been formed around the same time but had been inactive. SWIFT was designed explicitly as a network that would work for the benefit of its membership banks, not for the benefit of one particular bank or group of banks. After the MARTI ultimatum, the 68 banks that had funded the preparatory work for a rival system were joined by many more, and by the end of 1975, there were 270 member banks located in fifteen countries. Moreover, SWIFT was a diplomatic compromise. The standard ultimately adopted was not that of one bank. Everybody had to adapt to a common standard format.[9]

This is what made the success of SWIFT, not any superior technology. When SWIFT became operational, it was an instant success since so many banks supported it. First National City Bank closed down its MARTI system soon thereafter.

The location of SWIFT is thus no accident: It was part of the compromise. A nice suburb of Brussels was chosen because it was nowhere in terms of financial markets. The key point was that the headquarters was not in any financial center, which might have indicated a danger of one group dominating the rest, but still conveniently located for the larger European banks. Moreover, the legal form, that of a Belgian cooperative society, reinforced the point that it should work for the benefit of its members. This is what made it so attractive to so many banks worldwide. Joining SWIFT means joining a cooperative in which in principle every member has a vote.[10]

This standardized format started the real digitalization of international transfers. The reason for this revolutionary impact was simple: cost savings and speed. Standardization had an immediate impact on costs; SWIFT messages were cheaper than traditional telex and telegraph messages by an order of magnitude. Sending a letter of credit by telex might have cost about 13 dollars compared to 50 cents for a SWIFT. Other estimates differ, but it is clear that SWIFT allowed banks significant savings in personnel.[11]

Standardization and digitalization also increased speed, allowing SWIFT to manage a much larger volume of transactions. The growth in the volume of transactions was phenomenal. In 1979, 10 million messages were sent across 15 countries. A decade later the number of messages per year had risen thirtyfold to close to 300 million across 90 countries. Growth has continued, with every decade raking up a new record. The number of messages treated each year has now surpassed 10 billion covering over 200 countries and territories (areas that do not have a government that is recognized by the United Nations).[12]

SWIFT TODAY

Nowadays, SWIFT has become a large organization that has had a monopoly of global financial messaging for over forty years. It defines itself in this way:

> The Society for Worldwide Interbank Financial Telecommunication (SWIFT), legally S.W.I.F.T. SC, is a Belgian cooperative society providing services related to the execution of financial transactions and payments between certain banks worldwide. Its principal function is to serve as the main messaging network through which international payments are initiated. It also sells software and services to financial institutions, mostly for use on its proprietary "SWIFTNet," and assigns ISO 9362 Business Identifier Codes (BICs), popularly known as "SWIFT codes."[13]

The last element is essential for the standardization of international transfers. Virtually every bank has a Business Identification Coder or BIC, which is a key element in all international payments because it identifies the bank receiving the funds even if the name is not familiar to the sending bank in another country. Identifying banks by this code instead of the full name of the bank and the branch was one of the key innovations that allowed the digitalization of cross-border payments.

The cost advantage which made SWIFT so useful persists today. The annual revenue of SWIFT amounts to a bit under 1 billion dollars (2022 data), but the network also processed 10 billion transactions, meaning that the average cost per transaction is now somewhat below 10 cents.[14]

These low costs have a reason. The key, often misunderstood, point about SWIFT is that it does not execute payments – it does not substitute itself for the correspondent banking system. It provides only a standard for the billions of messages that are generated within the international banking system. This is also why SWIFT is so cheap. It does not provide transaction services. It does not settle any transactions. It merely provides a network over which it is possible to send billions of secure transactions in a format that every bank in the world accepts.

Security is never absolute. However, the security features of SWIFT seem to have been breached rather rarely over decades. The biggest breach came in 2006, allowing the hackers to initiate a false transaction from the Bangladesh central bank, leading to a loss of over 100 million dollars.[15]

SWIFT of course has its critics. It has a monopoly, and tales about slow transactions abound. It does not really make sense to criticize its monopoly position because its usefulness is exactly that it sets a universally recognized standard. English is so useful because it is the now universally used vehicular language – not because it is a more efficient language. What remains true is that international transactions remain costly and slow. In an era of real-time and, apparently free, payments, it seems inconceivable that international payments take days and cost dozens of dollars each. However, it would be wrong to fault SWIFT for these problems since SWIFT only provides a standard.

It is often tempting to shoot the messenger, but SWIFT is not even the messenger; it only provides the format for the message. The real problem is the correspondent banking system with its multiple stations and the need for multiple verifications.

What is true is that the banks that ultimately own SWIFT have little interest in changing the correspondent banking system because it generates substantial revenues for them. The revenues of SWIFT pale in comparison to the various fees banks levy on international transactions. As already mentioned in Chapter 7, transaction services constitute an important source of income, which they are loath to lose. Revenues from international transactions are particularly important and here one finds a large difference between wholesale (business) and retail (consumer) transactions. McKinsey estimates that banks take a margin of about 3 percent on international retail transactions, yielding a total revenue of close to 100 billion euros. The margin of banks is much lower on wholesale (business to business) transactions, about 0.2 percent. But since the market for international wholesale transactions is so much larger (more than fifty times that of consumers), this still yields close to 300 billion dollars. Comparing these numbers to those for domestic transactions in Chapter 7 shows that international transfers are about ten times more expensive than domestic ones.[16]

The correspondent banking system is one factor responsible for these high costs because it involves many more steps than domestic transfers. However, higher costs are not the only reason since the profit market of banks on international transfers is much higher. Customers have little choice when making an international transfer. Online services and apps like PayPal promise much cheaper and quicker service. But as we showed also in Chapter 7 the charges of PayPal also amount to about 2 percent of the value of the transaction, not much better than the charges of banks.

International transactions, especially at the retail level, thus remain an area that should be rife for radical cost reduction by fintech. In Chapter 9 we found that stablecoins are unlikely to provide a solution for workers' remittances. What is needed is thus not fancy new technology but some standard, going beyond SWIFT, that accelerates and simplifies the inherent complications of the correspondent banking system.

CRISIS AND FUTURE OF CORRESPONDENT BANKING

Correspondent banking thus represents the key obstacle to making international transfers quicker and cheaper. Moreover, correspondent banking is experiencing a crisis coming from another angle, namely cost and regulatory pressure. The cost element derives from the fact that each correspondent banking relationship has to be established through human contact and requires due diligence work that becomes worthwhile to undertake only if the expected revenues are substantial.

The Bank for International Settlements (BIS) observed recently:

> Banks have traditionally maintained broad networks of correspondent banking relationships, but there are growing indications that this situation might be changing. In particular, some banks providing these services are reducing the number of relationships they maintain and are establishing few new ones. The impact of this trend is uneven across jurisdictions and banks. As a result, some respondent banks are likely to maintain relationships, whereas others might risk being cut off from international payment networks. This implies a threat that cross-border payment networks might fragment and that the range of available options for these transactions could narrow. In addition, an analysis using SWIFT data shows that there seems to be a trend towards concentration in correspondent banking activities.[17]

What the BIS did not dare to say was that AML and countering the financing of terrorism regulations have become increasingly stringent. The need for banks to know their customers (KYC) to avoid becoming unwitting facilitators of illicit transactions has increased the compliance costs of keeping correspondent banking relationships in countries with known problems. This general trend has been well documented for countries that are perceived to have weaker regulatory regimes.[18] Banks know that they might face a problem if they keep a correspondent banking relationship with a country where there are problems with weak oversight. The laudable goal of global regulators to combat money laundering has thus some unforeseen side effects.

When in early 2018 it was discovered that banks in Latvia had laundered hundreds of billions of dollars (and euros) of Russian funds, it became difficult for banks worldwide to keep any correspondent banking relationship in that country, even with banks that had not participated in the money laundering operations. The trigger for this crisis actually came from the United States when the Financial Crimes Enforcement Network at the US Treasury proposed to ban activities in the United States of an important bank in the region, called ABLV, due to concerns related to money laundering, bribing officials, and breaching the North Korea embargo. This led to action by supervisors at the European Central Bank (ECB), and the bank in question was quickly liquidated and the local authorities initiated an in-depth reform of the entire national AML regime.[19] But it took some time before the reputational damage could be undone.

Another practical problem for the existing cross-border payment systems is the different, only partially overlapping, opening hours of the central bank settlement systems in the major reserve currency countries (United States, euro area, Japan, and China). This means that if a payment instruction originates in the afternoon in the United States it would arrive too late in the evening in Europe to settle even if it were received immediately because the payment system of the ECB would be closed at that point, meaning that there will be an unavoidable delay of at least one (business) day.

But the key issue for international banking is not technical; it is the trust or lack thereof across borders. As mentioned earlier, correspondent banking arose from the need to have a trusted partner abroad. Any proposal to improve correspondent banking must address the trust issue.

In principle, it should be straightforward to solve the trust issue via a global central counterparty for cross-border payments. Banks would then only have to trust this central counterparty, which would absorb the risk of the other side not completing the transactions. Such a global counterparty would have to be a public institution because no private sector entity would be able and willing to bear this risk at a global scale. But the political will to create such an institution does not exist, precisely because the appetite to cover risk abroad is very limited. The major international financial institutions, like the International Monetary Fund (IMF) or the World Bank, are very risk-averse and provide financing only under very stringent conditions.

A group of experts from the IMF has thus proposed to use wholesale central bank digital currencies (CBDCs) to create "trust bridges."[20] The underlying idea is that international transactions could consist of the exchange of (national) CBDCs. This would obviate the need to trust the creditworthiness of the other bank. Only the ownership of the CBDC in question would need to be certain, and this could be achieved through a permissioned ledger which could be run by central banks. Reducing the cost of international transactions is thus one potential benefit of wholesale CBDCs, particularly attractive for highly trade-dependent countries. This is why wholesale CBDCs have been proposed for Asia and for the euro area.[21]

It remains to be seen whether CBDC could be used to overcome the limitations of the correspondent banking system. It would take a big push to change a system that banks know and that despite its shortcomings yields an important stream of income.

All of this might remain moot as discussions about the most efficient international transactions system risk now being sidelined as geopolitics takes center stage. We now turn to consider the part money plays in the global power relations.

MONEY AND GEOPOLITICS

The first inescapable fact of the global monetary system is the dominance of the US dollar. The dollar is on one side of one-half of all foreign exchange transactions and accounts for more than 60 percent of foreign exchange reserves.[22] The dollar is also the currency of denomination for more than 60 percent of international debt and

50 percent of international loans. On all these dimensions, the international monetary role of the dollar far exceeds the weight of the United States in the global economy, which is around 20 percent. In most of these dimensions, the euro is the runner-up in that it is clearly also a global currency, but the share of the euro is only a fraction of that of the United States dollar, although the United States and the euro area are of similar size as trading powers (but not in terms of GDP).[23]

The euro is thus the second most important global currency, but its share of global transactions does not exceed the weight of the euro area in the global economy (except in payments through SWIFT, where the euro and dollar shares are roughly equal). The key difference is that the international role of the euro relies almost entirely on the importance of the euro area itself in global trade, with the euro little used in transactions in which the euro area itself is not one of the principals. The absence of the euro in "third country" transactions is especially pronounced in Asia. While the US dollar also dominates in Latin America, the economic weight of this region is low compared with Asia, and its growth prospects are more limited.

What explains this dominance of the dollar as the vehicular currency of choice almost everywhere? Economic research is converging on the "dominant currency paradigm,"[24] which implies that traders in non–reserve currency countries use the dominant currency, currently the dollar, in their international transactions for invoicing and financing – even in transactions that do not involve the country issuing the dominant currency. This is contrary to the traditional view that producers of manufacturing products, especially in developed economies, invoice their exports in their home currency because most costs, especially labor costs, are fixed in that currency. That continues to be the case for firms in the euro area but not in other countries, especially fast-growing emerging economies. This is yet an additional factor that favors the dollar over the euro.

The dominance of the US dollar in economic transactions that do not involve the United States has a simple explanation: There are over 190 sovereign countries in the world, most of which (the main exception is the euro area) have their own currencies. Accounting for the euro one can thus estimate that there are about 180 actively used national currencies. This means there are (180/179)/2 = 16,110 currency pairs. The market in most of these pairs would be very small with irregular transactions arriving each day or week. This is why a vehicle currency helps to reduce transaction costs. In reality, most currencies are thus traded only against the dollar. An exchange of Mexican pesos for Indian rupee would thus require two transactions: pesos into dollars and then dollars into rupee. However, the use of a vehicle (currency) is much more efficient than trying to fill the entire matrix of bilateral exchange rates.

The spread of international value chains reinforces this shift by traders (both exporters and importers) to dominant currency invoicing. Exporters require intermediate inputs. Exporters will thus prefer to price their products in the same currency as their inputs and will require and prefer finance in that same currency. Given that many such inputs are invoiced in dollars, also given the historical weight of the United States in the global economy, the "same currency" tends to be the dollar. This combination of network effects in invoicing and complementarity between invoicing and financing implies a considerable degree of inertia, absent major disturbances. Once most trade is invoiced and financed in a currency (the US dollar at present), it becomes difficult to change the status quo. No individual economic agent has an incentive to switch to another currency.

Dominance does not mean monopoly. Some have argued that there can only be one international reserve currency because of the network effects mentioned earlier. However, these network effects can become secondary in specific geographic or political situations. For example, the euro is the preferred vehicular currency in central and eastern Europe even for transactions between countries outside the euro area, such as Poland and Hungary. Even SWIFT is not an absolute monopoly as it is challenged by fintech upstarts, and other countries, notably China, have developed their own system.

The question is now whether a combination of changes in the structure of the global economy and government interventions motivated by geopolitics can overcome this inertia.

BENEFITTING FROM AN EXORBITANT PRIVILEGE?

The use as foreign exchange reserves represents the most visible part of the international role of a currency. When a foreign central bank puts a large part of its precious fund into the dollar or the euro, it signals a high level of trust that it will be able to use these funds quickly should it need them in an emergency.

Central banks usually hold their reserves in short-term government bonds. This implies that the dollar holdings of foreign central banks finance US public debt and its fiscal deficits. This is why a French president complained already over half a century ago about the "exorbitant privilege" of the United States.[25]

How important is the use of the dollar for the US government's ability to run up its debt? And does the same apply, maybe on a smaller scale, to the euro?

Total global reserves amount to about 11 trillion dollars. The 60 percent share of the dollar thus amounts to about 6.6 trillion dollars, and US federal debt stood at 33 trillion by the end of 2023. This implies that foreign central banks might hold about one-fifth of the total federal public debt of the United States.

For the euro, an equivalent calculation leads to a similar result. The share of the euro in global foreign exchange reserves is only one-third of that of the US dollar (about 20 percent, or 2.2 trillion dollars). But the public debt of the euro area is also much smaller, about 12.5 trillion dollars. This implies that foreign central banks hold a bit more than one-sixth of the public debt of the euro area – not far from the US value. Central banks usually require a rating of at least AA or AAA for their investments. Only Germany and the Netherlands have the top-notch AAA in the euro area. Even adding AA-rated France, one arrives at a total public debt that might be acceptable to foreign central banks of only about 5 trillion euros. This means that foreign central banks might hold up to 40 percent of the public debt of the highly rated eurozone countries. The conclusion is that the eurozone benefits from an exorbitant privilege similar to that of the United States and that the highly rated euro area countries might benefit even more than the United States.

While it is gratifying that foreign central banks hold one's own government debt, one should really ask what the value of the exorbitant privilege is. How should one measure the economic advantage of the fact that foreign central banks hold a large amount of one's own public debt? An answer may come from asking whether the US government has been paying a lower interest rate on its debt than other countries.

This does not seem to have been the case. Since 1999, when the euro was born, the interest rate on US long-term debt has been 3.3 percent, compared to 3.1 percent for the average of the euro area over the same time period of almost twenty-five years. The average for the euro area includes countries like Italy and Spain, which paid at times a considerable risk premium, and Germany, whose government paid only 2.4 percent over this period of almost a quarter of a century. The data on the averages for short-term rates would show the same pattern: Euro area countries paid somewhat lower rates than the United States.

Readers trained in international economics might object that one has to account for the trend in the euro/dollar exchange rate over this period, not only the interest rate differential. But the exchange rate between the euro and dollar is today very close to where it was when the euro started. The intervening years have seen very strong fluctuations, but they were temporary. What remains is the fact that the cost of public debt was considerably lower for Germany than for the United States. We have mentioned the data for Germany as the main example of a AAA-rated euro area issuer, but other highly rated euro area countries like Holland or France were also able to finance themselves at a lower cost than the United States. The difference in funding costs might appear to be small. Germany is paying "only"

0.9 percent less than the United States. But even this small difference cumulates over this long period to over 20 percentage points.

The explanation of this finding might be simple. Maybe the biggest advantage of the dollar's hegemony as a reserve currency is not a lower interest rate but that the United States maintains a high rating, even after the downgrading to AA+, despite the repeated drama when the federal government runs up against the debt ceiling and partisan bickering leads to brinkmanship that at times unnerves the markets and has considerable costs for US taxpayers.[26] One could thus argue that given the danger of US public debt from this increasing polarization of the US political system, the US government should pay a high-risk premium, but this has been much reduced through the demand for US government debt from foreign central banks.

EXORBITANT PRIVILEGE BEGETS EXORBITANT DUTY

Economists are famous for being "two-handed"; they regularly find offsetting effects. This also applies to the benefits of having a global currency. Some researchers have thus argued that the exorbitant privilege can become an exorbitant duty.[27] Their argument is that during periods of crisis in the global financial systems risk averse investors all want to go to the safe haven of the dollar. This leads to an appreciation of the dollar, which is of course bad for US exports. But the more important effect of the appreciation of the United States dollar during a crisis emphasized here is that it means the US assets owned by foreigners become suddenly more valuable than the foreign assets US investors own abroad. This is what happened during the Great Financial Crisis of 2008–09 and also, more briefly, in 2020 during the financial turbulences at the start of the COVID-19 pandemic and in 2022 after the Russian invasion of Ukraine. Other researchers following similar lines of arguments concentrating on crisis periods have argued that the status of key currency that the US dollar enjoys implies also an extraordinary risk.[28] The basic argument is thus that when times get tough the US dollar appreciates, helping the rest of the world but adding a burden for the US economy.

These arguments relating to the costs of having an international currency were already known to the German authorities before the euro was created. The Bundesbank never tried to increase the international role of the Deutschmark (DM).[29] On the contrary, on several occasions it imposed controls on inflows of capital, so-called hot money, in order to keep the DM from appreciating too much during crisis periods similar to those mentioned earlier.[30]

Upon closer inspection, the "exorbitant privilege" thus turns out to be much less of an unmitigated privilege than might appear at first sight.[31]

TANGIBLE BENEFITS FROM A CURRENCY'S INTERNATIONAL USE

However, there is one aspect of the international use of the currency which undeniably provides a benefit, albeit a small one. This is the use of national cash, that is, euro and dollar banknotes, abroad. As we showed in earlier chapters, a large part of euro and US dollar banknotes are held abroad. This use of cash abroad confers a substantial benefit for the home country when interest rates are high, as at present, because the national central bank pays no interest on the banknotes it issues but earns interest on the assets in which it can invest the value of the cash it has printed. The seigniorage or inflation tax is normally just a transfer inside the country from cash holders to the central bank. But in the case of the euro and the dollar, about one-half of the seigniorage is a net gain, that is, a transfer from the cash holders abroad to the ECB and thus the national treasuries.

International seigniorage can be substantial. One can assume that about 1 trillion dollar notes are held abroad. This implies that the benefit from foreign seigniorage equals 50 billion dollars per annum when the short-term interest rate is around 5 percent, as in the summer of 2023. Though 50 billion dollars is a large number in absolute, it represents only 0.2 percent of US GDP. For the euro area, the gain might be slightly larger, about 0.25 percent of GDP, because the ratio of cash to GDP is slightly higher. In the earlier years of low interest rates, this was different. As we showed, cash holdings were much smaller twenty years ago, and with zero, or even negative, interest rates, the zero-interest loans implicit in bank notes circulating abroad did not produce any economic benefit.

CAN THE CHINESE YUAN CHALLENGE THE US DOLLAR?

Whether the benefits of an international currency are large or small, one must now recognize that the economic factor has become less significant lately: Governments are less and less guided by economic considerations, as opposed to strategic ones. Geopolitics has now become more important, leading to politically motivated competition for global currency status. China might try to dethrone the US dollar just to reinforce its international status, and some EU policy-makers are looking for concrete steps to increase the international role of the euro, in the hope that this would increase the international power base of the European Union as well.

The main argument so far is that the US dollar continues to be the premier global currency not because of US governmental efforts to foster its use internationally but because of network effects and size of the US economy. This implies that it will continue to dominate as long as private operators engaged in international trade and finance find it the most convenient currency to use.

But in the current climate of geopolitical rivalry, the Chinese government might try to offer alternatives to the US dollar. China is of course the country not only with the strongest political motives to challenge the hegemony of the US dollar but also with the strongest economy (the Chinese GDP now surpasses that of the euro area, as already mentioned).

The international role of the renminbi has increased over the last two decades. For example, starting in 2013, the People's Bank of China has also taken some steps to foster the international use of its currency by extending swap lines to a number of foreign central banks, mostly from poorer countries. This has jumpstarted the role of the renminbi from 0 to about 3 percent of global foreign exchange reserves and a somewhat higher percentage in trade invoicing, but there has been little growth since then.[32]

China thus did undertake some steps to foster the international use of the renminbi. But there are also other actions it could undertake to decouple from the US dollar.

A natural first step would be for China to diversify its foreign exchange reserves away from the United States by investing in other countries. But this is easier said than done. There are few opportunities to invest hundreds or thousands of billions of dollars outside of the United States. BIS data show that the overall euro area bond market, including both public and private issues, is worth less than one-third of that of the United States. Moreover, as mentioned earlier, the euro area offers little in terms of highly rated government bonds since the public debt of Germany and other fiscally prudent euro area countries amounts only to a fraction of US government debt.

Another step could be to use the renminbi in government-to-government transactions; for example, trade in crude oil between China and Saudi Arabia could be denominated in yuan. At first sight, this would secure an important share for the renminbi in global transactions. But then the Saudi government would have to find something to do with the Chinese currency it receives. Some could be used to pay for imports from China, but Saudi Arabia imports a lot less from China than it exports to it. The interests of other governments to use the renminbi are thus limited.

The 600 billion dollar Public Investment Fund (PIF), Saudi Arabia's sovereign wealth fund, could of course use the renminbi to invest in China. But this is difficult on a large scale because the Chinese currency remains only partially "convertible." This means that the Chinese authorities still control many transactions in and out of China so the Saudi fund might not be able to use its yuan funds as and when it needs them. Moreover, with the Chinese state tightening its controls over the economy, formal convertibility restrictions might become secondary. Even without them, few private investors, and even fewer Western investment funds, would be keen to put a lot of money into China if they were at the mercy of the Communist Party.

Until recently it was thought that the renminbi could become an important global currency if China opened its financial market and allowed its currency to be freely traded, perhaps even actively encouraging its use in offshore trade and finance.[33] But so far, there is little sign of this happening. China tightened up on many cross-border transactions following a bout of financial turbulence in 2015, in response to which it prioritized domestic financial stability over currency internationalization. By a number of measures, the international role of the renminbi diminished subsequently.

Given the direction toward more state control, it is unlikely that China's convertibility restrictions will be lifted. But formal currency convertibility might no longer be the key question. If the world divides into competing blocks, some countries that want to be closer to the Chinese camp might favor the use of the renminbi in their economic relations. But it seems that most of countries with close economic relations with China, especially in Asia, prefer to keep their independence and their operators are likely to prefer using a currency without political control.

This argument applies also to another much-discussed threat, namely the spread of the Chinese CBDC, the e-yuan. We documented in Chapter 10 that the e-yuan has been a flop in China itself because Chinese consumers prefer the very efficient payment apps they already have. It is even more unlikely that the e-yuan may become a big success abroad. The fear that all transactions in e-yuan would be ultimately known to the Chinese state is likely to further limit its attractiveness abroad.

The increasing drift of China toward state (or rather party) control over the economy thus constitutes the major obstacle to the spread of the Chinese currency on the global scene. The post-COVID slowing down of the Chinese economy adds one further economic element to this assessment.

CAN THE EURO CHALLENGE THE US DOLLAR?

Is the global currency ambition harbored in some eurozone quarters realistic and desirable? As discussed earlier, one needs to keep in mind that the exchange rate of the euro might become more volatile if the euro's importance as a global currency were to increase. This was also the reason why the Bundesbank never actively encouraged the international use of the DM.

More recently, with the resurgence of geopolitical tensions, the ability of the United States to impose sanctions on the use of the US dollar has prompted discussion about whether the European Union could achieve a similar status through the international use of the euro. But if the dominant currency paradigm is correct, there is little chance that the euro could substitute the US dollar on a significant scale and the issuance of Eurobonds would make little difference. The key remains the combination of the geopolitical strengths of the United States and its central role in the international payment infrastructure.

Currently, the eurozone accounts for about 15 percent of global trade – a bit less than when the euro was introduced. The slight fall in the share of the euro is due to the rise of China, not a fall in extra euro area trade, which has remained strong. The euro is already the world's second-most-traded currency. Its share in foreign exchange flows is roughly the same as its share in global trade and falling only slightly given the small increase in the role of the Chinese renminbi moving from 4 percent in 2019 to 7 percent of all trades in 2022.[34]

The share of the euro in global reserves is presently around 21 percent, around one-third of that of the United States.[35] Maybe the role of the euro as a foreign exchange currency can increase somewhat, but one needs to be realistic because there are other contenders in a more diversified currency market. The combined share of the other currencies as global reserve currencies (yen, UK pound, and renminbi) is now equal to that of the euro.[36]

The increase in the shares of the other currencies has come mainly at the expense of the US dollar, whose share has declined by over 10 percentage points since the financial crisis.[37] The near constancy of the euro's share over more than twenty years and the rise of the rest suggests that there is little upside room for the euro (unless there is a run from the dollar). The motives of foreign exchange reserve holders, that is, central banks, all over the world in choosing the currency composition of their reserves are not well understood. It is thus difficult to know what measures would increase the share of the euro. It has been suggested that invoicing practices and exchange rate movements are key determinants of the currency composition of foreign exchange reserves.[38] These factors cannot be influenced by EU measures.

One should also factor in the overall trend that the share of the eurozone in global trade is likely to fall further due to the increase of other players (China, emerging market economies in general). In a multipolar economy, a balance between the major currencies is preferable so that the role of the dollar is reduced while no one has the power to fundamentally manipulate the exchange rate. Given these developments in global trade relations and financial markets, the best way to secure the international role of the euro is to reduce its vulnerability. But here again one needs to ask whether the status of a global currency confers power that can be used for geopolitical aims.

SWIFT SANCTIONS

The most direct use of international finance as a weapon came when Russia launched its full-scale invasion of Ukraine on February 24, 2022. The Western allies were then looking for ways to hit the Russian economy as a way to put pressure on Putin. One of the first issues to come up was the idea to exclude Russian banks from SWIFT.[39]

With virtually every bank in the world depending on SWIFT, it was thought that excluding Russia from the SWIFT network would incapacitate the Russian banking system. However, the move turned out to be a damp squib. Russian banks were initially inconvenienced but domestic payments continued with only minor initial problems mainly because the potential use of this type of sanctions had already been discussed after the 2014 annexation of Crimea and the subsequent invasion of the Donbass region. The Central Bank of Russia had thus had ample time to develop its own domestic payment system.[40]

The reason for this lack of a decisive impact is simple. Networks like SWIFT can become dominant even if they offer just a minor cost advantage over alternatives. The success of SWIFT was not based on some fancy new technology. It only offered a messaging system with a unified format to facilitate the sending and reception of payment messages that are machine-readable. This represented a decisive improvement in the 1970s and 1980s, but it is something one takes for granted today. Russia has its own domestic telecommunication system, and Russian banks could just continue to use this to transit to their domestic system to use the SWIFT format if they wanted.

The broader reason why control over SWIFT does not confer a lot of political power comes from the nature of the reasons for the monopoly. Saving a few cents on every transaction represents a potentially decisive competitive disadvantage in a competitive market with razor-thin margins, but it becomes negligible in a war economy where survival is at stake. Moreover, Russia sells abroad mostly raw materials that have liquid world markets (like oil and some minerals) that are formally exempted from sanctions, and it sells those products increasingly to countries that have not imposed any sanctions.

Russia in 2022 was not the first case of SWIFT being used as a geopolitical weapon. Already ten years earlier, in 2012, the European authorities instructed SWIFT to disconnect Iranian banks. But the case of Iran was very different. First of all, the Russian economy is ten times larger than that of Iran, giving the Russian government also the necessary resources to develop a domestic replacement. Secondly, the Iranian sanctions were imposed under a decision of the United Nations, which gave them greater legitimacy and forced all countries to participate. By contrast, no UN decision could be taken on Russia, which has veto power. A number of countries, including India and

China, refused to support even UN resolutions condemning the invasion. Banks in these countries soon found ways to establish relations with Russian banks, necessary also to pay for their imports of oil and gas. This did not happen in the case of Iran, whose ability to trade was thus crippled.

China is of course taking note of the use of access to SWIFT as a political instrument and has developed its own domestic and international payment system. However, the use of Cross-Border Interbank Payment System (CIPS[41]) has remained limited so far, with the transaction volume only a fraction of that of SWIFT. China could foster the use of its system given its weight in international trade. The Berkeley economist Barry Eichengreen describes in detail the potential significance of the Chinese system.[42] CIPS will face two handicaps in its competition with SWIFT: It does not have the network economies of scale, and it is associated with the Chinese government, which makes confidentiality a sore point.

For China itself the key point is that its homegrown system would provide an alternative to SWIFT in the case of a military conflict over Taiwan, which might lead to Western sanctions.

CBDCS' POTENTIAL ROLE IN GLOBAL CURRENCY DOMINANCE

As we showed in Chapter 10, the stage of preparation for CBDCs differs widely around the world, depending on local conditions and policy priorities. The key motive for China going ahead was one of control, and the timing was triggered essentially by the dominant market position achieved by the private platforms – Alipay, WeChat, and others. Given that the party has now reinforced its control over the private sector in general, it is possible that the Chinese government now sees much less of a need to have a governmental alternative to the two private sector payment giants.

As we also noted in Chapter 10, the decision by each central bank to actually introduce a CBDC is likely to be influenced by, and to influence in turn, the decision of others, leading to a group dynamic we called "Fear of Missing Out." A Federal Reserve staff research paper has examined this issue from an economic point of view and concluded that there should be no "first-mover advantage" for a country in launching a CBDC. On the contrary, one could argue that waiting to observe the experience of others could be the best strategy because in this way one can learn from the experience of the early adopters.[43]

From a purely economic point of view, it is difficult to see why issuing a CBDC should strengthen the international role of one's national currency. The availability of a CBDC is unlikely to have a significant effect on the relative attractiveness of currencies for invoicing or as reserve instruments. As explained earlier, the cross-border use of currencies depends on other aspects, such as economic size, the stability of the currency itself, and the breadth of the underlying financial markets. The use as a vehicle currency is subject to network economies which continue to favor the incumbent, the US dollar. Explicit government actions to favor the international use of the home currency might yield some minor gains in reserve or invoicing statistics but are unlikely to have a significant impact on the use of the US dollar as the only global vehicle currency. Moreover, as discussed, it is not clear what economic advantage the euro area (or China for that matter) will gain by gaining some market share in global reserves or invoicing.

That said, the decision to go for a CBDC is now unlikely to be made on economic considerations alone. Political and strategic considerations, whether well-grounded or not, are increasingly coming to the fore in discussions about the pros and cons of having a CBDC.

Some regard CBDCs as "monetary weapons" which can be used to promote the international role of currencies or to defend smaller countries against the overwhelming power of the large countries' currencies.[44] Accordingly, CBDCs are seen at times as instruments to defend monetary sovereignty. It is difficult to see how these hopes and fears would materialize in practice.

The intention of using CBDCs as a geopolitical weapon would also lead to awkward issues as to who would be allowed to obtain a

CBDC account and thus access to the national central bank: only citizens, all lawful residents, even foreigners, maybe only foreigners from countries considered friendly? The same conundrum faces the argument that a digital euro constitutes an expression of "European" sovereignty. Should the digital euro then be made available only to euro area citizens/residents only, to non–euro area EU citizens as well, or even to foreigners? Who would perform the onboarding of the latter?

Finally, the ongoing fragmentation of global politics makes it increasingly unlikely that major countries will allow wide use of a foreign CBDC at home. This might turn out to be the key reason why CBDCs will not shake up the global financial order.

CONCLUSIONS

Global trade and finance benefits from standards. The nineteenth century developed the Gold Standard, which, although never applied in its pure form, provided a framework for price stability and a huge expansion of international trade and finance. It was of course not the Gold Standard itself that caused this expansion, but it made steamships and telegraphs so much more useful. The SWIFT system of the last century, based on a private initiative, further facilitated cross-border transactions by providing a common standard transfer across hundreds of currencies and hundreds of thousands of banks worldwide.

The world is far from a new global monetary standard. This should not be surprising: The role of governments in the economy is much larger today than in the nineteenth century, so it is natural that the realm of money coincides with that of the nation-state – with the euro area the only major exception.

However, some standard is still needed for international trade and finance. At present this standard is mainly provided by the US dollar and the euro in some peripheral areas of Europe.

Using traditional metrics to compare the positions of the three major currencies to the size of their home economies, one finds that the United States punches above the weight of the US economy, the euro's international role is about as large as one would expect given the size of the European economy, and the role of the renminbi is much smaller than the weight of the Chinese economy, which is now much larger than that of the euro area.

When it comes to global trade and finance, currency use outside the orbit of these three major economic powers is underpinned by a self-reinforcing network of transactions. Because of this, and the size of the US financial market, the dollar's dominant position as the premier global vehicle currency remains something for the United States to lose rather than for others to gain.

Currency competition is not a new feature of the global financial system. According to some, the idea that the dollar should be able to compete with the then absolutely dominant pound sterling was one of the reasons why the US central bank, the Federal Reserve System, was created in the first place in the early 1900s.[45] However, at the time the driving forces were mainly economic and financial, as the United States and the United Kingdom were both democracies and allies. The French franc and the German Reichsmark had only a limited role within Europe. The Reichsmark disappeared in a blaze of hyperinflation whereas the French franc remained stable and continued to play an important, if secondary, role as a reserve currency until World War II. The postwar period then saw another reversal of fortunes within Europe, as the economy of the new democratic Germany was able to grow in an increasingly integrated Europe. Its currency, the DM, became an important competitor to the US dollar, eventually giving its legacy to the euro.

It shouldn't come as a surprise that democracies dominate the world financially. Companies and financial markets require trust and a well-established rule of law. Nondemocratic regimes have no basis for establishing the rule of law, and every investor is ultimately subject to the whims of the ruler. That said, trying to use one's currency or control over financial networks to exert power globally is a fool's errand as the small impact of the SWIFT sanctions on Russia has shown. The major economies would be well advised not to strive for a dominant global role of their currency but rather concentrate on keeping their monies and financial systems stable and reliable. Currencies have but a limited place in the geopolitical armory.

NOTES

1. Marina Dossena, "Building Trust through (Self-)Appraisal in Nineteenth-Century Business Correspondence," in Päivi Pahta, Minna Nevala, Arja Nurmi, and Minna Palander-Collin (eds.), *Social Roles and Language Practices in Late Modern English*, Pragmatics & Beyond New Series (John Benjamins, 2010), 191–209.

2. John M. Ward, "Information Planning for Strategic Advantage," *Journal of Information Technology* 3, no. 3 (September 1, 1988): 169–77.

3. Tom Standage, *The Victorian Internet: The Remarkable Story of the Telegraph and the Nineteenth Century's Online Pioneers* (Phoenix, 1999).

4. Bank for International Settlements (BIS), "Correspondent Banking," July 2016.

5. Catherine R. Schenk, "The Development of International Correspondent Banking in the USA 1970–1989," University of Oxford Global Correspondent Banking 1870–2000 Working Paper Series 1, no. 1, December 2021.

6. Jeffrey S. Tallackson and Norma Vallejo, "International Commercial Wire Transfers: The Lack of Standards," *North Carolina Journal of International Law and Commercial Regulation* 11 (1986): 639.

7. Susan V. Scott and Markos Zachariadis, "Origins and Development of SWIFT, 1973–2009," *Business History* 54, no. 3 (June 1, 2012): 462–82.

8. Scott and Zachariadis, "Origins and Development of SWIFT."

9. One could regard SWIFT as the first example of the recent concept of open strategic autonomy for the European Union. The main reason a group of European banks formed this consortium was to challenge a private American monopoly by the then only provider of the digitalized international transfer system.

10. "The Race to Redefine Cross-Border Finance," *The Economist*, October 21, 2021, seems to overlook the preexistence of the MARTI system when it states: "a string of 12 characters ushered in a new age of global finance. Until then a bank wiring money abroad needed to relay up to ten instructions on public phone lines, which were then typed into forms, taking time and causing errors."

11. Boris Kozolchyk, "The Paperless Letter of Credit and Related Documents of Title," *Law and Contemporary Problems* 55, no. 3 (January 1, 1992): 39; "New SWIFT Network Gives Banks an Instantaneous Link Worldwide," *Banking* (July 1977): 48; SWIFT Brochure, 80-3056-2, Barclays Group Archives, c. March 1980.

12. These data and the following ones are reported in the SWIFT website and Annual Reports.

13. SWIFT website.

14. "SWIFT Annual Review | SWIFT," SWIFT, 2022.

15. As reported in Wikipedia contributors, "2015–2016 SWIFT Banking Hack," *Wikipedia*, July 27, 2023.

16. "Rethinking Correspondent Banking," McKinsey & Company, June 1, 2016.

17. BIS, "Correspondent Banking."

18. Tara Rice, Goetz von Peter, and Codruta Boar, "On the Global Retreat of Correspondent Banks," BIS Quarterly Review (March 1, 2020).

19. "Latvia Cracks Down on Unscrupulous Banking | Think Tank | European Parliament," December 13, 2018.

20. Tommaso Mancini Griffoli, Tobias Adrian, Rodney Garratt, and Dong He, "Trust Bridges and Money Flows," *Fintech Notes* 2023, no. 001 (March 1, 2023): 1.

21. Robert Greene, "Asia's Interest in Wholesale Central Bank Digital Currency – and Challenges to Cross-Border Use," Carnegie Endowment for International Peace, February 7, 2023; and Maria Demertzis and Catarina Martins, "The Value Added of Central Bank Digital Currencies: A View from the Euro Area," Bruegel, June 12, 2023.

22. This should be qualified since it refers to those reserves for which the currency composition is known.

23. Angela Capolongo, Barry Eichengreen, and Daniel Gros, "Safely Increasing the Supply of Safe Assets: Internationalising the Euro in the Age of COVID-19," CEPR, October 23, 2020.

24. Gita Gopinath, Emine Boz, Camila Casas, Federico J. Díez, Pierre-Olivier Gourinchas, and Mikkel Plagborg-Møller, "Dominant Currency Paradigm," *The American Economic Review* 110, no. 3 (March 1, 2020): 677–719.

25. As so often, it is not clear whether the first use of this term came from the French president himself. The first documented utterance was by Valéry Giscard d'Estaing, then finance minister and only later

president in February 1965. Raymond Aron, *Les Articles de Politique Internationale Dans "Le Figaro" de 1947 à 1977*, vol. 2 (De Fallois, 1994), 147.

26. Wendy Edelberg and Noadia Steinmetz-Silber, "Debt Ceiling Brinksmanship Has Clear Negative Effects on Taxpayers," Brookings, May 23, 2023; and Lucas Rengifo-Keller, "US Debt Limit Brinkmanship and Potential Default Could Affect Everyone in the Country," PIIE, March 24, 2023.

27. Pierre-Olivier Gourinchas and Hélène Rey, "Exorbitant Privilege and Exorbitant Duty," CEPR Press Discussion Paper 16944, January 22, 2022.

28. Matthew B. Canzoneri, Robert Cumby, Behzad Diba, and David López-Salido, "Key Currency Status: An Exorbitant Privilege and an Extraordinary Risk," *Journal of International Money and Finance* 37 (October 1, 2013): 371–93.

29. Karl O. Pöhl, "International Monetary Stability," Deutsche Bundesbank, Auszüge aus Presseartikeln, February 3, 1988.

30. Jacob A. Frenkel, *The International Role of the Deutsche Mark* (Institute for International Economics, 1997).

31. See also Andrew Atkeson, Jonathan Heathcote, and Fabrizio Perri, "The End of Privilege: A Reexamination of the Net Foreign Asset Position of the United States," *NBER Working Papers* 29771, February 1, 2022.

32. Saleemand Bahaj and Ricardo Reis, "Jumpstarting an International Currency," London School of Economics, July 2022.

33. Alain Naef, Eric Monnet, Camille Macaire, Arnaud Mehl, and Barry Eichengreen, "The Renminbi's Unconventional Route to Reserve Currency Status," CEPR, October 31, 2022.

34. See Bank for International Settlements (BIS), "OTC Foreign Exchange Turnover in April 2022," October 27, 2022.

35. Capolongo, Eichengreen, and Gros, "Safely Increasing the Supply of Safe Assets," discusses the medium-term evolution of the euro's share. The ECB publishes each year a special report on the international role of the euro: European Central Bank, "The International Role of the Euro, June 2021," June 2, 2021. For the most recent data see: International Monetary Fund, "Currency Composition of Official Foreign Exchange Reserves."

36. See page 12 of European Central Bank, "The International Role of the Euro, June 2022," June 2022.

37. Part of this reduction in the share of the United States and the rise of the rest might be a statistical artifact since the statistics on foreign exchange reserves refer only to "identified" reserves, that is, the reserves held by countries which provide the IMF with the data on the composition of their foreign exchange reserves. The identified reserves now account for the bulk of all reserves, but this was not the case in the past. The statistics on the composition of foreign exchange reserves from more than a decade ago are thus not directly comparable to today's data.

38. Hiro Ito and Robert N. McCauley, "Currency Composition of Foreign Exchange Reserves," *Journal of International Money and Finance* 102 (April 1, 2020).

39. Similarly, in August 2014 the UK planned to press the European Union to block Russian use of SWIFT as a sanction due to Russian military intervention in Ukraine; see Wikipedia contributors, "Russo-Ukrainian War," Wikipedia, September 25, 2023; SWIFT refused to do so. SPFS, a Russian alternative to SWIFT, was developed by the Central Bank of Russia as a backup measure. See Wikipedia contributors, "SPFS," *Wikipedia*, August 13, 2023, and Wikipedia contributors. "Central Bank of Russia," *Wikipedia*, September 20, 2023.

40. The Russian system is of course much smaller than SWIFT as it has members almost exclusively from Russia itself and it therefore processes only a very small number of transactions. See "Number of Countries within Financial Messaging System to Reach 18 in 2023: Bank of Russia," TASS, November 25, 2022.

41. Wikipedia Contributors, "Cross-Border Interbank Payment System," *Wikipedia*, September 18, 2023.

42. Barry Eichengreen, "Sanctions, SWIFT, and China's Cross-Border Interbank Payments System," *CSIS*, October 13, 2022.

43. Ken Isaacson, Jesse Leigh Maniff, and Paul Wong, "An Examination of First-Mover Advantage for a CBDC," FEDS Notes, November 25, 2022.

44. See, for example, Maria Demertzis, "Central Bank Digital Currencies as Weapons of Finance?," *Bruegel*, October 10, 2023.

45. See Barry Eichengreen, "Sterling's Past, Dollar's Future: Historical Perspectives on Reserve Currency Competition," *NBER Working Papers* 11336, May 1, 2005.

13 The Return of Instability

Stability breeds instability.

Hyman Minsky

Earlier in this book we hinted at an important question, without going into details: How did the rise of the digital and crypto "revolution" in finance come about? In other words, what explains its occurrence and its timing? Understanding the origins sometimes helps prepare for a better future.

Actually, the term "revolution" is in some respects overstated. As we have seen, money has been largely digital for a long time. Paper currency is far from disappearing. The role of banks as payment providers may be declining in some areas but is still central. So is the position of central banks as guardians of the stability and the efficiency of the payment system. And the system works remarkably well. Admittedly, there are glitches: Payments are expensive and slow across borders and in certain jurisdictions. Market failures and human mistakes occasionally lead to inconvenience and costs for ordinary people. Frauds occur, that authorities and in-built checks cannot detect and sanction, let alone prevent. But these are imperfections calling for reform and gradual improvement, not for replacing the status quo with a hitherto unidentified "something else."

Yet the popular discourse and even expert debates often tend to overemphasize the shortcomings of traditional monetary arrangements, adding credence to the purported need for revolutionary changes. Even central banks, quintessential conservatives, have joined in the excitement, some of them appearing as if they want to be at the front of the revolution by issuing their own digital instruments.

What explains all this? To gain some understanding we need to broaden our focus. In recent decades, the role of central banks and the monetary arrangements built around them have changed. So have popular expectations regarding these institutions, the extent of their power, and the services they can provide. At first, expectations grew out of proportion: In many people's eyes, central banks became "masters of the universe" capable of delivering ideal economic outcomes under any circumstances.[1] The peak of central bankers' reputation was probably reached by the former US Federal Reserve chair Alan Greenspan, universally named "the master" after a popular 2000 book by the *Washington Post* journalist Bob Woodward, emphatically titled *Maestro*. Greenspan's prestige did not suffer, actually probably gained, from the obscurity of his language, which required huge interpretation efforts from observers and market participants.

Early in the twenty-first century, the cycle turned and disillusion started to set in. Financial crises, economic stagnation, eventually inflation – many complex and interconnected factors conjured to produce this change. While traditional monetary institutions were entering a state of crisis, people started looking out on the fringes for more exotic and "dark" alternatives. Such is, after all, the nature of monetary politics: As politics in general, it is cyclical, going back and forth in phases, subject to courses and recourses. Trends and reversals alternate and repeat themselves in different forms.

We call the most recent phase of this cycle the "return of instability" and argue that it has something to do with the digital and crypto hype we have discussed in the earlier chapters. Let's see how we got to it and what the consequences are.

BACK AND FORTH BETWEEN I-PHASES AND S-PHASES

As we noted in Chapter 3, the post–World War II monetary order rested on the so-called Bretton Woods system, where national currencies were linked to the US dollar and through the dollar indirectly to gold. All central banks except the US Federal Reserve exchanged dollars against their own monies to maintain the parities. They also could trade in dollars to the US Federal Reserve and receive gold; in practice, however, they rarely did so, preferring to keep dollars instead.

Designed before the end of World War II by the two leading wartime allies, the United States and Britain, that regime was meant to establish orderly conditions for postwar reconstruction and recovery based on free international trade. There was a prearranged crisis management mechanism centered on the International Monetary Fund (IMF), which could lend to deficit countries and adjust the parities if needed. International capital flows were tightly controlled and financial development was effectively repressed, domestically and globally. Domestically, financial innovation was hampered by legislation. Internationally, it was limited in size and de facto dominated by the official sector. Financial systems operated eminently within national borders.

All in all, this regime worked well and achieved its purpose; the Western world – what happened beyond the "Iron Curtain" is a different matter – enjoyed sustained economic growth, rising productivity, steady technological progress, and stable prices. That system lasted until 1971. A remarkable stretch of time: In history, periods of broadly shared prosperity lasting so long (we will call them "stability phases," or S-phases) are rare. It usually happens that during S-phases there are inner forces sowing the seeds of subsequent instability (I-phases).

In this particular case, the seed of instability was the "exorbitant privilege" of the US dollar, which we discussed in Chapter 12. The pivot currency of the system, used for international payments and as a reserve asset, exploited this privilege to conduct expansionary fiscal and monetary policy in the pursuit of its own domestic objectives – enlarging the social safety net and financing military expenses. In the 1960s, when inflation started to rise and pressure on the dollar rose, the system's days were numbered. After years of economic expansion under Democratic administrations, it fell on a Republican president, Richard Nixon, to suspend the dollar parity, effectively letting the US currency plunge in value and the price of goal soar. From its "Bretton Woods" value of 35 dollars per ounce, the market price of gold climbed almost continuously thereafter. Today its price is well above 2,000 dollars per ounce.

In 1971, the postwar S-phase ended. The ensuing I-phase lasted until the early 1980s and was marked by pronounced instability in many respects: major exchange rate fluctuations, currency crises, high and rising inflation, sharp interest rate increases, and banking crises. The first prominent postwar bank failure, of the German bank Herstatt, happened in 1974, a direct result of exchange rate instability. Inflation reached double-digit levels almost everywhere. In other respects, however, this was a fruitful period, rich in innovation, financial development, and institution building. The Herstatt failure led to the creation of the Basel Committee on Banking Supervision, until today the main forum of global coordination among banking supervisors. New instruments were devised to diversify and hedge the new risks generated by the more volatile financial environment. A key milestone was the introduction of financial derivatives on exchange rates and interest rates in the Chicago exchanges (Chicago Board of Trade and Chicago Mercantile Exchange). Another one was the creation of MMFs, which as discussed in Chapter 9 allowed investors to take advantage of rising market interest rates while retaining the liquidity of their investments. As invariably happens, instability sharpened ingenuity. The financial system was adapting to a new reality characterized by much higher volatility and risk.

A consequential development of this period was the rise in the status and reputation of central banks, followed by a strengthening of their legal status. During that period central banks acquired, in the popular perception, the role of "guardians of price stability." In the beginning, central banks were rather complacent: They hesitated to react, lacking either sufficient knowledge or sufficient political force to intervene.[2] An exception was the German Bundesbank, whose unwavering anti-inflationary stance contributed to Germany being the only advanced nation where inflation in the 1970s remained at single-digit levels. Other central banks joined later. By the early 1980s, following the example of Paul Volcker's Federal Reserve, all adopted anti-inflationary stances and acquired, formally or de facto, the necessary independence to pursue it.

The turmoils of the 1970s and the victory over the Great Inflation in the early 1980s opened the way to the next S-phase, which would last until the Great Financial Crisis of 2008–09. A distinct trait of this period was the liberalization and expansion of global capital markets, followed by an astronomical increase in domestic and international capital flows.[3] This period saw unprecedented growth in volume and diversification of financial instruments. The real side of the global economy grew fast as well: Between 1980 and 2008, global output more than doubled, and the volume of international trade grew by a factor of four. Such was the result of "globalization." Not only trade for finite products but also intermediate goods cross-border flows grew exponentially. Production chains in this period started diversifying internationally, as companies looked for cheaper labor costs, especially in developing countries. Trade globalization culminated with the accession to the World Trade Organization of China in 2001, and other Asian and Eastern European countries in the early 2000s.

Trade globalization in the late 1990s is key for understanding the monetary and financial developments that followed. Compounded by the rise of the internet and related digital technologies, the entry into the global production chains of low-cost producers from the Far East stabilized the global economy, guaranteeing higher output levels and lower prices. There was much debate at the time about the role played by the so-called new economy: the application of internet communication making for more efficient production chains and allowing increases in productivity. Internet technology may have played a role, but globalization was key. The world was living what economists call a "positive supply shock" – more goods available at a lower cost. With inflation anchored at low levels, central banks could conduct more expansionary monetary policies without triggering inflation.[4] Central bankers' prestige soared on the tailwinds of ample liquidity, easy and cheap credit, and booming stock markets.

Academic economists have coined for that era the term "great moderation." Heated discussions flourished on whether the merit for such moderation should be attributed to better corporate processes (in particular, more efficient inventory management), better monetary policies, or simply "luck" (fortuitous circumstances). Not unexpectedly, central bankers tended to put the weight on monetary policy improvements. They argued that central banks had become more systematic and predictable, for example, by adopting preannounced policy rules: most notably the celebrated "Taylor rule," according to which central bank rates adjust in response to measures of the output gap and expected inflation. An articulate statement of this view was provided in 2004 by Ben Bernanke, Fed governor at the time and future chair of the Federal Reserve and Nobel recipient. He concluded his statement as follows:

> I have argued today that improved monetary policy has likely made an important contribution not only to the reduced volatility of inflation (which is not particularly controversial) but to the reduced volatility of output as well. Moreover, because a change in the monetary policy regime has pervasive effects, I have suggested that some of the effects of improved monetary policies may have been misidentified as exogenous changes in economic structure or in the distribution of economic shocks. This conclusion on my part makes me optimistic for the future, because I am confident that monetary policymakers will not forget the lessons of the 1970s.[5]

The timing of that statement was not fortunate: Just three years later, the Great Financial Crisis brought global finance to the brink. With hindsight, we know today that at that time the seed of instability had already been sown.

One must not forget that globalization also had dramatically positive effects, unattainable in other circumstances. The number of poor people in the world, defined by the United Nations as those having an income lower than 1.25 dollars a day, declined by over a billion, mostly in developing countries. The United Nations was able in this way to attain its most important "development goal," extreme poverty reduction. As recognized by few economists in those times, however, in the economically advanced part of the world those conditions generated excessive financial risk-taking and facilitated the subsequent instability.[6] It took time for the process to develop. After a short-lived market crash in 2000, the euphoria in financial markets intensified, with the global investor community taking on increasing risks in the real estate sector, through new exotic and poorly understood financial instruments. The "bubble" eventually burst in 2008, with the failure of Lehman Brothers, the dramatic rescue of the insurer AIG by the US authorities, and the ensuing near-collapse and rescue of the entire US and global financial system.

The time of reckoning had come; a new I-phase was starting.

THE GREAT MONETARY EXPANSION AND THE REVIVAL OF INFLATION

The subsequent period – from 2008 to today and beyond – is when the boom of digital and crypto finance is temporally located. This period coincides with unprecedented activism of central banks aimed at supporting economic activity and fending off the risks of deflation – a downward spiral of falling prices and real economic activity. In Europe, the European Central Bank (ECB) had another purpose too, preserving the cohesion of the euro under threat from the sovereign debt crisis and the fragility of banks.

For our argument, we focus on three separate but related developments.

The first is the massive, unprecedented increase in market liquidity. From 2008 onward, monetary aggregates, relative to the size of the economies – which economists measure by the so-called velocity of money – increased sharply in the early postcrisis years and even more during the COVID pandemic. The increase was larger for the more liquid components of the money stock, directly usable for spending. The collapse in money's "velocity" reflects the fact that money was in fact stagnant, parked with banks and central banks, nervously searching for scarce profitable opportunities and willing to take more risk to find them.

At the base of the process were the central bank balance sheets. Measured in relation to GDP, the balance sheet of the US Federal Reserve rose from around 5 percent in 2008 to over 30 percent at the end of 2022. The comparable increase for the Eurosystem, combining the ECB and the national central banks of the eurozone, was from just over 10 percent to 60 percent.[7] The monetary expansion was accompanied by a decline in interest rates, close to or at zero first, then below zero in some countries. The ECB brought its pivot policy rate to zero in 2012 and below zero from 2014 onward. The Federal Reserve had already reduced its federal fund rate guidance to 0.25 percent in the end of 2008 and kept it there for seven years, until 2015, followed by a moderate (and at the time controversial) tightening cycle that lasted until the pandemic (2020), after which the rate was slashed again to 0.25 percent. During this whole period, market interest rates were close to or (in Europe) below zero on most maturities.

The "money binge" was successful in preventing another Great Depression like that of the 1930s. The 2008–09 crisis was remarkably short-lived and so was the deep recession that followed. The United States and the eurozone resumed growth already in 2010. We agree with the prevalent narrative according to which the central banks avoided the mistakes of the 1930s by providing prompt and unlimited monetary support. The other side of the coin is that their victory overburdened the perception of the central banks' abilities and responsibilities, among public opinions and political circles. An awkward position for central banks to be in, because their power to steer economic outcomes is not limitless.

The expansionary tone of economic policy in that period was not limited to money and central banks but extended to the whole financial sector. Indicators of "financial conditions," which combine developments in various compartments of the financial sector (equity markets, exchange rates, bank credit, etc.), signal a continuous expansion, starting after 2008 and continuing until the surge of inflation in 2021–22.[8] A large part derived from stock market prices, which rose steadily, especially in the technological compartments. The Dow Jones industrial index rose five times over this period, and the Nasdaq 100 composite index ten times.

The more recent part of this I-phase coincided with the return of inflation in the global economy. An old acquaintance and enemy of policymakers, inflation had remained out of sight for over forty years. By the end of 2022, it had risen globally to 8.8 percent and to 7 and 10 percent in the United States and the eurozone, respectively. In some traditionally less stable emerging countries, like Turkey and Argentina, inflation approached 100 percent.

Debates on the causes of all this have already started. The "monetarist" side emphasized the preceding monetary expansion, seeing a chance to regain the upper hand in the debate after decades of relegation in the academic fringes.[9] Competing explanations emphasize commodity shocks, supply constraints, deglobalization, and more. We expect this discussion to keep economists and their computers busy for many years. We also predict that it will not be settled, just like the "monetarist controversy," whose story we told in Chapter 6, was never fully settled.

Our reflection on this and earlier experiences leads us to believe that monetary accommodation and lax financial conditions do not necessarily *cause* inflation. There is no predictable mechanism linking inflation to them, no regularity one can count on to make accurate predictions. The long post-1980s S-phase along with its enduring price stability is the most recent demonstration. However, we do believe that monetary accommodation *permits* inflation to happen when *other* circumstances occur. Once those conditions materialize – whether due to a salary push, an excessive fiscal expansion, a commodity price increase, or something else – if monetary conditions are lax the rise of inflation is more likely to occur and its intensity is likely to be higher. The recent burst of inflation started in 2021, in the exceptional circumstances of the COVID pandemic. When it started, it could flare up more easily and persistently because the monetary "fuel" was abundantly available.

Another critical development we need to point concerns the state of the banking and financial sector. Following the Great Financial Crisis of 2008–09 the sector was, with few exceptions, bailed out by governments, with costs that are difficult to assess. Estimates vary, critically depending on the timing of the calculation, because most bailout funds were eventually reimbursed. The initial effects in both the United States and Europe were measured in the trillions (dollars or euros). Longer-term estimates are lower, especially in the United States.[10] What we want to emphasize here is that in spite of the public support, or perhaps also because of it, the traditional financial sector emerged from the experience critically weakened, in at least three ways. First was reputationally: The prestige of banks and their leaders sank to a historical low after the crisis. Bankers were seen as responsible for badly misperceiving if not deliberately misrepresenting the risks they were running for their own institutions and the economy at large. Second, they were also weakened financially, because of the losses they had incurred, and structurally, due to the inevitable downsizing with the ensuing loss of material and human resources. Finally, they were weakened from a regulatory viewpoint, because of the stricter legislation they came to be subject to after the crisis.

THE RETURN OF INSTABILITY AND THE RISE OF DIGITAL FINANCE: LINKS AND IMPLICATIONS

Lax monetary conditions, inflation, banks debilitated and on defense – all of these factors have created an easier ground for competitors to challenge a traditional financial sector in a state of crisis. An increasingly strong tech sector diversified into business areas traditionally occupied by banks. Alternative financial instruments, like crypto, compete with the existing ones for the favors and confidence of investors. It is tempting to connect all these elements, but such a connection is complex and tentative because the phenomena are recent and evolving.

Empirical economists – always in search of "puzzles" to be explained – have started examining the relationship between the postcrisis monetary expansion and the rise of crypto finance using data and advanced statistical methodologies.[11] The results are suggestive but not conclusive. There is a temporal coincidence between some episodes of monetary expansion and the biggest spikes in crypto prices. Such evidence is particularly evident in certain phases of the pandemic crisis (2021–22) when central banks engaged in the latest round of Quantitative Easing (massive purchases of securities) and almost simultaneously the prices of crypto assets exploded. But there are caveats to such findings. The movements of crypto are too erratic to allow any significant systematic link. Measured correlations explain at best a small part of the movements of crypto prices. And as mentioned already, the data are too recent to distinguish between a simple correlation and causal effects.

Circumstantial elements nonetheless suggest a link between the success of crypto and monetary developments of recent years.

Bitcoin's foundational document by the elusive Satoshi Nakamoto was published in October 2008, right after the peak of the financial crisis. It makes clear references to the goal of creating a new monetary sign that does not rely on trust in banks and central banks. While the most emphasis is given to privacy and to payment security, "trust" naturally extends also to the process of money creation. An upper limit to the number of Bitcoins is set at 21 million – though this limit does not seem insurmountable, as noted in Chapter 8. This supposed limit at least in part explains the attractiveness of the instrument and the rise in price since its creation. It is seen as a guarantee that this form of money will never be debased and inflated away. A not-so-implicit challenge to all monies in history managed by central banks in a discretionary way.

A central feature of cryptocurrencies is their volatility: They can provide extremely high returns at times but are subject to

correspondingly high losses in other periods. Neither is easily foreseeable. Therefore, crypto is favored by "risk-lovers": investors
comfortable taking high risks for the prospect of hefty returns.
Researchers have established a link between monetary policy and
risk-seeking: Monetary expansions induce investors, both individual
and institutional, to assume higher risks.[12] It seems therefore natural to infer that the added risk appetite induced by the money binge
in the postcrisis and postpandemic years may be a factor behind the
success of crypto in the same period. A large part of the crypto positions is likely to have been leveraged by borrowing through traditional financial channels. Cheap credit was available throughout this
period given the prevailing low or even negative rates. Systematic
data on leveraged crypto positions are not available – another trou-
blesome consequence of the opacity of the unregulated crypto world.
But one can easily convince oneself that this is the case by searching
on the internet for the words "leveraged trading crypto": Thousands
of offers pop out.

A hotly debated question is whether the volatility of crypto
assets may have had an effect on the riskiness of the traditional
financial sectors – stocks, bonds and related derivatives, commodities, and so on – and what the regulatory consequences may be. If
the volatility of crypto extends to other market segments, with ensuing, potential systemic instability, the case strengthens for regulating
those segments. Analysis by the IMF has shown that the correlation
between crypto asset volatility and US stock market volatility has
increased since 2020, coinciding with the monetary expansion during
the pandemic.[13] The channels underlying this correlation are complex and require further analysis. It has also been noted that crypto
prices seem to relate to other exotic asset classes, known to be coveted by novel millionaires, such as luxury watches.[14] It is unlikely
that the price of gold Rolexes is responsible for the ups and downs of
the financial sector. The opposite is more plausible.

Based on the evidence available, the IMF has recommended
strengthening the sector's regulation to preserve systemic stability

and protect financial institutions. The Basel Committee on Banking Supervision and some regional regulators (notably, in the European Union) have already followed up by recommending the application of maximum risk weights (1,250 percent) to bank exposures in crypto assets.[15]

Another question is whether there is a link between the economic and monetary conditions of the last few years and the development of the broader "fintech" industry, which among its products includes the popular payment applications and platforms increasingly used in retail commerce (PayPal, Apple Pay, Google Pay, etc.). Such a link may exist, but it is unlikely to be important. Many leveraged buyouts in the tech sector have been recorded recently, especially during the pandemic period where the restrictions to in-person activities have dramatically increased the use of online applications. This has resulted in a wave of consolidations in the fintech sector.[16] Financial conditions have undoubtedly influenced the leverage choice underlying these operations. That being said, the main driver of fintech in recent years has been the entry into the industry of "big techs," technological companies which benefit from superior technical expertise and synergies between the management of large data sets, online retail and marketing, and the payments world. Scale economies and network externalities allow them to expand while still realizing large profits. Their ability to raise capital has also been facilitated by the stellar performance of tech stocks throughout the period.

WHERE TO, NOW?

With the inversion of the monetary policy cycle, the monetary landscape is changing and many of the factors just listed are starting to go backward. The endpoint of the new cycle is not visible yet. Looking into the future at this juncture is difficult – but also tempting.

The return of interest rates above zero may look reassuring, like a return to a familiar past. But history shows that sudden monetary and financial reversals bring risks. Comparable episodes come to mind. The transition from the inflation of the 1970s to the monetary restriction of the 1980s led to temporary financial instability, bank failures (the Savings and Loan Crisis in the United States), and sovereign defaults (Mexico in 1982, followed by debt crises in Eastern Europe and Latin America). Financial crises almost invariably originate from excessive debt fueled by easy financial conditions, followed by sudden credit restrictions and higher interest rates. The present phase shares these features; the March 2023 banking turmoil in the United States may not remain an isolated case[17].

The crypto compartment, with its high riskiness and because of its unclear link to fundamental values, is vulnerable. The summer of 2022 saw a chain of high-profile failures, peaking with the demise of the negotiating platform FTX and its many associated trading and investment entities. The fallout from that episode has not ended yet: Other crypto failures are in progress and others will likely follow. The traditional financial sector by contrast seems, as we write, relatively unscathed. Two questions arise. One regards the future of crypto after the return to a "normal" financial environment, with interest rates back to historical norms and global liquidity reabsorbed. The other relates to the appropriate regulatory approach: whether and how should regulators step in.

Some contend that regulators should refrain from intervening at this stage because prospects are too uncertain and the authorities' action may even be seen as an official seal of approval, effectively supporting a moribund and socially useless activity. Authorities should wait for the crypto sector to extinguish itself, for its inherent flaws.[18] This line of thinking faces two objections. The first is that even a moribund crypto crisis can do much harm, especially among small unsophisticated investors. One cannot rule out adverse systemic effects either, though they seem much less likely. Unfortunately, the very lack of regulation has allowed, even encouraged, individuals without proper financial education and risk-bearing capacity to engage in crypto investment. Regulators cannot ignore the damage from regulatory gaps for the safety and soundness of the saving–investment environment.

The second objection is that the prospect of the sector "burning itself" is far from granted; as we write this line (October 2024), Bitcoin's market value has recuperated all of its losses and is above its previous historical peak. Another "bubble" may be in progress. Whatever it may be, the crypto asset class is proving remarkably resilient. The possibility of it spontaneously disappearing in our view can, at this point, be dismissed.

The more promising alternative is for regulators to intervene with eyes on both consumer protection and systemic risks. Access to crypto investment should be restricted to professional investors with appropriate risk control capabilities. Investment platforms should be required to enforce these limitations and to provide full transparency on the characteristics of the products they sell. Online advertisements and other publicity through investment platforms or elsewhere should indicate in clear and detailed terms the risks of each financial product. The possibility that warnings of this nature may be interpreted as "seals of approval" by the official sector is remote, much like the health warnings printed on cigarette packs do not discourage many smokers (though they do discourage some). As to systemic risks, as noted already, some supervisors have started applying stringent prudential requirements on bank exposures. But in a closely interconnected sector, ringfencing the banks is not sufficient. Requirements should be extended to the nonbank sector, including especially pension, mutual and MMFs, private credit institutions, and the like. In a phase where developments are still fluid and markets evolving, regulatory intervention can only be tentative. Regulators should accept the risk of erring on the side of caution, being more stringent than required, rather than the opposite. In setting prudential requirements, international consistency and coordination are important but not strictly necessary. Requirements would have some of the desired effects even if not fully harmonized or even confined to single jurisdictions.

Different considerations apply to the mainstream "fintech" sector. The growth of this sector in recent decades has been impetuous, but more gradual and fundamentally solid than that of crypto. Fintech has foundations rooted in the valuable services it provides to the financial and especially the payments ecosystem. While it competes with traditional banking in certain areas, it has also been demonstrated that it can be complementary to it, for example, integrating payment applications into the banking and central banking settlement structure. The favorable financial conditions that prevailed in the recent decades are likely to have influenced the growth of fintech as well, in various ways: for example, through their effects on stock markets and the abundance of liquidity and low borrowing costs. Corporate restructuring and buyouts were facilitated by those conditions.

It is too early to definitively judge if and how the turn of inflation and the monetary cycle will have an effect on the way the fintech sector develops. All in all, considering the rich multiple sources of financing available to big techs and their ability to adapt to changing conditions, we feel that any such effect should probably be small.

NOTES

1. Bob Woodward, *Maestro: Greenspan's Fed and the American Boom* (Simon & Schuster, 2000).
2. Athanasios Orphanides, "Monetary-Policy Rules and the Great Inflation," *The American Economic Review* 92, no. 2 (April 1, 2002): 115–20, emphasized statistical lags in his explanation of the "great inflation" of the 1970s.
3. Roy E. Allen, *Financial Crises and Recession in the Global Economy*, 4th ed. (Edward Elgar Publishing EBooks, 2016), chap. 1; Phillip R. Lane, "Financial Globalization and the Crisis," BIS Working Papers 397, December 2012, provides summary measures of financial globalization between 1980 and the Great Financial Crisis.
4. See, among others, Charles Goodhart and Manoj Pradhan, *The Great Demographic Reversal: Ageing Societies, Waning Inequality, and an Inflation Revival* (Palgrave Macmillan, 2020).
5. Ben S. Bernanke, "The Great Moderation," Washington, DC, February 20, 2004.

6. Among the few economists who recognized the dangers early on, the best known is Robert J. Shiller, *Irrational Exuberance* (Princeton University Press, 2000).

7. Data can be found in Isabel Schanbl, "Back to Normal? Balance Sheet Size and Interest Rate Control," New York City, March 27, 2023.

8. The best known among these indicators is that calculated by Goldman Sachs; see "The Case for a Financial Conditions Index," *Goldman Sachs*, July 16, 2018.

9. See Claudio Borio, Boris Hofmann, and Egon Zakrajšek, "Does Money Growth Help Explain the Recent Inflation Surge?," BIS Bulletin 67, January 26, 2023.

10. See, for the United States, Deborah Lucas, "Measuring the Cost of Bailouts," *Annual Review of Financial Economics* 11, no. 1 (December 26, 2019): 85–108; for the eurozone, Antonio Millaruelo and Ana del Río "The Cost of Interventions in the Financial Sector since 2008 in the EU Countries," Economic Bulletin, Banco de España, June 2017.

11. "The Impact of the Eurosystem Monetary Policy on Bitcoin and Other Crypto Assets," Deutsche Bundesbank Monthly Report, September 2021.

12. The most recent analysis, coauthored by the former Fed chairman and Nobel laureate Ben Bernanke, is Michael D. Bauer, Ben Bernanke, and Eric Milstein, "Risk Appetite and the Risk-Taking Channel of Monetary Policy," *Journal of Economic Perspectives* 37, no. 1 (February 1, 2023): 77–100; Earlier research includes Carlo Altavilla, Miguel Boucinha, José-Luis Peydró, and Frank Smets, "Banking Supervision, Monetary Policy and Risk-Taking: Big Data Evidence from 15 Credit Registers," ECB Working Paper 2349, 2020; Ignazio Angeloni, Ester Faia, and Marco Lo Duca, "Monetary Policy and Risk Taking," *Journal of Economic Dynamics and Control* 52 (March 1, 2015): 285–307.

13. Tobias Adrian, Tara Iyer, and Mahvash S. Qureshi, "Crypto Prices Move More in Sync with Stocks, Posing New Risks," IMF, January 11, 2022.

14. Andrea Felsted, "Crypto, Stock Meltdown Hits Rolex, Patek Philippe, Audemars Piguet Watches," *Bloomberg.Com*, July 1, 2022.

15. Basel Committee on Banking Supervision, "Prudential Treatment of Crypto Assets," December 2022.

16. Abby Latour, "Tech Sector Leads Leveraged Loan LBO Surge amid Search for Pandemic-Proof Deals," S&P Global Market Intelligence, April 2021.

17. The link between monetary policy and the 2023 banking turmoil in the United States is analyzed in Geneva Reports on the World Economy no. 27: Ignazio Angeloni, Stijn Claessens, Amit Seru, Sascha Steffen, and Beatrice Weder di Mauro, "Much Money, Little Capital, and Few Reforms: The 2023 Banking Turmoil," September 2024.

18. Stephen Cecchetti and Kim Schoenholtz, "Let Crypto Burn," *Financial Times*, November 17, 2022.

14 Money in Crisis and the Possible Future

In a crisis, be aware of the danger, but recognize the opportunity.

John F. Kennedy

The history of money is one of discovery: a never-ending search for secure, efficient, and attractive ways to store and trade our purchasing capability. Digitalization is only a milestone in this process but a formidable one: Nobody could imagine, three decades ago, that we would soon purchase by brandishing a cellphone, swaying our wristwatch, or – maybe soon – just thinking about it, with a chip implanted in our brain. Authorities, financiers, and scholars must embrace these novelties with confidence and openness but with a grain of caution. The fundamental nature of money, the reason why we need it, and the ways it can benefit or harm have not changed. These are the tracks on which the train of innovation must advance. It is our collective responsibility that that train does not go off the rails.

These were the ideas we had in mind when we started this book. We wanted to address questions like: What is "digital money"? Is the emphasis on it in today's public discourse justified or overstated, well-centered or biased? Can digital money improve our lives, and how? We wanted to address these questions from the viewpoint of ordinary people, especially the least advantaged. Like the rule of law, a good money is especially important for the less privileged; the wealthy, powerful, and influential ones do not need good monetary institutions to prosper. Money is eminently democratic: a means, with others, to an open and equal society.

As we moved ahead in our project, our perspective changed somewhat. We came to think of money's digitalization as part of a more general state of crisis that money and its institutions have entered into after the beginning of this century. We mean "crisis" not just in the way the word is commonly used ("a state of disease and danger") but also in its etymological meaning ("a turning point, a time for decision"). Making payments today is easier and quicker, thanks to the digital revolution. But managing money is also more difficult, complex, and risky, for a combination of reasons including the increasing complexity of the financial system, the mystery and opacity of crypto, geostrategic dangers, and inflation. Amid the promises and pitfalls of digital monies, we should stay clear of fads or bandwagons. As we embrace the digital future, we must beware of false promises and prospective dangers.

The history of money started some 5,000 years ago on the river shores of ancient Mesopotamia, as savvy merchants and priests devised a technology and a set of norms and techniques to facilitate the storage and transfer of wealth. Ever since, with highs and lows, amid progress and reversals, money has been a constant partner in human civilization and development. Its essential functions and the characteristics it needs to possess have changed little if at all. Economic theorists of the nineteenth century codified those functions, suggesting that money serves as a unit of account (metric to compare relative values), a means of payment (tool for transferring values among people), and a store of value (means for preserving and transferring values through time).

This classification, which we all as economics students have learned early in our university education, is exact but restrictive.

Money is a *bridge in time*. People receive monetary value when they part with something they own: valuable objects, worktime, or other. They keep it in order to procure, later, what they desire or need. Economists call this money's "store of value" function. Stability in value and ease of use are the most important requirements of this function. When people start fearing that money cannot be relied upon, or its use becomes awkward, trust starts eroding and the search for better alternatives begins.

Money is also *technology*. It involves the application of scientific knowledge to fulfil a practical need. Money therefore evolves in the form it takes: not because its purpose changes but because the way in which that purpose is served improves with scientific progress. The history of money is largely the history of how new technologies make money more useful and reliable. Embracing new technologies while preserving money's fundamental purposes is a constant challenge. The same challenge faces regulators now in addressing the opportunities and risks posed by digital money.

Taking a broader view, money is a *social construct*, a means to facilitate interaction among people. It displays its benefits in full when people cooperate and interact in an associated life. Its functioning requires trust among individuals and between the individuals and their institutions, rules, and leaders. For this reason a good money can never rely on private initiative alone: It will always require a quantum of publicly driven action, institutions, and rules to ensure that the collective interest is properly served. Establishing that quantum and setting the boundary between the public and private spheres are the essence of good monetary governance.

At the end of the twentieth century, a balance among those various elements seemed to have been found. Severing the link between money and gold in the 1970s had initially led to a bout of inflation. But global monetary stability was eventually reconquered, and new stability and functionality standards were reached. This state of equilibrium was based on a private–public partnership: a complementarity between central banks, technocratic institutions with a public mission, and a private profit-making financial sector. The former responsible for the pursuit of the collective interest, the latter leveraging on the market mechanism and contributing efficiency and technological advance.

The years preceding the Great Financial Crisis of 2008–09 marked the heyday of central banking: Central bank leaders, like modern "monetary sovereigns," enjoyed unprecedented success, reputation, and prestige. We know now that that situation was largely the result of fortunate or coincidental circumstances: free trade and more efficient production chains, the fall of the Iron Curtain, and a general improvement of global relations. The combination of these factors increased the supply of goods and services and helped keep their prices low. Those conditions were transient, though a wave of optimism made people think they may be permanent. This induced complacency and sowed the seeds of future instability.

The global financial crisis of 2008–09 (in Europe, lasting until 2013) marked the end of this "golden age." It dealt a serious reputational blow to both private financial institutions and the regulatory community, with central banks at its center. In the eyes of Main Street, banks could no longer be trusted to properly perform their core business, which ultimately is handling financial risks on behalf of ordinary people. Regulators could no longer be trusted either, because they allowed all that to happen under their watch.

With the financial crisis, central banks stopped acting as leaders and started chasing events from behind. Fears of deflation and repetition of the Great Depression of the 1930s, whether well-grounded or not, dominated policymaker concerns for a while, leading central bankers to engulf their balance sheets with government securities and expanding market liquidity without precedents.

The Great Monetary Expansion lasted fourteen years, from 2008 to 2022. It added to an already accommodative stance during earlier periods, creating an environment conducive to inflation. Old-fashioned monetarist theories implying a mechanical link between money and inflation are discredited, but the fact that lax money makes inflation more likely to arise when other circumstances are present can hardly be contested. Like fuel for the fire, liquidity does not cause inflation but permits it to develop when something else triggers it.

Cryptocurrencies arose during this period characterized by mistrust in the financial establishment and ample liquidity. The foundational concept was to provide a "peer-to-peer electronic cash system" that would work without trusted intermediaries. It is now clear that the technical characteristics of the underlying technology render cryptocurrencies unsuitable for retail payments. Bitcoin will never become money in the traditional sense. However, despite this limitation, investment in cryptocurrencies took off and acquired the hallmarks of a bubble, fueled by hype and by the liquidity created by central banks.

With interest rates probably headed to a higher "new normal," large segments of financial markets still insufficiently regulated, and amid high uncertainties regarding the future of geopolitics, international trade, and financial stability, central banks are at a crossroads. The direction they take may shape the future of money for generations.

We see three alternative avenues ahead.

One is for central banks to strengthen their links with governments and maintain them over the long term. This would inevitably mean a retreat of central bank independence, one of the tenets of monetary theories and practice in the late twentieth century. Central banks would become, effectively, *Banks of the State*. For many of them, it would be a return to their primeval function of financing cash-hungry sovereigns. In a way, this would mean a continuation of the status quo: Already now, the share of government debt they hold in the United States, Europe, United Kingdom, let alone Japan, is at levels that are unprecedented in peacetime. Making this permanent, however, would remove the vital separation between monetary and fiscal powers that has helped ensure price stability for a long time, even in a global regime of pure fiat currencies. With large holdings of public securities in central bank balance sheets on a stable basis, the pressure to finance governments further could only increase, along with the danger that inflation would resurface in times of fiscal problems.

Another option is for central banks to change their job profile in a different direction, becoming *Banks for Everybody*. This would happen if they decided to issue all-purpose retail central bank digital currencies (CBDCs). Far from being a return to the past, this would be a bold leap forward. It would mark a departure from a time-tested tradition in which they offer their services to ordinary people only indirectly, otherwise relying on private markets. Becoming direct payment providers would imply major organizational changes for central banks, even if central banks decided to outsource all front-office functions to banks, limiting themselves to recording transactions on their balance sheets.

By issuing retail CBDCs, central banks would start competing with commercial banks in their traditional business segment, that of deposit collection and provision of payment services. With consequences along at least three dimensions.

First, competition between central banks and commercial banks would blur and distort business incentives. Banks traditionally make a profit by offering attractive conditions on the deposits they offer and the related services. They would continue to do that, but in addition, they would start offering deposit products on behalf of central banks, presumably for a fee. They would face a dilemma between promoting their own products, for the benefit of the shareholders, and promoting CBDCs, whose profit margins would accrue to the central banks. All of that in a situation in which central banks supervise, and have sanctioning power on, the provision of payment services and the prudential soundness of banks. A regulatory mess whose outcome is hard to discern.

Second, and relatedly, the entry of central banks in the retail payment sector would likely discourage private sector innovation by banks and nonbank providers, such as fintech and big-tech companies. Given their different expertise and mission, it is unlikely that central banks can match the technical expertise of the private sector. That expertise in recent years has given rise to formidable advances through online platforms, payment apps, contactless technologies, and the like. Central banks are more likely either to discourage this process or to fail in the competition, suffering reputation losses.

Third, in stressed financial conditions the coexistence of traditional bank deposits and CBDCs would create problems in the implementation of monetary policy and exacerbate systemic risk. When bank risk rises, a riskless alternative to bank deposit would become highly attractive, encouraging large shifts of funds outside of the banking sector and possibly a bank run. With CBDCs, the adverse impact of banking crises on the real sector of the economy is likely to be more severe than without them.

From a user-case perspective, the arguments cited on the potential advantages of retail CBDCs remains unconvincing. Private sector initiative in the last few years has greatly increased the efficiency, attractiveness, and convenience of the traditional retail payment sector. Any officially sponsored retail payment instrument is unlikely to add much to what the market already offers and may turn out to be a business flop.

The alternative option sometimes advocated across the Atlantic, of wholesale CBDCs as a means to improve the global payment system, is worth studying. On the one hand, wholesale CBDCs, if not well-designed, may be even more damaging to financial stability than retail CBDCs, because they would not likely be subject to strict holding limits. On the other hand, however, current international payment practices, still largely based on correspondent relations across large banks, are not ideal from both efficiency and security viewpoints. As we have seen in our historical overview, early in the twentieth century the introduction of central bank settlements brought great improvements in domestic payment systems. One can argue that a similar development should take place today. Whether a good compromise between risks and advantages can be struck depends, once again, on design and regulation and on the quantum of international cooperation that the new system would gather.

The third avenue is for central banks to be *Banks of the Banks*, the dominant model that prevailed until the Great Financial Crisis. Central banks would continue to exert rigorous surveillance and use their regulatory powers to encourage further progress and foster efficiency and stability in the underlying settlement infrastructures. By concentrating on these tasks, they would reaffirm and strengthen their position as Banks of the Banks.

Far from being a rear-guard strategy, this avenue requires bold action and involves multiple challenges.

One challenge for them as well as other authorities is to properly regulate crypto assets. One cannot rely on market forces alone to mitigate or ringfence the risks that this sector implies for retail investors and potentially for the financial system as a whole. In the main, regulating crypto does not require new rules. The risks involved are in most cases not specific to crypto. They stem from the fact that this segment suffers to a high degree from failures present elsewhere in finance: complexity, lack of transparency, poor internal controls, insufficient or distorted corporate culture. Existing instruments dealing with these problems elsewhere in the financial sector should be utilized to the fullest possible extent. Devising new broad-ranging regulatory frameworks ad hoc is risky because the crypto industry is constantly evolving: It would mean aiming at a moving target. The principle should be "same activity, same risk, same regulation."[1] And this industry being global as probably no other, the maximum possible international harmonization and international supervisory cooperation should be sought.

Over time central banks will probably need to abandon their exclusive focus on banks and broaden their financial and supervisory scope to the whole financial sector. The experience of recent crises has demonstrated that financial stability depends not on banks alone but on all intermediaries that perform maturity transformation. The postcrisis reform program was concentrated largely on the banking sector and its effect was to shrink the share of banks in financial intermediation, enlarging that of so-called shadow banks. This category includes all subjects that, while not called banks and not being regulated as such, perform comparable functions. The notion of "same activity, same risk, same regulation" should apply here as well, and be extended to include "same lending-of-last-resort."

Digitalization is yet another factor, among many experienced in monetary history, contributing to blur traditional barriers in finance. The scope and responsibility of central banks can only increase as a consequence, evolving from guardians of monetary stability to custodians of the broader financial sector.

NOTE

1. Financial Stability Board (FSB), "International Regulation of Crypto-Assets Activities," *Executive Summary*, July 17, 2022.

Index

ABBA (pop group), 105
Adams, Henry, 46, 51, 74
Afghanistan, 292
Africa, 71, 117, 274
Ahr (river), 125
Ahrtal (region of Germany), 125, 127
Alibaba, 168, 176, 192, 224
Alighieri, Dante, 100, 104
Alipay, 3, 8, 71, 174, 238, 263, 276, 278–79,
        327
Amsterdam, 33
Ant Financial, 168
anti–money laundering (AML), 120, 264–65,
        271, 312
app (smartphone application), 10, 53, 63,
        164–65, 171–72, 194, 220, 254, 276,
        278
Apple, 8, 12, 71, 167–68, 262, 347
        Apple Pay, 3, 8, 12, 71, 167, 347
Aristophanes, 23, 43
as (Roman coin), 24–25
Ashurbanipal, 17–18, 20
Asia, 117, 256, 314–15, 323, 332
Associated Press, 53
Assyria, 17
AT&T Corporation, 54
Athens, 23, 43, 295, 302
ATM (Automated Teller Machine), 68, 76,
        89, 108, 111, 122, 126, 129, 169, 189,
        224, 280, 302
Augustus, 25–26
aureus, 25
Australia, 108
Austria, 42, 114

Bain, Alexander, 53
Banca Romana, 38
Bank of America (BofA), 61–65, 135
Bank of England, 10, 35, 75, 255
BankAmericard, 64
Bankman-Fried, Sam, 232

banknotes, 6, 24, 29, 32, 34, 39, 56, 72, 107,
        121, 125–26, 128, 169, 295
Banque Générale Privée, 36
Banque Royale, 36
Bardi (family), 31
base money, 147
Basel Accord, 159
Basel Committee on Banking Supervision,
        159, 338, 347, 351
Baumol, William J., 107–9, 115, 129
Becker, Gary, 133
Belgium, 50, 99, 304
Bell Telephone, 54
Bell, Alexander Graham, 54
Bentham, Jeremy, 296
Berkeley (University of California camps),
        287, 327
Berlin, 81, 83, 86, 103
Binance (crypto exchange), 232
BIS (Bank for International Settlements),
        115, 130, 158–61, 176, 224–26, 228,
        250, 256–57, 283, 285–86, 288, 312,
        322, 331–33, 350–51
Bismarck, Otto von, 37
Bitcoin, 2–3, 9, 12, 105, 120, 124, 178–203,
        206–29, 232, 244–45, 252, 294,
        299–300, 302, 345, 349, 351, 357
        Bitcoin Gold, 209–10, 218
        Bitcoin SV, 209
black economy, 118–19, 127
blockchain, 93, 145, 176, 180–81, 183,
        190–96, 198–200, 203–8, 210, 213,
        216–17, 221, 226–27, 232–33, 245,
        248–49, 260, 282
BMW, 88
BNP Paribas, 239
Bosphorus, 27
Brandeis, Louis, 291
Brazil, 71
breaking of the buck, 240
Bretton Woods, xi, 159, 336–37

Britain, 37, 46–47, 50, 82, 108, 296, 337
Brunnermeier, Markus, 218
Brussels, 159, 304–5, 308
Bundesrepublik (BRD), 85
Buterin, Vitalik, 217, 223, 226–28

California, 61, 287
Cambridge Analytica, 259
Canada, 50, 130–31
Capitol (Rome), 26–27
Caracalla, 27, 96
Carthage, 24, 96
cash, 5–6, 8–9, 22, 24, 61, 63, 65, 68–69,
    73, 84, 87, 105–31, 134–36, 146–52,
    162, 169–70, 174–75, 179, 184, 189,
    202–3, 208–9, 212–16, 222, 224, 231,
    238, 242, 244, 250–51, 253–54, 257,
    259–60, 262–64, 269–72, 275–77,
    279–82, 284, 287, 290, 292–95, 300,
    302, 320, 356–57
CBDCs (Central Bank Digital Currencies),
    4, 8–11, 13, 70, 157, 257–61, 263–76,
    279–87, 314, 323, 327–29, 332, 334,
    357–59
CBOT (Chicago Board of Trade), 338
central banks, xi, 2, 4–13, 32–38, 40, 46,
    48–50, 56, 58, 60–61, 69–70, 72–73,
    75–76, 93–94, 98, 102, 105–7, 114,
    120, 126, 129, 134–38, 141–42,
    145, 147–48, 150–53, 155, 157–62,
    166–67, 174–75, 181, 219, 231, 236,
    257, 260–74, 280–88, 294–95, 297,
    299, 301, 306, 310, 313–14, 317–21,
    325, 327, 329–30, 335–36, 338–42,
    345, 355–61
Chappe, Claude, 42
checks (personal), 8, 19, 33–34, 58, 61–63,
    68–69, 72, 75, 113, 135, 162–66, 173,
    176, 241, 271, 284, 335
Chicago, 56, 133, 136, 139, 338
Chicago Plan, 142
China, 4, 6, 12, 22, 28, 30, 32, 39, 64, 71,
    96, 103, 113, 117, 121, 147, 150,
    167–68, 170, 174, 176, 192, 201, 222,
    238, 262–63, 274, 276–79, 281, 284,
    288, 295, 313, 316, 321–25, 327–28,
    334, 339
    People's Bank of, 10, 262
CHIPS (Clearing House Interbank payments
    System), 60

Churchill, Winston, 145
CME (Chicago Mercantile Exchange), 338
Coin USD, 235
coins, 4, 16, 20–25, 27, 41, 43–44, 48, 55, 73,
    88–89, 93–98, 105, 107, 110–13, 115,
    123, 126, 130, 144, 185, 213, 218,
    227, 245, 253–55, 295, 302
Compiègne, 82
Constantinople, 27, 30
correspondent banking, 57, 304–6, 310,
    311–14
corruption, 119, 279
COVID-19, 112, 218, 224, 241, 319
Croesus, 20
Crusades, 33
cryptocurrencies, 1, 3, 8–9, 13, 93, 124, 144,
    176, 178–83, 189, 194, 196, 199–200,
    204, 206–14, 217–29, 232, 235,
    244–45, 252, 255–57, 280, 283, 287,
    293–94, 300, 351–52, 356–57

Dai USD (stablecoin), 235
Dawes Plan, 83
denarius, 24–27, 96–98
Denmark, 112, 116, 201
deposit insurance, 141, 266, 273
Detroit, 56
Diem, 9, 257–58
digital money, xii, 1–8, 10, 12, 39, 61, 63,
    69–70, 72, 93–94, 106, 114, 146,
    160, 257, 260, 286, 295, 298, 300,
    353–55
Diners Card, 64
Diocletian, 27
distributed ledger, 176, 180, 189–90, 206,
    208, 217, 233, 244–45, 260, 280,
    282, 293
D-Mark (Deutschmark or DM), 84–85,
    87–88, 90, 103, 213, 227, 320
Do Kwon, 234

Edinburgh, 53
Eichengreen, Barry, 74, 327, 332–34
Einstein, Albert, 52
El Salvador, 219–20, 228, 249
e-Naira, 279–80
ERMA (Electronic Recording Machine
    Accounting), 62–63
Ethereum, 179, 182–83, 195, 203–6, 209,
    211, 217–18, 222, 226, 232

euro, 8, 11, 24, 38, 88–91, 97, 99–103, 108, 110, 113, 115–17, 120–22, 125, 127, 130, 150–53, 157, 159, 213, 218, 230, 258, 261–63, 267–69, 271, 277, 281–82, 286, 293, 297, 313–18, 320–22, 324–25, 328–30, 333, 341

Europe, 4, 7, 12, 22, 27, 30–31, 33, 39–41, 46, 54, 68, 71–72, 81, 87, 89, 96, 100–1, 103, 111, 112, 116, 119–20, 130–31, 145, 147, 149–50, 152, 158–59, 162, 165, 167, 169, 177, 201, 207, 215, 237–38, 243–44, 249, 268–69, 281, 297, 303, 305–6, 313, 316, 329–30, 341–42, 344, 348, 356–57

European Central Bank (ECB), 10, 37, 88, 90, 110–11, 113, 116, 122, 125–26, 130, 132, 147–48, 153, 157, 159, 246, 254–55, 262, 264, 281, 286–87, 293, 313, 320, 333, 341–42, 351

European Monetary System (EMS), 159

e-wallet, 63, 165

e-yuan, 276

Facebook, 9, 100, 252, 257–59, 283, 285

FBI (Federal Bureau of Investigation), 214–15, 227

Fedwire, 57, 59, 75, 282

finality of payment, 8, 58–60, 69, 72–73, 75, 129, 161, 233, 266–67, 284

financial inclusion, 267

Financial Stability Board (FSB), 160, 241, 248, 250, 255, 352

fintech, 12, 138, 154, 170, 174–75, 229, 254, 300, 311, 316, 347, 349–50, 358

float, 163

Florence, 31–32

France, 35–37, 42, 45, 50, 52–53, 72, 74, 113, 163, 238–39, 284, 297, 317–18
Banque de, 35, 37

Frankfurt, 159

Friedman, Benjamin, 138

Friedman, Milton, 78, 102, 133, 155

FTX (crypto exchange), 143, 221, 228, 232, 234, 242, 275, 348

Fugger (family), 31

General Electric, 62

Genoa, 28, 31

German Democratic Republic (GDR), 85, 103

Germany, 30–31, 37–38, 50, 82–85, 87, 91, 102–3, 112–14, 125, 127, 130, 158, 297, 306, 317–18, 322, 330, 338
Bundesbank, 37, 103, 126, 130, 132, 177, 227, 320, 324, 333, 338, 351
hyperinflation, 81, 83, 98, 102
Reichsbank, 37, 75
Reichsmark, 81–84, 102, 330

Giannini, Amedeo, 61–63

Glasgow, 53

Glass–Steagall Act, 143

Gorbachev, Mikhail, 86

gold, 16, 19–20, 22, 24–25, 29, 38, 44, 48–50, 55–59, 69, 72, 74, 76, 96–97, 198, 202–3, 219, 222, 225–26, 296–97, 299, 303, 329, 336, 338, 346, 355
Gold Settlement Fund, 57, 74
Gold Standard, 37–38, 47–50, 56, 58–59, 74, 81

Google, 12, 71, 167–68, 178, 183, 347
Google Pay, 3, 8, 12, 71, 167, 347

Grand Kahn, 41

Great Depression, 58, 114, 142, 158, 236, 342, 356

Great Financial Crisis (GFC), 67, 140, 143–44, 147, 152–53, 159, 182, 232, 235, 244, 259, 299, 319, 339–40, 344, 350, 355, 359

Great War (World War I or WWI), 47

Greece, x, 23, 90, 102

Greenspan, Alan, 336

gray economy, 118–19, 150, 214, 250

Gutenberg, Johannes, 33

Harvard University, 51, 118, 138, 176, 216, 225–26, 302

hash, 182–83, 190, 217

Hayek, Friedrich von, 296–97

Hemingway, Ernest, 96

Herstatt, 338

Hitler, Adolf, 38, 82, 158

Holland, 31, 33, 318

Honduras, 249

Hume, David, 134, 155

Hydra (darknet marketplace), 216, 227

India, 98, 122, 251, 280, 326

Industrial Revolution, 51

International Monetary Fund (IMF), 80, 113,
    130–31, 220, 228, 250, 256, 264, 280,
    283, 285–86, 288, 314, 333–34, 337,
    346, 351
iPhone, 164
Iraq, 17, 249
Ireland, 102, 238
Iron Curtain, 85, 337, 356
Italy, 24, 30–31, 37, 39, 50, 54, 61, 113, 297,
    318
    Banca d'Italia, 39

Japan, 50, 118, 121, 145, 150, 179, 211, 238,
    261, 313, 357

Kansas City, 56
Kant, Immanuel, 100, 104
Kardashian, Kim, 178
Keynes, John Maynard, 78, 135, 296
Keynesians, 94, 133–38, 155
King Louis XIV, 36
King Louis XV, 36
Klarna, 94, 167
Know Your Customer (KYC), 210, 264–65,
    271, 280, 312
Kraken (crypto exchange), 245
Kuwait, 249

Latin America, 117, 315, 348
Law, John, 36, 45
Lehman Brothers, 239, 341
Leonardo da Vinci, 31
Libra, 9, 252, 256–59, 274, 283,
    285
Liebknecht, Karl, 82
liquidity constraints, 65
Luxemburg, Rosa, 82
Lydia, 20
Lyngstad, Frida, 105

M0, 146–48
M1, 115, 146, 148
M2, 146, 148
M3, 114, 146, 148, 150–53
Marco Polo, 28, 30, 31, 41, 44
Marconi, Guglielmo, 54
marginalist approach, 296
Marshall Plan, 84
Marshall, Alfred, 296
MARTI (Machine Readable Telegraphic
    Input), 307–8, 331

Mastercard, 64, 66, 75, 167, 171, 173, 250,
    262
McKinnon, Ronald, 100
means of payment (function of money),
    63–64, 73, 79, 81, 85, 91, 96, 102,
    106, 145–46, 174, 187, 221, 238, 245,
    278, 284, 354
Medici (family), 31–32
Mediterranean (sea), 21, 24, 33, 96
Menger, Carl, 78, 296
Mercedes, 88
Mesopotamia, 4, 17, 32, 41, 43, 48, 166, 354
Metcalfe's law, 170
Mexico, 251–52, 256, 348
Miami, 251
Michelangelo Buonarroti, 31
Midas, 20
Middle Ages, 4, 6, 28, 30–31
miners, 138, 180, 182–83, 187, 190, 192,
    195–98, 200–4, 208–9, 217, 219,
    229, 301
Modigliani, Franco, 137, 155–56
Monero, 213–15
monetarists, 133–38, 152–53, 155, 343, 356
money demand, 80, 98
money market funds, 68, 144, 151, 229,
    235–44, 246–48, 338, 349
money multiplier, 135–39, 152–53
money transfer operator, 251–52
MoneyGram, 252, 256
Morse, Samuel, 42, 53
    Morse (alphabet, code, system), 42, 60
M-Pesa, 71, 146
Mussolini, Benito, 39, 137
mutual funds, 237

Nakamoto, Satoshi, 12, 184–87, 190–91,
    202, 224, 299, 345
Napoleon Bonaparte, 37, 45, 52
    Napoleonic Wars, 47
NAV (net asset value), 238–40, 243
Nazi (National Socialist party or regime),
    82, 84, 159
Nero, 26
Netherlands, 50, 317–18
New Haven, 133
New Orleans, 56
New York, 53–56, 63, 74, 82, 102–3, 131,
    255, 306, 351
Nigeria, 251, 267, 274, 279–80, 288
    National Bank of, 280

Nixon, Richard, 76, 337
Nobel (prize, laureates), 78, 109, 133, 136, 139, 155, 223, 255, 296, 340, 351
North Korea, 214, 313

off-chain (stablecoins), 247
Office of the Controller of the Currency (OCC), 47
Omaha, 56
on-chain (stablecoins), 247

payment service providers (PSPs), 265
PayPal, 3, 8, 12, 71–72, 94, 167, 170–72, 174, 195, 250, 252–53, 262, 276, 311, 347
Peloponnesian War, 23
Philippines, 251
PIN (Personal Identification Number), 67–68, 166, 211–12
Pix, 71
Ponzi scheme, 179, 198
POS (point-of-sales), 68, 199, 226
Princeton University, 107, 130, 139, 218, 351
privacy, 6, 11, 95, 181, 187, 214–15, 259, 270–71, 291–95, 300–1, 345
programmable money, 206
Proof of Stake, 182, 203–5, 217
Proof of Work, 182, 186, 190, 193, 204, 208, 217, 223
Prussia, 37, 42
public–private partnership, 40

quetzal, 253

Raffaello Sanzio, 31
rational inattention, 150
real bills doctrine, 36–37
Regulation Q, 236–37
Reign of Terror, 42
Renaissance, 4, 7, 31–33, 39–40, 51
renminbi (yuan), 333. See also yuan (renminbi)
required reserves, 99, 147–48, 157
Reserve Primary Fund (RPF), 238–40, 242, 255
Restoration, 47
Reuters, Paul Julius, 53
Revolut, 167, 172
Riksbank, 35, 105–6, 112, 129–30, 132

Robespierre, Maximilien, 42
Rogoff, Kenneth, 104, 118, 216, 227
Roman Empire, 23, 27, 44, 96, 104
Roman Republic, 96
Rome, 23–27, 38–39, 61, 251
Ronalds, Francis, 52
Roosevelt, Franklin D., 289
Russia, ix, 11, 53, 99, 116, 120, 222, 292, 301, 325–26, 330, 334

Sand Dollars, 274–76
Savannah, 56
scalability (of blockchain), 193, 217
Schabowski, Günther, 86
Schacht, Hjalmar, 81–83, 102
Schultz, Theodore, 133
SEC (Securities and Exchange Commission), 197, 240, 255
seigniorage, 6, 16, 34, 98
SEPA (Single European Payments Area), 8, 71–72, 194
Septimus Severus, 26, 97
sestertius, 25, 44
Shiller, Robert, 223
Smith, Adam, 14, 36, 43, 77
Solow, Robert, 78
Spain, 31, 102, 113, 318
St. Petersburg, 53
stablecoins, 8–9, 13, 144, 151, 178, 206, 221, 229–36, 238, 242, 244–49, 252–54, 260, 294, 299, 311
Stanford University, 62, 100, 104
Stigler, George, 133
Stiglitz, Joseph, 139
Stockholm, 35, 140
store of value (function of money), 5, 79–80, 89, 93, 102, 146, 148, 179, 218, 222, 284, 354
Stresemann, Gustav, 81
Stuart Mill, John, 100, 104, 289, 296
Sustainable Development Goals, 252
Sweden, 50, 105–6, 112, 115, 120, 126, 129–31, 170
SWIFT (Society for Worldwide Interbank Financial Telecommunication), 11, 65, 99, 304, 308–12, 315–16, 325–27, 329–32, 334
Swift, Taylor, 178
Switzerland, 50, 114–16, 118, 121, 170

Target (euro payment system), 8, 282

technology, xii, 4, 6, 14, 16, 21–22, 24, 32, 35, 41, 46, 51, 54, 57–58, 60, 65, 67–68, 70, 73, 85, 90, 93–95, 107, 113, 128, 138, 140, 145, 152, 164, 166, 168–69, 175, 178, 182–83, 193–94, 208, 216, 220, 223, 226, 232–33, 253, 260–61, 280, 286, 301, 306, 308, 311, 326, 339, 354–55, 357

telex (machine), 307–8

Tencent, 71

Terra USD, 234–35

Terra USD (stablecoin), 234

Tether (stablecoin), 229–30, 232–35, 245–46, 253–54, 256

theory of turnings, x, 43

Tobin, James, 80, 109, 115, 136–37, 139, 150, 154, 156

Tombstone (Arizona), 53

Treaty of Versailles, 83

Trotsky, Leon, 53

True USD, 235

Truman, Harry, 84

Trump, Donald, 259

Ukraine, ix, 99, 222, 319, 325, 334

UnionPay, 64

unit of account (function of money), 5, 79–80, 83–85, 88–91, 98, 102, 139, 179, 220, 285, 290, 354

United Kingdom, 50, 357

United States, 6, 34, 41–42, 47, 50, 55, 58, 67, 69, 78, 102, 108, 142, 157, 163–64, 176, 229, 236, 301, 315–16, 333, 348, 357

   Civil War, 34, 43, 47, 53, 55–56, 298

   Second Bank of the, 55

   US dollar, 76, 303

US Federal Reserve, 10, 34, 44, 47, 54–55, 57–60, 62, 68, 70, 74–76, 111, 130, 138, 153, 155–57, 163–65, 176, 202, 230, 262–63, 268, 287, 305, 328, 330, 336–38, 340, 342, 350–51

US dollar, 11, 25, 55, 58–59, 98–99, 110–11, 117, 121, 184, 191, 197–98, 200–2, 211–12, 216, 218–19, 230–31, 234, 246, 258, 274, 310, 314–17, 319–22, 324–25, 328–30, 336–37

USD Coin (stablecoin), 230, 234

Venezuela, 6

Venice, 28, 31–33

Venmo, 167, 171

Visa, 65–66, 75, 167, 171, 173, 177, 192, 224, 262

Volkswagen, 88

Walras, Léon, 78

Warren, Samuel, 291, 302

WeChat, 174, 263, 276, 278–79, 327

Weimar Republic, 81

Western Union, 176, 250

World Bank, 114, 129–30, 146, 149, 156–57, 249–52, 256, 288, 314

World War II or WWII, 11, 37, 59, 61, 85, 97, 159, 162, 285, 303, 336, 337

WTO (World trade Organization), 339

WWI. *See* Great War (World War I or WWI)

Wyatt Earp, 53

Xoom, 167

Yale University, 48, 109, 133, 136, 223

yuan (renminbi), 121, 174, 263, 276–77, 279–82, 321–23

For EU product safety concerns, contact us at Calle de José Abascal, 56–1°,
28003 Madrid, Spain or eugpsr@cambridge.org.

www.ingramcontent.com/pod-product-compliance
Ingram Content Group UK Ltd.
Pitfield, Milton Keynes, MK11 3LW, UK
UKHW020432240426
470322UK00017B/481